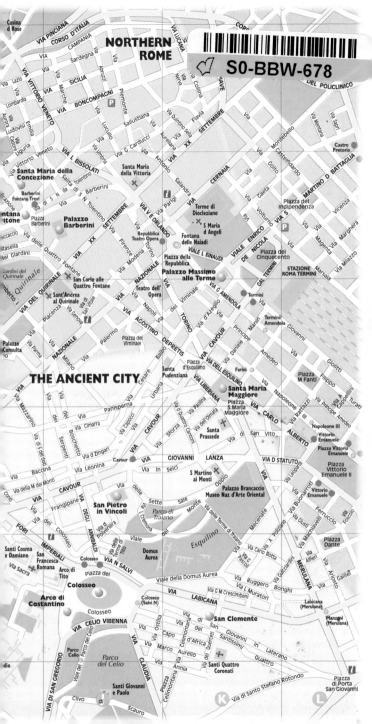

How to Use This Book

KEY TO SYMBOLS

✚ Map reference to the accompanying fold-out map

✉ Address

☎ Telephone number

🕐 Opening/closing times

🍴 Restaurant or café

🚃 Nearest rail station

Ⓜ Nearest subway (Metro) station

🚌 Nearest bus route

⛴ Nearest riverboat or ferry stop

♿ Facilities for visitors with disabilities

❓ Other practical information

▷ Further information

ℹ Tourist information

✋ Admission charges: Expensive (over €7), Moderate (€4–7), and Inexpensive (€4 or less)

★ Major Sight   ★ Minor Sight

👣 Walks   🚐 Excursions

🏬 Shops

🎵 Entertainment and Nightlife

🍽 Restaurants

This guide is divided into four sections

• **Essential Rome:** an introduction to the city and tips on making the most of your stay.

• **Rome by Area:** We've broken the city into six areas, and recommended the best sights, shops, entertainment venues, nightlife and restaurants in each one. Suggested walks help you to explore on foot.

• **Where to Stay:** the best hotels, whether you're looking for luxury, budget or something in between.

• **Need to Know:** the info you need to make your trip run smoothly, including getting about by public transport, weather tips, emergency phone numbers and useful websites.

Navigation In the Rome by Area chapter, we've given each area its own colour, which is also used on the locator maps throughout the book and the map on the inside front cover.

Maps The fold-out map accompanying this book is a comprehensive street plan of Rome. The grid on this fold-out map is the same as the grid on the locator maps within the book. We've given grid references within the book for each sight and listing.

Contents

Introducing Rome

Rome is one of the world's great cities, the city of the Caesars, of romance and *la dolce vita*, of long, hot sunny days, of endless art galleries, churches and museums, of fountain-splashed piazzas and majestic monuments to its golden age of empire.

It is also a city with all the myriad pleasures of any Italian destination—notably superb food and wine—as well as great bars, cafés, and shopping, vibrant nightlife and numerous cultural events. At the same time, Rome is very much a contemporary city—traffic rumbles around medieval cobbled streets and the skyline bristles not with glittering skyscrapers but with the domes of churches and palaces.

But how to visit a city where there is so much to see? First of all don't rush to the Colosseum, St. Peter's or the Sistine Chapel on your first morning. Rome for much of the year is hot and crowded. If you try to cram in too much, or soldier on through the heat, the chances are you'll emerge battered rather than enraptured. Instead, start with a stroll around the Ghetto or Trastevere, two of the city's quaintest old quarters, or

have a cappuccino in one of Rome's loveliest squares, Campo de' Fiori or Piazza Navona. Or maybe head for one of the lesser-known art-filled churches, such as Santa Maria del Popolo, crammed with masterpieces by Raphael, Pinturicchio and Caravaggio.

Once gently acclimatized, and hopefully charmed by the city's quieter side, then you can begin to think about the Trevi Fountain, the Spanish Steps, the Roman Forum or the Vatican Museums. And, of course, the newer but still relatively unsung museums that have opened in the last decade—notably the Palazzo Altemps and Palazzo Massimo alle Terme. But bear in mind this is a living city with over 3,000 years of history. One, two, even ten visits aren't enough to do it justice. However much you see, one thing for certain, you'll be back.

Facts + Figures

● **Population in 2003: 2,810,931.**
● **The official age of Rome in 2007 is 2,760 years.**
● **There have been 169 popes and 73 emperors.**
● **The area of the city covers 1,494sq km (577sq miles).**

SECRET KEYHOLE

Rome's most charming view is from Piazza dei Cavalieri di Malta on Aventine Hill. To find it, go to the left of the church of Santa Sabina and to the end of the piazza; look through the keyhole of the door (No. 3) of the Priory of the Knights of Malta. Through this tiny hole you will see a secret garden and an avenue of trees framing… but let's not spoil the surprise: see for yourself.

WATERY WASTE

More than 50 of Rome's fountains are fed by the waters of the Aqua Virgo, a source that the Romans first brought into the city in 19BC. It flows from the countryside outside the city, and feeds the Barcaccia fountain at the foot of the Spanish Steps, before supplying many others, including the most famous of them all, the Fontana di Trevi.

SWISS GUARD

The pope's official bodyguards are recruited from Switzerland's four predominantly Catholic cantons. Each must be between 19 and 25, at least 1.75cm (5ft 8in) tall and remain unmarried during their tour of duty. Their distinctive uniforms were designed by Michelangelo in the colours of the Medici popes—red, yellow and blue.

A Short Stay in Rome

DAY 1

Morning Take breakfast in a café in **Campo de' Fiori** (▷ 48), a pretty square whose market makes a lively start to the day. Then glance at Piazza Farnese before walking east through the quiet streets of the Ghetto to Piazza Venezia and up the ramp to **Piazza del Campidoglio** (▷ 34).

Mid-morning Look around the piazza, dipping into the church of **Santa Maria in Aracoeli** (▷ 35) and the **Musei Capitolini** (▷ 28–29). Or make straight for the **Foro Romano** (▷ 26–27), the **Palatino** (▷ 34) and the **Colosseum** (▷ 24–25)—take the alley and steps to the rear left of Piazza del Campidoglio for a wonderful view of the Forum.

Lunch There are several restaurants near the Colosseum, notably **Nerone** and **Pasquilino** (▷ 38). Alternatively, buy a snack in **Cavour 313** (▷ 37) or the café at the Monumento a Vittorio Emanuele II—it has great views over the Foro Romano and **Fori Imperiali** (▷ 33).

Afternoon Visit the **Palazzo Doria Pamphilj** (▷ 44–45) and see the **Colonna di Marco Aurelio** (▷ 51) before walking to the **Fontana di Trevi** (▷ 78). Then walk to **Piazza di Spagna** for the Spanish Steps (▷ 81). If you want to shop, now is the time to do so, for the streets on and around nearby Via Condotti contain Rome's best stores. If not, and you want more culture, take a short walk east to the **Palazzo Barberini** (▷ 80), passing **Santa Maria delle Concezione** (▷ 87) on the way.

Dinner Take a bus or taxi to Trastevere, which has a wide choice of places to eat (▷ 73–74).

Evening Trastevere is not the cutting-edge nightlife district it once was, but its streets remain some of Rome's prettiest places to wander after dark.

DAY 2

Morning Today explore central Rome and the **Vatican** (▷ 96–97). If you want to do the museums justice, and beat some of the crowds, you'll need at least a morning and may wish to start the day there—or save them for another, longer visit. Otherwise, have breakfast in **Piazza Navona** (▷ 49) Rome's grandest square (or in **Bar della Pace**, ▷ 58, just off it), before the crowds arrive. Then walk east to the **Pantheon** (▷ 46–47) via San Luigi dei Francesi, also seeing **Santa Maria sopra Minerva** (▷ 50).

Mid-morning Take a coffee in **La Tazza d'Oro** (▷ 60). Then walk down Via delle Coppelle to see **Sant'Agostino** (▷ 52) and the superb **Palazzo Altemps** (▷ 42–43). Walk back towards Piazza Navona and explore Via dei Coronari and/or Via del Governo Vecchio or Via dei Banchi Nuovi, three of central Rome's most interesting streets.

Lunch The streets around Piazza Navona have plenty of bars and restaurants for lunch or a snack.

Afternoon Depending on time, and whether you want to see the Vatican museums, visit the **Castel Sant'Angelo** (▷ 95). Then make for the museums, or, for a more leisurely time, confine yourself to **St. Peter's** (▷ 94).

Dinner The area around St. Peter's is not great for dining, so take the 64 bus back to the heart of the city. The streets around Piazza Navona and Campo de' Fiori have plenty of restaurants.

Evening Join the throng in Piazza Navona, indulging in a famous *tartufo* ice cream from **Tre Scalini** (▷ 60). Or have a drink in one of the area's many bars. For peace and quiet, walk east to the **Ghetto** (▷ 67), whose streets are often deserted, despite being minutes from the night-time hubbub.

Top 25

►►►

ESSENTIAL ROME **TOP 25**

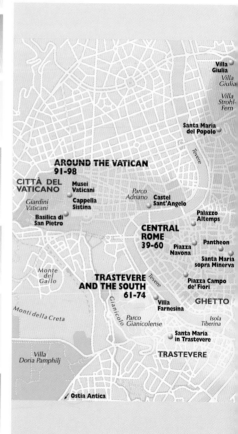

Villa Giulia
Villa Giulia
Villa Strohl-Fern

Santa Maria del Popolo

Tevere

AROUND THE VATICAN
91–98

CITTÀ DEL VATICANO
Giardini Vaticani
Basilica di San Pietro

Musei Vaticani
Cappella Sistina

Parco Adriano
Castel Sant'Angelo

Palazzo Altemps

CENTRAL ROME
39–60
Piazza Navona

Pantheon

Santa Maria sopra Minerva

Monte del Gallo

TRASTEVERE AND THE SOUTH
61–74

Tevere

Villa Farnesina

Piazza Campo de' Fiori

GHETTO

Monti della Creta

Gianicolo

Parco Gianicolense

Isola Tiberina

Santa Maria in Trastevere

Villa Doria Pamphilj

TRASTEVERE

Ostia Antica

These pages are a quick guide to the Top 25, which are described in more detail later. Here they are listed alphabetically and the tinted background shows which area they are in.

Fontana di Trevi ▷ 78
Nicola Salvi's baroque masterpiece and Rome's most popular fountain.

Foro Romano ▷ 26–27
The heart of ancient Rome and one of the city's most evocative sites.

Museo e Galleria Borghese ▷ 79 Beloved museum with great art in beautiful surroundings.

Musei Capitolini ▷ 28–29 The oldest collection in the world, with over 1,300 works.

Musei Vaticani & Cappella Sistina ▷ 96–97 Supreme treasures spanning more than 3,000 years.

Ostia Antica ▷ 102–103 Ancient ruins, pine trees and wild spring flowers make the perfect setting.

Palazzo Altemps ▷ 42–43 A superb Renaissance building with top-class Classical sculpture.

Palazzo Barberini ▷ 80 Beautiful piazza named after the powerful Barberini family.

Palazzo-Galleria Doria Pamphilj ▷ 44–45 An important art collection displayed in a beautiful palace.

Palazzo Massimo alle Terme ▷ 82–83 Some of Rome's most magnificent Classical treasures.

Piazza di Spagna ▷ 81
Site of the city's most stunning stairway, the Spanish Steps.

Piazza Campo de 'Fiori ▷ 48 A picturesque and atmospheric square in the heart of the city.

Pantheon ▷ 46–47 The best-preserved building from the Roman world; the last resting place of Raphael.

◀ ◀ ◀

9

Shopping

Rome was once the market place of an empire that embraced much of the known world. These days it has a more humble place in the shopping firmament. This said, all the great Italian retail staples—food, wine, fashion, shoes, leatherware and clothing—are well represented, and the city is a good source of art, antiques, traditional crafts and artisan products such as furniture.

More for your Money

Mid-price shoes and clothes represent good value for money; you will find them in countless shops around the new city, but particularly Via Nazionale, Via del Tritone and Via del Corso. The same streets are also dotted with small specialist shops selling good-quality bags, gloves and other leatherware. The sprawling market in an ex-barracks near Piazza Vittorio Emanuele II, where most Romans do their shopping, is also a good source of clothes and shoes, as well as pots, pans and kitchenware with an Italian stamp (such as coffee makers). In stylish Rome, even inexpensive clothes tend to be good quality and well-cut.

Designer Names

At the other sartorial extreme, most of the great Italian and European fashion houses have shops in the city: Gucci, Prada, Armani are all here, mostly in the grid of streets around Via

ANTIQUES

It is no wonder, given Rome's long history, that the city is a treasury of antiques. Prices are often high, but the range of objects—Etruscan, Roman, Renaissance, baroque and other items—is unrivalled. For paintings and prints, head for Via Margutta, which also has a scattering of galleries selling contemporary art and carpets, while for general antiques try Via Giulia, Via del Babuino (particularly for Persian carpets), Via dei Coronari, Via dell'Orso and Via del Monserrato. Also good, and with lower prices and less exclusive stock, are Via del Panico, Via del Pellegrino and Via dei Banchi Nuovi.

Great fashion houses sit side by side on Via Condotti, with the occasional gelaterie in between for refreshment

Condotti, an excellent source of high-class clothes, shoes, lingerie and accessories. Department stores have not really caught on, and only Coin and Rinascente are worth a visit.

Tempt your Taste Buds

Shopping for food has a unique charm in Rome, whether in the small area shops known as *alimentari*, or the specialist delicatessens in streets such as Via della Croce. The city's ancient markets, particularly Campo de' Fiori, are colourful sources of provisions. Pasta in every shape and size, the finest extra virgin oil, *funghi porcini* (dried cep mushrooms), truffle oil and spices made good food buys.

Catholic Paraphernalia

The range of shops selling ecclesiastical items is vast. The largest concentration is around St. Peter's—look out for ceramic Swiss Guards and fluorescent rosaries. On Via dei Cestari all manner of ecclesiastic garb is available—if you ever daydreamed about buying a bishop's robe or a cardinal's hat, this is the place.

Fun for the Tourist

Rome has any number of shops and stalls selling plaster and plastic casts of famous statues. Around the tourist traps are plenty of souvenirs, from figures of gladiators to models of the Colosseum. Better-quality items, plus books, prints and artistic replicas, are sold in museum and gallery shops.

Something to take home—a culinary delight, a designer bag or an exclusive little number from a top name

MARBLED PAPER
Notebooks and other stationery items covered with marbled paper make wonderful souvenirs, which you can find in shops all over the city. The paper originated in Venice, where the technique arrived from the East in the 15th century, and is still handmade. The process involves floating multicolour pigments on liquid gum and combing the different colours, separated by ox-gall, into distinctive patterns. The paper is placed delicately on top, then lifted and hung up to dry.

Shopping by Theme

Whether you're looking for a department store, a quirky boutique, or something in between, you'll find it all in Rome. On this page shops are listed by theme. For a more detailed write-up, see the individual listings in Rome by Area.

ACCESSORIES AND LEATHER GOODS

Gucci (▷ 89)
Mondello Ottica (▷ 56)
La Perla (▷ 89)
Sergio di Cori (▷ 89)

BOOKS AND STATIONERY

Almost Corner Bookshop (▷ 71)
Antica Libreria Croce (▷ 55)
Feltrinelli (▷ 55)
Pineider (▷ 89)
Poggi (▷ 56)
Il Sigillo (▷ 56)

DEPARTMENT STORES

Coin (▷ 37)

INTERIORS

Almaxxura (▷ 71)
Bassetti (▷ 55)
Casimon (▷ 71)
Culti (▷ 55)
Ginori (▷ 89)
House & Kitchen (▷ 56)
Lumières (▷ 71)
Maria Grazia Luffarelli (▷ 56)
Ornamentum (▷ 56)
Pandora (▷ 71)
Spazio Sette (▷ 56)

FOOD AND WINE

Antica Enoteca (▷ 89)
Al Monasteri (▷ 55)
Bottega del Cioccolata (▷ 37)
Castroni (▷ 98)
Enoteca al Goccetto (▷ 55)
Panella (▷ 37)
Pietro Franchi (▷ 98)
La Renella (▷ 71)

FOOTWEAR

AVC di Adriana Campanile (▷ 89)
Fausto Santini (▷ 89)
Ferragamo (▷ 89)

MEN'S FASHION

Battistoni (▷ 89)
Ermenegildo Zegna (▷ 89)
Prada (▷ 89)

OUTDOOR MARKETS

Campo de' Fiori (▷ 55)
Mercato Andrea Doria (▷ 98)
Mercato di Via Sannio (▷ 37)
Piazza Coppelle (▷ 56)
Piazza San Cosimato (▷ 71)
Porta Portese (▷ 71)

WOMEN'S FASHION

Ethic (▷ 55)
Fabindia (▷ 55)
Giorgio Armani (▷ 89)
Marella (▷ 89)
Prada ▷ (89)

Rome by Night

After dark the heat of a summer day gives way to balmy evenings and life takes to the streets, allowing you to share in the soft, sweet blandishments of *la dolce vita,* still as vibrant and seductive as in the heady 1950s. Bars and cafés fill with Romans at their sleek and well-dressed best, while Lotharios and lean-limbed starlets and wannabes glide around the city on snarling Vespas and in open-topped sports cars.

Roman Illuminations

The Pantheon and Colosseum are spectacular under floodlights and romantic under moonlight. St. Peter's takes on a different hue under Rome's velvety night skies—come at midnight or later and you may well have Piazza San Pietro to yourself. The experience is magical. Much the same can be said of Rome's other great set-pieces, Piazza Navona, the Trevi Fountain and Spanish Steps. Piazza Navona, like a great nocturnal salon, fills with street performers, food stalls, artists and locals and visitors there to see and be seen.

Under the Stars

If you prefer tranquillity then walk from one sleepy fountain-splashed piazza to the next, sip an aperitif in a flower-decked terrace or eat alfresco—one of Rome's pleasures. Alternatively, take in an open-air concert amid ancient Roman ruins or a beautiful Renaissance garden.

As night falls, and you move from café to bar, enjoy the city's illuminated sights along the way

NOCTURNAL STROLLS

Rome's trendiest after-dark areas are San Lorenzo, a student and working-class district east of the city, and working-class Testaccio, to the south. Both are some way from the heart of town. So if you don't need to be at the cutting edge, spend the night in Trastevere, an established area full of small squares and pretty streets. To escape its crowds, walk to the Pincio from the top of the Spanish Steps for great sunset views, or wander through the old Ghetto area south of Via delle Botteghe Oscure, beautifully deserted after dark.

Eating Out

In Rome prepare yourself for rich, sun-drenched tastes. Thousands of restaurants cater to every budget and provide every kind of dining experience. Eating is so much a social way of life that it is quite normal to spend several hours over a meal.

When to Eat

If you are eating breakfast in a bar, as many Romans do, you will find that most bars open at around 7–7.30am for cappuccino and a croissant. In hotels, breakfast usually starts at 8am, and includes cereal, cold meat and cheeses. Restaurants open for lunch at 12.30 or 1pm, and serve until about 3pm. Romans generally eat dinner late, so many restaurants don't open for evening meals until 8pm, although you will find some that open earlier. Many places, especially cafés and bars, stay open all day.

Where to Eat

There are several different types of eating establishments in Rome. A *ristorante* tends to be the most expensive, with pristine table linen and waiters. The *trattoria* is less formal, less expensive and often family-run. An *osteria* or *hostaria* can be basic, sometimes with paper tablecloths and no written menu, but can serve some of the best food. A *rosticceria* or *tavola calda* is a fast-food outlet serving mostly cold foods. If you want pizza, look for the sign *pizzeria forno a legno* to make sure that it is traditionally cooked in a wood-fired oven.

PRICE MATTERS

Although in theory restaurants are no longer allowed to add a bread and cover charge, many feign oblivion to this and just charge for the bread anyway. Normally service is not included, although a minority of establishments do still add it as a fixed item. In everyday pizzerias, a tip of 5 per cent is perfectly adequate, but in *ristoranti*, if the service has been good, 10 per cent would be acceptable. You should always be given a receipt after paying the bill as the restaurant could be fined if they don't issue one.

Pizza, pasta or something more substantial, whatever your choice, finish it off with an espresso coffee

Restaurants by Cuisine

There are restaurants to suit all tastes and budgets in Rome. On this page they are listed by cuisine. For a more detailed description of each restaurant, see Rome by Area.

BARS BY DAY

Antica Birreria Fratelli
  Tempe Ra (▷ 58)
Bar della Pace (▷ 58)
Gran Caffé Martini e Rossi
  (▷ 38)
Latteria del Gallo (▷ 59–60)
Sacchetti (▷ 74)
Salotto 42 (▷ 60)
San Clemente (▷ 38)

COFFEE/PASTRIES

Antico Caffè Brasile
  (▷ 38)
Babington's Tea Rooms
  (▷ 90)
Bibli (▷ 73)
Caffè Farnese (▷ 58)
Sant' Eustachio (▷ 60)
La Tazza d'Oro (▷ 60)
Trastè (▷ 74)

FINE DINING

Bramante (▷ 58)
Checchino dal 1887
  (▷ 73)
Il Convivio (▷ 58)
Sabatini (▷ 74)
Vecchia Roma (▷ 60)

FISH/SEAFOOD

Alberto Ciarla (▷ 73)
Dur Filettaro a Santa
  Barbara (▷ 59)
La Rosetta (▷ 60)

GELATERIE

Alberto Pica (▷ 73)
Da Mirella (▷ 73)
Gelateria della Palma
  (▷ 59)
Giolitti (▷ 59)
Tre Scalini (▷ 60)

PIZZA/PASTA

Baffetto (▷ 58)
Corallo (▷ 58)
Dar Poeta (▷ 73)
Da Vittorio (▷ 73)
Est! Est! Est! (▷ 90)
Ivo (▷ 74)
Leoncino (▷ 90)
Panattoni (▷ 74)
Pizza Ciro (▷ 90)

ROMAN/ITALIAN

Adriano (▷ 106)
Agate e Romeo (▷ 38)
Augusto (▷ 73)
Il Bacaro (▷ 58)
Borgo Nuovo (▷ 98)
Cacciani (▷ 106)
Ciccia Bomba (▷ 59)
Da Francesco (▷ 59)
Dal Toscano (▷ 98)
Ditirambo (▷ 59)
Grappolo d'Oro (▷ 59)
Il Grottino della Sibil la dal
  1826 (▷ 106)
'Gusto (▷ 59)
Nerone (▷ 38)
Paris (▷ 74)
Pasquilino (▷ 38)
Sora Lella (▷ 74)
Taverna Angelica (▷ 98)
Tucci (▷ 60)
Zarazzà (▷ 106)

WORLD CUISINES

Charly's Saucière (▷ 38)
Giggetto (▷ 73)
Hasekura (▷ 38)
L'Eau Vive (▷ 60)
Piperno (▷ 74)
Thien Kim (▷ 60)
Zen Sushi (▷ 98)

If You Like...

However you'd like to spend your time in Rome, these top suggestions should help you tailor your ideal visit. Each sight or listing has a fuller write-up in Rome by Area.

BURNING THE MIDNIGHT OIL

Sit up late with the beautiful people in Bar della Pace (▷ 58).
Share a glass or two of wine with the characters in the bars around Campo de' Fiori (▷ 48).
Visit one or more of the many clubs in the Testaccio (▷ 72) nightlife district.

THE LAP OF LUXURY

Go mad in the chic designer stores in the streets around Via dei Condotti (▷ 89).
Stay in one of the city's opulent five-star hotels, notably the Hassler (▷ 112).
Eat at Convivio or La Rosetta (▷ 58, 60), two of the city's best restaurants.

Cafés in Campo dei Fiori buzz at night (top). Spoil yourself and stay in one of Rome's top hotels (above)

TO KEEP YOUR CHILDREN HAPPY

Take them to the Bioparco in the Villa Borghese (▷ 87).
Buy lots of ice cream, especially from Giolitti or Gelateria della Palma (▷ 59).
Introduce them to the characters dressed as centurions and gladiators outside the Colosseum (▷ 24–25).

SAVING FOR A RAINY DAY

Buy an integrated travel pass (▷ 118–119) and save on public transport.
Visit Rome's art-crammed churches— such as Santa Maria sopra Minerva (▷ 50)—they are virtually all free.
Time your visit for the last Sunday of the month, when the normally expensive Vatican museums (▷ 96–97) are free.

Posing outside the Colosseum (above right). Visit Santa Prassede for free (right)

A night of jazz (below). A hotel offering unparalleled views of the city (below middle)

AN EVENING OF ENTERTAINMENT

See what's playing at the Teatro dell'Opera di Roma (▷ 90).

Enjoy a night of blues or jazz at Big Mama's (▷ 72).

Look out for posters advertising church recitals and other classical music concerts. In summer, many are held outdoors (▷ 37).

A MEMORABLE PLACE TO STAY

De Russie (▷ 112) broke the mold for luxury Rome hotels with its sleek and clean-lined contemporary design.

You want history? The Albergo del Sole al Pantheon (▷ 112) has been a hotel for over 500 years.

The pretty, ivy-covered Raphael (▷ 112) is a tranquil, perfectly situated gem.

ROMANTIC SUPPERS

Dine outdoors in summer; try Panattoni (▷ 74), but almost any restaurant or pizzeria will do.

Vecchia Roma (▷ 60) may not have Rome's best food, but its lovely setting is delightful.

Buy a picnic and take it to the Pincio gardens (▷ 87) to watch the sunset over St. Peter's.

Eat Italian at a traditional trattoria (above) and shop in style on Via Condotti (below)

SPECIALTY SHOPPING

Via dei Coronari (▷ 55–56) and the streets nearby are the places for antiques and sumptuous fabrics.

Stroll down Via Margutta to take in its various art galleries (▷ 10, panel 55).

For designer clothes and accessories, it has to be Via Condotti (▷ 89).

ESSENTIAL ROME IF YOU LIKE...

A BREATH OF FRESH AIR

*Get away from it all—
Villa Borghese and Colle
Oppio (below)*

The Villa Borghese (▷ 87) park offers
numerous walks and shady nooks.
Escape the crowds around the Forum
by climbing the Palatine Hill (▷ 34).
If you don't have time to see the
Gianicolo and Villa Doria Pamphilj above
Trastevere, how about the closer Orto
Botanico (▷ 68).

A TASTE OF TRADITION

Long-established Giggetto (▷ 73)
and Piperno (▷ 74) serve classic
Roman-Jewish cuisine.
As its name suggests,
Checchino dal 1887 (▷ 73)
has been serving traditional
Roman food for over 120 years.
To sample pizza at its best, try Ivo
(▷ 74) and Baffetto (▷ 58), who have served
pizza to generations of Romans.

A GREAT CUP OF COFFEE

La Tazza d'Oro (▷ 60), a stone's throw from
the Pantheon, is a temple to the espresso.
Sant' Eustachio (▷ 60) serves what many locals
consider to be Rome's best cup of coffee.
Antico Caffè Brasile (▷ 38) knows its beans—
Pope John Paul II once bought his coffee here.

THE WORLD'S BEST CLASSICAL SCULPTURE

*After visiting the Musei
Capitolini (below) move
on to La Tazza d'Ore
(above) for a great coffee*

Visit the Palazzo Altemps (▷ 42–43) and
Palazzo Massimo alle Terme (▷ 82–83),
which have manageable and beautifully
presented collections.
To see individual sculptural works go
to the Museo Capitolini (▷ 28–29), with
some of the city's most significant pieces.
The Laocoön (▷ 96) is the most celebrated of the Vatican museums' immense
collection of sculptures.

The Ancient City is where Rome began, first as a series of settlements on the Palatine Hill, and then as the site of the Foro Romano, the civic, social and political heart of the empire for over 500 years.

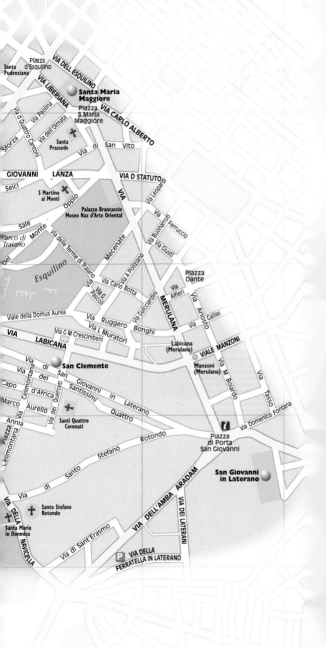

Colosseo

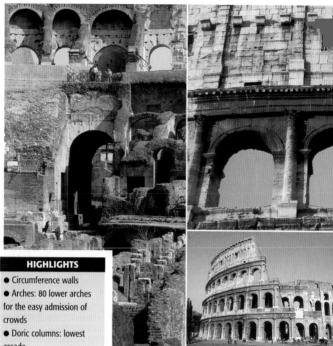

HIGHLIGHTS

- Circumference walls
- Arches: 80 lower arches for the easy admission of crowds
- Doric columns: lowest arcade
- Ionic columns: central arcade
- Corinthian columns: upper arcade
- Underground cells
- Sockets that once housed binding metal clamps
- Vomitoria: interior exits and entrances
- Views from the upper levels

TIP

- The Colosseum's ticket office can be very busy—buy your ticket at the Palatine to avoid waiting, or online.

The Pantheon may be better preserved and the Forum more historically important, but no monument in Rome rivals the majesty of the Colosseum, the largest surviving structure from Roman antiquity.

Awe-inspiring The Colosseum was begun by Emperor Vespasian in AD72 and inaugurated by his son, Titus, in AD80 with a gala that saw 5,000 animals slaughtered in a day (and 100 days of continuous games thereafter). Finishing touches to the 55,000-seat stadium were added by Domitian (AD81–96). Three types of columns support the arcades, and the walls are made of brick and volcanic tufa faced with marble blocks, which were once bound together by metal clamps. Its long decline began in the Middle Ages, with the pillaging of stone to build churches and palaces. The

Inside the Colosseum the various tiers are still very evident (far left). The magnificent Colosseum is a daunting sight from all perspectives: close up, from a distance, illuminated at night or under an Italian sunset

desecration ended in 1744, when the structure was consecrated in memory of the Christians supposedly martyred in the arena (later research suggests they weren't). Clearing of the site and excavations began late in the 19th century.

Games Armed combat at the Colosseum went on for some 500 years. Criminals, slaves and gladiators fought each other or wild animals, often to the death. Women and dwarfs also wrestled, and mock sea battles were waged (the arena could be flooded via underground pipes). Spectators exercised the power of life and death over defeated combatants, by waving handkerchiefs to show mercy or by displaying a down-turned thumb to demand the finishing stroke. Survivors' throats were often cut anyway, and the dead were poked with a red-hot iron to make sure they had expired.

THE BASICS

✚ J7
✉ Piazza del Colosseo, Via dei Fori Imperiali
☎ 06 3996 7700; online booking www.pierreci.it
🕐 May–end Sep daily 9–7.30; Apr and Oct 9–6.30; Nov–end Mar 9–4.30. Last admission 1 hour before closing
🚇 Colosseo
🚌 3, 60, 75, 85, 87, 117, 175 to Piazza del Colosseo
♿ Poor to the interior; limited access from Via Celio Vibenna entrance
💰 Expensive (joint ticket with Palatino)

Foro Romano

HIGHLIGHTS

● Temple of Antoninus and Faustina (AD141)
● Colonna di Foca (AD608)
● Arch of Septimius Severus (AD203)
● Curia (Senate House, 80BC)
● 12 columns from the Portico of the Dei Consentes (AD367)
● 8 columns from the Temple of Saturn (Tempio di Saturno, 42BC, AD284)
● House of the Vestal Virgins

TIPS

● Making sense of the Forum is quite a challenge—use an audioguide to get more out of your visit.
● Take something to drink as there are no bars in the Forum area.

The civic and political heart of the Roman Empire was Rome's Forum. Its ruins can be difficult to decipher, but the site is one of the most evocative in the city, the standing stones and fragments conjuring up echoes of a once powerful state.

History The Forum (Foro Romano) started life as a marsh between the Palatine and Capitoline hills, taking its name from a word meaning 'outside the walls'. Later, unfortunately, it became a rubbish dump, and then, having been drained, a marketplace and a religious shrine. In time it acquired all the structures of Rome's burgeoning civic, social and political life. Over the many centuries consuls, emperors and senators have embellished it with magnificent temples, courts and basilicas.

Lone columns and fallen masonary give few clues to the Forum's former impressiveness (far left). Marble Arch of Titus (middle). Detail of relief decoration and frieze on the remains of the Forum market (bottom left). A remaining Corinthian column (bottom right). The view across the Forum, with the Colosseum in the background (right)

Forum and Palatine Two millennia of plunder and decay have left a mish-mash of odd pillars and jumbled stones, which nonetheless can begin to make vivid sense given a plan and some imagination. This strange, empty space is romantic, especially on the Palatine Hill to the south, once covered by a palace.

What to see Today orange trees, oleanders and cypresses line the paths, and grasses and wildflowers flourish among the ancient remains. Worth a visit are the Temple of Antoninus and Faustina, the Colonna di Foca, the Curia, the restored Arch of Septimius Severus, the Portico of the Dei Consentes, the Temple of Saturn, Santa Maria Antiqua (the Forum's oldest church), the aisle of the Basilica of the Emperor Maxentius, the House of the Vestal Virgins and the Arch of Titus.

THE BASICS

✚ H7

✉ Entrances alongside Arco di Settimio Sevoro, near Arco di Tito and Largo Romolo e Remo on Via dei Fori Imperiali

☎ 06 699 0110 or 06 3996 7700

🕐 Daily 9 to 1 hour before dusk

🚇 Colosseo

🚌 60, 75, 84, 85, 87, 117, 271, 571, 810, 850 to Via dei Fori Imperiali

♿ Access difficult to much of site

💶 Forum free. Palatine expensive (joint ticket with Colosseum)

Musei Capitolini

HIGHLIGHTS

Palazzo Nuovo
● Statue of Marcus Aurelius
● Sculpture: *Capitoline Venus*
● Sculpture: *Dying Gaul*
● Sculpture: *Wounded Amazon*
● Sculpture: *Discobolus*
● Sala degli Imperatori

Palazzo dei Conservatori
● *St. John the Baptist*, Caravaggio
● Bronze: *Lupa Capitolina*
● Bronze: *Spinario*
● Marble figure: *Esquiline Venus*

TIP
● Allow plenty of time and be prepared to concentrate. This is not the easiest museum and not for the fainthearted.

Few in number, but outstanding, the Greek and Roman sculptures in the Capitoline Museums (Palazzo Nuovo and Palazzo dei Conservatori) make a far more accessible introduction to the subject than the Vatican Museums.

Palazzo Nuovo The Capitoline Museums occupy two palaces on opposite sides of the Piazza del Campidoglio and are linked by an underground passage. Both have recently been restored. Designed by Michelangelo, the Palazzo Nuovo (on the north side) contains most of the finest pieces, none greater than the magnificent 2nd-century AD bronze equestrian statue of Marcus Aurelius (just off the main courtyard). Moved here from outside San Giovanni in Laterano in the Middle Ages, it is now restored

Ancient statuary, such as the remains of Constantine's giant statue (far left and middle) and a Satyr (right), make up the collection. Sculpture in the Palazzo dei Conservatori, which holds the largest part of the collection (bottom left). A closer look demonstrates the amazing detail on these works of art (bottom middle and right)

and covered. Among the sculptures inside are celebrated Roman copies in marble of Greek originals, including the *Dying Gaul*, *Wounded Amazon*, *Capitoline Venus* and the discus thrower *Discobolus*. In the Sala degli Imperatori is a portrait gallery of busts of Roman emperors.

Palazzo dei Conservatori This former seat of Rome's medieval magistrates contains an art gallery (the Pinacoteca Capitolina) and a further rich hoard of Classical sculpture. Bronzes include the 1st-century BC *Spinario*, a boy removing a thorn from his foot, and the 5th-century BC Etruscan *Lupa Capitolina*, the famous she-wolf suckling Romulus and Remus (the twins were added by Antonio Pollaiuolo in 1510). Paintings include works by Caravaggio, Velázquez, Titian, Veronese and Van Dyck.

THE BASICS

www.museicapitolini.org
✚ G6
✉ Musei Capitolini, Piazza del Campidoglio 1
☎ 06 6710 2475 or 06 3996 7800
🕐 Tue–Sun 9–8
🚌 40, 44, 64 and all other services to Piazza Venezia
♿ Poor: steps to Piazza del Campidoglio
💶 Expensive; combined Capitolini Card available

San Clemente

Two of San Clemente's treasures: 12th-century mosaics (left) and the Mithraic temple (right)

THE BASICS

☐ K7
✉ Via di San Giovanni in Laterano
☎ 06 7045 1018
🕐 Mon–Sat 9–12.30, 3–6, Sun 10–12.30, 3–6
🚌 60, 85, 87, 117, 175 to Piazza del Colosseo or 85, 117, 850 to Via di San Giovanni in Laterano
♿ Church free; excavations moderate

HIGHLIGHTS

● Choir screen
● Chapel of St. Catherine: fresco cycle
● Ciborio: altar canopy
● Apse mosaic: *The Triumph of the Cross*
● Monument to Cardinal Roverella, Giovanni Dalmata (upper church)
● Fresco: *Miracle of San Clemente*
● Fresco: *Legend of Sisinnio*
● Triclinium
● Altar of Mithras: bas-relief of Mithras slaying the bull

No site in Rome reveals as vividly the layers of history that underpin the city as this beautiful medieval ensemble built over a superbly preserved 4th-century church and the remains of a 3rd-century Mithraic temple.

The upper church The present San Clemente, which was named after Rome's fourth pope, was built between 1108 and 1184 to replace an earlier one that was sacked by the Normans in 1084. Almost untouched since, its medieval interior is dominated by the 12th-century marble panels of the choir screen and pulpits and the glittering 12th-century apse mosaic, *The Triumph of the Cross*. Equally captivating are the *Life of St. Catherine* frescos (1428–31) by Masolino da Panicale.

Below ground Steps descend to the lower church, which retains traces of 8th- to 11th-century frescos of San Clemente and the legends of Sts. Alessio and Sisinnio. More steps lead deeper into the twilight world of the best-preserved of the 12 Mithraic temples uncovered in Rome. (Mithraism was a popular, men-only cult, eclipsed by Christianity.) Here are an altar with a bas-relief of Mithras ritually slaying a bull, and the triclinium, used for banquets and rites. Excavations are revealing parts of the temple, and the 1,900-year-old remains of buildings, streets and an underground stream, which you can hear even today, that may have formed part of ancient Rome's drainage system.

San Giovanni in Laterano

Statues on top of the façade seen from afar (left). The beautiful ornate ceiling (right)

San Giovanni's soaring façade can be seen from afar, its distinctive statues rising over the rooftops—a deliberate echo of St. Peter's—reminding us that this is the cathedral church of Rome and the pope's titular see in his role as bishop of Rome.

In the early days A 4th-century palace here provided a meeting place for Pope Miltiades and Constantine (the first Christian emperor), later becoming a focus for Christianity. Earthquakes, fires and Barbarians destroyed the earliest churches on the site, so the façade, modelled on St. Peter's, dates from 1735, and Borromini's interior from 1646. It was the papal residence in Rome until the 14th century, when the popes moved to the Vatican.

Interior treasures Bronze doors from the Forum's Curia usher you into the cavernous interior, its chill whites and greys redeemed by a fabulously ornate ceiling. Other highlights include an apse mosaic by Jacopo Torriti (1288–94) and the beautiful cloister (off the north transept). A high altar reliquary is supposed to contain the heads of St. Peter and St. Paul, and a frescoed tabernacle is attributed to Arnolfo di Cambio and Fiorenzo de Lorenzo.

Step outside Outside are the Scala Santa, reputedly the steps ascended by Christ at his trial in Jerusalem. The octagonal baptistery dates back to the time of Constantine and was the model for many subsequent baptisteries.

THE BASICS

➕ L8

✉ Piazza di San Giovanni in Laterano

☎ 06 6988 6433

🕐 Church Apr–end Sep daily 7–7 (Oct–end Mar until 6/6.30). Cloisters daily 9–12, 4–6 (until 5 in winter). Scala Santa daily 6.15–12, 3–6.30. Baptistery daily 9–12, 4–7

Ⓜ San Giovanni

🚌 3, 16, 81, 85, 87, 117, 850 to Piazza di San Giovanni in Laterano

♿ Poor: steps to church

🎫 Church, Scala Santa, baptistery free. Cloister inexpensive

HIGHLIGHTS

- Central portal: bronze doors
- Fresco: *Boniface VIII*, attributed to Giotto
- Cappella Corsini
- Frescoed tabernacle
- High altar reliquary
- Apse mosaic, Jacopo Torriti
- Cloister: columns and inlaid marble mosaics
- Papal altar: only the pope can celebrate mass here
- Scala Santa
- Baptistery

Santa Maria Maggiore

Ferdinando Fuga's 18th-century façade (right) conceals a beautiful interior (left)

THE BASICS

📍 K5

✉ Piazza di Santa Maria Maggiore and Piazza dell'Esquilino

☎ 06 483 195 or 06 581 4802

🕐 Apr–end Sep daily 7–7/8; Oct–end Mar 7–6.30/7. Loggia: guided tours Mar–end Oct daily 9–6.30; Nov–end Feb 9–1

🚇 Termini or Cavour

🚌 C3, 16, 70, 71, 75, 84, 360 to Piazza di Santa Maria Maggiore

♿ Poor: access is easiest from Piazza di Santa Maria Maggiore

🎫 Church free; Loggia inexpensive

HIGHLIGHTS

● Mosaics
● Coffered ceiling
● Four reliefs from a papal altar, Mino del Reame
● Fresco fragments attributed to Cimabue, Pietro Cavallini or Giotto (apse)
● Cappella Sistina
● Cappella Paolina
● Tomb of Cardinal Rodriguez

Santa Maria Maggiore is, justifiably so, considered Rome's finest Early Christian basilica, which is largely thanks to its magnificent mosaic-swathed interior.

History According to a myth, the Virgin appeared to Pope Liberius on 5 August AD352, and told him to build a church exactly where snow would fall the next day. Although it was summer, snow fell, marking the outlines of a basilica on the Esquiline Hill. Legend aside, the church probably dates from AD430, though the campanile (the tallest in Rome at 75m/246ft) was added in 1377 and the interior and exterior were altered in the 13th and 18th centuries. The coffered ceiling, attributed to Giuliano da Sangallo, was reputedly gilded with the first gold to arrive from the New World, a gift from Spain to Alexander VI (note his Borgia bull emblems).

Rich decoration Beyond the general grandeur, the main treasures are the 36 mosaics in the architraves of the nave, 5th-century depictions of the lives of Moses, Abraham, Isaac and Jacob, framed by some 40 ancient columns. Also compelling are the mosaics in the loggia and on the triumphal arch. In the 13th-century apse are mosaics by Jacopo Torriti, the pinnacle of Rome's medieval mosaic tradition. Other highlights include the Cappella Sistina (tomb of Pope Sixtus V) by Domenico Fontana, 1588; the Cappella Paolina, built by Paul V (1611); and Giovanni di Cosma's tomb of Cardinal Rodriguez (1299). The high altar reputedly contains a relic of Christ's crib.

More to See

ARCO DI COSTANTINO
Triumphal arches, like celebratory columns, were usually raised as monuments to military achievement, in this case the victory of Emperor Constantine over his imperial rival Maxentius. It was one of the last great monuments to be built in ancient Rome, and at 21m (69ft) high and 26m (85ft) wide it is also the largest and best-preserved of the city's arches. Most of its reliefs were taken from earlier buildings, partly out of pragmatism and partly out of a desire to link Constantine's glories with those of the past. The battle scenes of the central arch show Trajan at war with the Dacians, while another describes a boar hunt and sacrifice to Apollo.

➕ J7 ✉ Piazza del Colosseo-Via di San Gregorio, Via dei Fori Imperiali 🕓 Always open 🚇 Colosseo 🚌 60, 75, 85, 87, 117, 175, C3 to Piazza del Colosseo ✋ Free

CIRCO MASSIMO
This enormous grassy arena follows the outline of a stadium once capable of seating 300,000 people. Created to satisfy the passionate Roman appetite for chariot racing, and the prototype for almost all subsequent racecourses, it was begun around 326BC and modified frequently before the occasion of its last recorded use under Totila the Ostrogoth in AD549. Much of the original structure was robbed of its stone—old monuments were often ransacked for building materials—but the *spina* (the circuit's dividing wall) remains, marked by a row of cypresses, the ruins of the imperial box and the open arena, now a public park. Avoid after dark.

➕ H8 ✉ Via del Circo Massimo 🕓 Always open 🚇 Circo Massimo 🚌 60, 75, 81, 175, 628, 673, C3 to Piazza di Porta Capena ✋ Free

FORI IMPERIALI
The five colonnaded areas just down the road from the Colesseum were once the Imperial Fora, built as commercial and political meeting places by successive emperors. Plundered remorselessly over the centuries, today's ruins seem at first glance little more

Cast in evening light, the Arch of Constantine

Imperial Forum with the Trajans Market in the foreground

★

than a jumble of columns and tumbled stone, so take time to get your bearings. Excavations are still ongoing, and over 15,000sq m (160,000sq ft) have been unearthed, representing more than half the original fora—and there's still more to discover.

✚ H6 ✉ Via dei Fori Imperiali ☎ 06 679 7786; Visitor Centre 06 679 7702 🕐 Guided tour only, check with Visitor Centre for times 🚇 Colosseo 🚌 75, 84, 87, 117, 175 to Via dei Fori Imperiali 💵 Moderate

MERCATI TRAIANEI

Trajan's markets were a group of commercial buildings constructed at the beginning of the 2nd century AD as a semicircular range of halls on three levels. Two survive in excellent condition, together with many of the 150 booths that once traded rare and expensive commodities.

✚ H6 ✉ Via IV Novembre 94 ☎ 06 679 0048; reservations 06 6978 0532 🕐 Apr–end Sep, Tue–Sun 9–6.30; Oct–end Mar, Tue–Sun 9–4.30 🚇 Cavour 🚌 H, 40, 60, 64, 70, 117, 170 and other routes to Via IV Novembre 💵 Expensive

PALATINO E ORTI FARNESIANI

After a stroll around the Forum it's worth making time to climb the Palatine Hill to enjoy this peaceful spot. Orange groves, cypresses and endless drowsy corners, all speckled with flowers and ancient stones, make up the Orti Farnesiani, which were laid out in the 16th century over the ruins of the palace that once stood here.

✚ H7 ✉ Entrances from Via di San Gregorio 30 and other entrances to the Roman Forum ☎ 06 3996 7700 🕐 Daily 9–1 hour before dusk 🚇 Colosseo 🚌 75, 84, 87, 117, 175 to Via dei Fori Imperiali 💵 Expensive (joint ticket with Colosseum)

PIAZZA DEL CAMPIDOGLIO

This piazza was designed by Michelangelo for Emperor Charles V's triumphal entry into Rome in 1536 on the Capitoline, the most famous of Rome's seven hills and the hub of the Roman Empire. The magnificent buildings that stand on three sides of the square—the Palazzo Senatorio, the Palazzo Nuovo and the Palazzo dei Conservatori, were part of his scheme.

Mercati Trainei terraced up the Quirinal Hill

Remains laid out beneath the ruins on Palatine Hill

🚉 G6 ✉ Piazza del Campidoglio
🚇 Colosseo 🚌 All services to Piazza
Venezia

SAN PIETRO IN VINCOLI

Hidden in a narrow back street, San
Pietro in Vincoli is a thoroughly appealing church. Drop by to admire
Michelangelo's statue of Moses, one
of the most powerful of all the artist's
monumental sculptures. San Pietro in
Vincoli takes its name from the chains
(*vincoli*) proudly kept in the coffer
with bronze doors under the high altar. According to tradition they are the
chains used to bind St. Peter while he
was held captive in the Mamertine
prison. The 20 columns of its interior
arcade came from a Roman temple.

🚉 J6 ✉ Piazza di San Pietro in Vincoli 4a
☎ 06 488 2865 🕐 Daily 8–12/12.30,
3/3.30–6/7 🚇 Colosseo or Cavour 🚌 75,
84 to Via Cavour or 60, 75, 85, 87, 117, 175 to
Piazza del Colosseo ♿ Good 🎟 Free

SANTA MARIA IN ARACOELI

Perched atop the Capitoline Hill, Santa
Maria in Aracoeli, with its glorious
ceiling, fine frescos and soft chande-
lier-lit interior, is a calm retreat from
the ferocious traffic of Piazza Venezia.
The flight of 124 steep steps approaching Santa Maria was built in
1348 to celebrate either the end of a
plague epidemic or the Holy Year pro-
claimed for 1350. The church is first
recorded in AD574, but even then it
was old. Most of the present structure
dates from 1260.

🚉 G/H6 ✉ Piazza d'Aracoeli ☎ 06 679
8155 🕐 Daily 7–12, 4–6 or dusk 🚌 40, 44,
46, 62, 64, 70, 80 and all other services to
Piazza Venezia ♿ Poor: steep steps to main
entrance or steps to Piazza del Campidoglio
🎟 Free

VILLA CELIMONTANA

Set on one of the southern hills of
ancient Rome and scattered with the
remains of ancient buildings, this is
one of Rome's lesser-known parks,
easily accessible from the Colosseum
and San Giovanni in Laterano.

🚉 J8 ✉ Piazza della Navicella 🕐 Daily
7–dusk 🚌 3 to Via dei Parco del Celio or
117, 673 to Via Claudia 🎟 Free

*A statue of Marcus Aurelius takes centre
stage in Piazza del Campidoglio*

*Michelangelo's monumental statue of
Moses, in the church of San Pietro in Vincoli*

Shopping

BOTTEGA DEL CIOCCOLATO

A blissful Italian chocolate shop. Most goodies are produced from a 19th-century Piedmont recipe; others are 'secrets of old masters'. Period cupboards and shelves, and a large mirror reflecting the chocolate creations along the wall in jars.

🔼 J6 ✉ Via Leonina 82 ☎ 06 482 1473 🕐 Mon–Sat 9.30–7.30

COIN

www.coin.it
One of Rome's most popular department stores is a modern, mainly glass building with cosmetics, home furnishings, kitchenware, toys and fashions. The top floor is dedicated to home exhibitions. Prices are higher than in the average store.

🔼 M8 ✉ Piazza Appio 7 ☎ 06 709 0020 🕐 Daily 9.30–8

MERCATO DI VIA SANNIO

This market in the shadow of San Giovanni in Laterano sells bags, belts, shoes, toys and inexpensive clothes. Other stands nearby peddle more interesting bric-a-brac.

🔼 M8 ✉ Via Sannio 🕐 Mon–Fri 10–1.30, Sat 10–6

PANELLA

For over a century, Panella has sold dozens of varieties of bread and cakes, and it has the largest selection of homemade *grissini* (bread stick) in Rome. The back rooms are packed with hard-to-find ingredients.

🔼 K6 ✉ Via Merulana 54–55 ☎ 06 487 2344 🕐 Mon–Sat 8–2, 5–8, Sun 8–2

Entertainment and Nightlife

CAVOUR 313

At the Forum end of Via Cavour, this easily missed wine bar has a relaxed, student feel. Good snacks from the bar and wine by the glass or bottle.

🔼 H6 ✉ Via Cavour 313 ☎ 06 678 5496 🕐 Mon–Sat 12.30–2.30, 7.30–12.30 (also Sun 7.30–12.30 Oct–end May) 🚌 75, 84, 117 to Via Cavour or 84, 85, 87, 175 to Via dei Fori Imperiali

DRUID'S DEN

Friendly and realistic Irish pub that appeals to Romans and expats alike. Also try The Fiddler's Elbow, a popular sister pub around the corner at Via dell'Olmata 43.

🔼 K6 ✉ Via San Martino ai Monti 28 ☎ 06 4890 4781

MUSIC OUTDOORS

Alfresco recitals often take place throughout the city in summer. Locations include the cloisters of Santa Maria della Pace; the Villa Doria Pamphilj; in the grounds of the Villa Giulia; and in the Area Archeologica del Teatro di Marcello from July to September (as part of the Estate al Tempietto, also known as the Concerti del Tempietto). Note that the venues may change from year to year.

🕐 Mon–Fri 5pm–12.30am, Sat–Sun 4pm–1am 🚇 Cavour 🚌 75, 84, 117 to Via Cavour or 16, 70, 71, 360 to Piazza Santa Maria Maggiore

TEATRO COLOSSEO

www.teatrocolosseo.it
In the shadow of the mighty Colosseum, this venue is a rarity for Rome—a theatre that sometimes stages English-language plays. It showcases young directors and actors, and the small stage suits one-man shows.

🔼 J7 ✉ Via Capo d'Africa 5 ☎ 06 700 4932 🕐 Sep–end Jun Mon–Sat 10–1, 3–7 🚇 Colosseo 🚌 30

Restaurants

AGATA E ROMEO (€€€)

www.agataeromei.it

It is worth putting up with a less-than-perfect position south of Termini because this cosy, family-run restaurant serves some of the city's best and most imaginative modern Roman cooking.

➕ K6 ✉ Via Carlo Alberto 45 ☎ 06 446 6115 🕐 Mon–Fri 12.30–2.30, 7.30–10; closed 2 weeks in Jan and Aug 🚌 70, 71, 360 to Via Carlo Alberto

ANTICO CAFFÈ BRASILE (€)

Superb variety of beans and ground coffee sold from huge sacks or at the bar. Try the 'Pope's blend': John Paul II bought his coffee here before his pontificate.

➕ J6 ✉ Via dei Serpenti 23 ☎ 06 488 2319 🕐 Mon–Sat 6am–8pm, Sun 7–7 🚌 60, 63, 64, 70, 117, 170 to Via Nazionale or 75, 84, 117 to Via Cavour

CHARLY'S SAUCIÈRE (€€)

Homey and established, offering reliable French and Swiss staples.

➕ L8 ✉ Via di San Giovanni in Laterano 268–270 ☎ 06 7049 5666 🕐 Tue–Fri 12.30–2.30, Mon–Sat 7.30–10.30; closed 2 weeks in Aug 🚌 85, 117, 850 to Via San Giovanni in Laterano

GRAN CAFFÈ MARTINI E ROSSI (€)

Bar/restaurant popular with locals, and what better location could it have than looking across to the Palatine Hill, with the Colosseo across the road? Good-value all-inclusive menus, plus snacks and vegetarian dishes.

➕ J7 ✉ Piazza del Colosseo ☎ 06 700 4431 🕐 Daily 9am–1am 🚌 85, 87, 117

HASEKURA (€–€€)

Rome's best Japanese food; good set-price menus, with the Forum

ROMAN SPECIALTIES

Roman favourites—though they are by no means confined to the city—include pastas like *bucatini all'amatriciana* (tomato sauce, salt pork and chilli peppers); *spaghetti alla carbonara* (egg, bacon, pepper and cheese); and *gnocchi alla Romana* (small potato or semolina dumplings with tomato or butter). The best-known main course is *saltimbocca alla Romana* (veal scallops with ham and sage, cooked in wine and butter). Also traditional are *trippa* (tripe), *cervelli* (brains) and *coda alla vaccinara* (oxtail).

and Colosseum close by.

➕ J6 ✉ Via dei Serpenti 27 ☎ 06 483 648 🕐 Mon–Sat noon–2.30, 7–10.30; closed Aug 🚇 Cavour 🚌 71, 84 to Via Cavour

NERONE (€€)

A small, friendly, old-fashioned *trattoria* just a few steps north of the Colosseum that is best known for its antipasti buffet and simple Abruzzese cooking. Has a handful of outside tables.

➕ J7 ✉ Via delle Terme di Tito 96 ☎ 06 481 7952 🕐 Mon–Sat 12–3, 7–11; closed Aug 🚇 Colosseo 🚌 60, 75, 85, 87, 117, 175, 810, 850 to Piazza del Colosseo

PASQUILINO (€€)

A simple, long-established *trattoria* with good, robust food a few minutes east of the Colosseum.

➕ K7 ✉ Via dei Santissimi Quattro 66 ☎ 06 700 4576 🕐 Tue–Sun 12.30–2.30, 7.30–11; closed 2 weeks in Aug 🚇 Colosseo 🚌 85 to Via di San Giovanni in Laterano

SAN CLEMENTE (€)

This bar/pizzeria is a great place to refuel between the Colosseo and the basilica of San Giovanni in Laterano. Three vaulted rooms and a terrace offer decent inexpensive food.

➕ K7 ✉ Via di San Giovanni Laterano 124 ☎ 06 7045 0944 🕐 Daily 7am–1am 🚇 Colosseo or San Giovanni 🚌 85, 87, 117 to Via di San Giovanni in Laterano

Here, most of the great churches, palaces and squares of the city's medieval, baroque and Renaissance heyday sit beside museums, monuments and cobbled streets filled with cafés, shops and restaurants.

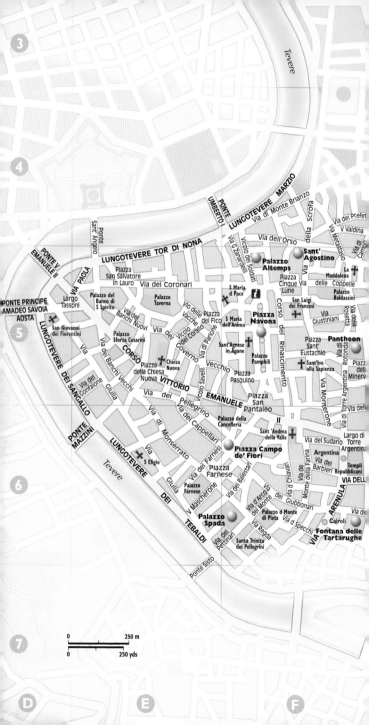

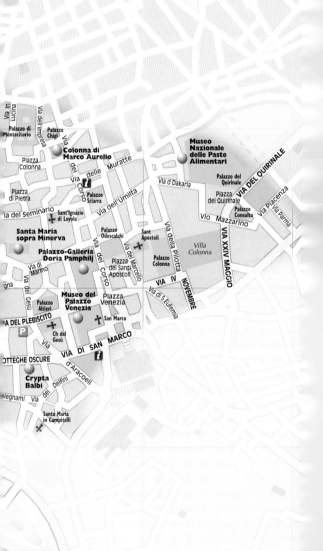

Palazzo di
Montecitorio

Palazzo
Chigi

Via dell'Impresa

Piazza
Colonna

Colonna di
Marco Aurelio

Palazzo
Sciarra

Via delle Muratte

Via del Corso

Via dell'Umiltà

Museo
Nazionale
delle Paste
Alimentari

Via d'Dakaria

Palazzo del
Quirinale

Piazza
del Quirinale

VIA DEL QUIRINALE

Via Placenza

Via Parma

Piazza
di Pietra

Via del Seminario

Sant'Ignazio
di Loyola

Santa Maria
sopra Minerva

Palazzo
Odescalchi

Sant'
Apostoli

Palazzo
Consulta

Vlo Mazzarino

VIA XXIV MAGGIO

Palazzo-Galleria
Doria Pamphilj

Via di
Marino

Piazza
del Santi
Apostoli

Via del Corso

Via del Marcello

Palazzo
Colonna

Villa
Colonna

Via della Pilotta

Via del Gesù

Via di Sbogna

Palazzo
Altieri

Museo del
Palazzo
Venezia

Piazza
Venezia

VIA IV

Via di S Eufemia

NOVEMBRE

A DEL PLEBISCITO

Ch del
Gesù

Via

VIA DI SAN MARCO

San Marco

OTTEGHE OSCURE

d'Aracoeli

Crypta
Balbi

Via dei Delfini

Legnami   Via

Santa Maria
in Campitelli

G   H

Palazzo Altemps

HIGHLIGHTS

- Aphrodite's Throne
- Galatian Soldier statue
- Courtyard loggia
- Satyr pouring wine
- Head of Aphrodite

TIPS

● A combined ticket is available, which includes entry to the Palazzo Altemps, Palazzo Massimo alle Terme and other sights.

● Tickets can be prebooked at www.pierreci.it or call ☎ 06 3996 7700 (Mon–Sat).

This beautiful building epitomizes the best of Renaissance urban architecture, while its series of elegant rooms provides the perfect setting for some of the finest of Rome's Classical sculpture.

The building Rome's Museo Nazionale Romano (National Roman Museum) is housed in two superbly restored buildings; the Palazzo Massimo alle Terme (▷ 82–83) near the station and here in the Palazzo Altemps, whose odd-sounding name is the Italian corruption of the German name von Hohenemps. Mainly constructed in the 15th century, the building houses a series of charming and intimate rooms, many with vaulted ceilings. One gives access to a splendidly frescoed loggia overlooking the comings and goings of a harmonious inner courtyard. The best time to get

A colossal exhibit, just one example from this top-class collection of Classical sculpture (left). Statues watch over the Palazzo Altemps' peaceful courtyard (middle). Statuary exhibited in the arcades (bottom middle). The Painted Loggia on the upper floor (right)

a sense of the building's history is as dusk falls, when the rooms and exhibits are imaginatively lit.

The collections The *palazzo* is home to the famous Ludovisi Collection, amassed by Cardinal Ludovico Ludovisi in the 17th century, as well as the Altemps collection, Egyptian antiques and portraits. Downstairs look for the *Tiber Apollo*, so called because it was found in the bed of the river in the late 19th century, and the two gigantic statues of Athena. Upstairs, the star of the collection the Ludovisi Throne, is probably a Greek sculpture dedicated as a throne for Aphrodite, the protectress of sailors. From the 5th century BC, the delicate carving portrays the goddess rising from the sea foam, her draperies clinging to her. Do not miss the statue of the *Galatian Soldier and His Wife Committing Suicide*, apparently commissioned by Julius Caesar.

THE BASICS

✚ F5
✉ Piazza Sant' Apollinare 44
☎ 06 683 3759 or 06 3996 7700
🕐 Tue–Sun 9–7.45
🚌 30, 70, 87, 116, 492, 628 to Corso del Rinascimento
♿ Moderate

Palazzo-Galleria Doria Pamphilj

HIGHLIGHTS

● *Religion Succoured by Spain* (labelled 10) and *Salome* (29), Titian
● *Portrait of Two Venetians* (23), Raphael
● *Maddalena* (40) and *Rest on the Flight into Egypt* (42), Caravaggio
● *Birth and Marriage of the Virgin* (174/176), Giovanni di Paolo
● *Nativity* (200), Parmigianino
● *Innocent X*, Velázquez
● *Innocent X*, Bernini
● *Battle of the Bay of Naples* (317), Pieter Brueghel the Elder
● Salone Verde
● Saletta Gialla

TIPS

● Use the audioguide, which is included in the price and helps make sense of what you're seeing.
● The paintings are not well lit so it is better to visit during the daylight hours.

One of Rome's largest palaces that contains one of the city's finest patrician art collections and offers the chance to admire some of the sumptuously decorated rooms of its private apartments.

A dynasty Little in the bland exterior of the Palazzo Doria Pamphilj prepares you for the glory of the beautiful rooms that lie within. The core of the building, which was built over the foundations of a storehouse dating back to ancient times, was erected in 1435, and it has withstood countless alterations and owners. The Doria Pamphilj dynasty was formed by yoking together the Doria, a famous Genoese seafaring clan, and the Pamphilj, a Rome-based patrician family. Most people come here for the paintings, but—when open—you can enjoy a guided tour around some

This magnificent palace is at the middle of lovely parkland laid out by Prince Camillo Pamphilj in the mid-17th century (left). Inside the galleries are lavishly decorated with painted ceilings and the walls adorned with golden framed mirrors (right)

of the private apartments in the 1,000-room palace. The most impressive is the Saletta Gialla (Yellow Room), decorated with 12 Gobelin tapestries made for Louis XV. In the Salone Verde (Green Room) are three important paintings: *Annunciation* by Filippo Lippi, *Portrait of a Gentleman* by Lorenzo Lotto and *Andrea Doria* (a famous admiral) by Sebastiano del Piombo.

Labyrinth of masterpieces The Pamphilj's art collection is displayed in ranks in four broad galleries. As the works are numbered, not labelled, it's worth investing in a guidebook from the ticket office. The finest painting is the famous Velázquez portrait, *Innocent X* (1650), a likeness that captured the pope's weak and suspicious nature so adroitly that Innocent is said to have lamented that it was 'too true, too true'.

THE BASICS

www.doriapamphilj.it

✚ G5

✉ Piazza del Collegio Romano 1a

☎ 06 679 7323

🕐 Fri–Wed 10–5. Apartments currently closed for restoration

Ⓜ Barberini

🚌 60, 62, 85, 95, 160, 492 and all other services to Piazza Venezia

♿ Good

✋ Gallery expensive. Apartments moderate

Pantheon

TOP 25

HIGHLIGHTS

- Façade inscription
- The pedimented portico
- Original Roman doors
- Marble interior and pavement
- Coffered dome and oculus
- Tomb of Raphael
- Royal tombs

TIP

- The Pantheon is often very crowded. To make the most of your visit, go on a week-day or early in the morning.

No other monument suggests the grandeur of ancient Rome as magnificently as this temple whose early conversion to a place of Christian worship has rendered it the most perfect of the city's ancient monuments.

Temple and church The greatest surviving complete Roman structure, built by Emperor Hadrian from AD118–28, the Pantheon replaced a temple of 27BC by Marcus Agrippa, son-in-law of Augustus. (Modestly, Hadrian retained the original inscription proclaiming it as Agrippa's work.) It became the church of Santa Maria ad Martyres in AD609 (the bones of martyrs were brought here from the Catacombs) and is now a shrine to Italy's 'immortals', including the artist Raphael and kings Vittore Emanuele II and Umberto I.

The sun pours through the opening in the Pantheon's roof (far left and bottom middle). Raphael's Tomb (middle). Giacomo della Porta's fountain in Piazza della Rotonda (bottom). Sixteen massive Egyptian granite columns support the portico (bottom left and right)

An engineering marvel Massive and simple from the outside, the Pantheon is at its most breathtaking inside, where the scale, harmony and symmetry of the dome in particular are more apparent. The world's largest dome until 1882 (when it was surpassed in the English spa resort of Buxton), it has a diameter of 43.3m (142ft)—equal to its height from the floor. Weight and stresses were reduced by rows of coffers in the ceiling, and the use of progressively lighter materials from the base to the crown. The central oculus, 9m (30ft) in diameter and clearly intended to inspire meditation on the heavens above, lets light (and rain) fall onto the marble pavement far below. Take time to relax in one of Piazza della Rotonda's many cafés to enjoy and admire the exterior view of the Pantheon and the atmosphere of the lively piazza.

THE BASICS

+ F5
✉ Piazza della Rotonda
☎ 06 6830 0230
🕐 Mon–Sat 8.30–7.30, Sun 9–6, public holidays 9–1
Ⓜ Spagna
🚌 116, 119 to Piazza della Rotonda or 40, 64, 70 and all other services to Largo di Torre Argentina
♿ Good
🎫 Free

Piazza Campo de' Fiori

Vibrant market stalls surround the statue of Giordano Bruno in Campo dei Fiori

THE BASICS

⊞ F6

✉ Piazza Campo de' Fiori

🕐 Market Mon–Sat 7–1.30

🚌 40, 46, 62, 64 to Corso Vittorio Emanuele II or H, 8, 46, 62, 64, 70, 87 to Largo di Torre Argentina

♿ Cobbled streets and some curbs around piazza

💲 Free

HIGHLIGHTS

● Street market
● Wine bar Vineria Reggio
● Statue of Giordano Bruno
● Palazzo Farnese, Piazza Farnese
● Palazzo della Cancelleria, Piazza della Cancelleria
● Palazzo Pio Righetti
● Via Giulia
● Santa Maria dell'Orazione e Morte: church door decorated in stone skulls
● Via dei Baullari

There is nowhere more relaxing in Rome to sit and watch the world go by than Campo de' Fiori, a lovely old piazza whose fruit, vegetable and fish market makes it one of the liveliest and most vivid corners of the old city.

Ancient square Campo de' Fiori, or the 'Field of Flowers', was turned in the Middle Ages from a meadow facing the ancient Theatre of Pompey (55BC; now Palazzo Pio Righetti) into one of the city's most exclusive residential and business districts. By the 15th century it was surrounded by busy inns and bordellos, some run by the infamous courtesan Vannozza Catanei, mistress of the Borgia pope Alexander VI. By 1600 it had also become a place of execution; Giordano Bruno was burned for heresy on the spot marked by his cowled statue.

Present day Just sit back and soak up the atmosphere. Students, foreigners, locals and tramps mingle with the market vendors shouting their wares, while the cafés, bars and the wonderfully dingy wine bar at No. 15 will have you relishing the street life. One block south lies Piazza Farnese, dominated by the Palazzo Farnese, a Renaissance masterpiece partly designed by Michelangelo and begun in 1516. It is now home to the French Embassy. One block west is the Palazzo della Cancelleria (1485), once the papal chancellery. The nearby Via Giulia, Via dei Baullari, the busy Via dei Cappellari and Via del Pellegrino are all wonderful streets to explore.

Bernini's fountain and obelisk lie at the heart of Piazza Navona

Piazza Navona

Piazza di Spagna may be more elegant and Campo de' Fiori more vivid, but Piazza Navona, with its atmospheric echoes of a 2,000-year history, is a glorious place to amble or stop for a drink at a sun-drenched table.

Shaping history Piazza Navona owes its unmistakable elliptical shape to a stadium and racetrack built here in AD86 by Emperor Domitian. From the Circus Agonalis—the stadium for athletic games—comes the piazza's present name, rendered in medieval Latin as *in agone*, and then in Rome's strangulated dialect as *'n 'agona*. The stadium was used until well into the Middle Ages for festivals and competitions. The square owes its present appearance to its rebuilding by Pope Innocent X in 1644.

Around the piazza Bernini's spirited Fontana dei Quattro Fiumi (1651), the 'Fountain of the Four Rivers', dominates. Unveiled in 1651, it has four figures that represent the four rivers of Paradise (the Nile, Ganges, Danube and Plate), and the four 'corners' of the world (Africa, Asia, Europe and America). On the west side is the baroque Sant' Agnese (1652–57), its façade designed by Borromini. Beside it stands the Palazzo Pamphilj, commissioned by Innocent X and now the Brazilian Embassy. Further afield, San Luigi dei Francesi is famous for three superlative Caravaggio paintings, and Santa Maria della Pace for a cloister by Bramante and Raphael's frescos of the four *Sybils*.

THE BASICS

🔳 F5
✉ Piazza Navona
🚇 Spagna
🚌 30, 70, 51, 87, 116, 492, 628 to Corso del Rinascimento or 40, 46, 62, 64 to Corso Vittorio Emanuele II

HIGHLIGHTS

● Fontana dei Quattro Fiumi
● Fontana del Moro (south)
● Fontana del Nettuno (north)
● Palazzo Pamphilj
● San Luigi dei Francesi (Via Santa Giovanna d' Arco)
● Santa Maria dell'Anima (Via della Pace)

Santa Maria sopra Minerva

Soaring Gothic arches (left). Bernini's elephant (middle). Tomb of St. Catherine (right)

THE BASICS

- ✚ G5
- ✉ Piazza della Minerva 42
- ☎ 06 679 3926
- 🕐 Mon–Sat 7–7, Sun 8–7 (10–6 in winter)
- 🚇 Spagna
- 🚌 H, 8, 30, 40, 46, 62, 64, 70, 81, 87 to Lago di Torre Argentina or 119 to Piazza della Rotonda
- ♿ Stepped access to church
- 🎟 Free

HIGHLIGHTS

- Porch to the Cappella Carafa
- Frescos: *St. Thomas Aquinas* and *The Assumption*, Filippino Lippi, in the Cappella Carafa
- *Risen Christ*, Michelangelo
- Relics of St. Catherine of Siena, and preserved room in sacristy where she died
- Tombs of Clement VII and Leo X, Antonio da Sangallo
- Tomb slab of Fra Angelico
- Tomb of Giovanni Alberini, Mino da Fiesole or Agostino di Duccio
- Monument to Maria Raggi
- Tomb of Francesco Tornabuoni, Mino da Fiesole

Remarkable in having retained many Gothic features despite Rome's love for the baroque, behind its plain façade Santa Maria sopra Minerva is a cornucopia of tombs, paintings and Renaissance sculpture.

Florentine influences Originally founded in the 8th century over ruins of a temple to Minerva, the church was built in 1280 to a design by two Florentine Dominican monks who modelled it on their own church, Santa Maria Novella. Before entering the church, notice its strange but charming statue of an elephant supporting an ancient Greek obelisk in the piazza outside. It was designed by Bernini in the 17th century.

Inside The interior of the church abounds with beautiful works such as the Cappella Carafa (whose fine porch is attributed to Giuliano da Maiano), and Michelangelo's calm statue *The Risen Christ* (1521), left of the high altar. Filippino Lippi painted the celebrated frescos *St. Thomas Aquinas* and the *Assumption* (1488–93). Among other sculptures are the tombs of Francesco Tornabuoni (1480) and that of Giovanni Alberini, the latter decorated with reliefs of Hercules (15th century). Both are attributed to Mino da Fiesole. Other works include Fra Angelico's tomb slab (1455); the tombs of Medici popes Clement VII and Leo X (1536) by Antonio da Sangallo the Younger; and Bernini's monument to Maria Raggi (1643). St. Catherine of Siena, one of Italy's patron saints, is buried beneath the high altar.

More to See

COLONNA DI MARCO AURELIO

The Column of Marcus Aurelius (AD180–96) was built to celebrate Aurelius's military triumphs over hostile north European tribes. It is composed of 27 separate drums of Carrara marble welded into a seamless whole, and is done with a continuous spiral of bas-reliefs commemorating episodes from the victorious campaigns. Aurelius is depicted no fewer than 59 times, though curiously never actually in battle. The summit statue is of St. Paul, crafted by Domenico Fontana in 1589 to replace the 60th depiction of Aurelius.

➕ G5 ✉ Piazza Colonna, Via del Corso ⏰ Always open 🚇 Barberini 🚌 62, 63, 85, 95, 117, 119 and all routes to to Via del Corso ✋ Free

CRYPTA BALBI

This museum, part of the Museo Nazionale Romano, contains part of a theatre built in 13BC, along with a rich collection of objects to illustrate social, economic and urban planning changes from ancient times, through the Middle Ages up to the present day. Two other sections have displays of vases, glassware, mosaics and other items dating from between the 5th and 8th centuries.

➕ G6 ✉ Via delle Botteghe Oscure 31 ☎ 06 3996 7700 ⏰ Tue–Sun 9–7.45 🚇 Barberini 🚌 30,40, 46, 62, 64, 70, 492, 628, 780, 787, 916 to Largo di Torre Argentina ✋ Expensive

FONTANA DELLE TARTARUGHE

This tiny fountain (1581–84) is one of Rome's most delightful sights, thanks to the tortoises, probably added by Bernini in 1658 (the current bronze sculptures are copies).

➕ F6 ✉ Piazza Mattei 🚌 H, 8, 63, 630, 780 to Via Arenula or 30, 70, 87, 116 and other services to Largo di Torre Argentina

MUSEO NAZIONALE DELLE PASTE ALIMENTARI

www.pastainmuseum.it

An unusual museum dedicated to Italy's best-loved and best-known food—pasta. It traces the history and evolution of pasta and of the

Colonna di Marco Aurelio

Detail of the Fontana delle Tartarughe showing a boy reaching up to a tortoise

manufacturing processes, from early grindstones for milling the wheat to modern industrial pasta machinery.

🔶 H5 ✉ Piazza Scanderberg 117 📞 06 699 1119 🕐 Daily 9.30–5.30 Ⓜ Barberini 🚌 52, 53, 61, 62, 63, 71, 80, 85, 160, 850 to Piazza San Silvestro 👆 Expensive

MUSEO DEL PALAZZO VENEZIA

Built in 1455 for Pietro Barbo (later Pope Paul II), and one of the first Renaissance palaces, the former Venetian Embassy became the property of the state in 1916; Mussolini harangued the crowds from the balconies. The museum hosts travelling exhibitions and a fine permanent collection that includes Renaissance paintings, sculpture, armour, ceramics, silverware and objets d'art.

🔶 G6 ✉ Palazzo Venezia, Via del Plebiscito 118 📞 06 6999 4318; reservations 06 328101 🕐 Tue–Sun 8.30–7.30; closed holidays 🚌 All services to Piazza Venezia 👆 Moderate

PALAZZO SPADA

This pretty *palazzo*, with a creamy stucco façade (1556–60), has four rooms where you can admire the 17th- and 18th-century Spada family paintings. Cardinal Spada is portrayed by Guido Reni; there's a fine Borromini *Perspective* and works by Albrecht Dürer, Andrea del Sarto and others.

🔶 F6 ✉ Piazza Capo di Ferro 13–Vicolo del Polverone 15b 📞 06 687 4893/4896 or 06 683 2409 🕐 Tue–Sat 8.30–7.30 🚌 H, 8, 63, 630, 780 to Via Arenula 👆 Moderate

SANT'AGOSTINO

One of the first Renaissance churches in Rome, Sant'Agostino still maintains its Latin-cross plan with apse, chapels and dome. Even if 19th-century additions have ruined its elegance, it is still worth visiting to see the works of Caravaggio, Raphael and other fine artists. The first chapel on the left contains Caravaggio's magnificent *Madonna di Loreto*.

🔶 F5 ✉ Piazza di Sant'Agostino 🕐 Daily 8–12, 4.30–7.30 🚌 116 to Via Zanardelli; 30, 40, 46, 62, 63, 64, 70 to Largo di Torre Argentina; 30, 70, 87, 130, 186 to Corso del Rinascimento

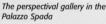

The perspectival gallery in the Palazzo Spada

Sant'Agostino, one of Rome's earliest Renaissance churches

The Medieval City

Explore the tangle of streets around some of Rome's most popular piazzas, taking in some of the best-known sights along the way.

DISTANCE: 2.5km (1.5 miles)   **ALLOW:** 2 hours

START

CAMPO DE' FIORI (▷ 48)
✚ F6 🚌 40, 60, 62, 116 and other services to Corso Vittorio Emanuele II

1 Walk east on Via dei Giubbonari and take the third right, Via d'Arco del Monte. Continue down Via dei Pettinari and and right through the arch into Via Giulia.

2 Take the fourth right opposite the church with the skull-adorned façade and admire Piazza Farnese before following Vicolo Gallo back into Campo de' Fiori.

3 Take Via dei Cappellari out of the campo and go left on Via del Pellegrino and then right on Via dei Banchi Vecchi. Cross Corso Vittorio Emanuele II into Via Banco Santo Spirito, then go immediately right on Via del Governo Vecchio.

4 Continue to the end to visit Piazza Navona (▷ 49). Or explore the tangle of lovely streets to the west of this piazza by turning sixth left on Vicolo del Corallo to Piazza del Fico.

END

PIAZZA DELLA ROTONDA
✚ F5 🚌 116, 116T to Piazza della Rotonda

8 Otherwise, go north on Via della Scrofa, then right on Via Stelletta to Piazza Campo Marzio. Turn right on Via Uffici del Vicario, then right on Via Maddalena to Piazza della Rotonda.

7 Take the southeast corner of Piazza Sant'Apollinare into Piazza Sant' Agostino to see the church (▷ 52). Go past the church and left into Via della Scrofa. Turn right on Via della Scrofa and cross Largo Toniolo to see the Caravaggios in San Luigi dei Francesi.

6 Turn left to look at antiques shops on Via dei Coronari, or right and cross Piazza di Tor Sanguigna, and then left into Piazza Sant' Apollinare, to the Palazzo Altemps (▷ 42–43).

5 Take Via della Fossa east out of Piazza del Fico and turn left on Via del Parione, then left on Vicolo delle Volpe to Via dei Coronari.

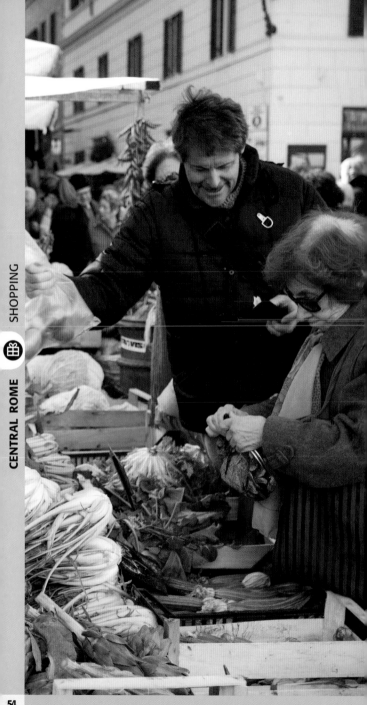

Shopping

AI MONASTERI

This unusual, large and rather dark old shop sells the products of seven Italian monasteries, from honeys, wines, natural preserves and liqueurs to herbal cures and elixirs.

✚ F5 ✉ Piazza Cinque Lune 76 ☎ 06 6880 2783 🕐 Fri–Wed 9–1, 4.30–7.30, Thu 9–1; closed 1st week of Sep

ANTICA LIBRERIA CROCE

This primarily Italian bookshop, with some titles in English, specializes in books on all aspects of Classical and contemporary art and photography. Over two floors; from time to time exhibitions are held here.

✚ F6 ✉ Corso Vittorio Emanuele II 56, corner of Corso del Rinascimento ☎ 06 6880 2269 🕐 Mon–Sat 10–8, Sun 10–1.30, 4–8.30

BASSETTI

Central shop with a dazzling collection of quality Italian silks and other luxurious fabrics, plus everyday materials.

✚ E5 ✉ Corso Vittorio Emanuele II 73 ☎ 06 689 2326 🕐 Tue–Sat 9–7.30 (Jul–end Aug 9–1, 4–6), Mon 4–6 (hours can vary)

CAMPO DE' FIORI

This picturesque market is in a pretty, central square. Fruit and vegetables dominate, but you can also buy fish, flowers and beans.

✚ F6 ✉ Piazza Campo de' Fiori 🕐 Mon–Sat 7am–1.30pm

CULTI

Shop near Piazza Navona packed with linens, well-designed kitchen utensils, plates, glasses, vases, towels, sheets and a host of other articles for the home.

SHOPPING AREAS

Most of the city's quality and specialty shops are concentrated in specific areas. Via Condotti and its surrounding grid of streets (Via Frattina, Via Borgognona and Via Bocca di Leone) contain most of the big names in men's and women's fashion, accessories, jewellery and luxury goods. In nearby Via del Babuino and Via Margutta, the emphasis is on top antiques, paintings, sculpture and modern glassware and lighting. Via della Croce, which runs south from Piazza di Spagna, is known for its food shops, while Via del Corso, which bisects the northern half of central Rome, is home to bargain mid-range clothes, shoes and accessories shops. For inexpensive shops visit Via del Tritone and Via Nazionale. Nice areas to browse for antiques, even if you are not buying, include Via Giulia, Via dei Coronari, Via dell'Orso, Via dei Soldati and Via del Governo Vecchio.

✚ F5 ✉ Via della Vetrina 16a ☎ 06 683 2180 🕐 Tue–Sat 10–1.30, 4–7.30, Mon 4–7.30

ENOTECA AL GOCCETTO

Wines from all over Italy are sold in this old bishop's *palazzo*, complete with original floors and wooden ceiling.

✚ E5 ✉ Via dei Banchi Vecchi 14 ☎ 06 686 4268 🕐 Mon–Sat 11.30–2, 7–11, closed 3 weeks in Aug

ETHIC

One of many inexpensive stores with good mid-range fashion just east of Campo de' Fiori.

✚ F6 ✉ Piazza Benedetto Cairoli 11–12 ☎ 06 6830 1063 🕐 Tue–Sat 10–8, Sun–Mon 12–8

FABINDIA

www.fabindia.it

Facing the Ponte Sant'Angelo is this delightful emporium selling Indian fabrics, scarves and garments, all handwoven and made in Indian villages. The company is devoted to developing fair and equitable relationships with the producers. The style is both traditional and more contemporary.

✚ E5 ✉ Via del Banco di Santo Spirito 40 ☎ 06 6889 1230 🕐 Mon–Sat 10–1.30, 3–7.30

FELTRINELLI

An Italy-wide bookshop chain with well-designed

shelves displaying a broad range of Italian titles, and usually a reasonable choice of French- German- and English-language books.

🚩 F6 ⊠ Largo di Torre Argentina 7–10 ☎ 06 6866 3001 ⏰ Mon–Sat 9–8, Sun 10–1.30, 4–7.30

🚩 G3 ⊠ Via del Babuino 39–41 ☎ 06 3600 1873 ⏰ Mon–Sat 9–8, Sun 10–1.30, 4–7.30

🚩 J4 ⊠ Via Vittorio Emanuele II Orlando 78–81/84 ☎ 06 484 430 or 06 487 0171 ⏰ Mon– Sat 9–8, Sun 10–1.30, 4–7.30

HOUSE & KITCHEN

More traditional than Spazio Sette (▷ below). This shop sells a range of household goods, notably a selection of kitchen utensils and kitchenware.

🚩 G6 ⊠ Via del Plebiscito 103 ☎ 06 679 4208 ⏰ Mon–Sat 9.30–8, Sun 10.30–2.30, 4–8; closed Sun in Jul and Aug

MARIA GRAZIA LUFFARELLI

Bright watercolour landscapes of hills, sea and sun. Prices range from very low to moderate for original works by the eponymous artist. Also on sale is a lovely range of Rome watercolour reproductions in postcard format, plus prints of Luffarelli's work mounted on brightly painted tables.

🚩 E5 ⊠ Via dei Banchi Vecchi 29 ☎ 06 683 2494 ⏰ Mon–Sat 11–8

MONDELLO OTTICA

www.mondelloottica.it Eyewear with a difference: This minimalist boutique has regular installations by local artists. Prices may be higher than average, but the glasses are superlative in quality and sheer chic. All have that little extra something special that makes the price worth paying.

🚩 E5 ⊠ Vial del Pellegrino 98 ☎ 06 686 1955 ⏰ Tue–Sat 9.30–1, 4–7.30

ORNAMENTUM

A beautiful shop selling silks and other sumptuous fabrics, tassels, brocades and other furnishing accessories.

🚩 E5 ⊠ Via dei Coronari 227 ☎ 06 687 6849 ⏰ Tue–Fri 9–1, 4–7.30, Sat 9–1, Mon 4–7.30; closed Aug

GIFTS WITH A TWIST

For a souvenir with a difference, visit the extraordinary shops on Via dei Cestari, just south of the Pantheon, which specialize in all sorts of religious clothes, candles and vestments. Crucifixes, rosaries, statues of saints and other religious souvenirs can be found in shops on Via di Porta Angelica near the Vatican. Alternatively, visit the Farmacia Santa Maria della Scala (⊠ Piazza Santa Maria della Scala), an 18th-century monastic pharmacy that sells herbal remedies.

PIAZZA COPPELLE

This tiny, attractive local food market is an oasis among the cars and tourists. Close to the Pantheon.

🚩 F5 ⊠ Piazza Coppelle ⏰ Mon–Sat 7am–1pm

POGGI

Vivid pigments, lovely papers and exquisitely soft brushes have been on sale at Poggi's since 1825. The second shop almost opposite sells high-quality paper.

🚩 G5 ⊠ Via del Gesù 74–5 ☎ 06 678 4477 ⏰ Mon–Sat 9–1, 4–7.30

🚩 G5 ⊠ Via Piè di Marmo 40–1 ☎ 06 6830 8014 ⏰ Mon–Fri 9–1, 4–7.30, Sat 9–1

IL SIGILLO

Close to the Pantheon, this little shop specializes in fine pens, hand-printed stationery and a wide variety of objects covered in marbled paper.

🚩 F5 ⊠ Via della Guglia 69 ☎ 06 678 9667 ⏰ Daily 11–8

SPAZIO SETTE

Housed in a 17th-century cardinal's palace, this is one of the few stores in Rome that will make even the most hardened shopper salivate over furnishings for the kitchen, living room and bathroom.

🚩 F6 ⊠ Via dei Barbieri 7 ☎ 06 6880 4261 ⏰ Tue–Sat 9.30–1, 3.30–7.30, Mon 3.30–7.30

Entertainment and Nightlife

ANIMA
At the heart of a small buzzing nightlife area, Anima is a welcoming bar and club that plays an eclectic assortment of music and attracts a clientele of all ages and types.
🔢 F5 ⊠ Via Santa Maria dell'Anima ☎ 06 6889 2806 🕐 Daily 12am–4am 🚌 30, 70, 87 and other services to Corso del Rinascimento

ASSOCIAZIONE MUSICALE ROMANA
www.assmusrom.it
Stages a summer season of chamber recitals at a number of venues, including the French Academy in the Villa Medici.
🔢 G3 ⊠ Via Gregorio 216 ☎ 06 3936 6322

BEVITORIA
Friendlier and more intimate than most large or touristy bars on Piazza Navona. Primarily a wine bar (the cellar is part of Domitian's former stadium). Gets busy.
🔢 F5 ⊠ Piazza Navona 72 ☎ 06 6880 1022 🕐 Daily 11am–1am 🚌 46, 62, 64 to Corso Vittorio Emanuele II or 30, 70, 81, 87, 116 to Corso del Rinascimento

CUL DE SAC
An established informal wine bar near Piazza Navona with pine tables and a big marble bar. More than 1,400 wines, plus snacks, light meals and cheese and salami from every region in Italy.
🔢 F5 ⊠ Piazza Pasquino 73

☎ 06 6880 1094 🕐 Daily 12–4pm, 6–12.30 🚌 46, 62, 64 to Corso Vittorio Emanuele II

IL GONFALONE
A small but prestigious company that hosts chamber music and other small-scale recitals.
🔢 E5 ⊠ Oratorio del Gonfalone, Via del Gonfalone 32a; Information ⊠ Vicolo della Scimmia 1b ☎ 06 687 5952; www.romeguide.it/musica 🕐 Concerts Oct–Jun, call for times; box office Mon–Fri 9am–1pm, day of concert 9–9 🚌 46, 62, 64 to Corso Vittorio Emanuele II or 23, 116, 280 to Lungotevere di Sangallo

MAD JACK'S
www.madjacks.com
This Irish pub will suit

WHAT TO DRINK
The most inexpensive way to drink beer in Italy is from the keg (*alla spina*). Measures are *piccola*, *media* and *grande* (usually 33cl, 50cl and a litre respectively). Foreign canned or bottled beers (*in lattina* or *in bottiglia*) are expensive. Italian brands like Peroni are a little less expensive: a Peroncino (25cl bottle) is a good thirst-quencher. Aperitifs (*aperitivi*) include popular non-alcoholic drinks like Aperol, Crodino and San Pellegrino bitter. A glass of red or white wine is *un bicchiere di vino rosso/bianco*.

those looking for a festive place in which to pass the night hours. The music is loud and drinks are flowing.
🔢 F6 ⊠ Via Arenula 20 ☎ 06 6880 8223 🕐 Daily 11.30am–2am 🚌 40, 64 to Largo di Torre Argentina 🎵 Free

IL PICCOLO
Intimate wine bar close to Piazza Navona, ideal for a romantic interlude.
🔢 E5 ⊠ Via del Governo Vecchio 74–5 ☎ 06 6880 1746 🕐 Daily noon–2am 🚌 46, 62, 64 to Corso Vittorio Emanuele II

TRINITY COLLEGE
English and Irish-style pubs are all the rage—this is one of the better ones. Its serves inexpensive food as well as Guinness.
🔢 G5 ⊠ Via del Collegio Romano ☎ 06 678 6472 🕐 Daily noon–3am 🚌 62, 63, 85, 95, 117, 119 to Via del Corso and all services to Piazza Venezia

LA VINERIA REGGIO
The quainter side of nighttime drinking. Fusty and old-fashioned inside, with characters to match; tables on the city's most evocative square. Also try the popular Drunken Ship pub virtually next door.
🔢 F6 ⊠ Campo de' Fiori 15 ☎ 06 6880 3268 🕐 Mon–Sat 8.30am–2am, Sun 5pm–2am 🚌 46, 62, 64 to Corso Vittorio Emanuele II, 116 to Via Baullari or 70, 81, 87 to Corso del Rinascimento

Restaurants

PRICES

Prices are approximate, based on a 3-course meal for one person.

€€€   over €50
€€   €30–€50
€   under €30

ANTICA BIRRERIA FRATELLI TEMPERA (€)

Ideal for a simple lunch or dinner. Original art nouveau interior and a large beer hall.

➕ G5 ✉ Via di San Marcello 19 ☎ 06 678 6203 🕑 Mon–Sat 12–12 🚌 44, 46, 64, 70, 87 and all other buses to Piazza Venezia

IL BACARO (€€)

www.ilbacaro.com

Tiny but gracious restaurant. It can be noisy, but the light, modern pan-Italian cooking is great.

➕ F5 ✉ Via degli Spagnoli 27, near Piazza delle Coppelle ☎ 06 686 4110 or 06 687 2554 🕑 Mon–Sat 8am–11.30pm; closed Aug 🚇 Spagna 🚌 119

BAFFETTO (€)

A tiny, hole-in the wall classic that has retained its atmosphere and low prices. Expect to wait for a table.

➕ E5 ✉ Via del Governo Vecchio 114 ☎ 06 686 1617 🕑 Daily 6.30 –1am; closed Aug 🚌 46, 62, 64 to Corso Vittorio Emanuele II

BAR DELLA PACE (€)

Extremely trendy bar, which is quieter by day, when you can eat outside or enjoy the 19th-century mahogany interior.

➕ F5 ✉ Via della Pace 3, off Piazza Navona ☎ 06 686 1216 🕑 Daily 9am–2am; closed Mon am 🚌 30, 70, 87, 116 to Corso del Rinascimento

BRAMANTE (€€€)

The setting of this chic restaurant, complete with an art nouveau window, could scarcely be bettered: It's on one of the city's most prestigious and beautiful baroque squares, Piazza Navona. Inside, you could be in a Tuscan villa, softly lit with oil lamps; the walls are frescoed with local scenes and classical music plays. The food is not the most imaginative

THE MENU

Starters are called antipasti; first course (soup, pasta or risotto) is *il primo*; and main meat and fish dishes are *il secondo*. Salads (*insalata*) and vegetables (*contorni*) are ordered (and often eaten) separately. Desserts are *dolci*, with cheese (*formaggio*) or fruit (*frutta*) to follow. If no menu card is offered, ask for *la lista* or *il menù*. A set-price menu (*un menù turistico*) may seem good value, but portions are usually small and the food is invariably poor—usually just spaghetti with a tomato sauce, followed by a piece of chicken and fruit.

but good and the service is first class.

➕ F5 ✉ Via della Pace 25 ☎ 06 6880 3916 🕑 Mon–Sat 6.30pm–2am, Sun 12.30–2pm (summer only) 🚌 46, 62, 64, 87, 116, 492 to Corso del Rinascimento

CAFFÈ FARNESE (€)

Quieter and more elegant than the bars on the nearby Campo de' Fiori. Serves cakes, ice creams and light snacks as well as drinks. Also has tables on the cobbled street outside.

➕ E6 ✉ Via dei Baullari 106–7, at Piazza Farnese ☎ 06 6880 2125 🕑 Daily 7am–2am 🚌 8, 46, 62, 64

IL CONVIVIO (€€€)

www.ilconviviotroiani.com

The Troiani brothers from Italy's Marche region have created a tranquil little restaurant with a reputation for innovative and subtle tasting modern dishes.

➕ F4 ✉ Vicolo dei Soldati 31 ☎ 06 686 9432 🕑 Mon–Sat dinner only 8–10.30 🚌 30, 70, 87, 116, 492 to Corso del Rinascimento

CORALLO (€)

This stylish pizzeria is convenient to Piazza Navona. Full meals also available.

➕ F5 ✉ Via del Corallo 10, off Via del Governo Vecchio ☎ 06 6830 7703 🕑 Mon 7.30pm–11.30pm, Tue–Sun 12–2.30, 7–1am; closed 1 week in Aug 🚌 46, 62, 64 to Corso Vittorio Emanuele II

CICCIA BOMBA (€€)

An excellent option amid the plethora of restaurants around Piazza Navona. Simple wooden tables, efficient service, and good Roman food at good prices for this area.
⊞ E5 ⊠ Via dell Governo Vecchio 76 ☎ 06 6880 2108 ⏰ Thu–Tue 12.30–3, 7.30–11.30; closed 2 weeks in Aug 🚌 All services to Corso del Rinascimento or Corso Vittorio Emanuele II

DA FRANCESCO (€)

A simple restaurant near Piazza Navona, which over the years has never lost its appeal, thanks to a warm, friendly atmosphere, good food and low prices. No reservations so arrive early to be sure of a place.
⊞ E5 ⊠ Piazza del Fico ☎ 06 686 4009 ⏰ Wed–Mon 12–3, 7–1, Tue 7pm–1am 🚌 64 and other services to Chiesa Nuova on Corso Vittorio Emanuele II

DITIRAMBO (€€)

www.ristoranteditirambo.it
Downtown *trattoria* that far transcends the tourist menu, even satisfying the difficult-to-please *bel mondo* of Rome. The kitchen uses organic ingredients, and produces homemade bread, pasta and desserts. Reservations essential.
⊞ F6 ⊠ Piazza della Cancelleria 74 ☎ 06 687 1626 ⏰ Tue–Sun 1–3, 7.30–11.30, Mon 8pm–11.30pm; closed Aug

🚌 46, 62, 64, 87, 116, 492 to Corso Vittorio Emanuele II

DUR FILETTARO A SANTA BARBARA (€)

At this tiny place with Formica tables you wash down cod with plenty of beer or crisp local wine.
⊞ F6 ⊠ Largo dei Librari 88, off Via dei Giubbonari ☎ 06 686 4018 ⏰ Mon–Sat 5.30–11; closed Aug and 1 week Dec–Jan 🚌 H, 8, 63, 630, 780 to Via Arenula

GELATERIA DELLA PALMA (€)

A big, brash place just behind the Pantheon. Cakes and chocolates, plus over 100 flavours of ice cream—many of them a little wild.
⊞ F5 ⊠ Via della Maddalena 20 ☎ 06 6880

THE BILL

The bill (check), *il conto*, usually includes extras such as *servizio* (service). Iniquitous cover charges (*pane e coperto*) have now been outlawed, but some restaurants still try to get round the regulations. Only pay for bread (*pane*) if you have asked for it. Proper receipts—not a scrawled piece of paper—must be given by law. If you receive a scrap of paper, which is more likely in a pizzeria, and have doubts about the total, be sure to ask for a proper receipt (*una fattura* or *una ricevuta*).

6752 ⏰ Daily 8am–midnight 🚌 116 to Piazza della Rotonda

GIOLITTI (€)

For years Giolitti was the king of Roman ice cream. Standards have slipped slightly, but the ice cream is still excellent value.
⊞ F5 ⊠ Via Uffici del Vicario 40 ☎ 06 699 1243 ⏰ Mon–Fri, Sun 7am–12.30am, Sat 7am–2am 🚌 119 to Piazza della Rotonda or 62, 80, 81, 85, 95, 117, 119, 160, 175 and other services to Via del Corso

GRAPPOLO D'ORO (€)

Unspoiled *trattoria* loved by locals and foreign residents for decades. The menu has *pasta all' Amatriciana* and *scaloppine* any way you like.
⊞ F6 ⊠ Piazza della Cancelleria 80 ☎ 06 689 7080 ⏰ Daily 12.30–2.30, 7.30–10.30; closed lunch Tue–Fri in winter 🚌 46, 62, 64 to Corso Vittorio Emanuele II

'GUSTO (€€)

A chic, modern restaurant on two levels where you can eat pizzas, salads and other light meals downstairs or fuller meals upstairs. There is also a good kitchenware shop.
⊞ F3 ⊠ Piazza Augusto Imperatore 9 ☎ 06 322 6273 ⏰ Daily 1–3, 7.30–1 🚌 117, 119 to Via del Corso

LATTERIA DEL GALLO (€)

Marble tables and 1940s decor. Try the big, sticky cakes and steaming

hot chocolate.
🔳 E6 ✉ Vicolo del Gallo 4
☎ 06 686 5091 🕐 Thu–Tue
8.30–2, 5–midnight 🚌 46,
62, 64 to Corso Vittorio
Emanuele II

L'EAU VIVE (€€)

Expect a bizarre dining
experience here. The
predominantly French
food is served by nuns.
Politicians, celebrities and
locals come to enjoy the
food and the beautiful
16th-century frescoed
dining rooms.
🔳 F5 ✉ Via Monterone 85
☎ 06 654 1095 or 06 6880
1095 🕐 Mon–Sat 12.30–3.30,
7.30–10; closed Aug 🚌 8, 46,
62, 63, 64, 70, 87, 186, 492 to
Largo di Torre Argentina

LA ROSETTA (€€€)

An exclusive fish and
seafood restaurant whose
popularity means
reservations are a must.
🔳 F5 ✉ Via della Rosetta
8–9 ☎ 06 686 1002
🕐 Mon–Sat 1–3, 8–11.30;
closed 2 weeks in Aug 🚌 119
to Piazza della Rotonda or 70,
87, 90 to Corso del
Rinascimento

SALOTTO 42

Warm and relaxed place
for drinks or light meals,
especially at lunch (the
kitchen closes at
9.30pm). In the evening
it transforms into a stylish
cocktail bar.
🔳 G5 ✉ Piazza di Pietro 42
☎ 06 678 5804 🕐 Tues–Sun
🕐 10am–2am (earlier on
Sun) 🚌 C3, 62, 63, 85, 91,

117, 119 and other services to
Via del Corso

SANT' EUSTACHIO (€)

Excellent coffee served in
a pleasant interior and
tables outside.
🔳 F5 ✉ Piazza Sant'
Eustachio 82 ☎ 06 6880
2048 🕐 Daily 8.30am–1am
🚌 119 to Piazza della Rotonda
or 30, 70, 87, 116 to Corso del
Rinascimento

LA TAZZA D'ORO (€)

The 'Cup of Gold' sells
only coffee, and probably
the city's best espresso.
🔳 G5 ✉ Via degli Orfani 84
☎ 06 678 9792 🕐 Mon–Sat
7am–8pm 🚌 119 to Piazza
della Rotonda or 30, 70, 87,
116, 186 to Corso del
Rinascimento

THIEN KIM (€)

More adventurous
Romans have been
visiting this calm and

UNUSUAL WAITRESSES

You are served at the L'Eau
Vive by nuns from a third
world order known as the
Vergini Laiche Cristiane di
Azione Cattolica Missionaria
per Mezzo del Lavoro
(Christian Virgins of Catholic
Missionary Action through
Work). With restaurants in
several parts of the world,
their aim is to spread the
message of Christianity
through the medium of
French food. To this end, dining is interrupted by prayers
each evening at 9.

---

courteous restaurant for
Thai food since 1976.
Very good value.
🔳 E6 ✉ Via Giulia 201
☎ 06 6830 7832 🕐 Mon–
Sat 7.30–10.30 🚌 46, 64 to
Corso Vittorio Emanuele II

TRE SCALINI (€)

Known for its chocolate-
studded *tartufo* (the
best chocolate-chip
ice cream).
🔳 F5 ✉ Piazza Navona
28–32 ☎ 06 6880 1996
🕐 Daily Thu–Tue 8am–1am
🚌 30, 70, 87, 116 and other
services to Corso del
Rinascimento

TUCCI (€)

You can sit here for hours
facing Bernini's Fontana
dei Quattro Fiumi, but
watch your bill.
🔳 F5 ✉ Piazza Navona
94–100 ☎ 06 686 1547
🕐 Wed–Mon 8.30am–
12.30am 🚌 46, 62, 64 to
Corso Vittorio Emanuele II or
30, 70, 87, 116 to Corso del
Rinascimento

VECCHIA ROMA (€€€)

In a pretty piazza and
perfect for an alfresco
meal on a summer
evening. Although the
18th-century interior is
also captivating, prices are
rather high for what is
only straightforward and
reliable Roman cooking.
🔳 F6 ✉ Piazza Campitelli 18
☎ 06 686 4604 🕐 Mon,
Tue, Thu–Sun 1–3, 8–11;
closed 3 weeks in Aug 🚌 All
services to Via Arenula or
Piazza Venezia

Trastevere and the South

Trastevere—literally 'across the Tiber'—is Rome's working-class district, an enclave of appealing streets and leafy corners full of cafés, bars and restaurants, as well as a handful of churches and galleries.

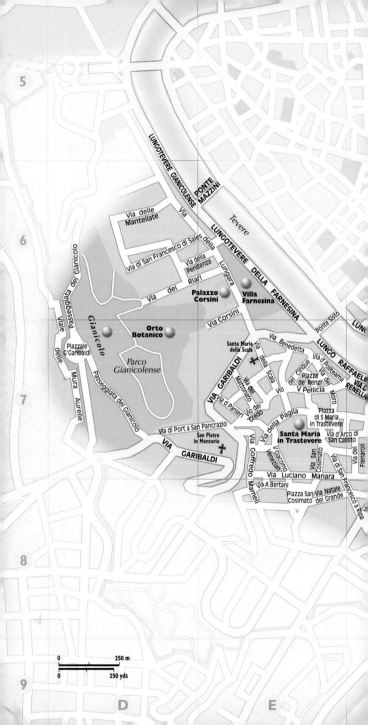

5

6

Via delle Mantellate

Via di San Francesco di Sales

Via della Penitenza

Via del Riari

Via della Lungara

PONTE MAZZINI

LUNGOTEVERE GIANICOLENSE

Tevere

LUNGOTEVERE DELLA FARNESINA

Passeggiata de Gianicolo

Gianicolo

Palazzo Corsini

Villa Farnesina

Via Corsini

Ponte Sisto

LUNGO

Orto Botanico

Piazzale G'Garibaldi

Parco Gianicolense

Via Benedetta

Santa Maria della Scala

Via d Politeama

LUNGO RAFFAELL

VIA C

VIA GARIBALDI

Via della Scala

Via de Cinque

Via del Moro

Piazza de' Renzi

RENELL

V Pellicia

Viale delle Mura Aurelie

Passeggiata del Gianicolo

Via de Mattonato

Vio del Cedro

Piazza di S Maria in Trastevere

7

Via di Port a San Pancrazio

Via d Panieri

Via della Paglia

Santa Maria in Trastevere

Via d'Arco di San Calisto

VIA GARIBALDI

San Pietro in Montorio

Via Goffredo

V Giacomo Venezian

Via San Cosimato

Via di San Francesco a Ripa

Via Fienaroli

Via Luciano Manara

Via A Bertani

Piazza San Via Natale Cosimato del Grande

Mameli

8

0   250 m

0   250 yds

9

D   E

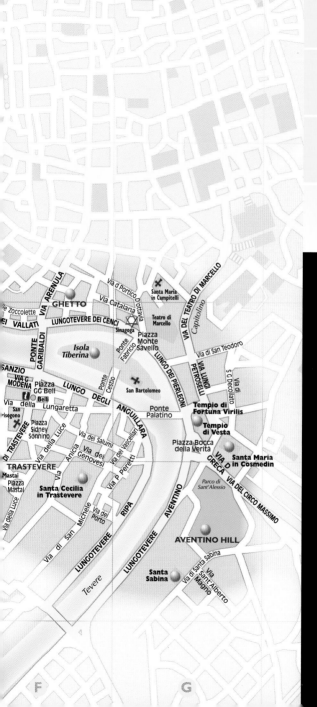

Via Zoccolette

DEI VALLATI

VIA ARENULA

GHETTO

LUNGOTEVERE DEI CENCI

Via d'Portico D'Ottavia

Via Catalana

Santa Maria in Campitelli

Teatro di Marcello

VIA DEL TEATRO DI MARCELLO

Capitolino

Sinagoga

Piazza Monte Savello

PONTE GARIBALDI

Isola Tiberina

Ponte Fabricio

Ponte Cestio

LUNGO DEI PIERLEONI

Via di San Teodoro

VIA LUNGO PETROSELLI

Via di S. Decollato

SANZIO

VIA C. MODENA

Piazza GG Bell

Belli

LUNGO DEGLI

ANGUILLARA

San Bartolomeo

Via della Lungaretta

Via San Crisogono

Piazza Sidney Sonnino

DI TRASTEVERE

Ponte Palatino

Tempio di Fortuna Virilis

Tempio di Vesta

TRASTEVERE

Via della Luce

Via Anicia

Via dei Genovesi

Via del Salumi

Via dei Vascellari

Via P. Pereffi

Piazza Bocca della Verità

VIA D. GRECA

Santa Maria in Cosmedin

VIA DEL CIRCO MASSIMO

Mastai

Piazza Mastai

Santa Cecilia in Trastevere

Via di San Michele

Via del Porto

RIPA

AVENTINO

Parco di Sant'Alessio

Via della Luce

LUNGOTEVERE

LUNGOTEVERE

AVENTINO HILL

Tevere

Santa Sabina

Via di Santa Sabina

Via Sant'Alberto Magno

F

G

Santa Maria in Trastevere

HIGHLIGHTS

- Romanesque campanile
- Façade mosaics
- Portico
- Ceiling, designed by Domenichino
- Cosmati marble pavement
- Wall tabernacle by Mino del Reame (central nave)
- Byzantine mosaics, upper apse
- Mosaics: *Life of the Virgin* (lower apse)
- *Madonna della Clemenza* in Cappella Altemps
- Cappella Avila: baroque chapel

TIP

- Visit in the evening, then have a drink in one of the outdoor cafés, from where you can appreciate the lit piazza and basilica.

One of the most memorable sights of night-time Rome is the 12th-century gold mosaics on the façade of Santa Maria in Trastevere, their floodlit glow casting a gentle light over the piazza below.

Early church Santa Maria in Trastevere is among the oldest officially sanctioned places of worship in Rome. It was reputedly founded in AD222, allegedly on the spot where a fountain of olive oil had sprung from the earth on the day of Christ's birth (symbolizing the coming of the grace of God). Much of the present church was built in the 12th century during the reign of Innocent II, a member of the Papareschi, a prominent Trastevere family. Inside, the main colonnade of the nave is composed of reused and ancient Roman columns. The portico, containing fragments of Roman reliefs and

A fountain graces the piazza outside the church (far left). The apse mosaics are a highlight of this medieval church (left, bottom right and middle). Night time in Piazza di Santa Maria in Trastevere (right). Twenty-two columns from ancient monuments divide the nave from the aisles (bottom left)

inscriptions and medieval remains, was added in 1702 by Carlo Fontana, who was responsible for the fountain that graces the adjoining piazza.

Mosaics The façade mosaics probably date from the mid-12th century, and depict the Virgin and Child with 10 lamp-carrying companions. Long believed to portray the parable of the Wise and Foolish Virgins, their subject matter is contested, as several 'virgins' appear to be men and only two are carrying unlighted lamps (not the five of the parable). The mosaics of the upper apse inside the church, devoted to the glorification of the Virgin, date from the same period and are Byzantine-influenced works by Greek or Greek-trained craftsmen. Those below, depicting scenes from the life of the Virgin (1291), are by the mosaicist and fresco painter Pietro Cavallini.

THE BASICS

✚ E7

✉ Piazza Santa Maria in Trastevere

☎ 06 361 0836 or 06 581 4802

🕐 Daily 7.45–8/9 (may close 12.30–3.30 in winter)

🚌 H, 8, 780 Viale di Trastevere, 125 to Via Manara or 23, 280 to Lungotevere Raffaello Sanzio

♿ Wheelchair accessible

🖐 Free

Villa Farnesina

The Salone delle Prospettive (left). Villa Farnesina's gardens, ideal for a walk (right)

THE BASICS

www.francopanini.it

✚ E6

✉ Via della Lungara 230

☎ 06 6802 7268

🕐 Mon–Sat 9–1

🚌 23, 125, 280 to Lungotevere della Farnesina

✋ Moderate

HIGHLIGHTS

● The Loggia of Cupid and Psyche, decorated with frescos by Raphael
● Sodoma's Scenes from the Life of Alexander the Great
● Salone delle Prospettive
● Peruzzi's trompe l'oeil views of Rome
● The gardens

This is one of the most intimate and charming of all Rome's grand houses, known as much for its peaceful gardens as for its beautifully decorated interior, which contains works commissioned from Raphael and other artists by the villa's original owner, Agostino Chigi.

All to impress In 1508, Agostino Chigi, a wealthy banker from Siena, commissioned Baldasssare Puruzzi to build him a suburban villa. Here, Chigi entertained artists, princes and cardinals. His banquets were memorable: After the meal, Chigi would have the gold and silver dishes thrown into the Tiber to impress his guests with his wealth. What they did not know was that the plates were caught by safety nets and returned to the kitchens. In 1580, the villa was bought by the Farnese family, and it has been known as Villa Farnesina ever since.

Lots to admire On the ground floor are the Loggia of Galatea, with a much admired fresco by Raphael of the Triumph of Galatea, and the Loggia of Cupid and Psyche, frescoed to Raphael's designs by some of his pupils (including the future star of Mannerist painting, Giulio Romano). On the upper floor is the beautiful Salone delle Prospettive, with a fresco by Baldassare Peruzzi of a trompe l'oeil colonnade through which can be seen rural landscapes, villages and a town. Finally, visit Chigi's former bed chamber, decorated with an erotic fresco, The Wedding Night of Alexander the Great and Roxane, by Il Sodoma.

More to See

AVENTINO HILL

The most southernly of Rome's seven hills and one of the most beautiful quarters. Here the traffic and chaos of the city are left far behind, replaced by peaceful churches, charming cloisters, beautiful gardens and panoramic views over Trastevere and St. Peter's.

🞣 G8 🚇 Circo Massimo 🚌 C3, 81, 160, 628, 715 to Via del Circo Massimo

✓ GHETTO

This picturesque place, its narrow streets full of Jewish restaurants, pastry shops and workshops, is still a meeting place for the Roman-Jewish community. The Synagogue, built in 1904 overlooking the Tiber, its great dome visible from all over the city, houses the Jewish Museum.

🞣 F6 ☎ Synagogue 06 6400 0661
🕐 Mon–Thu 9–4.30, Fri 9–1.30, Sun 9–12.30
🚌 23, 63, 280, 630, 780 💷 Moderate

GIANICOLO (out of view)

Not one of Rome's original seven hills, but the best view of Rome has to be from the Janiculum Hill. There are spectacular views all the way up from the Passeggiata del Gianicolo, a fine avenue that runs around the hill. En route visit the little Tempietto designed by Bramante in 1508, and the church of San Pietro in Montorio.

🞣 D7 ✉ Passeggiata del Gianicolo
🕐 Tempietto Tue–Sun 9.30–12.30, 4–6 (2–4 Nov–end Apr); church daily 9–12, 4–6
🚌 44, 75, 115, 125 to the Gianicolo or Via Garibaldi

ISOLA TIBERINA

This small island in the Tiber with its medieval buildings and Roman bridges, feels like a safe haven, protected from the chaos of the city. The island is on a volcanic rock and its shape resembles that of a ship. Two bridges join the Isola Tiberina to the riverbanks: the Ponte Cestio dates back to the first century BC, and leads to Trastevere; while the Ponte Fabricio, built in 62BC, the only Roman bridge to survive intact, joins the island to the Ghetto.

🞣 F7 🚌 H, 23, 63, 280, 780 to Lungotevere dei Cenci and all services to Via Arenula and Largo di Torre Argentina

From Gianicolo a panorama of Rome opens up before you

The narrow streets of the Ghetto Quarter

ORTO BOTANICO

Trastevere has few open spaces, so these university gardens and their 7,000 or so botanical species provide a welcome oasis of green shade.

🏛 D7 ✉ Largo Cristina di Svezia 24, off Via Corsini ☎ 06 4991 7107 🕐 Tue–Sat 9.30–6.30 (5.30 in winter). Closed holidays and Aug 🚌 23, 280 to Lungotevere Farnesina ✋ Moderate

PALAZZO CORSINI

Though in a separate building, this gallery is part of the Palazzo Barberini's Galleria Nazionale. Originally part of the Corsini family's 17th-century collection, it became state property in 1883. Pictures from the 16th to 18th century hang alongside bronzes and sculptures in a series of elegant rooms.

🏛 E6 ✉ Via della Lungara 10 ☎ 06 6880 2323, reservations 06 328 101; www.ticketeria.it 🕐 Tue–Fri entrance at 9.30, 11, 12.30, Sat–Sun 8.30–1.20 🚌 23, 280, 870 to Lungotevere Farnesina ✋ Moderate

SANTA CECILIA IN TRASTEVERE

Enter the church through a delightful courtyard, with a portico supported by old granite columns and a lily garden with a central fountain. Next you pass a façade designed by Ferdinando Fuga in 1741. Crypt excavations and splendid 9th-century apse mosaics depicting Jesus with saints Paul, Agata, Peter, Paschal, Valeriano and Cecilia are among Santa Cecilia's treasures. Another is the beautiful fresco *Last Judgement* (1293) by Pietro Cavallini, the remains of a medieval masterpiece that once covered the walls of the central nave but was mostly lost in an 18th-century restoration of the church. The fresco was moved to the nuns' choir where it can be viewed.

🏛 F8 ✉ Piazza di Santa Cecilia 22 ☎ 06 589 9289 or 06 581 2140 🕐 Daily 9.30–12.30, 4–6.30. Cavallini fresco Mon–Sat 10.15–12.15, Sun 11–12.30 🚌 23, 44, 125, 280, 780 to Viale Trastevere or Lungotevere Ripa ✋ Church free; Cavallini fresco inexpensive; crypt expensive

SANTA MARIA IN COSMEDIN

This lovely old medieval church is best known for the Bocca della Verità, a

A charming courtyard fronts Santa Cecilia in Trastevere

Framed by overhanging branches, the ancient bridge linking Isola Tiberina with Trastevere

weather-beaten stone face (of the sea god Oceanus) once used by the ancient Romans as a drain cover. Inside, the church has a beautiful floor, twin pulpits, a bishop's throne and a stone choir screen, all done in fine Cosmati stone inlay. Most date from the 12th century, a little earlier than the impressive *baldacchino* (altar canopy), which was built by Deodato di Cosma in 1294. In a room off the right aisle is a mosaic depicting the *Adoration of the Magi*, almost all that remains of an 8th-century Greek church on the site.

➕ G7 ✉ Piazza Bocca della Verità 18 ☎ 06 678 1419 🕐 Daily 9–1, 2–7 (6 in winter) 🚌 30, 44, 81, 95, 170 and other routes to Piazza Bocca della Verità or Lungotevere Pierleoni 👊 Free

SANTA SABINA

The lovely basilica of Santa Sabina, on the Aventine Hill, has kept its original 5th-century early Christian plan almost intact. Next to the church is a beautiful medieval cloister where St. Dominic is said to have planted the first orange tree in Rome, the descendants of which still perfume the monk's garden. At the entrance, behind a front portico, is one of the church's main treasures. The entrance doors are divided into wooden panels, many of them survivors from the 5th-century church, carved with scenes from the Old and New Testaments.

➕ G8 ✉ Via di Santa Sabina 2 ☎ 06 5794 0660 🕐 Daily 7–12.30, 3.30–7 🚇 Circo Massimo 🚌 C3, 81, 160, 628, 715 to Via del Circo Massimo 👊 Free

TEMPLES

The Tempio di Vesta and Tempio di Fortuna Virilis are the two best-preserved ancient temples in Rome—all but one of the 20 columns of the former remain standing. Both date from the 2nd century BC, the first named after its resemblance to a similar temple in the Roman Forum. The origins of the second, and the god to whom it was dedicated, remain a mystery.

➕ G7 ✉ 7 Piazza Bocca della Verità 🚌 C3, H, 81, 160, 175 and other services to Via del Teatro del Marcello and Piazza Bocca della Verità

Inside Santa Sabina, Rome's finest surviving 5th-century Basilica

The Bocca della Verità or 'Mouth of Truth', Santa Maria in Cosmedin

Ghetto to Trastevere

Discover two of Rome's less explored areas, the Ghetto and the Isola Tiberina, before crossing the Tiber to the unspoilt Trastevere.

DISTANCE: 3.5km (2 miles)   **ALLOW:** 2–3hours

START

PIAZZA DEL CAMPIDOGLIO
➕ G6 🚌 C3, 40, 63, 70 and all other services to Piazza Venezia

END

PIAZZA DI SANTA MARIA IN TRASTEVER[
➕ E7 🚌 H, 8, 170 to Viale Trastevere or 125 to ˈ
della Sc

① Walk west down the ramp from Piazza del Campidoglio. Cross the road and go down Via d'Aracoeli. Take the second left alley just after the fountain directly into Piazza Margana.

② Cross the piazza into Via dei Delfini and follow the street as it curves right into Via dei Funari. Walk along Via dei Funari to Piazza Mattei, home to the Fontana delle Tartarughe (▷ 51).

③ Continue past the fountain on Via dei Falegnami to busy Via Arenula. Turn left and then immediately left again on Via Santa Maria di Pianto.

④ Continue along Via Santa Maria di Pianto as it becomes Via del Portico d'Ottavia, named after the gateway on the left. Follow the road as it bears right.

⑧ In Piazza Sidney Sonnino go left down Via della Lungaretta to Piazza di Santa Maria in Trastevere. Some of the prettiest streets are north of here.

⑦ Continue to the church of Santa Cecilia (▷ 68) on your right. With your back to the church, turn left and then first left down Via del Genovesi. Continue straight as this street becomes Via G. C. Santini and turn right at Viale Trastevere.

⑥ Go over the Lungotevere and cross the Ponte Fabricio to the Isola Tiberina (▷ 67). Leave the island on the Ponte Cestio and cross over the Lungotevere. Go left and bear right through Piazza Piazza dei Ponziani and right on Via dei Vascellari.

⑤ Note the Teatro di Marcello to your left and Rome's main synagogue on your right.

Shopping

ALMAXXURA
A treasure trove of objects is to be found here, all chosen with the greatest care, and of the finest quality. Everything is made in Italy, and some famous names are represented, such as Capodimonte, Marzi and Murano. There is china, porcelain and glass, as well as collectors' dolls and model cars.
🔒 F8 ☎ 06 580 6303 ✉ Viale di Trastevere 83 ⏰ Mon 4–8, Tue–Sat 10–8

ALMOST CORNER BOOKSHOP
Interesting and unusual selection of books, especially considering the shop's small size. Competitively priced and particularly good on biography and history, with a strong emphasis on Rome and Italy. Helpful and knowledgeable staff.
🔒 E7 ✉ Via del Moro 45 ☎ 06 583 6942 ⏰ Mon–Sat 10–1.30, 3.30–8, Sun 11–1.30, 3.30–8; closed Sun in Aug

CASIMON
This glorious shop sells a variety of objects in marble, stone, glass and semi-precious stones, from ornamental marble balls and bookends to tables and lampshades.
🔒 F7 ✉ Via della Lungaretta 90 ☎ 06 581 4860 ⏰ Daily 11am–midnight

LUMIÈRES
Unassuming shop crammed with goods. If an interesting lamp from the French art deco or Italian Liberty periods is what you're after, this is the place to come. Choose from dozens of antique lamps, all fully restored. Or bring your own lamp to be restored by an artisan.
🔒 E7 ✉ Vicolo del Cinque 48 ☎ 06 580 3614 ⏰ Mon–Sat 10–1, 4–8.30, Sun 4–8

PANDORA
This is an unusual but tasteful store, with a great selection of contemporary Venetian glass items,

LOCAL SHOPPING

Roman supermarkets are few and far between and most food is still bought in tiny local shops known as *alimentari*. Every street of every 'village' or district in the city has one or more of these general shops, a source of everything from olive oil and pasta to candles and corn and bunion treatments. They are also good places to buy picnic provisions—many sell bread and wine—and most have a delicatessen counter that will make you a sandwich (*panino*) from the meats and cheeses on display. For something a little more special, or for food gifts to take home, visit Via della Croce, a street renowned for its wonderful delicatessens.

Italian handmade ceramics, ethnic and handmade jewellery, small antique pieces, and accessories such as scarves and bags.
🔒 E7 ✉ Piazza Santa Maria in Trastevere 6 ☎ 06 581 7145 ⏰ Daily 10–10

PIAZZA SAN COSIMATO
It is a great shame that very few visitors manage to discover what this excellent mid-size general food market in Trastevere has to offer.
🔒 E8 ✉ Piazza San Cosimato ⏰ Mon–Sat 7am–1pm

PORTA PORTESE
Everything and anything is for sale at this famous flea market, though the few genuine antiques are highly priced. By mid-morning crowds are huge, so come early and guard your belongings.
🔒 F8 ✉ Via Porta Portese-Via Ippolito Nuevo ⏰ Sun 6.30am–2pm

LA RENELLA
Wonderful freshly baked bread and pizza all day, every day. This also means it is crowded at all hours. Try freshly baked, thick, unctuous slices of simple pizza *bianca*, topped with olive oil and rosemary, or opt for a number of different fresh toppings. Excellent cakes as well.
🔒 E7 ✉ Via del Moro 15–16 ☎ 06 581 7265 ⏰ Daily 7am–10pm

Entertainment and Nightlife

AKAB-CAVE
www.akabcove.it
In the lively Testaccio area, this very popular and long-established club is on two levels (one underground—hence Cave) with a garden area and varied music policy. International DJs and live rock bands.

➕ Off map at G9 ✉ Via Monte Testaccio 68–69 ☎ 06 578 2390 🕐 Tue–Sat 11pm–4.30am 🚇 Piramide 🚌 23, 44, 170, 280 to Piazza di Porta San Paolo or Via Monte Testaccio 💷 Expensive

L'ALIBI
Primarily a gay disco, but not exclusively, L'Alibi is one of the most reliable (and most established) clubs now mushrooming in trendy Testaccio.

➕ Off map at G9 ✉ Via Monte Testaccio 40–44 ☎ 06 574 3448 🕐 Wed–Sun 11pm–4.30am 🚇 Piramide 🚌 23, 44, 170, 280 to Piazza di Porta San Paolo or Via Monte Testaccio 💷 Expensive

BIG MAMA
www.bigmama.it
This is Rome's best blues club, which also hosts rock and jazz.

➕ F8 ✉ Vicolo San Francesco a Ripa 18 ☎ 06 581 2551 🕐 Oct–end Jun, Tue–Sat 9pm–1.30am 🚌 H, 8, 780 to Viale di Trastevere 💷 Yearly membership (moderate) plus fee for concerts

CAFFÈ LATINO
Testaccio oldest club, devoted to eating, drinking, live music and dance sessions. Mostly jazz, but rap, blues and other genres are here.

➕ Off map at G9 ✉ Via Monte Testaccio 96 ☎ 06 5728 8556 🕐 Sep–end Jul, Tue–Thu, Sun 10.30pm–2.30am, Fri, Sat 10.30pm–4.30am 🚇 Piramide 🚌 3, 23, 30, 75, 280, 716 to Via Marmorata 💷 Membership (expensive)

ENOTECA TRASTEVERE
Tavern-like wine bar with more than 900 wines. During weekends, a pianist plays soft jazz and swing. Outdoor tables in summer.

➕ F7 ✉ Via della Lungaretta 86 ☎ 06 588 5659 🕐 Daily 6pm–2am; closed Wed Dec–end Feb 🚌 H, 175 to Piazza Sidney Sonnino

---

LICENSING LAWS

Laws are much more liberal in Italy than in many countries. The legal age for buying alcoholic drink in bars or shops is 18, but it is very rare for proof of age to be demanded. Laws against drinking and driving, however, are firmly enforced. Opening times for premises licensed to sell alcohol are not set, and correspond to the individual opening times of each establishment. The only occasion on which restrictions on opening are set are before, during and after some football (soccer) matches.

PASQUINO
A Roman institution near Santa Maria in Trastevere, with three screens. Films are in their original language. Crowded espresso bar before screenings.

➕ E7 ✉ Piazza Sant'Egidio 10 ☎ 06 581 5208 🕐 Daily; closed Jun–end Sep 🚇 Piramide 🚌 H, 23, 44, 56, 75, 280 to Viale Trastevere

RIPARTE CAFÉ
Popular modern and stylish nightspot; be sure to reserve ahead, particularly if you want to eat. Part of a four-star hotel.

➕ F8 ✉ Via Orti di Trastevere 7 ☎ 06 586 1816 🕐 Mon–Sat 7.30am–12.30/1am 🚌 8, 780 💷 Expensive

LA SCALA
La Scala is one of the most popular bars and clubs in Trastevere. Loud, lively and young, it offers wine, beer, snacks and light meals and occasional live music. There are a few outside tables.

➕ E7 ✉ Via della Scala 4 ☎ 06 580 3763 🕐 Daily noon–12.30am 🚌 H, 8, 780 to Piazza Sidney Sonnino or 23, 125, 280 to Lungarno Sanzio 💷 Free

TEATRO VASCELLO
On the edge of Trastevere, this is a small but good venue for experimental dance and some classic ballet.

➕ D8 ✉ Via Giacinto Carini 72 ☎ 06 588 1021 🕐 Sep–end Jun, Tue–Sat 5.30–9, Sun 3–5 🚌 44, 75, 115, 710, 870

Restaurants

ALBERTO CIARLA (€€€)

This is among Rome's best fish restaurants, with a fine wine list. The food is elegantly presented, the candlelight lovely and the service impeccable.
🚇 E8 ✉ Piazza San Cosimato 40 ☎ 06 581 8668 or 06 581 6068 🕐 Dinner only Mon–Sat; closed 2 weeks in Aug and Jan 🚌 H, 8, 630, 780 to Viale di Trastevere

ALBERTO PICA (€)

Around 20 flavours of excellent quality ice cream; try the house specialties like green apple (*mele verde*) and Sicilian citrus (*agrumi di Sicilia*).
🚇 F6 ✉ Via della Seggiola 12, Cenci ☎ 06 686 8405 🕐 Mon–Sat 8am–1.30am (also Sun 4pm–2am Apr–end Oct); closed 2 weeks in Aug 🚌 8 to Via Arenula and 8, 46, 62, 63, 64, 70, 87, 186, 492 to Largo di Torre Argentina

AUGUSTO (€) ✅

One of Trastevere's last remaining inexpensive and authentic family-run *trattorie*, with 50 places. No credit cards.
🚇 E7 🕐 10 ✉ Piazza de' Renzi 15 ☎ 06 580 3798 🕐 Daily 12–3.30, 8–11; closed

Aug 🚌 23, 280 to Lungotevere Sanzio or H, 8, 780 to Piazza Sidney Sonnino

BIBLI (€€)

www.bibli.it
This Trastevere bookshop-cum-cafeteria is particularly popular for Sunday brunch. A selection of pastas, quiches, coucous with vegetable dishes are served buffet style.
🚇 F7 ✉ Via dei Fienaroli 28 ☎ 06 588 4097 🕐 Daily 11am–midnight; Mon 5.30–11.30 buffet-style dinner 🚌 H, 23, 44, 56, 75, 280 to Viale Trastevere or Piazza Sonnino

CHECCHINO DAL 1887 (€€€)

www.checchino-dal-1887.com
Robust appetites are required for the menu at this Testaccio establishment. Quintessential Roman dishes relying largely on offal are the

specialty. Reservations advisable.
🚇 Off map G9 ✉ Via Monte Testaccio 30 ☎ 06 574 6318 🕐 Tue–Sat 12.30–3, 8–11; closed Aug 🚌 3, 60, 75, 118 to Piramide

DA MIRELLA (€)

Sells *granita*: crushed ice drenched in juice or syrup. The flavourings in this ice cream kiosk have been refined over many years; the ice is still ground by hand.
🚇 F7 ✉ Lungotevere Anguillara, Ponte Cestio 🕐 May–end Sep daily 8am–late 🚌 23, 280

DAR POETA (€)

A very popular and long-established little pizzeria hidden in a quiet street. The interior is simple but the pizza (and puddings) are excellent.
🚇 E7 ✉ Vicolo di Bologna 45 ☎ 06 588 0516 🕐 Daily dinner only 7.30–11 🚌 8, 870 and all services to Trastevere

DA VITTORIO (€)

Tiny Neapolitan-run Trastevere pizzeria that makes a good standby if Ivo (▷ 74) is busy.
🚇 E7 ✉ Via di San Cosimato 14a, off Piazza San Calisto ☎ 06 580 0353 🕐 Mon–Sat 7.30pm–midnight 🚌 H, 8, 780 to Viale di Trastevere

GIGGETTO (€)

A famous Romano-Jewish restaurant in the Ghetto district; almost as good and cheaper than Piperno (▷ 74).

73

⊞ G6 ⊠ Via Portico d'Ottavia 21a ☎ 06 686 1105 ⏱ Tue– Sun 12.30–2.30, 7.30–10.30 🚌 H, 8, 63 to Via Arenula and 46, 62, 63, 70 and other services to Largo di Torre Argentina

IVO (€) ✓

The best-known of Trastevere's pizzerias. Lines are common but turnover is quick.
⊞ E7 ⊠ Via di San Francesco a Ripa 158 ☎ 06 581 7082 ⏱ Wed–Mon 5.30–2am; closed 3 weeks in Aug 🚌 H, 8, 780 to Viale di Trastevere

PANATTONI (€)

Big, bright and often busy, Panattoni is known locally as 'L'Obitorio' (The Morgue) on account of its characteristic cold marble-topped tables. Watch the chef flip the pizzas at the oven. Arrive early to get a table outside.
⊞ F8 ⊠ Viale di Trastevere 53 ☎ 06 580 0919 ⏱ Thu–Tue 6.30pm–2am; closed 3 weeks in Aug 🚌 H, 8, 780 to Viale di Trastevere

PARIS (€€) ✓

An extremely popular and elegant little restaurant just south of Piazza Santa Maria in Trastevere, and known for its fish, pastas and Roman cuisine. Outside tables for alfresco dining. Reserve ahead.
⊞ E7 ⊠ Piazza San Callisto 7a ☎ 06 581 5378 ⏱ Tue–Sat 12.30–3, 8–11, Sun 12.30–3; closed 3 weeks in Aug 🚌 H, 8, 780 to Piazza

Sidney Sonnino or 23, 280 to Lungotevere Sanzio

PIPERNO (€€) ✓

Much Roman cuisine is based on the city's Jewish culinary traditions. The famous and resolutely traditional Piperno has been a temple to Romano-Jewish cuisine for over a century. Reserve ahead.
⊞ F6 ⊠ Via Monte de' Cenci 9 ☎ 06 6880 6629/ 2772 ⏱ Tue–Sat 12.15–2.30, 8–10.30, Sun 12.15–3; closed Aug 🚌 H, 8, 63 to Via Arenula and 8, 46, 62, 63, 64, 70, 87, 492 to Largo di Torre Argentina

SABATINI (€€€)

Once Rome's most famous restaurant, Sabatini is still preferred for its reliable food and lovely setting, though

BAR ETIQUETTE

You almost always pay a premium to sit down (inside or outside) and to enjoy the privilege of waiter service in Roman bars. If you stand—which is less expensive—the procedure is to pay for what you want first at the cash desk (*la cassa*). You then take your receipt (*lo scontrino*) to the bar and repeat your order (a tip slapped down on the bar will work wonders in attracting the bar person's attention). Pastry shops, cafés and ice cream shops often double as excellent all-around bars to be enjoyed during the day.

prices are higher than the cooking deserves. Reserve ahead.
⊞ E7 ⊠ Piazza Santa Maria in Trastevere 13 (and Vicolo Santa Maria in Trastevere 18) ☎ 06 581 2026 or 06 581 8307) ⏱ Daily 12–2.30, 7.30–11; closed Aug 🚌 H, 8, 780 to Piazza Sidney Sonnino or 23, 280 to Lungotevere Sanzio

SACCHETTI (€)

Family-run bar in Trastevere also good for cakes and pastries.
⊞ E8 ⊠ Piazza San Cosimato 61–62 ☎ 06 581 5374 ⏱ Tue–Sun 5am–11pm 🚌 H, 8, 780 to Viale di Trastevere

SORA LELLA (€€)

Founded by the actress Sora Lella, and now presided over by her son and nephews, this is a two-room, wood-panelled former *trattoria* on the Isola Tiberina. Roman cooking, with menu and daily specials.
⊞ G7 ⊠ Via Ponte Quattro Capi 16 ☎ 06 686 1601 ⏱ Mon–Sat 12.30–2.30, 7.30–10.30; closed Aug 🚌 23, 23, 63, 280 to Lungotevere dei Cenci or Lungotevere degli Anguillara

TRASTÈ (€)

Chic tea and coffee shop serving light meals. Come to chat, read the papers and pass the time.
⊞ F7 ⊠ Via della Lungaretta 76 ☎ 06 589 4430 ⏱ Daily 5pm–2am 🚌 H, 8, 780 to Piazza Sidney Sonnino

Northern Rome is a wonderful medley of open spaces, notably the Villa Borghese, historical and cultural attractions such as the Fontana di Trevi and the Spanish Steps, and Rome's finest shopping streets.

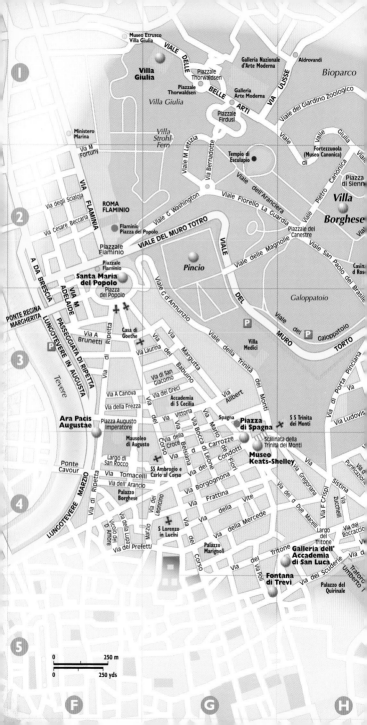

Museo Etrusco
Villa Giulia

VIALE DELLE

Villa
Giulia

Piazzale
Thorwaldsen

Galleria Nazionale
d'Arte Moderna

Aldrovandi

Villa Giulia

Piazzale
Thorwaldsen

BELLE

Galleria
Arte Moderna

Bioparco

Villa
Strohl-
Fern

ARTI

Viale del Giardino Zoologico

Ministero
Marina

Via M
Fortuny

Viale M Letizia

Viale Bernadotte

Tempio di
Esculapio

Viale

Viale Giardino Zoologico

Fortezzuoola
(Museo Canonica)

di

Piazza
di Sienn

ROMA
FLAMINIO

Via degli Scialoja

VIA FLAMINIA

Via Cesare Beccaria

Viale G Washington

Viale dell'Arandera

Viale Fiorello La Guardia

Villa
Borghese

Viale Piero Canonica

Flaminio
Piazza del Popolo

VIALE DEL MURO TOTRO

VIALE

Piazzale
del Canestre

Casin
di Ros

A DA BRESCIA

VIA M ADELAIDE

Piazzale
Flaminio

Pincio

Viale delle Magnolie

Viale San Paolo del Brasile

Galoppatoio

Piazzale
Flaminio

Santa Maria
del Popolo

Piazza
dei Popolo

Viale G d'Annunzio

DEL

PONTE REGINA
MARGHERITA

PASSEGGIATA DI RIPETTA

Via A
Brunetti

Casa di
Goethe

Via del Babuino

Via

Viale della Trinità dei Monti

MURO

Galoppatoio

LUNGOTEVERE IN AUGUSTA

Via
di
Ripetta

Via Laurina

Villa
Medici

TORTO

Via A Canova

Via della Frezza

Via di San
Giacomo

Via del Greci

Via Margutta

Accademia
di S Cecilia

Via Albert

Via di Porta Pinciana

Tevere

Ara Pacis
Augustae

Piazza Augusto
Imperatore

Vittoria

Via Bocca di Leone

Via Mario de' Fiori

Spagna

Piazza
di Spagna

S S Trinita
dei Monti

Via Ludovis

Mausoleo
di Augusto

C Via della
Croce

Via
Belsiana

Via delle Carrozze

Scalinata della
Trinita dei Monti

Ponte
Cavour

Largo di
San Rocco

SS Ambrogio e
Carlo al Corso

Via Tomacelli

Via del Corso

Via
Condotti

Museo
Keats-Shelley

Via di Ripetta

Via dell' Aranclo

Palazzo
Borghese

Via Borgognona

Via Gregoriana

LUNGOTEVERE MARZIO

Via del Leoncino

Via Frattina

Via della

Vite

Via F Crispi

Via d. Due Macelli

Sistina

Via del Due Macelli

Via del
Boccaccio

Via Zucchelli

Vicolo del
'D Amore'

Via della Lupa

S Lorenzo
in Lucini

Via del Corso

Via della Mercede

Largo
del
Tritone

Via del Prefetti

Palazzo
Marignoli

Via del Poli

Via del Tritone

Galleria dell'
Accademia
di San Luca

Via d

Via del Scuderie

Traforo
Umberto I

Fontana
di Trevi

Palazzo del
Quirinale

0 ——— 250 m

0 ——— 250 yds

F

G

H

1

2

3

4

5

Fontana di Trevi

TOP
25

Remember to toss a coin in the fountain (left). The Trevi in all its floodlit glory (right)

THE BASICS

⊞ G5
✉ Piazza Fontana di Trevi
🕒 Always open
Ⓢ Spagna or Barberini
🚌 C3, 52, 53, 61, 62, 71, 95, 117, 119 and other routes to Via del Corso and Via del Tritone
♿ Access via cobbled street
💲 Free

HIGHLIGHTS

● *Oceanus* (Neptune)
● *Allegory of Health* (right of *Oceanus*)
● *Virgin Indicating the Spring to Soldiers*
● *Allegory of Abundance* (left of *Oceanus*)
● *Agrippa Approving the Design of the Aqueduct*
● *Triton with Horse* (on the right, symbolizing the ocean in repose)
● *Triton with Horse* (on the left, symbolizing a tempestuous sea)
● Façade of Santi Vincenzo e Anastasio
● Baroque interior of Santa Maria in Trivio

There is no lovelier surprise than that which confronts you as you emerge from the tight warren of streets around the Fontana di Trevi, the city's most famous fountain—a sight 'silvery to the eye and ear', in the words of Charles Dickens.

Virgin discovery In its earliest guise the Fontana di Trevi lay at the end of the Aqua Virgo, or Acqua Vergine, an aqueduct built by Agrippa in 19BC (supposedly filled with Rome's sweetest waters). The spring that fed it was reputedly discovered by a virgin, hence its name. (She is said to have shown her discovery to some Roman soldiers, a scene—along with Agrippa's approval of the aqueduct's plans—described in bas-reliefs on the fountain's second tier.) The fountain's liveliness and charm is embodied in the pose of *Oceanus*, the central figure, and the two giant tritons and their horses (symbolizing a calm and a stormy sea) drawing his chariot. Other statues represent Abundance and Health and, above, the Four Seasons, which each carry gifts.

The fountains A new fountain was built in 1453, ordered by Pope Nicholas V who paid for it by taxing wine. Its name came from the three roads (*tre vie*) that converged on the piazza. The present fountain was commissioned by Pope Clement XII in 1732 and finished in 1762: Its design was inspired by the Arch of Constantine and is attributed to Nicola Salvi, with possible contributions from Bernini. Those wishing to return to Rome toss a coin (over the shoulder) into the fountain.

Museo e Galleria Borghese

The Galleria Borghese may be small, but what it lacks in quantity it makes up for in quality. It combines paintings and sculptures, including many masterpieces by Gian Lorenzo Bernini, Raphael, Caravaggio and others.

Seductress The Villa Borghese was designed in 1613 as a summer retreat for Cardinal Scipione Borghese, nephew of Pope Paul V, who accumulated most of the collection (acquired by the state in 1902). Scipione was an enthusiastic patron of Bernini, whose works dominate the gallery. The museum's foremost masterpiece is Antonio Canova's *Paolina Borghese* (1804), Napoleon's sister and wife of Camillo Borghese. Depicted bare-breasted, with a come-hither hauteur, Paolina was just as seductive in life. Her jewels, clothes, lovers and the servants she used as footstools all excited gossip.

Bernini His *David* (1623–24) is said to be a self-portrait, while *Apollo and Daphne* (1622–25), in the next room, is considered his masterpiece. Other Bernini works include the *Rape of Proserpine* (1622) and *Truth Unveiled by Time* (1652).

The paintings Foremost in this wonderful collection are works by Raphael (*The Deposition of Christ*, 1507), Titian (*Sacred and Profane Love*, 1512), Caravaggio (*Boy with a Fruit Basket* and *Madonna dei Palafrenieri*, 1605) and Correggio (*Danae*, 1530).

THE BASICS

www.galleriaborghese.it

➕ J2

✉ Piazzale Scipione Borghese 5

☎ 06 841 7645; obligatory reservations 06 328 101; www.ticketeria.it

🕐 Tue–Sun 9–7. Closed public holidays

🚇 Spagna or Flaminio

🚌 116 to Viale del Museo Borghese, or 52, 53, 910 to Via Pinciana or C3, 19 to Via delle Belle Arti

♿ Steps to front entrance

✋ Expensive

HIGHLIGHTS

- *Paolina Borghese*, Canova
- *David*, Bernini
- *Apollo and Daphne*, Bernini
- *Madonna dei Palafrenieri*, Caravaggio
- *Sacred and Profane Love*, Titian
- *Deposition of Christ*, Raphael

Palazzo Barberini

TOP 25

Frescoes outlined in gold adorn the palazzo (left). Raphael's La Fornarina (right)

THE BASICS

- ✚ J4
- ✉ Via Barberini 18
- ☎ 06 482 4184; online booking www.ticketeria.it
- 🕐 Tue–Sun 9–7
- Ⓜ Barberini
- 🚌 52, 53, 61, 62, 63, 71, 80, 95, 116, 119 to Via del Tritone or H, 40, 60, 64, 70, 71, 116T, 170 to Via Nazionale
- ♿ Few
- 💶 Moderate

HIGHLIGHTS

- Elicoidale
- *Madonna and Child* and *Annunciation*, Filippo Lippi
- *Holy Family* and *Madonna and Saints*, Andrea del Sarto
- *Madonna and Child*, Beccafumi
- *La Fornarina*, Raphael
- *Adoration of the Shepherds* and *Baptism of Christ*, El Greco
- *Judith and Holofernes* and *Narciso*, Caravaggio
- *Beatrice Cenci*, attributed to Guido Reni
- *Henry VIII*, attributed to Holbein
- *The Triumph of Divine Providence*, Pietro da Cortona (Gran Salone)

The magnificent Palazzo Barberini— designed by Bernini, Borromini and Carlo Maderno—houses a stupendous ceiling fresco and one of Rome's finest art collections, the Galleria Nazionale d'Arte Antica.

Urban's grandeur The palace was commissioned by Maffeo Barberini for his family when he became Pope Urban VIII in 1623. It was begun by Carlo Maderno and completed by Bernini. The epitome of Rome's high baroque style, it is a maze of suites, apartments and staircases, many still swathed in their sumptuous original decoration. Overshadowing all is the Gran Salone, dominated by Pietro da Cortona's rich ceiling frescos, glorifying Urban as an agent of Divine Providence. The central windows and oval spiral staircase (Scala Elicoidale) are the work of Borromini.

The collection '*Antica*' here means old rather than ancient. Probably the most popular painting in the collection is Raphael's *La Fornarina* (also attributed to Giulio Romano). It is reputedly a portrait of one of the artist's several mistresses, identified later as the daughter of a *fornaio* (baker). It was executed in the year of the painter's death, a demise brought on, it is said, by his mistress's unrelenting passion. Elsewhere, eminent Italian works from Filippo Lippi, Andrea del Sarto, Caravaggio and Guido Reni stand along-side paintings by leading foreign artists. Also here is a rich collection of paintings, furniture, ceramics and other beautiful decorative arts.

This popular meeting
place (left and right) is
used as a stage for
fashion shows (middle)

TOP 25

Piazza di Spagna

Neither old nor particularly striking, the Spanish Steps are nonetheless one of Rome's most popular meeting points, thanks largely to their views, at the heart of Piazza di Spagna in the city's exclusive shopping district.

Spanish Steps Despite their name, the Spanish Steps were commissioned by the French ambassador, Étienne Gueffier, who in 1723 sought to link Piazza di Spagna with the French-owned church of Trinità dei Monti on the hill above. A century earlier the piazza had housed the headquarters of the Spanish ambassador to the Holy See, hence the name of the steps and the square.

Around the steps At the base of the steps is the Fontana della Barcaccia, commissioned in 1627 by Urban VIII and designed either by Gian Lorenzo Bernini or by his less famous father, Pietro. The eccentric design represents a half-sunken boat. As you face the steps from below, to your right stands the Museo Keats–Shelley, a fascinating collection of literary memorabilia and a working library housed in the lodgings where the poet John Keats died in 1821. At the top of the steps you can enjoy views past Palazzo Barberini (▷ 80) and towards the Quirinal Hill; walk into the simple Trinità dei Monti, with its outside double stairs by Domenico Fontana; and visit the beautiful gardens of the 16th-century Villa Medici, the seat of the French Academy in Rome, where scholars study painting, sculpture, architecture, engraving and music.

THE BASICS

✚ G4
✉ Piazza di Spagna
☎ Caffè Greco 06 679 1700. Villa Medici 06 679 8381
🕐 Spanish Steps always open. Trinità dei Monti daily 10–12.30, 4–6. Villa Medici occasionally open for exhibitions.
🍴 Babington's Tea Rooms (▷ 90)
Ⓜ Spagna
🚌 119 to Piazza di Spagna
♿ None for the Spanish Steps
👐 Free

HIGHLIGHTS

● Spanish Steps
● Museo Keats–Shelley (▷ 87)
● Trinità dei Monti
● Fontana della Barcaccia
● Babington's Tea Rooms (▷ 90)
● Villa Medici gardens
● Pincio Gardens (▷ 87)

Palazzo Massimo alle Terme

HIGHLIGHTS

- *Niobid from the Hortus Sallustiani* (Room VIII)
- *The Lancellotti Discobolus* (Room VI)
- *The Sleeping Hermaphrodite* (Room VII)
- House of Livia (Room II)
- The Villa Farnesina (Gallery II, Rooms III–V)

TIP

- The combined ticket is valid for all parts of the Museo Nazionale Romano, notably the Palazzo Altemps.

A sublime collection of Greek and Roman sculpture with outstanding and unique displays of ancient Roman wall paintings and mosaics dating from end of the Republican age to the late Imperial age.

The building The Palazzo Massimo is an elegant and airy 19th-century palace, beautifully renovated for the millennium. The palace, designed by Camillo Pistrucci, was built in the late 19th century by the Massimo family to replace an earlier one demolished to make way for the Termini station. In 1981 the palace was acquired by the state, and in the 1990s it was transformed into one of Rome's most attractive museums. The palace has four floors of museum space, a modern library, a conference room and a computer-based documentation area.

Lovingly restored, the Palazzo Massimo was a Jesuit college until 1960 (left) but now houses outstanding displays of ancient Roman wall paintings and mosaics (right)

The collection One of the two buildings (the other being Palazzo Altemps, ▷ 42–43) housing Rome's magnificent Classical collections, here you'll find some of Rome's greatest Classical treasures, ranging from naked gods and games players to sarcophagi and goddesses. Don't miss the superb portrait busts or the wonderful Roman frescos and mosaics on the upper floor.

Lancellotti Discobolus This fine marble copy of the great *Discus Thrower* dates from the mid-second century AD, and is one of the most famous copies of the 5th-century BC works. Discovered in the 18th century, it was sent to Germany during World War II and returned in 1948. It reproduces an original bronze, showing an athlete throwing a discus—probably the work of Myron, a Greek sculptor renowned for his portraits of athletes.

THE BASICS

www.pierreci.it
✚ K4–5
✉ Piazza dei Cinquecento 67–Largo di Villa Peretti 1
☎ Reservations 06 3996 7700
🕐 Tue–Sun 9–7.45
🚇 Repubblica
🚌 All services to Termini and Piazza dei Cinquecento
💶 Expensive (joint pass available with Palazzo Altemps, Crypta Balbi and Terme di Diocleziano)

Santa Maria del Popolo

Carracci's Assumption of the Virgin *(left). Inside is a wealth of artistic works (right)*

Santa Maria del Popolo's appeal stems from its intimate size and location, and from a wonderfully varied and rich collection of works of art ranging from masterpieces by Caravaggio to some of Rome's earliest stained-glass windows.

Renaissance achievement Founded in 1099 on the site of Nero's grave, Santa Maria del Popolo was rebuilt by Pope Sixtus IV in 1472 and extended later by Bramante and Bernini. The right nave's first chapel, the Cappella della Rovere, is decorated with frescos–*Life of San Girolamo* (1485–90)–by Tiberio d'Assisi, a pupil of Pinturicchio whose *Nativity* (c1490) graces the chapel's main altar. The apse contains two fine stained-glass windows (1509) by the French artist Guillaume de Marcillat. On either side are the greatest of the church's monuments: the tombs of the cardinals Ascanio Sforza (1505, left) and Girolamo Basso della Rovere (1507, right). Both are the work of Andrea Sansovino. High on the walls are superb and elegant frescos (1508–10) of the Virgin, Evangelists, the Fathers of the Church and Sybils by Pinturicchio.

North nave The first chapel of the left transept, the Cappella Cerasi, contains three major paintings: the altarpiece, *Assumption of the Virgin,* by Annibale Carracci; and Caravaggio's dramatic *Conversion of St. Paul* and the *Crucifixion of St. Peter* (all 1601). The famous Cappella Chigi (1513), the second chapel in the north aisle, was commissioned by the Sienese banker Agostino Chigi.

Villa Giulia, built to a design by Giacomo da Vignola, displays beautiful frescos

Villa Giulia

The Museo Nazionale Etrusca di Villa Giulia houses the world's greatest collection of Etruscan art and objects. The exhibits are not always perfectly presented, but it is a revelation to discover this mysterious civilization.

The villa Built in 1550–55 as a country house and garden for the hedonistic Pope Julius III, the Villa Giulia was designed by some of the leading architects of the day, including Michelangelo and Georgio Vasari.

The collection The exhibits are generally divided between finds from Etruscan sites in northern Etruria (western central Italy) and from excavations in the south (Nemi and Praeneste), including objects made by the Greeks. Most notable are the Castellani exhibits, which include vases, cups and ewers, and jewellery from the Minoan period (the latter collection is one of the villa's special treasures). To see the most striking works of art, be selective. Pick through the numerous vases noting the *Tomba del Guerriero* and the *Cratere a Volute*. Note also the *Sarcofago degli Sposi*, a 6th-century BC sarcophagus with figures of a married couple reclining together on a banqueting couch; the engraved marriage coffer known as the *Cista Ficoroni* (4th century BC); the giant terra-cotta figures, *Hercules and Apollo*; the temple sculptures from Falerii Veteres; and the valuable 7th-century BC relics in gold, silver, bronze and ivory from the Barberini and Bernardini tombs in Praeneste, 39km (24 miles) east of Rome.

THE BASICS

✚ G1

✉ Piazzale di Villa Giulia 9

☎ 06 322 6571; reservations 06 824 620 online booking, www.ticketeria.it

🕐 Tue–Sun 8.30am–7.30pm

🍴 Café and shop

Ⓜ Flaminio

🚌 3 or 19 to Viale delle Belle Arti

♿ Good

💷 Moderate

HIGHLIGHTS

● *Lamine d'Oro*, Sala di Pyrgi: a gold tablet
● Vase: *Tomba del Guerriero*
● Terra-cottas: *Hercules and Apollo*
● Sarcofago degli Sposi
● Castellani Collection
● Vase: *Cratere a Volute*
● Finds from Falerii Veteres
● Tomb relics: Barberini and Bernardini
● Marriage coffer: *Cista Ficoroni*
● Gardens with Nymphaeum and reconstructed 'Temple of Alatri'

More to See

ARA PACIS AUGUSTAE
www.arapacis.it
The Altar of Peace, now contained within architect Richard Meier's controversial glass pavilion (opened in 2006) is decorated with bas-reliefs from 9BC. It was built to celebrate Augustus's triumphal return to Rome after campaigns in Spain and Gaul, and to commemorate the peace he had established throughout the Roman world. The outside of the enclosure is decorated with mythological scenes and grand processional friezes in which life-size figures portray Augustus, the imperial family, officials and other notables. The altar has recently reopened to the public within a new building.

➕ F4 ✉ Lungotevere in Augusta ☎ 06 8205 9127 ⏰ Tue–Sun 9–7 🚌 224, 913 to Piazza Augusto Imperatore or 224, 590, 628, 926 to Lungotevere in Augusta or 117, 119 to Via di Ripetta 🖐 Moderate

FONTANA DEL TRITONE
Like its companion piece, the Fontana delle Api, the Fountain of Triton (1643) was also designed by Bernini for Urban VIII. One of the sculptor's earliest fountains, the Fontana del Tritone depicts four dolphins supporting twin scallop shells bearing the Barberini coat of arms, on which the triumphant Triton is enthroned.

➕ H4 ✉ Piazza Barberini 🅜 Barberini 🚌 52, 53, 61, 62, 80, 95, 116, 119 to Piazza Barberini or Via del Tritone

GALLERIA DELL'ACCADEMIA DI SAN LUCA
www.accademiasanluca.it
This gallery was founded to promote the training of artists in Renaissance techniques. From 1633, every artist member of the academy had to donate a work of art, resulting in a wonderful collection that includes paintings by Raphael, Canova, Van Dyck, Rubens and Titian, to name a few.

➕ H4 ✉ Piazza dell'Accademia di San Luca 77 ☎ 06 679 8850 ⏰ Call for latest openings or visit website 🚌 52, 53, 60, 61, 62, 71, 80, 85, 160, 850 to Piazza San Silvestro 🖐 Free

Ara Pacis Augustae, a memorial to the peace brought about by Augustus

A feature at the Galleria dell'Accademia di San Luca

MUSEO KEATS–SHELLEY

www.keats-shelley-house.org
Since 1909 this has been a museum and library for students of the Romantic poets Keats and Shelley. Books, pictures and essays lie scattered around the 18th-century house.

✚ G4 ✉ Piazza di Spagna ☎ 06 678 4235 🕐 Mon–Fri 9–1, 3–6, Sat 11–2, 3–6 🚇 Spagna 🚌 119 to Piazza di Spagna ✋ Inexpensive

PINCIO

The park was laid out in the early 19th century. Walk to the Pincio from Piazza del Popolo or Piazza di Spagna to enjoy wonderful views (best at dusk) across the rooftops to St. Peter's.

✚ G2 ✉ Piazza del Pincio 🕐 Daily dawn–dusk 🚌 95, 117, 119 to Piazzale Flaminio or Piazza del Popolo ✋ Free

SANTA MARIA DELLA CONCEZIONE

Lying in the crypt of Santa Maria della Concezione, built in 1624, are the remains of 4,000 Capuchin monks, some still dressed in jaunty clothes, the bones of others crafted into macabre chandeliers and bizarre wall decorations. The bodies were originally buried in soil especially imported from Jerusalem. When this ran out they were left uncovered, a practice that continued until 1870.

✚ H4 ✉ Via Vittorio Veneto 27 ☎ 06 487 1185 🕐 Church daily 7–12, 3/4–7. Crypt (Cimitero dei Cappuccini) Wed–Mon 9–12, 3–6 🚌 52, 53, 80, 95, 116, 119 and other services to Via Vittorio Veneto ✋ Free (donation to visit crypt)

VILLA BORGHESE

Rome's largest central park (▷ 88) was laid out between 1613 and 1616 as the grounds of the Borghese family's summer villa. Redesigned in the 18th century, it still provides a shady retreat. Walkways, woods and lakes are complemented by fountains, a racetrack and children's playgrounds. There is also a zoo (Bioparco).

✚ H2 ✉ Porta Pinciana-Via Flaminia 🕐 Daily dawn–dusk; Bioparco daily 9.30–5/6 🚇 Flaminio 🚌 3, 19, 88, 95, 116, 117, 119, 495 ✋ Free; Bioparco expensive

The crypt, Santa Maria della Concezione

The Temple of Esculapio, at the Villa Borghese

Villa Borghese

A stroll in this park, once the estate of Cardinal Scipione Borghese, is the perfect antidote to the turmoil of Rome's busy streets.

DISTANCE: 2km (1.2 miles) **ALLOW:** 2 hours

START

PIAZZA DEL POPOLO
F2 117, 119

END

PIAZZALE FLAMINIO
F2 95, 120 to Piazzale Flaminio or 117, 119 to Piazza del Popolo

❶ Piazza del Popolo is the site of two almost identical churches, standing on the corners of Via di Ripetta and Via del Babuino. With your back to the churches, take Viale G. d'Annunzio, on the right-hand side of the square.

❷ Follow the road as it snakes up, turning left onto Viale Mickievicz into Giardino del Pincio (▷ 87). Continue to Piazzale Napoleone I for a view over the city. Retrace your steps to Viale del'Obelisco and turn left.

❸ Carry straight on, crossing Viale del'Orologio, with its fascinating water-clock, until you reach Piazzale dei Martini and the entrance to the Villa Borghese park (▷ 87).

❹ Keep walking straight along Viale delle Magnolie until you reach Via de Casina di Raffaello. Follow this road up to the 18th-century Classical Tempietto di Diana. Turn left at the temple, onto Viale dei Pupazzi.

❽ Continue straight down to Viale Washington, which ends with the spectacular gate in Piazzale Flaminio, or on the left the gate back to Piazza del Popolo.

❼ Climb the steps to the Tempio di Esculapio. Take the next lane on the right to emerge onto Piazza Paolina Borghese. To leave the park, retrace your steps to Piazza Paolina Borghese, and take the road in front, Via Bernadotte, leading down to Piazzale Fiocco and the Esculapio Fountain.

❻ To the right is the Museo e Galleria Borghese (▷ 79). Go left on Piazzale del Giardino Zoologico and pass the entrance to the zoo. Keep on Viale del Giardino Zoologico until you reach Largo P. Picasso.

❺ When you reach Piazzale dei Cavalloi Marini, continue straight on to the end of the path.

WALK

NORTHERN ROME

ANTICA ENOTECA

An old-fashioned shop where you can purchase wine by the bottle or by the glass amid trickling fountains.

G3 Via della Croce 76b 06 679 0896 Daily 11.30am–midnight

AVC DI ADRIANA CAMPANILE ✓

Bright, modern and wearable styles for women with the distinctive red heart logo of Adriana Campanile.

G3 Piazza di Spagna 88 06 6992 2355 Mon–Sat 10.30–7.30, Sun 11–1, 2–7.30

BATTISTONI

Traditional tailor's shop in business for over half a century.

G4 Via Condotti 61a 06 697 6111 Tue–Sat 10–7, Mon 3–7.30

ERMENEGILDO ZEGNA

Informal suits and jackets in exquisite, expensive fabrics. Also stocks shirts, sweaters and accessories.

G4 Via Borgognona 7e 06 678 9143 Mon–Sat 10–7.30, Sun 3.30–7.30

FAUSTO SANTINI

An iconoclast who designs witty, innovative and bizarre shoes.

G4 Via Frattina 120–1 06 678 4114 Mon–Sat 10–7.30, Sun 12–7.30

FERRAGAMO ✓

An established family firm; probably Italy's most renowned shoe shop.

G4 Via Condotti 73–4 (women's) 06 679 1565; Via Condotti 65 (men's) 06 678 1130 Mon–Sat 10–7, last Sun of month 12–7

GINORI

One of the top Italian names in modern and traditional glass and china.

G3 Piazza Trinita dei Monti 18b 06 679 3836 Tue–Sat 10–7.30

GIORGIO ARMANI

King of cut and classic, understated elegance.

G4 Via Condotti 77 06 699 1460 Mon–Sat 10–7

GUCCI

Expensive and high-quality bags, shoes and leather goods are a feature of this famous name.

G3 Via Condotti 8 06 679 0405 Mon–Sat 10–7, Sun 2.30–7

MARELLA

The showcase shop for the Marella label offers classic, well-made designs at reasonable prices.

G4 Via Frattina 129–31 06 6992 3800 Tue–Sat 10–7.30, Mon, Sun 11–2, 3–7

LA PERLA

Italian lingerie is among the best in the world, and this reputation is more than upheld by La Perla.

G4 Via Condotti 79 06 6994 1934 Tue–Sat 10–7, Mon 3–7

PINEIDER

Rome's most expensive and exclusive stationers. Virtually any design can be printed onto personalized visiting cards.

H4 Via dei Due Macelli 68 06 678 9013 Mon–Sat 10–7, Sun 10–2, 3–7

PRADA ✓

The Rome flagship store of the celebrated Milan-based designer.

G4 Via Condotti 92–5 06 679 0897 Daily 10–7

SERGIO DI CORI

Romans who need gloves look no further than this tiny shop.

G3 Piazza di Spagna 53 06 678 4439 Mon–Sat 9.30–7.30, Sun 11–7

SALES AND BARGAINS

Sales (*saldi*) in Rome are not always the bargains they seem. That said, many shoe shops and top designers cut their prices drastically during summer and winter sales (mid-Jul to mid-Sep and Jan to mid-Mar). Other lures to get you into a shop, notably the offer of *sconti* (discounts) and *vendite promozionali* (promotional offers), rarely save you any money. It can occasionally be worth asking for a discount (*uno sconto*), particularly if you are paying cash for an expensive item, or buying several items from one shop.

Entertainment and Nightlife

GILDA

The louche and languid atmosphere at this club has been attracting stars and VIPs for years. Smart jacket required.

➕ G4 ✉ Via Mario de' Fiori 97 ☎ 06 678 4838 🕐 Thu–Sun 11pm–4am 🚇 Spagna 🚌 52, 53, 61, 71, 85, 160, 850 to Piazza San Silvestro 🍴 Expensive

GREGORY'S

www.gregorysjazzclub.it

Relaxed club, and one of the few places in central Rome where you can listen to jazz.

➕ H4 ✉ Via Gregoriana 54/a ☎ 06 679 6386 🕐 Tue–Sun 8pm–2/3.30am 🚌 119 to Piazza di Spagna 🍴 Variable

TEATRO DELL'OPERA DI ROMA

www.opera.roma.it

One of Italy's top opera houses; also an official venue for the ballet.

➕ J–K5 ✉ Piazza Beniamo Gigli 8 ☎ 06 481 7003; box office 06 481 601 🚇 Termini 🚌 H, 40, 60, 64, 70, 71, 170 to Via Nazionale or services o Termini

TEATRO OLIMPICO

This is where the Filarmonica di Rome performs, as well as other international dance and music ensembles.

➕ Off map at F1 ✉ Piazza Gentile da Fabriano ☎ 06 323 4890 Box Office 06 326 5991 🚌 225 Piazza Mancini

ZEST

The sleek, modern bar of the ES Hotel. Sip drinks in the stylish minimalist interior, or in summer outside on the terrace.

➕ L5 ✉ ES Hotel, Via Filippo Turati 171 ☎ 06 444 841 🕐 Daily 10am–1.30pm 🚇 Vittorio Emanuele 🚌 70, 71 🍴 Free

Restaurants

PRICES

Prices are approximate, based on a 3-course meal for one person.

€€€	over €50
€€	€30–€50
€	under €30

BABINGTON'S TEA ROOMS (€€€)

Mix with the well-heeled at Babington's, set up by a pair of English spinsters in 1896. Prices are sky-high, but the tea is the best in Rome.

➕ G3 ✉ Piazza di Spagna 23 ☎ 06 678 6027 🕐 Daily 9am–8.15pm 🚇 Spagna 🚌 119 to Piazza di Spagna

√EST! EST! EST! (€)

Among Rome's oldest and best pizzerias.

➕ J5 ✉ Via Genova 32 ☎ 06 488 1107 🕐 Tue–Sun 6.30–11.30pm; closed Aug 🚇 Repubblica 🚌 H, 40, 60, 64, 70, 117, 170 to Via Nazionale

RESTAURANT ETIQUETTE

Italians have a strong sense of how to behave, which applies in restaurants as much as anywhere It is considered bad form to order only one course in more sophisticated restaurants–if that is what you want, go to a pizzeria or *trattoria*.

LEONCINO (€)

Little has changed at this wonderful old-fashioned pizzeria for over 30 years.

➕ G4 ✉ Via del Leoncino 28, Piazza San Lorenzo in Lucina ☎ 06 687 6306 🕐 Mon–Tue, Thu–Fri 1–2.30pm, 7pm– midnight, Sat 7pm–midnight 🚇 Spagna 🚌 81, 119 to Via del Corso-Via Tomacelli

PIZZA CIRO (€)

The pizzas and pasta here are far better than the lurid wall murals.

➕ G4 ✉ Via della Mercede 43 ☎ 06 678 6015 🕐 Daily noon–1/2am 🚇 Spagna 🚌 All services to Via del Corso and Via del Tridente

Vatican City is a separate sovereign state within Rome, and home to the great basilica of St. Peter's and a series of museums with some of the world's richest and most varied collections of art and objects.

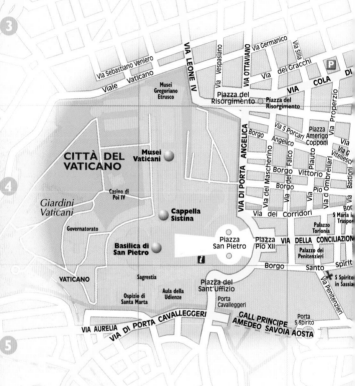

CITTÀ DEL
VATICANO

Giardini
Vaticani

Musei
Vaticani

Cappella
Sistina

Basilica di
San Pietro

Casino di
Poi IV

Governatorato

VATICANO

Sagrestia

Ospizio di
Santa Marta

Aula della
Udienze

Piazza
San Pietro

Piazza del
Sant'Uffizio

Porta
Cavalleggeri

Musei
Gregoriano
Etrusco

Viale   Vaticano

Via Sebastiano Veniero

VIA LEONE IV

Via Vespasiano

VIA OTTAVIANO

Via Germanico

Via Sila

Via del Gracchi

COLA   DI

Piazza del
Risorgimento

Piazza del
Risorgimento

VIA

Via Properzio

P

VIA DI PORTA ANGELICA

Borgo

Via S Porcari

Angelico

Borgo

Via del Mascherino

Falco

del

Via

Plauto

Pio

Vittorio

Via d'Ombrellari

Piazza
Amerigo
Capponi

Via G
Vitelleschi

Via

Bastioni

S Maria i
Traspor

Bor

Via dei Corridori

Palazzo
Torlonia

Piazza
Pio XII

VIA   DELLA   CONCILIAZION

Palazzo dei
Penitenzieri

Borgo   Santo   Spirit

S Spirito
in Sassi

Via Penitenzieri

Porta
S Spirito

VIA AURELIA

VIA DI PORTA CAVALLEGGERI

GALL PRINCIPE
AMEDEO SAVOIA AOSTA

0   250 m

0   250 yds

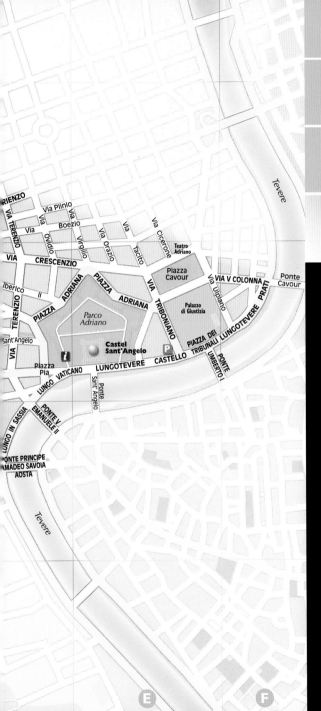

RIENZO
VIA TERENZIO
Via Plinio
Via
Boezio
Via Ovidio
Via Virgilio
Via
Via Orazio
VIA
CRESCENZIO
Via Cicerone
Via Tacito
Teatro
Adriano
Piazza
Cavour
VIA V COLONNA
Via Ulpiano
Iberico II
PIAZZA ADRIANA
PIAZZA ADRIANA
VIA TRIBONIANO
Ponte
Cavour
PIAZZA
TERENZIO
Parco
Adriano
Palazzo
di Giustizia
PIAZZA DEI TRIBUNALI
LUNGOTEVERE PRATI
VIA
Sant'Angelo
Castel
Sant'Angelo
P
LUNGOTEVERE CASTELLO
PONTE UMBERTO I
Piazza
Pia
LUNGO VATICANO
Ponte
Sant'Angelo
Tevere
LUNGO IN SASSIA
PONTE V
EMANUELE II
PONTE PRINCIPE
AMADEO SAVOIA
AOSTA
Tevere

E

F

Basilica di San Pietro

The famous dome of St. Peter's viewed from the inside (right) and out (left)

THE BASICS

🔹 B–C4

✉ Piazza San Pietro, Città del Vaticano

☎ 06 6988 1662/3462

🕐 Mid-Mar–end Sep daily 7–7 (Oct–end Feb until 6). Dome Apr–end Sep 8am–5.45; Oct–end Mar 8am–4.45. Grottos Apr–end Sep daily 7–6 (Oct–end Mar until 5). Treasury Apr–end Sep daily 9–6 (Oct–end Mar until 5)

🍴 Shop

Ⓜ Ottaviano

🚌 64 to Porta Cavalleggeri or 23, 32, 49, 492, 990 to Piazza del Risorgimento

♿ Wheelchair access

💶 Basilica free. Dome and Treasury moderate. Grottos expensive

HIGHLIGHTS

● Façade
● Dome
● *Pietà*, Michelangelo
● *Baldacchino*, Bernini
● *St. Peter*, Arnolfo di Cambio
● Tomb of Paul III, Guglielmo della Porta
● Tomb of Urban VIII, Bernini
● Monument to Alexander VII, Bernini

Although some of the works of art in St. Peter's can be rather disappointing, the interior impresses as the spiritual capital of Roman Catholicism with an overwhelming sense of scale and decorative splendour.

The creators The first St. Peter's was built by Constantine around AD326, reputedly on the site where St. Peter was buried following his crucifixion in AD64. Between 1506 and 1626, it was virtually rebuilt to plans by Bramante, and then again to designs by Antonio da Sangallo, Giacomo della Porta, Michelangelo and Carlo Maderno. Michelangelo was also responsible for much of the dome, and Bernini finished the façade and the interior.

What to see Michelangelo's unforgettable *Pietà* (1499)— which is behind glass following an attack in 1972—is in the first chapel of the right nave. At the end of the same nave stands a statue of St. Peter: His right foot has been caressed by millions since 1857 when Pius IX granted a 50-day indulgence to anyone kissing it following confession. Bernini's high altar canopy, or *baldacchino* (1624–33), was built during the papacy of Urban VIII, a scion of the Barberini family; it is decorated with bees, the Barberini's dynastic symbol. To its rear are Guglielmo della Porta's Tomb of Paul III (left) and Bernini's influential Tomb of Urban VIII (right). Rome seen from the dome (entrance at the end of the right nave) is *the* highlight of a visit.

Castel Sant'Angelo

The route to the fortified castle, Ponte Sant'Angelo, watched over by Bernini's angels

Castel Sant'Angelo, rising above the river, has served as an army barracks, papal citadel, imperial tomb and medieval prison. Today the 58-room museum traces the castle's near 2,000-year history, providing a contrast to the Vatican Museums.

Many incarnations The Castel Sant'Angelo was built by Emperor Hadrian in AD130 as a mausoleum for himself, his family and his dynastic successors. It was crowned by a gilded chariot driven by a statue of Hadrian disguised as the sun god Apollo. Emperors were buried in its vaults until about AD271, when under threat of invasion from Germanic raiders it became a citadel and was incorporated into the city's walls. Its present name arose in AD590, after a vision by Gregory the Great, who while leading a procession through Rome to pray for the end of plague saw an angel sheathing a sword on this spot, an act thought to symbolize the end of the pestilence.

Castle and museum In AD847 Leo IV converted the building into a papal fortress, and in 1277 Nicholas III linked it to the Vatican by a passageway, the *passetto*. A prison in the Renaissance, and then an army barracks after 1870, the castle became a museum in 1933. Exhibits, spread over four floors, are scattered around a confusing but fascinating array of rooms and corridors. Best of these is the beautiful Sala Paolina, done with stucco, fresco and *trompe-l'oeil*. The most memorable sight is the 360-degree view from the castle's terrace, the setting for the last act of Puccini's Tosca.

THE BASICS

✚ E4

✉ Lungotevere Castello 50

☎ 06 681 9111

🕐 Tue–Sun 9–7.30

🍴 Café

Ⓜ Lepanto

🚌 30, 49, 70, 87, 130, 186, 224, 492, 926, 990 to Piazza Cavour or the Lungotevere

♿ Poor

💶 Expensive

HIGHLIGHTS

● Spiral funerary ramp
● Staircase of Alexander VI
● Armoury
● Hall of Justice
● Chapel of Leo X: façade by Michelangelo
● Sale di Clemente VII with wall paintings
● Cortile del Pozzo: wellhead
● Prisons (Prigione Storiche)
● Sala Paolina
● View from Loggia of Paul III

Musei Vaticani & Cappella Sistina

The largest, richest and most impressive museum complex in the world incorporating one of Michelangelo's most supreme masterpieces in the Sistine Chapel.

Treasures of 12 museums At least two days (and 7km/4 miles of walking) are needed to do justice to the Vatican Museums. Egyptian and Assyrian art; Etruscan artefacts; the more esoteric anthropological collections; or modern religious art—whatever your priorities, several sights should not be missed. Most obvious are the four rooms of the Stanze di Raffaello, each of which is decorated with frescos by Raphael. Further fresco cycles by Pinturicchio and Fra Angelico adorn the Borgia Apartment and Chapel of Nicholas V, and are complemented by an almost unmatched collection of paintings in the Vatican Art Gallery. The

Galleria della Carte Geografiche decorated with 16th-century map frescos (far left and bottom left). Michelangelo's masterpiece, the ceiling of the Sistine Chapel (left, right and bottom right). An exhibit at the Vatican Museum (bottom middle)

THE BASICS

www.vatican.va

✚ C3

✉ Viale Vaticano, Città del Vaticano

☎ 06 6988 3322

🕐 Mar–end Oct Mon–Fri 8.45–4.45, Sat and last Sun of month 8.45–1.45; Nov–end Feb Mon–Sat and last Sun of month 8.45–1.45. Closed holidays

🍴 Café, restaurant and shop

Ⓜ Cipro–Musei Vaticani

🚌 23, 32, 49, 81, 492, 990 to Piazza del Risorgimento, 40 to Piazza Pia or 64 to Porta Cavalleggeri

♿ Wheelchair access

💶 Very expensive (includes entry to all Vatican museums); free last Sun of month

best of the Greek and Roman sculpture is the breathtaking Laocoön group in the Cortile Ottagono of the Museo Pio-Clementino. The list of artists whose work is shown in the Collezione di Arte Religiosa Moderna is a roll call of the most famous in the last 100 years, from Pablo Picasso to Salvador Dalí and Henry Moore.

Sistine Chapel Built by Pope Sixtus IV between 1475 and 1483, Pope Julius II commissioned Michelangelo to paint the ceiling of the Sistine Chapel in 1508. The frescos, comprising over 300 individual figures, were completed in four years, during which Michelangelo worked in appalling conditions, lying on his back and in extremes of heat and cold. The extraordinary fresco behind the high altar, the *Last Judgment*, was begun for Pope Paul III in 1534 and completed in 1541.

Shopping

CASTRONI

Castroni boasts Rome's largest selection of imported delicacies, a mouthwatering array of Italian specialties and an amazing range of coffees.
➕ D3 ✉ Via Cola di Rienzo 196, corner of Via Terenzio ☎ 06 687 4383
🕒 Mon–Sat 8–8

MERCATO ANDREA DORIA

A large, local market that serves the area northwest of the Vatican. Stands mostly sell meat, fish, fruit and vegetables, but there are a few with shoes and quality clothes.
➕ B3 ✉ Via Andrea Doria-Via Tunisi 🕒 Mon–Sat 7am–1pm

PIETRO FRANCHI

A rival to nearby Castroni as Rome's best delicatessen. Offers a selection of regional food and wines, and dishes to take out—anything from cold antipasti to succulent roast meats.
➕ D3 ✉ Via Cola di Rienzo 204 ☎ 06 686 4576
🕒 Mon–Sat 8am–9pm

RELIGIOUS ARTEFACTS

For religious art and souvenirs, both serious and light-hearted, you should head to the streets around St. Peter's, notably Borgo Pio, Via del Mascherano and Via Porta di Porta Angelica.

Restaurants

PRICES

Prices are approximate, based on a 3-course meal for one person.
€€€ over €50
€€ €30–€50
€ under €30

BORGO NUOVO (€€)

This place is ideal after a visit to the Basilica or the Vatican museums for a quiet sit down and some tasty, freshly prepared Italian food.
➕ D4 ✉ Borgo Pio 104 ☎ 06 689 2852
🕒 Wed–Mon 12–10
🚇 Ottaviano 🚌 81 to Piazza del Risorgimento

DAL TOSCANO (€)

This large trattoria in Vatican City serves Tuscan food, and is particularly known for its meats and its wood-fired grill.
➕ C3 ✉ Via Germanico 58 ☎ 06 3972 5717
🕒 Tue–Sun 12.30–2.30, 7.30–11 🚇 Ottaviano
🚌 23, 49, 81 to Piazza del Risorgimento

COFFEE

Breakfast in Rome is washed down with a cappuccino or the longer and milkier caffè latte. At other times espresso, a short kick-start of caffeine, is the coffee of choice or caffé macchiato, with a drop of milk—Italians never drink cappuccino after lunch or dinner. Decaffeinated coffee is caffè Hag and iced coffee caffè freddo.

TAVERNA ANGELICA (€€)

Popular restaurant, the best mid-priced option in the area. Minimalist interior and delicate and innovative cooking.
➕ D4 ✉ Piazza Amerigo Capponi 6 ☎ 06 687 4514
🕒 Mon–Sat 7–midnight, Sun 12.30–2.30, 7.30–midnight; closed 2 weeks Aug
🚇 Ottaviano 🚌 23 to Via San Porcari or to Piazza del Risorgimento

ZEN SUSHI (€€€)

Minimalist Japanese restaurant. Select tempting dishes from the constantly replenished conveyor belt.
➕ D3 ✉ Via degli Scipioni 243 ☎ 06 321 3420
🕒 Tue–Fri 1–3, 6.30–11, Sat 7.30–11 🚇 Lepanto 🚌 30

If you're short of time, you can join an organized tour to enjoy some of the popular day trips from Rome. However, places such as the ancient ruins at Ostia Antica, can easily be made using public transport.

Ostia Antica

HIGHLIGHTS

- Decumanus Maximus
- Piazzale delle Corporazioni
- The Insule and Forum
- The Borgo

TIPS

- Allow a whole day for the site, perhaps bring a picnic.
- In summer, take water with you and rest in the shade during the early afternoon.
- Buy a plan of the site and spend time when you arrive planning your visit.

Ancient Rome's port is one of the top three best-preserved Roman towns in Italy, and is a haven of romantic ruins and soothing greenery.

Living in the past Untrumpeted Ostia Antica, 25km (15 miles) southwest of Rome, is Italy's best-preserved Roman town after Pompeii and Herculaneum, and its extensive ruins and lovely rural site are as appealing as any in Rome itself. Built at the mouth (*ostium*) of the Tiber as ancient Rome's seaport, it became a vast and bustling colony before silt and the Empire's decline together hastened its demise. By the 17th century Ostia Antica was all but forgotten. Roman legend puts Ostia's founding in the seventh century BC; factual dating of the ruins points to the fourth century BC.

The well-preserved amphitheatre, a major part of this archaeological site (left and bottom right). An intact fragment of wall decoration (bottom far left). Excavations, some more intact than others (bottom left and middle). A surviving mosaic (right)

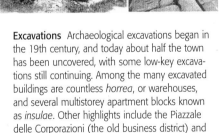

Excavations Archaeological excavations began in the 19th century, and today about half the town has been uncovered, with some low-key excavations still continuing. Among the many excavated buildings are countless *horrea*, or warehouses, and several multistorey apartment blocks known as *insulae*. Other highlights include the Piazzale delle Corporazioni (the old business district) and the 4,000-seat amphitheatre.

Lovely picture Ostia is a quintessentially romantic classical ruin, complete with umbrella pines, grassy slopes and spreads of wildflowers. These certainly contribute to its evocative allure, but they make its preservation a nightmare, damaging walls and foundations. The size and scale of Ostia are more impressive by far than the capital's Forum, and it gives far better idea of ancient Roman life.

THE BASICS

www.itnw.roma/ostia

➕ Off map

✉ Viale di Romagnoli 717

☎ 06 5635 8099

🕐 Apr–end Sep, Tue–Sun 9–6; Oct–end Mar, Tue–Sun 8.30–4 (last admission 60–90 min before closing). Closed holidays

🍴 Restaurant

🚇 Metro line B to Piramide, then trains from adjoining Roma–Lido train station every 10–30 minutes (covered by BIG ticket ▷ 119)

👐 Moderate

More to See

CATACOMBE DI SAN CALLISTO
www.catacombe.roma.it
These catacombs are the largest and most impressive in Rome—and thus the most popular. They extend over 20km (12 miles) on five levels, with over 170,000 burial places. You can explore claustrophobic tunnels and numerous *loculi*, or burial niches, carved from the soft tufa stone.
⊞ Off map at J9 ⊠ Via Appia Antica 110 ☎ 06 5130 1580 ⏰ Thu–Tue 8.30–12, 2.30–5.30 (5 in winter). Closed Feb 🚌 118, 628 to Via delle Terme di Caracalla ⏳ Moderate

CATACOMBE DI SAN SEBASTIANO
The accessibility of the catacombs of San Sebastiano, once a 1st-century BC pagan cemetery, has made them vulnerable to pillage over the years. They were some of the most important burial places in early Christian Rome, and may even have housed the bodies of saints Peter and Paul.
⊞ Off map at K9 ⊠ Via Appia Antica 136 ☎ 06 785 0350 ⏰ Mon–Sat 8.30–12, 2.30–5.30 (5 in winter). Closed part of Nov and Dec 🚌 118, 628 to Via delle Terme di Caracalla ⏳ Moderate

TERME DI CARACALLA
Rome's most luxurious baths that could hold as many as 1,600 bathers. Started by Septimius Severus in AD206, and completed 11 years later by his son, Caracalla, they were designed as much as a gathering place as for hygiene. The site is now best known as a stage for outdoor opera.
⊞ J9 ⊠ Via delle Terme di Caracalla 52 ☎ 06 3996 7700 ⏰ Tue–Sun 9–1 hour before sunset, Mon 9–2; closed holidays 🚇 Circo Massimo 🚌 60, 75, 81, 175, 673 to Via di San Gregorio-Via delle Terme di Caracalla ⏳ Moderate (combined Appia Antica card gives admission to tombs on Via Appia Antica)

VILLA DORIA PAMPHILJ
If you have time to spare, and fancy a good long walk away from the crowds, there is nowhere better than this huge area of parkland.
⊞ B8 ⊠ Via di San Pancrazio ⏰ Dawn–dusk 🚌 44, 75, 870 to the Gianicolo or 115, 125 to Via Garibaldi

The finest baths ever built in Rome, Terme di Caracalla

Laid out in 1650, the gardens of Villa Doria Pamphilj

Excursions

FRASCATI

Frascati is the loveliest of the Castelli Romani towns of the Colli Albani hills, famous for its wine and dominated by a majestic villa and its gardens.

The grandest of Frascati's villas is the Villa Aldobrandini, designed in 1598 by Giacomo della Porta. The vast palace, all faded majesty, is surrounded by a superb example of an early baroque garden, from where there are fabulous views. The town is scattered with other palaces and the baroque cathedral is notable, but leave time to sample the local wine. Made here since the 3rd century BC, Frascati is a worldwide seller; it's a revelation to drink it in its birthplace.

THE BASICS

Distance 20km (12 miles)
Journey time 40 min
🚆 Train from Termini
🚌 COTRAL bus from Anagnina metro station Villa Aldobrandini
✉ Via Cardinale Massaia
🕐 Garden only Apr–end Nov, Mon–Fri 9–1, 3–6; Dec–end Mar, Mon–Fri 9–1, 3–4

TIVOLI

Tivoli is the most popular excursion from Rome, thanks to the town's lovely wooded position, the superlative gardens of the Villa d'Este and the ruins and grounds of Hadrian's Roman villa.

The Este gardens were laid out in 1550 as part of a country retreat for Cardinal Ippolito d'Este, son of Lucrezia Borgia and the Duke of Ferrara. The highlights among the beautifully integrated terraces and many fountains are Gian Lorenzo Bernini's elegant Fontana di Bicchierone and the vast Viale delle Cento Fontane ('Avenue of the Hundred Fountains'). Hadrian's Villa (Villa Adriana) is an exceptional complex of Classical buildings, the largest ever conceived in the Roman world. It was built between AD118 and AD135 by Emperor Hadrian as an imperial palace away from the city and covered an area as great as the middle of imperial Rome.

THE BASICS

Distance 31km (19 miles)
Journey time 40 min
🚆 Train from Termini
🚌 COTRAL bus from Via Gaeta or metro line B to Ponte Mammolo and then COTRAL bus to Tivoli
Villa d'Este
✉ Piazza Trento
☎ 0424 600 460
🕐 Tue–Sun 8.30–4/7.30
💶 Expensive
Villa Adriana
✉ Via di Villa Adriana–Via Tiburtina
☎ 0774 530 203
🕐 Apr–end Jan 9–5
🚌 Local bus 4 or 4x from Tivoli 💶 Moderate

Entertainment and Nightlife

ALEXANDERPLATZ
www.alexanderplatz.it
A restaurant and cocktail bar north of St. Peter's with live jazz.
🚇 Off map ✉ Via Ostia 9
☎ 06 3974 2171
🕐 Sep–Jun, Mon–Sat 9–2
🚇 Ottaviano 🚌 29N, 30N, 99N and 23, 70, 490, 913, 991, 994, 999 to Largo Trionfale-Viale delle Milizie
💵 4-month membership (expensive); usually free to tourists (passport required)

PIPER
Open since the 1960s, Piper is consistently popular, thanks partly to its schedule of constant updating.
🚇 L1 ✉ Via Tagliamento 9
☎ 06 855 5398 or 06 841 4459 🕐 Hours erratic. Sat and Sun only in winter
🚌 63, 86, 92, N29, N30 to Via Tagliamento 💵 Very expensive

STADIO OLIMPICO
Home to Rome's two big football (soccer) teams, AS Roma and Lazio. Games are played here on alternate Sundays.
🚇 Off map ✉ Viale dei Gladiatori ☎ 06 323 7333

(box office) or 06 36851
🚌 32, 48, 69, 220, 225, 271, 280, 911 to Lungotevere Maresciallo Cadorna
AS Roma information:
Tickets available at many outlets around Rome. A full list is available on the official AS Roma website at www.asromacalcio.it. Also from Lottomatica stores and the AS Roma shop (✉ Via Colonna 360 ☎ 06 678 6514)
Lazio information:
Tickets can be bought online at www.sslazio.it. Also at Lottomatica stores or Lazio point at ✉ Via Farini ☎ 34 06 482 6768

Restaurants

PRICES

Prices are approximate, based on a 3-course meal for one person.
€€€   over €50
€€   €30–€50
€   under €30

ADRIANO (€€)
www.hoteladriano.it
Large restaurant and hotel in a 19th-century *palazzo*, with the same family since 1930. Classic and innovative Roman cooking, and alfresco dining during good weather.
🚇 Off map ✉ Via Villa Adriano 194, Tivoli ☎ 0774 382 235 🕐 Daily 12.30–2.30,

7–10.30 (closed Sun 7–10.30 winter)

CACCIANI (€€)
www.cacciani.it
In business for over half a century, serving Roman and classic Italian dishes. Lovely terrace with views as far as Rome. Try the house specialty, *pollo all Romana* (chicken in the Roman manner).
🚇 Off map ✉ Via A. Diaz 13, Frascati ☎ 06 942 0378 🕐 Tue–Sun 12.30–2.30, 7–10.30; closed Sun evening Oct–end May

IL GROTTINO DELLA SIBILLA DAL 1826 (€)
Well-priced, simple and

tasty regional food presented in two intimate dining rooms (with a terrace for summer dining). The wine and olive oil used is home-produced.
🚇 Off map ✉ Piazza Rivarola 21, Tivoli ☎ 06774 433 2606 🕐 Daily 12.30–2.30, 7–10

ZARAZZÀ (€)
Appealing terrace plus three attractive dining rooms. Traditional Roman cooking with a light touch.
🚇 Off map ✉ Via Regina Margherita 45, Frascati ☎ 06 6942 2053 0378 🕐 Tue–Sun 12.30–2.30, 7–10.30 (closed Sun 7–10.30 Oct–end May and part of Aug)

Rome has a vast range of hotels in every price category, including some of Italy's most prestigious establishments. Many hotels are over-priced and poorly located; if you are on a short visit it pays to choose a hotel in or close to the historic area.

Introduction

Following Rome's renaissance in the wake of the Jubilee Year in 2000, the number of luxury five-star hotels in the city is now almost double what it was. Previously crumbling *palazzi* and many of the longer-established hotels have been restored.

Location, Location

As in any city, Rome has a wide range of accommodation types, from small, low-budget places around the Termini to grand, five-star luxury establishments on the Via Veneto. What to expect in terms of price and quality depends largely on location. Staying in the *centro storico* means that you are close to all of Rome's sights, but also to its sounds. Narrow streets and tall buildings tend to amplify the noise. Quiet places can be found, on the edge of the popular areas or in hotels with double glazing. If you really value your sleep, book a room in the quieter Aventino, Celio or Prati districts. The disadvantage here is that you will have to travel, but public transport is inexpensive, and hotels are often cheaper than in the heart of the city.

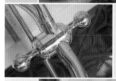

What you get for your Money

The familiar star system operates in Italy, with five stars denoting the highest standard of comfort, luxury and facilities. A one-star hotel has few facilities and frequently does not include a private bathroom. Normally both television and telephone will be in the lobby. These establishments tend not to accept credit cards and do not have a 24-hour desk service.

RESERVATIONS

As Rome is an eternally popular destination, it pays to reserve well in advance, especially if your stay is over the peak periods, which, nowadays, tend to be the greater part of the year. However, January to March and August are the least crowded months and you should be able to get some deals in this period. Consult hotel websites for details of special offers. If you arrive without a reservation, do ask to see the room first before you commit. Information agencies are always a useful resource.

After a hectic day sight-seeing, its nice to come back to a welcome smile and home comforts

Budget Hotels

ABRUZZI

www.hotelabruzzi.it
Twenty-five large rooms (and eight shared bath-rooms), some with a view of the Pantheon; rooms at the rear are quieter.

F5 ✉ Piazza della Rotonda 69 ☎ 06 679 2021; fax 06 6978 8076; 🚌 119 to Piazza della Rotonda or 46, 62, 63, 64, 70, 87, 186 to Largo di Torre Argentina

DELLA LUNETTA

www.albergodellalunetta.it
A plain 35-room hotel; it lacks panache but makes up for it with its position just off Campo de' Fiori.

F6 ✉ Piazza del Paradiso 68 ☎ 06 686 1080; fax 06 689 2028 🚌 40, 64 and other services to Corso Vittorio Emanuele II

HOTEL TRASTEVERE

www.hoteltrastevere.net
One of only a few hotels in the Trastevere quarter. Twenty bright rooms, all with private bathrooms, plus 4 apartments.

E7 ✉ Via Luciano Manara 24 ☎ 06 581 4713; fax 06 588 1016 🚌 H, 8, 780 to Piazza S. Sonnino or Viale Trastevere

KATTY

Less grim than most of the countless inexpensive hotels in the unsavoury area near Rome's train station. 28 rooms.

L4 ✉ Via Palestro 35 ☎ 06 444 1216; fax 06 444 1216 Ⓜ Termini 🚌 64, 65, 170 and all other services to Termini

NAVONA

www.hotelnavona.com
Twenty-six simple rooms, friendly owners and a superb central location. Reserve well in advance.

F5 ✉ Via dei Sediari 8 ☎ 06 686 4203; fax 06 6880 3802 🚌 30, 70, 87, 116, 186 to Corso del Rinascimento

PERUGIA

www.hperugia.it
Little-known, quiet and well placed between the Colosseum and Via Cavour; very convenient

for the sights of the Ancient City. All 11 doubles have private bathrooms.

J6 ✉ Via del Colosseo 7 ☎ 06 679 7200; fax 06 678 4635 🚌 75, 84, 117 to Via Cavour or 75, 85, 87, 117, 175 to the Colosseum

POMEZIA

www.hotelpomezia.it
Close to Campo de' Fiori with 25 small rooms (some have private bathrooms). Roof terrace and small bar. Specially adapted room for people with disabilities.

F6 ✉ Via dei Chiavari 12 ☎ 06 686 1371; fax 06 686 1371 🚌 46, 62, 64 to Corso Vittorio Emanuele II or 8, 46, 62, 63, 64, 70, 80 to Largo di Torre Argentina

SMERALDO

www.hotelsmeraldoroma.com
Thirty-five plain and clean rooms. In a back street close to Campo de' Fiori.

F6 ✉ Vicolo dei Chiodaroli 11 ☎ 06 687 5929; fax 06 6880 5495 🚌 46, 62, 64 to Corso Vittorio Emanuele II or 8, 46, 62, 63, 64, 70, 80 to Largo di Torre Argentina

SOLE

www.solealbiscione.it
A popular choice on the edge of Campo de' Fiori with 59 rooms and a small garden terrace.

F6 ✉ Via del Biscione 76 ☎ 06 6880 6873; fax 06 689 3787 🚌 46, 62, 64 to Corso Vittorio Emanuele II or 8, 46, 62, 63, 64, 70, 80 to Largo di Torre Argentina

WHERE TO STAY BUDGET HOTELS

Mid-Range Hotels

PRICES

Expect to pay between €100 and €250 per night for a double room in a mid-range hotel.

CAMPO DE' FIORI

www.hotelcampodefiori.com
Good value and position close to Campo de' Fiori. The 27 rooms are rather small and vary in decor, from exposed brick to funky blues. The roof garden is a pleasant bonus.
➕ F6 ✉ Via del Biscione 6 ☎ 06 6880 6865; fax 06 687 6003 🚌 46, 62, 64 to Corso Vittorio Emanuele II

CASA HOWARD

www.casahoward.com
The success of the first Casa Howard, a lovely residence close to Piazza di Spagna, spawned this second Casa Howard II, which opened in 2003. The five rooms all have private bathrooms. The location is excellent for shopping and the sights near the Spanish Steps and Fontana di Trevi.
➕ G4 ✉ Via Capo le Case 18 ☎ 06 6992 4555; fax 06 6794 6444 🚇 Spagna 🚌 116, 116T, 117, 119, 590 to Via dei Due Macelli or all services to Via del Tritone

CESARI

www.albergocesari.it
Friendly and straightforward three-star hotel with a loyal clientele and 47 elegant rooms that were renovated in 1999. Very

long-established—there has been a hotel here since 1787. Excellent position at the heart of the historic city.
➕ G5 ✉ Via di Pietra 89a ☎ 06 674 9701; fax 06 6749 7030 🚌 60, 62, 85, 117, 119, 160 to Via del Corso

COLUMBUS

www.hotelcolumbus.net
A converted monastery very close to St. Peter's—preferred by visiting cardinals. The 92 rooms are clean and functional, but the position is the hotel's real strength.
➕ D4 ✉ Via della Conciliazione 33 ☎ 06 686 5435; fax 06 686 4874 🚌 23, 34 to Via della Conciliazione or 64 to Piazza San Pietro

COMFORT INN BOLIVAR

www.bolivarhotel.com
This three-star hotel is perfectly positioned for sights of the Ancient City, in a quiet alley just off busy Via IV Novembre. 35 decent, modern rooms. Breakfast is taken

AGENCIES

Two good sources for all kinds of accommodation, from hotels to bed-and-breakfast in all price ranges, are the Hotel Reservation Agency (☎ 06 699 1000; www.hotelreservation.it) and Enjoy Rome (☎ 06 445 1843 or 06 445 0734; www.enjoyrome.com 🕐 Mon–Fri 8.30–7, Sat 8.30–2).

on the roof terrace.
➕ H6 ✉ Via della Cordonata 6, between Via IV Novembre and Via XXIV Maggio ☎ 06 679 1614; fax 06 679 1025 🚇 Cavour 🚌 H, 40, 60, 64, 70, 116T, 117, 170 to Via IV Novembre or Via Nazionale

DUE TORRI

www.hotelduetorriroma.com
A real find, in a perfect position hidden in a tiny alley between Piazza Navona and the Tiber. The 26 adequate rooms vary from stylish to plain. Some have small terraces with good views.
➕ F5 ✉ Vicolo del Leonetto 23–25 ☎ 06 687 6983; fax 06 686 5442 🚌 30, 70, 81, 87, 116, 186 to Lungotevere Marzio or Corso del Rinascimento

HOTEL PORTOGHESI

www.hotelportoghesiroma.com
A well-known hotel in a baroque *palazzo* with a roof terrace. Has been updated while retaining the 19th-century period feel of its 27 rooms. In a cobbled street north of Piazza Navona.
➕ F4 ✉ Via dei Portoghesi 1 ☎ 06 686 4231; fax 06 687 6976 🚌 30, 70, 87, 116 to Corso del Rinascimento

IL PICCOLO DI PIAZZA SPAGNA

www.piazzadispagna.com
A little-known three-star hotel in a small (*piccolo*) town house 300m southeast of Piazza di Spagna. It has 11 charming rooms, some with Jacuzzis, and a small

terrace where breakfast is served in fine weather.
⊞ H4 ✉ Via dei Due Macelli 47 ☎ 06 6929 0847; fax 06 6920 0560 🚇 Spagna 🚌 116, 116T, 117, 119, 590 to Via dei Due Macelli or all services to Via del Tritone

LOCARNO

www.hotellocarno.com
In a quietish side street close to Piazza del Popolo. Much genuine 1920s art nouveau decor, but with a feel of old-world elegance plus nice touches such as an open fire in winter and a garden and roof terrace. Ask for the better rooms in the eastern annexe, not the downbeat rooms in the main building.
⊞ F3 ✉ Via della Penna 22 ☎ 06 361 0841; fax 06 321 5249 🚇 Flaminio 🚌 926 to Via di Ripetta, or 81 to Lungotevere in Augusta

MANFREDI

www.hotelmanfredi.it
Quiet family-run hotel with charming service and 18 pretty rooms, in a cobbled street of galleries and antiques shops.
⊞ G3 ✉ Via Margutta 61 ☎ 06 320 7676; fax 06 320 7736 🚇 Spagna 🚌 119 to Piazza di Spagna

NERVA

www.hotelnerva.com
Unbeatable position for the sights of the Ancient City—this is one of only a few hotels within a stone's throw of the Roman Forum. Renovated rooms, some with original

features, amiable service and a warm welcome.
⊞ H6 ✉ Via Tor de'Conti 3 ☎ 06 678 1835; fax 06 6992 2204 🚇 Colosseo or Cavour 🚌 60, 84, 85, 87, 175 and all other services to Via dei Fori Imperiali, Piazza Venezia or Via IV Novembre-Via Nazionale

PONTE SISTO

www.hotelpontesisto.it
At the top end of the mid-range price, this four-star hotel is in a peaceful street just steps from the bridge to Trastevere. 106 simple rooms with fine marble bathrooms and a palm-lined courtyard.
⊞ F6 ✉ Via dei Pettinari 64 ☎ 06 686 310; fax 06 6830 1712 🚌 23, 271, 280 to

RESERVATIONS

Rome's peak season runs from Easter to October, but the city's hotels (in all categories) are almost invariably busy. Telephone, write or fax well in advance to reserve a room (most receptionists speak some English, French or German). Leave a credit card number or send an international money order for the first night's stay to be certain of the booking. Reconfirm a few days before your trip. If you arrive without a reservation then get to a hotel early in the morning; by afternoon most vacated rooms will have been snapped up. Don't accept rooms from touts at Stazione Termini.

Lungotevere dei Vallati or H, 8, 63, 271, 630 to Via Arenula

LA RESIDENZA

www.hotel-la-residenza.com
Good choice, close to Via Vittorio Veneto (but away from the hustle and bustle) and reasonably priced for this expensive area. 26 airy and stylish rooms. Combines the luxury of a five-star hotel with the intimacy and easy going charm of a private house. Terrace and roof garden.
⊞ H3 ✉ Via Emilia 22–24 ☎ 06 488 0789; fax 06 485721 🚇 Barberini 🚌 52, 53, 80, 95, 116, 119 to Via Vittorio Veneto

LA RESIDENZA FARNESE

www.residenzafarneseroma.it
A superb position in an ivy-hung alley and in the shadow of the great Palazzo Farnese. Part of a former convent, the rooms vary from modest former nuns' cells with small bathrooms to large, pastel-decorated salons.
⊞ E6 ✉ Via del Mascherone 59 ☎ 06 6821 0980; fax 06 8032 1049 🚌 116, 116T to Via Giulia and Via dei Farnesi

SISTINA

www.leonardihotels.com
Small, efficient and close to the Piazza di Spagna. Lovely terrace for drinks and breakfast. 23 rooms.
⊞ H4 ✉ Via Sistina 136 ☎ 06 474 4176; fax 06 481 8867 🚇 Spagna or Barberini 🚌 119 to Piazza di Spagna or 52, 53, 61, 62, 80, 95, 116, 119, 175 to Piazza Barberini

Luxury Hotels

PRICES

Expect to pay over €250 per night for a double room in a luxury hotel.

ALBERGO DEL SOLE AL PANTHEON

www.hotelsolealpantheon.com
Chic and old—open since 1467. Opposite the Pantheon; if you can stand the crowds, the location is one of the best. 25 rooms.

🚇 F5 ✉ Piazza della Rotonda 63 ☎ 06 678 0441; fax 06 6994 0689 🚌 119 to Piazza della Rotonda or 70, 87 to Corso del Rinascimento

AMBASCIATORI PALACE

www.ambasciatoripalace.com
One of the more venerable and stately of Via V. Veneto's large luxury hotels, with a traditional feel and opulent appearance. 110 rooms.

🚇 H–J3 ✉ Via Vittorio Veneto 62 ☎ 06 47493; fax 06 474 3601 🚇 Barberini 🚌 52, 53, 95, 116, 119 to Via Vittorio Veneto

ATLANTE STAR

www.atlantehotels.com
Luxury hotel between Vatican City and the Castel Sant'Angelo exuding class and elegance.

🚇 D4 ✉ Via G. Vitelleschi 34 ☎ 06 687 3233 🚇 Ottaviano 🚌 32, 81, 492

DE RUSSIE

www.roccofortehotels.com
A glorious hotel just off Piazza del Popolo that is distinguished by its modern and stylish design. The 123 rooms are calm and bright, and most have views of the delightful gardens, a lovely spot to dine alfresco.

🚇 F3 ✉ Via del Babuino 9 ☎ 06 328 881; fax 3288 8888 🚇 Flaminio 🚌 117, 119 to Piazza del Popolo

HASSLER-VILLA MEDICI

www.hotelhasslerroma.com
Well-located longtime jet-set and VIP haunt, just above the Spanish Steps. 86 rooms and 13 suites.

🚇 H4 ✉ Piazza Trinità dei Monti 6 ☎ 06 699 340; fax 06 678 9991 🚇 Spagna 🚌 119 to Piazza di Spagna

WHAT TO PAY

Hotels are classified by the Italian state into five categories from one star (basic) to five stars (luxury). The prices each can charge are set by law and must be displayed in the room (you will usually find them on the door). However, prices within a hotel can vary from room to room (and some hotels have off- and peak-season rates). If a room is too expensive, do not be afraid to ask for a less expensive one. Watch for extras like air-conditioning and obligatory breakfasts. Single rooms cost about two-thirds the price of doubles, and to have an extra bed in a room adds 35 per cent to the bill.

LORD BYRON

www.lordbyronhotel.com
Small, refined and very chic in leafy Parioli. Noted for its excellent restaurant Relais Le Jardin. 32 rooms, plus 3 suites.

🚇 G1 ✉ Via Giuseppe de Notaris 5 ☎ 06 322 4541; fax 06 322 0405 🚇 Flaminio 🚌 52 to Via Bruno Buozzi

RAPHAEL

www.raphaelhotel.com
Intimate, charming and ivy covered—hidden away yet near Piazza Navona. The 73 rooms are a little small but immaculate. Reserve ahead.

🚇 F5 ✉ Largo Febo 2 ☎ 06 682 831; fax 06 687 8993 🚌 70, 81, 87 to Corso del Rinascimento

ST. REGIS GRAND

www.stregis.com
Not in the most salubrious or convenient spot, but immensely lavish and luxurious. 138 rooms, plus 35 suites.

🚇 K4 ✉ Via Vittorio Emanuele Orlando 3 ☎ 06 47091/474 709; fax 06 474 7307 🚇 Repubblica 🚌 H, 40, 170, 492, 910 to Piazza della Repubblica

WESTIN EXCELSIOR

www.westin.com
Large and grand: Everything is on an enormous scale, from the vast silk rugs to the 284 palatial bedrooms (32 suites).

🚇 H–J3 ✉ Via Vittorio Veneto 125 ☎ 06 47081; fax 06 482 6205 🚇 Barberini 🚌 52, 53, 95, 116, 119 to Via Vittorio Veneto

Rome can be a busy and intimidating place, but behind the bustle it is easy to access the city from its two airports, while public transport, on the few occasions you will need it, is reliable and straightforward.

Planning Ahead

When to Go

The best time to visit Rome is April to early June or mid-September to October, when the weather is not uncomfortably hot. Easter weekend is very busy. Many restaurants and businesses close for the entire month of August. January and February are the quietest months.

TIME

Italy is one hour ahead of GMT in winter, six hours ahead of New York and nine hours ahead of Los Angeles.

AVERAGE DAILY MAXIMUM TEMPERATURES

JAN	FEB	MAR	APR	MAY	JUN	JUL	AUG	SEP	OCT	NOV	DEC
44°F	46°F	52°F	58F	64°F	74°F	79°F	77°F	72°F	64°F	55°F	48°F
7°C	8°C	11°C	14°C	18°C	23°C	26°C	25°C	22°C	18°C	13°C	9°C

Spring (March to April) can be muggy and rainy in April and May.
Summer (June to August) is hot and dry, with sudden thunderstorms. July and August are uncomfortably hot.
Autumn (September to November) is mixed but can produce crisp days with clear skies.
Winter (December to February) is short and cold.

WHAT'S ON

January *La Befana* (6 Jan): Epiphany celebrations; fair and market in Piazza Navona.
February *Carnevale* (week before Lent): Costume festivities; parties on Shrove Tuesday.
March *Festa di San Giuseppe* (19 Mar): Street stalls in the Trionfale area north of the Vatican.
April *Good Friday* (Mar/Apr): Procession of the Cross at 9pm to the Colosseum, led by the Pope.
Easter Sunday: The Pope addresses the crowds at noon in Piazza di San Pietro.

May *International Horse Show* (early May): Concorso Ippico in Villa Borghese.
June *Festa della Repubblica* (2 Jun): Military parade along Via de' Fiori Imperiali.
July *Tevere Expo* (last week Jun/Jul): Food and handicrafts fair on the banks of the Tiber.
August *Ferragosto* (15 Aug): Feast of the Assumption; everything closes.
September *Art Fair*: Via Margutta.
Sagra dell'Uva (early Sep): Wine and harvest festival in the Basilica di Massenzio.

October *Antiques Fair* (mid-Oct): Via dei Coronari.
November *Ognissanti* (1–2 Nov): All Saints' Day.
Festa di Santa Cecilia (22 Nov): In the catacombs and church of Santa Cecilia in Trastavere.
December *Festa della Madonna Immacolata* (8 Dec): Pope and other dignitaries leave flowers at the statue of the Madonna in Piazza di Spagna.
Christmas Eve Midnight Mass: Most striking are at Santa Maria Maggiore and Santa Maria in Aracoeli.

Useful Websites

www.romaturismo.it
Rome's official website for tourist information, has mostly generalized information on the city.

www.adr.it
The official site of Rome's main airports, Fiumincino and Ciampino, with useful contacts and details of transport links to the city.

www.vatican.va
Vatican City's polished official website offers multilingual information on the Musei Vaticani, a calendar of religious events, an online version of its official newspaper and other general information on the Vatican.

www.comune.roma.it
Aimed primarily at tourists, the official website of Rome's city council contains transport and other useful general information.

www.romaclick.com
A general site useful for checking up-to-the-minute information on events and exhibitions. It offers a user-friendly accommodation reservation service with last-minute reductions.

www.romeguide.it
An Italian-based site with a wealth of daily updated information; use it for reserving museum passes and to find out what's on.

www.enjoyrome.com
This friendly English-language site is run from Rome and has a quirkier approach than most; use it for general information, as well as tips on discovering Rome on foot and by public transport. Excellent links and daily updates.

www.museionline.it
Informative and easy-to-navigate site that will fill you in on what the city's museums have to offer. Lots of practical information as well. Opening times and prices are not always current.

PRIME TRAVEL SITES

www.atac.roma.it
Rome's bus company website gives every scrap of information about public transport, including maps and how to buy the best ticket for your needs—Italian and English.

www.capitolium.org
Devoted to the Roman Forum and the Imperial Fora, this site includes a wide range of historical material, including reconstructions of how the Fora might have looked in its original state.

www.catacombe.roma.it
The official site of Rome's catacombs.

www.fodors.com
A travel-planning site where you can research prices and weather, book tickets, cars and rooms, and ask questions; links to other sites.

CYBERCAFÉS

easyInternetcafe
www.easyinternetcafe.com
✉ H4 ✉ Via Barberini 2
🕐 Daily 7am–1am

Globalservice
✉ F7 ✉ Piazza S. Sonnino 27 ☎ 06 5833 3316
🕐 Daily 8am–midnight

Getting There

VISAS AND INSURANCE

Check visa and passport requirements before travelling, see www.britishembassy. gov.uk or www.american embassy.com. EU citizens are covered for medical expenses with an EHIC card; insurance to cover illness and theft is still strongly advised. Visitors from outside the EU should check their insurance coverage and, if necessary, buy a supplementary policy.

TIPS

● Avoid taxi and hotel touts who will approach you at the airport. Use only licensed (yellow or white) taxis.

● Buy your return (round-trip) train ticket when you arrive at Fiumicino. The queues are much longer at Termini, and the ticket will not become valid until you stamp it on your return journey.

● You will find suitcases with wheels a godsend at Fiumicino. It is quite some distance between baggage reclaim and the exit, and for some stretches you cannot use a baggage trolley, particularly on the home-ward journey.

AIRPORTS

There are direct flights into Rome from Europe and North America to Leonardo da Vinci and Ciampino airports. Visitors from Europe can also arrive by rail to Stazione Termini, or by bus.

60KM (37 miles)

⊠ **Leonardo da Vinci Airport**
36km (22 miles) to city centre
Train 45 min, €9.50

⊠ **Ciampino Airport**
15km (9 miles) to city centre
Bus/Metro 35 min

FROM LEONARDO DA VINCI

Scheduled flights arrive at this airport 36km (22 miles) southwest of the city, better known as Fiumicino (☎ switchboard 06 65951, 24hr recorded 06 6593 3640, flight information 06 6563 4956 (international), 06 65643 (domestic). The website for both main Rome airports is www.adr.it. The most economical way to reach the heart of Rome from the airport is by rail into Stazione Termini. Trains leave every 30 or 60 minutes (6.37am–11.37pm) at 7 and 37 minutes past the hour and take about 35 minutes. Buses depart outside train hours and take up to 50 minutes to Rome's Termini and Tiburtina train stations. Taxis take from 30 minutes to two hours depending on traffic, and are expensive (€40–€55). Take only licensed cabs (white or yellow) or a prepaid car with driver available from the SOCAT desk in the International Arrivals hall.

FROM CIAMPINO

This smaller airport, which handles mostly low-cost and charter flights, is 15km (9 miles) southeast of the city. There are good facilities but the airport doesn't have a direct rail link to

the heart of Rome. To get there take a 15-minute bus journey by COTRAL bus to the Metro (underground) station at Anagnina, then the 20-minute journey to Termini on Metro line A. Taxis take between 30 and 40 minutes and cost around €40. Bus shuttles (☎ 06 7949 4572; www.terravision.it) serve various no-frills and other airlines' flights and run to Termini (€8 one-way, €14 round-trip). Terravision also operates from Fiumicino airport to Termini (€7 one-way, €12 round-trip).

ARRIVING BY BUS

Most long-distance buses terminate at Tiburtina, to the northeast of the city. Although the station is somewhat way out of the city, it is well served by the Metro (line B) and by numerous bus services (for example. No. 492). Eurolines run buses from more than 100 European cities. For details of routes and tickets, see their website (www.eurolines.com).

ARRIVING BY CAR

In the days of the empire, all roads led to Rome, but in these modern times, all roads lead to the Gran Raccordo Anulare, known as the GRA. This 70km (43-mile) road encircles the city, and is always busy. From Fiumicino airport, take the Autostrada Roma Fiumicino, which leads to the GRA. If you are coming from Ciampino you will need to follow the Via Appia Nuova. From Florence or Pisa, take the A1, also known as the Autostrada del Sole. Visitors arriving from Naples should also use the A1, while those coming from Abruzzo or the Adriatic coast should follow the A24. Wherever you join the GRA, make sure you know which exit you need; your hotel can tell you which one is best.

ARRIVING BY RAIL

Most trains arrive and depart from Stazione Termini, which is convenient for most of central Rome. Taxis and buses leave from the station forecourt, Piazza dei Cinquecento. Train information ☎ 8488 88088; www.trenitalia.com.

DRIVING PERMIT

If you are arriving by car and staying in central Rome, you will need a permit to drive in the city. If you are staying in a hotel, the staff can arrange this.

LONG-TERM PARKING

If you are arriving by car, but don't want to use your car in Rome, you can leave it in the long-term parking area (*lungo sosta parcheggio*) at Fiumicino airport and take the train into the city. Parking costs €18 for 24 hours or €69 for seven days. Short-stay costs €28 daily (☎ 06 6595 5175).

CAR RENTAL

All major rental firms, and some local ones, have desks at both airports and also in town. Car rental is expensive in Italy and you can often get a better deal if you arrange it before you leave home. The minimum age for renting a car is between 21 and 25 (depending on which company), and you will need a have held a driver's licence for a least a year. Most firms require a credit card as a deposit. Accidents rates are high in Rome, so make sure you have adequate insurance cover. Most car rental contracts include breakdown cover.

Getting Around

VISITORS WITH DISABILITIES

Rome is not an easy place for visitors with physical disabilities. However, Vatican City has ramps and elevators and some hotels have rooms for visitors with disabilities. Staff at airports, museums and places of interest are willing to help and taxis usually accept wheel-chairs, although it is a good idea to phone ahead. The B line Metro is generally accessible (apart from Circo Massimo, Colosseo and Cavour) but the A line and most buses are not. For details contact RADAR (✉ Unit 12, City Forum, 250 City Road, London ECU 8AF ☎ 020 7250 3222; www.radar.org.uk) in the UK or Society for the Advancement of Travel and Hospitality (SATH) (✉ 347 5th Avenue, Suite 610 NY 10016 ☎ 212/447 7284; www.sath.org) in the US.

BUSES

Service is frequent and inexpensive on Rome's orange, green or red-grey regional and blue suburban buses run by ATAC/COTRAL.

🚇 K4 ✉ Piazza dei Cinquecento ☎ 800 431784 (freephone) or 06 4695 2057; www.atac.roma.it 🕓 Mon–Fri 9–1, plus Tue and Fri 2.30–5 🚇 Termini

The buses are often crowded and slow. Buy BIT tickets (*Biglietto Integrato a Tempo*; €1) before boarding, available from tobacconists, automatic machines and shops displaying an ATAC sticker. Your ticket must be stamped at the rear of the bus or tram, and is valid for any number of bus rides and one Metro ride within the next 75 minutes. Day (€4) and three-day (€11) BTI passes are available. These need only be validated the first time they are used. There are large fines if you are caught without a ticket. Daytime services run from 5.30am to 11.30pm, depending on the route. The night service consists of buses on key routes from midnight to 5.30am; night buses have a conductor selling tickets. Remember to enter buses by back doors and to leave by middle doors (if you have a pass or validated ticket with unexpired time you can also use the front doors). Buy several tickets at once as some outlets close early or the 5-ticket 5BIT-Multibit pass (€5), which must be validated for each journey. There are large fines if you are caught without a ticket. Bus stops (*fermate*) list routes and bus numbers and note that one-way streets often force buses to return along different routes.

USEFUL SERVICES

● 23 Piazza del Risorgimento (for the Vatican Museums)–Trastevere–Piramide
● 75 Termini–Roman Forum–Colosseum–Piramide
● 40, 64 Termini–Piazza Venezia–close to Piazza San Pietro/St. Peter's
● 110 Sightseeing service from Stazione Termini and other key monuments
● 81 Piazza del Risorgimento (Vatican

Museums)–Piazza Venezia
● 117, 119 Circular minibus service in the historic centre: Piazza Augusto Imperatore–Piazza della Rotonda (Pantheon)–Via del Corso–Piazza di Spagna
● 780 Piazza Venezia–Trastevere

SUBWAY
Rome's subway, the Metro, has two lines, A and B, which intersect at Stazione Termini. Mainly a commuter service and of limited use in the city, it is good for trans-city rides. Station entrances are marked by a large M and each displays a map of the network. Services run 5.30am to 11.30pm (12.30am on Saturday). Tickets are valid for one ride and can be bought from tobacconists, bars and shops displaying ATAC or COTROL stickers, and from machines at stations.

TAXIS
Official taxis are yellow or white, with a 'Taxi' sign on the roof. Use only these and refuse touts at Fiumicino, Termini and elsewhere. Drivers are not supposed to stop on the streets so it is difficult to hail a cab. Taxis congregate at stands, indicated by blue signs printed with 'Taxi'. Make sure the meter is reset when you start your journey (note one part of the meter will display the minimum-fare starting rate). Ranks are available in the area at Termini, Piazza S Sonnino, Pantheon, Piazza di Spagna and Piazza San Silvestro.
Calling a taxi: the company will give you a taxi code name, a number and the time it will take to get to you. The meter starts running as soon as they are called. Companies include: Samaranda ☎ 06 5551; Autoradio Taxi ☎ 06 3570; Capitale Radio ☎ 06 4994. The minimum fare is valid for 3km (2.5 miles) or the first 9 minutes of a ride. Surcharges are levied between 10pm and 7am, all day Sunday, on national holidays, for airport trips and for each piece of luggage larger than 35 x 25 x 50cm (13 x 9 x 19in).

HANDY HINT
An integrated ticket, the *Biglietto Integrato Giornaliero* (BIG) is valid for a day's unlimited travel on ATAC buses, the Metro, COTRAL buses and suburban trains (except to Fiumicino airport). The *Carta Integrata Settimanale* pass (€16) is valid for a week as for BIG tickets (see above).

LOST PROPERTY
Report lost or stolen property to a police station, which will issue a signed declaration for your insurance company. The central police station is the Questura
✉ Via San Vitale 15
☎ 06 46861 (tourist department) or ☎ 06 4686 2102
ATAC lost property
✉ Via Niccolò Bettoni 1
☎ 06 581 6040
🕐 Mon–Sat 8.30–1
Metro lost property
Line A ☎ 06 487 4309;
Line B ☎ 06 5735 2264
🕐 Mon, Wed, Fri 9–12
COTRAL lost property
Inquire at the route's origin or telephone ☎ 06 57531 or 06 591 5551
Rail lost property
✉ Stazione Termini, Via Giovanni Giolitti 24 ☎ 06 4782 5543 🕐 Mon–Fri 7am–10pm
Airport lost property
☎ 06 6595 3343 🕐 Mon–Fri 9–1, also Thu 2–3.30

Essential Facts

NATIONAL HOLIDAYS

- 1 Jan (New Year's Day)
- 6 Jan (Epiphany)
- Easter Monday
- 25 Apr
- 1 May (Labour Day)
- 29 Jun (St. Peter & St. Paul's Day)
- 15 Aug (Assumption)
- 1 Nov (All Saints' Day)
- 8 Dec (Immaculate Conception
- 25 Dec (Christmas Day)
- 26 Dec (St. Stephen's Day)

MONEY

The euro is the official currency of Italy. Banknotes come in denominations of 5, 10, 20, 50, 100, 200 and 500 euros and coins in 1, 2, 5, 10, 20, 50 cents and 1 and 2 euros.

10 euros

50 euros

200 euros

500 euros

ELECTRICITY

- Current is 220 volts AC, 50 cycles; plugs are the two-round-pin type.

NEWSPAPERS & MAGAZINES

- Most Romans read the Rome-based *Il Messaggero*, the mainstream and authoritative *Corriere della Sera* or the middle-left and popularist *La Repubblica* (which has a special Rome edition). Sports papers (such as *Corriere dello Sport*) and news magazines (like *Panorama* and *L'Espresso*) are also popular.
- Foreign newspapers can usually be bought after 2.30pm on the day of issue from booths (*edicole*) on and close to Termini, Piazza Colonna, Largo di Torre Argentina, Piazza Navona, Via Vittoria Veneto and close to several tourist sights. European editions of the *International Herald Tribune*, *USA Today* and the *Financial Times* are also available.

OPENING HOURS

- Shops: Tue–Sat 8–1, 4–8, Mon 4–8 (with seasonal variations) or, increasingly Mon/Tue–Sat 9.30–7.30. Food shops open on Monday morning but may close on Thursday afternoon.
- Restaurants: daily 12.30–3, 7.30–10.30. Many close on Sunday evening and half- or all day Monday. Most bars and restaurants also have a statutory closing day (*riposo settimanale*) and many close for much of August.
- Churches: variable, but usually daily 7–12, 4.30–7. Most churches close Sunday afternoon.
- Museums and galleries: vary considerably; usually close on Monday.
- Banks: Mon–Fri 8.30–1.30. Major branches may also open 3–4 and Saturday morning.
- Post offices: Mon–Fri 8.15 or 9–2; Sat 8.15 or 9–12 or 2

POSTAL SERVICE

- Buy stamps from post offices and tobacconists.
- Post boxes are red and have two slots, one for Rome (marked *Per La Città*) and one for other destinations (*Per Tutte Le Altre*

Destinazioni). New boxes, usually blue, are for the priority mail service, or *Posta Priorita*.

● Vatican post can be posted only in the Vatican's blue *Poste Vaticane* post boxes. The Vatican postal service is quicker (although tariffs are the same), but stamps can be bought only at the post offices in the Vatican Museums 🕐 Mon–Fri 8.30–7 and in Piazza San Pietro 🕿 06 6988 3406 🕐 Mon–Fri 8.30–7, Sat 8.30–6

● Main post office (*Ufficio Postale Centrale*) ✉ Piazza San Silvestro 18–20 🕿 06 6771; www.poste.it 🕐 Mon–Fri 9am–6.30/7.30pm, Sat 8.30–1 (9–12 last Sat of month).

TELEPHONES

● Telephone numbers listed in this book include the city area code (06), which must be dialled even when calling from within Rome.

● Public telephones are indicated by a red or yellow sign showing a telephone dial and receiver. They are found on the street, in bars and restaurants and in special offices (*Centri Telefoni*) equipped with banks of phones.

● Phones usually accept phone cards (*schede telefoniche*) available from tobacconists, post offices and some bars in a variety of denominations. Break off the card's corner before use.

● To call Italy from the UK, dial 00 44 and from the US or Canada dial 011, followed by 39 (the country code for Italy) then the number, including the relevant city code.

TOURIST INFORMATION

● Azienda di Promozione Turistica di Roma ✉ Via Parigi 11 and Via Parigi 5 🕿 06 3600 4399 or 06 488 991 🕐 Mon– Sat 8am–7pm

● Information kiosks (daily 9–6) are at ✉ Largo Goldoni 🕿 06 6813 6061; ✉ Piazza Tempio della Pace 🕿 06 6992 4307; ✉ Piazza delle Cinque Lune 🕿 06 6880 9240; ✉ Palazzo delle Esposizioni, Via Nazionale 🕿 06 4782 4525; ✉ Piazza San Giovanni in Laterano 🕿 06 7720 3535; ✉ Lungotevere Castel Sant'Angelo-Piazza Pia 🕿 06 6880 9707

MEDICAL TREATMENT

There are emergency rooms at these centres: Ospedale Fatebenefratelli ✉ Isola Tiberina 🕿 06 683 7299/06 68371; Policlinico Umberto I ✉ Viale del Policlinico 155 🕿 06 446 2341 or 06 49971; www.policlinicoumberto1.it. The George Eastman Clinic (✉ Viale Regina Elena 287/b 🕿 06 844 831) provides an emergency dentist service. No credit cards.

Pharmacies are indicated by a large green cross. Opening times are usually Mon–Sat 8.30–1, 4–8, but a rotating schedule (displayed on pharmacy doors) ensures at least one is open 24 hours a day, seven days a week. The most central English-speaking pharmacist is Internazionale (✉ Piazza Barberini 49 🕿 06 482 5456).

EMERGENCY NUMBERS

Police, Fire and Ambulance (general SOS) 🕿 113
Police (Carabinieri) 🕿 112
Central Police 🕿 06 46861
UK Embassy 🕿 06 4220 0001
US Embassy 🕿 06 46741
Information 🕿 12
International information (Europe) 🕿 176
International information (rest of the world) 🕿 170
ACI Auto Assistance (car breakdowns) 🕿 116
General info-tourist line 🕿 06 8205 9127

Language

All Italian words are pronounced as written, with each vowel and consonant sounded. Only the letter *h* is silent, but it modifies the sound of other letters. The letter *c* is hard, as in English 'cat', except when followed by *i* or *e*, when it becomes the soft *ch* of 'cello'. Similarly, *g* is soft (as in the English 'giant') when followed by *i* or *e*–*giardino*, *gelati*; otherwise hard (as in 'gas')–*gatto*. Words ending in *o* are almost always masculine in gender (plural: -*i*); those ending in *a* are generally feminine (plural: -*e*). Use the polite second person (*lei*) to speak to strangers and the informal second person (*tu*) to friends or children.

USEFUL WORDS	
yes	*sì*
no	*no*
please	*per piacere*
thank you	*grazie*
you're welcome	*prego*
excuse me! !	*scusi*
where	*dove*
here	*qui*
there	*là*
when	*quando*
now	*adesso*
later	*più tardi*
why	*perchè*
who	*chi*
may I/can I	*posso*
good morning	*buon giorno*
good afternoon	*buona sera*
good evening	*buona notte*
hello/goodbye (informal)	*ciao*
hello (on the telephone)	*pronto*
I'm sorry	*mi dispiace*
left/right	*sinistra/destra*
open/closed	*aperto/chiuso*
good/bad	*buono/cattivo*
big/small	*grande/piccolo*
with/without	*con/senza*
more/less	*più/meno*
hot/cold	*caldo/freddo*
early/late	*presto/ritardo*
now/later	*adesso/più tardi*
today/tomorrow	*oggi/domani*
when?/do you have?	*quando?/avete?*

NUMBERS	
1	*uno, una*
2	*due*
3	*tre*
4	*quattro*
5	*cinque*
6	*sei*
7	*sette*
8	*otto*
9	*nove*
10	*dieci*
20	*venti*
30	*trenta*
40	*quaranta*
50	*cinquanta*
100	*cento*
1,000	*mille*

EMERGENCIES

help!	*aiuto!*
stop, thief!	*al ladro!*
can you help me, please?	*può aiutarmi, per favore?*
call the police/an ambulance	*chiami la polizia/ un'ambulanza*
I have lost my wallet/ passport	*ho perso il mio portafoglio/il mio passaporto*
where is the police station?	*dov'è il commissariato?*
where is the hospital?	*dov'è l'ospedale?*
I don't feel well	*non mi sento bene*
first aid	*pronto soccorso*

COLOURS

black	*nero*
brown	*marrone*
pink	*rosa*
red	*rosso*
orange	*arancia*
yellow	*giallo*
green	*verde*
light blue	*celeste*
sky blue	*azzuro*
purple	*viola*
white	*bianco*
grey	*grigio*

USEFUL PHRASES

how are you? (informal)	*come sta/stai?*
I'm fine	*sto bene*
I do not understand	*non ho capito*
how much is it?	*quant'è?*
do you have a room?	*avete camere libere?*
how much per night?	*quanto costa una notte?*
with bath/shower	*con vasca/doccia*
when is breakfast served?	*a che ora è servita la colazione?*
where is the train/bus station?	*dov'è la stazione ferroviaria degli autobus?*
where are we?	*dove siamo?*
do I have to get off here?	*devo scendere qui?*
I'm looking for...	*cerco...*
where can I buy...?	*dove posso comprare...?*
a table for... please	*un tavolo per... per favore*
the bill, please?	*il conto, per favore*
we didn't have this	*non abbiamo avuto questo*
where are the toilets?	*dove sono i bagni?*

DAYS/MONTHS

Monday	*lunedì*
Tuesday	*martedì*
Wednesday	*mercoledì*
Thursday	*giovedì*
Friday	*venerdì*
Saturday	*sabato*
Sunday	*domenica*
January	*gennaio*
February	*febbraio*
March	*marzo*
April	*aprile*
May	*maggio*
June	*giugno*
July	*luglio*
August	*agosto*
September	*settembre*
October	*ottobre*
November	*novembre*
December	*dicembre*

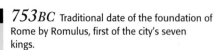

Timeline

PUNIC WARS

The First Punic War against Carthage (North Africa) started in 264BC and lasted for around 23 years. In the Second Punic War (218–201BC) Rome was threatened by Hannibal, leader of the Carthaginian army. But Rome finally defeated Carthage in the Third Punic War (149–146BC).

RELIGION

There are 280 churches within the city walls and 94 per cent of Romans have had their children baptized. However, only 23 per cent of Romans attend Mass. Forty per cent of Romans favour women priests; the same number believe in hell.

Caius Julius Caesar (left)
Map of the Roman Empire (middle)
Charlemagne—his coronation as Holy Roman Emperor (right)

753BC Traditional date of the foundation of Rome by Romulus, first of the city's seven kings.

616–578BC Tarquinius Priscus, Rome's first Etruscan king.

509BC Etruscans expelled and the Republic founded.

60BC Rome ruled by a triumvirate of Pompey, Marcus Licinius Crassus and Julius Caesar.

48BC Caesar declared ruler for life but assassinated by rivals in 44BC.

27BC–AD14 Rule of Octavian, Caesar's great nephew, who as Augustus becomes the first Roman emperor.

98–117 Reign of Emperor Trajan. Military campaigns extend the Empire's boundaries.

284–286 Empire divided into East and West.

306–337 The Emperor Constantine reunites the Empire legalising Christianity. St. Peter's and the first Christian churches are built.

410 Rome is sacked by the Goths.

476 Romulus Augustulus is the last Roman Emperor.

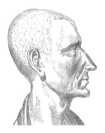

800 Charlemagne awards some territories to papacy; Pope Leo III crowns him Holy Roman Emperor.

1452–1626 The construction of a new St. Peter's begins and spans over 150 years.

1508 Michelangelo begins the Sistine Chapel ceiling.

1527 Rome is sacked by German and Spanish troops under Charles V.

1848 Uprisings in Rome under Mazzini and Garibaldi force Pope Pius IX to flee. The new 'Roman Republic' is defeated by the French.

1870 Rome joins a united Italy.

1929 The Lateran Treaty recognises the Vatican as a separate state.

1940 Italy enters World War II.

1960 Rome hosts the Olympic Games.

2000 Some 30 million pilgrims visit Rome for the millennial jubilee year.

2005 Pope John Paul II dies and is succeeded by Pope Benedict XVI.

2006 Romano Prodi of the centre left party takes the Italian presidency from Silvio Berlusconi in the April elections.

WHAT'S IN A NAME

Many of Rome's street names include dates that allude to significant events in the city's history. Via XX Settembre (20 September) remembers that day in 1870 when Italian troops liberated Rome: the city became the city's capital in the same year. Via XXIV Maggio (24 May) recalls the day in 1915 that Italy declared war in 1915 during World War I. Via IV Novembre (4 November) alludes to the date of the Italian armistice and victory in 1918 after World War I. And Via XXV Aprile (25 April) commemorates the day in 1944 that the Allies liberated the city from the Nazi rule.

Gladiators at a Funeral (left)
Charlemagne et ses ecoliers (middle)
Garibaldi, a popular leader (right)

Index

Rome's
25 Best

WRITTEN BY Tim Jepson
DESIGN CONCEPT AND DESIGN WORK Kate Harling
COVER DESIGN Tigist Getachew
INDEXER Marie Lorimer
IMAGE RETOUCHING AND REPRO Sarah Butler
EDITORIAL MANAGEMENT Apostrophe S Limited
REVIEWING EDITOR Jacinta O'Halloran
SERIES EDITOR Paul Mitchell

ISBN 978-1-4000-1830-7

SEVENTH EDITION

IMPORTANT TIP
Time inevitably brings changes, so always confirm prices, travel facts, and other perishable information when it matters. Although Fodor's cannot accept responsibility for errors, you can use this guide in the confidence that we have taken every care to ensure its accuracy.

SPECIAL SALES
This book is available for special discounts for bulk purchases for sales promotions or premiums. Special editions, including personalized covers, excerpts of existing books, and corporate imprints, can be created in large quantities for special needs. For more information, write to Special Markets/Premium Sales, 1745 Broadway, MD 6–2, New York, NY 10019 or email specialmarkets@randomhouse.com.

Colour separation by Keenes
Printed and bound by Leo, China
10 9 8 7 6 5 4 3 2 1

A03143
Maps in this title produced from:
 map data © 1998 – 2005 Navigation Technologies BV. All rights reserved.
 with map updates courtesy of MAIRDUMONT, Ostfildern, Germany
 mapping © ISTITUTO GEOGRAFICO DE AGOSTINI S.p.A., NOVARA - 2006
Transport map © Communicarta Ltd, UK

The Automobile Association wishes to thank the following photographers, companies and picture libraries for their assistance in the preparation of this book.

Abbreviations for the picture credits are as follows – (t) top; (b) bottom; (l) left; (r) right; (c) centre; (AA) AA World Travel Library

1 AA/C Sawyer; 2 AA/A Kouprianoff; 3 AA/A Kouprianoff; 4t AA/A Kouprianoff; 4c AA/S McBride; 5t AA/A Kouprianoff; 5c AA/D Miterdiri; 6t AA/A Kouprianoff; 6cl AA/C Sawyer; 6c AA/S McBride; 6cr AA/S McBride; 6bl AA/C Sawyer; 6cbl AA/C Sawyer; 6bc AA/S McBride; 6br AA/A Kouprianoff; 7t AA/A Kouprianoff; 7cl AA/S McBride; 7c AA/S McBride; 7cr AA/S McBride; 7bl AA/S McBride; 7bc AA/S McBride; 7br AA/S McBride; 8 AA/A Kouprianoff; 9 AA/A Kouprianoff; 10t AA/A Kouprianoff; 10ct AA/S McBride; 10c AA/S McBride; 10cb AA/C Sawyer; 10/11 AA/S McBride; 11t AA/A Kouprianoff; 11ct AA/C Sawyer; 11c AA/C Sawyer; 12t AA/A Kouprianoff; 12b AA/C Sawyer; 13t AA/A Kouprianoff; 13tct AA/A Kouprianoff; 13ct AA/D Miterdiri; 13c AA/A Kouprianoff; 13cb AA; 13b AA/S McBride; 14t AA/A Kouprianoff; 14ct AA/C Sawyer; 14c AA/J Holmes; 14cb AA/M Jourdan; 14b AA/C Sawyer; 15 AA/A Kouprianoff; 16t AA/A Kouprianoff; 16ct AA/A Kouprianoff; 16c AA/C Sawyer; 16cb AA/A Kouprianoff; 16b AA/D Miterdiri; 17t AA/A Kouprianoff; 17ct Digital Vision; 17c AA/C Sawyer; 17cb AA/C Sawyer; 17b AA/S McBride; 18t AA/A Kouprianoff; 18ct AA/P Wilson; 18c AA/A Kouprianoff; 18cb AA/C Sawyer; 18b AA/S McBride; 19i AA/A Kouprianoff; 19ii AA/J Holmes; 19iii AA/J Holmes; 19iv AA/S McBride; 19v AA/J Holmes; 19vi AA/T Souter; 20/21 AA/A Kouprianoff; 24l AA/J Holmes; 24/25 AA/S McBride; 24c AA/C Sawyer; 24tr AA/A Kouprianoff; 24cl AA/S McBride; 25cr AA/A Kouprianoff; 26l AA/A Kouprianoff; 26/27 AA/C Sawyer; 26c AA/P Wilson; 27c AA/P Wilson; 27r AA/S McBride; 28l AA/S McBride; 28/29 AA/S McBride; 28c AA/S McBride; 29tr AA/S McBride; 29cl AA/S McBride; 29cr AA/S McBride; 30l AA/J Holmes; 30r AA/J Holmes; 31l AA/S McBride; 31r AA/M Jourdan; 32l AA/D Miterdiri; 32r AA/S McBride; 33t AA/D Miterdiri; 33bl AA/T Souter; 33br AA/S McBride; 34t AA/D Miterdiri; 34bl AA/J Holmes; 34br AA/P Wilson; 35t AA/D Miterdiri; 35bl AA/A Kouprianoff; 35br AA/D Miterdiri; 36 AA/J Holmes; 37t AA/C Saywer; 37c AA/S McBride; 38 AA/J Holmes; 39 AA/A Kouprianoff; 40l Alamy/Pieter Estersohn; 42/43t AA/S McBride; 42/43b AA/S McBride; 43 Alamy/CuboImages srl; 44 AA/J Holmes; 44/45 AA/P Wilson; 46l AA/S McBride; 46tr AA/S McBride; 46/47 AA/S McBride; 47t AA/S McBride; 47bl AA/S McBride; 47br AA/S McBride; 48l AA/C Sawyer; 48c AA/C Sawyer; 48r AA/C Sawyer; 49l AA/C Sawyer; 49r AA/P Wilson; 50l AA/C Sawyer; 50c AA; 50r AA/C Sawyer; 51t AA/D Miterdiri; 51bl AA/C Sawyer; 51br AA/J Holmes; 52t AA/D Miterdiri; 52bl AA/D Miterdiri; 52br AA/J Holmes; 53 AA/D Miterdiri; 54 AA/C Sawyer; 55 AA/P Wilson; 56 AA/C Sawyer; 57 AA/A Kouprianoff; 58 AA/C Sawyer; 59 AA/C Sawyer; 60 AA/C Sawyer; 61 AA/A Kouprianoff; 64l AA/A Kouprianoff; 64tr AA/S McBride; 64/65 AA/S McBride; 65t AA/D Miterdiri; 65cl AA/S McBride; 65cr AA/S McBride; 66l AA/D Miterdiri; 66r AA/A Kouprianoff; 67t AA/D Miterdiri; 67bl AA/S McBride; 67br AA/S McBride; 68t AA/D Miterdiri; 68bl AA/J Holmes; 68br AA/J Holmes; 69t AA/D Miterdiri; 69bl AA/J Holmes; 69br AA/J Holmes; 70 AA/D Miterdiri; 71 AA/M Chaplow; 72 Digital Vision; 73 Brand X Pictures; 74 AA/T Harris; 75 AA/C Sawyer; 78l AA/S McBride; 78c AA/S McBride; 78r AA/S McBride; 79l AA/P Wilson; 79r AA/D Miterdiri; 80l AA/P Wilson; 80r AA/P Wilson; 81l AA/C Sawyer; 81c AA/J Holmes; 81r AA/C Sawyer; 82 AA/S McBride; 82/83 Alamy/Rough Guides; 84l AA/J Holmes; 84r AA/J Holmes; 85l AA/D Miterdiri; 85r Alamy/Peter Horree; 86t AA/D Miterdiri; 86bl AA; 86br AA/D Miterdiri; 87t AA/D Miterdiri; 87bl AA/D Miterdiri; 87br AA/P Wilson; 88 AA/D Miterdiri; 89 Photodisc; 90t Digital Vision; 90c AA/E Meacher; 91 AA/J Holmes; 94l AA/S McBride; 94r AA/J Holmes; 95l AA/C Sawyer; 95r AA/S McBride; 96l AA/S McBride; 96tr AA/S McBride; 96cr AA/S McBride; 97t AA/S McBride; 97cl AA/S McBride; 97cr AA/S McBride; 98t AA/S McBride; 98c AA/C Sawyer; 99 AA/S McBride; 102t AA/S McBride; 102cl AA/C Sawyer; 102cr AA/C Saywer; 103t AA/S McBride; 103cl AA/C Sawyer; 104t AA/D Miterdiri; 104bl AA/S McBride; 104br AA/J Holmes; 105t AA/S McBride; 105bl AA/S McBride; 105bc AA/S McBride; 105br AA/S McBride; 106t Photodisc; 106c AA/C Sawyer; 107 AA/P Wilson; 108t AA/C Sawyer; 108ct Photodisc; 108c AA/C Sawyer; 108cb AA/C Sawyer; 108b AA; 109 AA/C Sawyer; 110 AA/C Sawyer; 111 AA/C Sawyer; 112 AA/C Sawyer; 113 AA/J Holmes; 114 AA/S McBride; 115 AA/S McBride; 116 AA/S McBride; 117 AA/S McBride; 118 AA/S McBride; 119 AA/S McBride; 120 AA/S McBride; 121 AA/S McBride; 122t AA/S McBride; 122b AA/J Holmes; 123 AA/S McBride; 124bl AA; 124bc AA; 124br AA; 125t AA/S McBride; 125bl AA; 125bc AA; 125br AA

Every effort has been made to trace the copyright holders, and we apologise in advance for any unintentional omissions or errors. We would be pleased to apply any corrections in any following edition of this publication.

*It was time he had it out with her,
Griffin thought to himself.*

Who was this woman to so provoke him, his
mind demanded. Who was this damn Yankee
female, with her airs and principles. . . She
was his wife, by God. His wife! And as such,
he was entitled to his rights, and his
privileges.

He strode in her direction, full of purpose,
his jaw set with new determination.

Griffin paused before her, looking down at
Morgana's face as if he had never seen it
before. Then he grabbed her shoulders, none
too gently, and pulled her toward him. His
mouth sought hers, forcing her soft lips to
part. His tongue tasted the sweetness of her
mouth and he could feel himself becoming
aroused almost beyond control.

For a moment, Morgana remained passive
within his embrace. Then she began to
struggle, placing her small hands against his
chest, trying to push him from her.

He tore his mouth away, breathing heavily.
"Goddamn you," he muttered. "You're my
wife. You belong to me!"

"I belong to no one," she spat, twisting away
from him. "I'm not one of your wenches," she
said. The words were low and contemptuous.
"You can command Serena," she declared, her
eyes still blazing. "But you can't command me!"

STRANGER IN MY HEART

Helene Sinclair

WARNER BOOKS

A Warner Communications Company

WARNER BOOKS EDITION

Warner Books, Inc.
666 Fifth Avenue
New York, N.Y. 10103

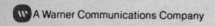 A Warner Communications Company

Printed in the United States of America

First Printing: December, 1985

10 9 8 7 6 5 4 3 2 1

For Doris and Don Lewandowski

and for a friendship that
has survived both time
and distance

Chapter
1

"At least give it some thought, Griffin," Nathaniel Kynes urged his grandson. He stirred restlessly in his chair and ran a hand through his silver hair.

The young man standing before the desk viewed his grandfather with angry eyes, his hard expression making him appear somewhat older than his twenty-five years. Dressed in tan breeches and a white cotton shirt, open at the neck, Griffin Kynes stood just over six feet tall. A darkly handsome man, his lean, well-muscled body was deeply suntanned, attesting to the many hours spent beneath the South Carolina sun.

"You're asking me to marry a woman I've never seen?" he demanded. "And a Yankee, at that?" His tone wavered with incredulity.

Nathaniel issued a long, drawn out sigh as he let his gaze travel about the study. It was a pleasant room; his late wife Anne had selected the pale pink marble that graced the mantel over the tiled hearth. She had also purchased the horsehair sofa and dark leather chairs, all with an eye toward his comfort. The rosewood desk, a massive piece with brass ornaments and intricately carved legs, had been imported from Italy more than fifty years ago, when Nathaniel had first built Albemarle.

The morning sun slanted in through tall windows, warming everything it touched—except Nathaniel, who felt the chill of despair penetrate his very bones. He closed the ledger book in front him, then viewed his grandson a moment before speaking again.

"The last crop failed," he murmured in a quiet voice. "And the previous one was barely enough to make ends meet." Nathaniel felt a twinge of conscience as he presented that argument. Griffin was well aware of their financial difficulties and they both knew that the failure of the crop had played only a small part in their present dire circumstances.

"You know the weather was against us," Griffin protested. He placed his hands, palms down, on the polished surface of the desk, his dark eyes intent. "The crop failed, but so did just about everyone else's. This year will be better," he went on, almost pleading. He couldn't quite believe that his grandfather actually wanted him to marry a stranger. "And by spring, we'll be able to send a coffle to Charleston, or even up to New Orleans." He waited hopefully.

Another sigh greeted that. "We can't wait that long. The money's overdue now. Aleceon Edgewood has made it plain that he won't give us anymore time." Nathaniel paused a moment, then, in a low voice, added, "If you

2

don't do this thing, we'll lose Albemarle." He ran his fingertips over the smooth leather of the ledger book as though the volume held all that was dear to him.

"You should never have gotten involved with that old reprobate," Griffin declared heatedly, straightening. "You know what he wants...."

"I do," his grandfather acknowledged sadly. "He wants Albemarle. Unfortunately, he's in a position to get it, one way or the other."

"That man is completely without honor. Not that any Yankee is so endowed," Griffin muttered in reply. He walked toward the fireplace. Putting a hand on the mantel, he stared, brooding, into the black and empty grate. "I should have called him out long ago."

"On what grounds?" his grandfather asked quietly, casting a look in Griffin's direction. "For demanding payment of his debts? Be reasonable, Griff. This could be the way out for all of us. Your sister is now seventeen. In January she'll be presented at Saint Cecelia's. Ah...." He leaned back in his chair in an attitude of dejection. "If only your mother were still alive. I worry about Cammy, I don't mind tellin' you. As for Albemarle, it's been too long without a woman's touch."

"And you expect me to supply the woman." Griffin knew his tone was bitter but he couldn't help himself. The hard look returned as he stared at his grandfather. "A woman I've never even seen!"

A pained expression crossed Nathaniel's creased face. "I'd do this myself, if it were possible," he replied softly, looking away from those accusing eyes.

Contrite now, Griffin crossed the room, coming quickly to his grandfather's side. Feeling ashamed of his outburst,

3

he placed a hand on the thin shoulder, his eyes softening as he viewed the older man. At seventy-one, Nathaniel Kynes was an active man, with a mind that was just as keen and intelligent as it had been fifty years before. His dark brown eyes were speculative and clear, his back ramrod straight, his silver hair adding a touch of distinction rather than age to his overall appearance. Yet, to Griffin's sharp eye, these past twelve months had taken their toll on the man he so dearly loved.

"You mustn't think I blame you," Griffin said at last, tightening the pressure of his hand. "I know that none of this is your fault."

"It's all my fault," Nathaniel observed simply and with a touch of weariness. "I should've gotten out of that game once I began to lose. But I was so certain . . ." He rapped the arm of his chair with a clenched fist and his brows knitted into an anguished scowl. "That last hand—I held four queens . . ." His voice trailed off, but Griffin, having heard it all before, made no comment.

And he *had* been sure, Nathaniel was thinking with a bitter recollection. So confident had he been, in fact, that he had wagered better than twenty thousand dollars on that one hand of cards—money he didn't have. And so he had put up Albemarle as collateral. Aleceon Edgewood, an experienced and well-known gambler, had been the only other player in the game, which had gone on all night long. When Nathaniel had placed his cards on the table, face up, Aleceon had regarded them for a moment with that small, cold smile of his. Nathaniel had known then, without even looking at the four kings held by his opponent, that he had lost.

That had been over a year ago, a year in which their rice

crop had failed, forcing Nathaniel further into debt to buy seed. That money, too, had come from Aleceon Edgewood, who by that time was such a frequent visitor at Albemarle that he had been given his own room on the second floor.

Some months ago, in an effort to pay their debts, Nathaniel had sent a coffle of slaves to market to be sold. But even that resource was being depleted. Last year, there had been better than three hundred slaves to work Albemarle; now there were barely one hundred and sixty.

"All my fault," Nathaniel murmured in fresh anguish. Then, with a sound of resignation, he reached up and patted the hand that still rested on his shoulder. What could he have been thinking of? he chastised himself. Better to let Albemarle go than to ruin his grandson's life. "Never mind, Griff," he said softly. "When Mr. Edgewood arrives later today, I'll tell him that his conditions are unacceptable. We'll just have to make other arrangements—"

"No," Griffin interrupted. But he couldn't prevent the deep sigh that followed. He knew that no bank would lend them the money. Albemarle was already mortgaged to the hilt. "We'll inform Mr. Edgewood that I'll marry his daughter. But only," he added in a terse voice, "if he wipes out every debt, every note in our name."

"Beggin' yore pardon, Masta Nathaniel, suh. . . ."

Both men looked toward the door, viewing the dark-skinned Hausa, who was standing there in respectful submission, waiting for permission to speak.

"What is it, Thomas?" Nathaniel asked, irritated with the interruption.

"It's Jonah, suh. They done caught him." Thomas nodded his head with its graying fringe of woolly hair surrounding his broad forehead. He was almost the same age as his master and was, in fact, the first Negro that Nathaniel had ever purchased.

A nod of satisfaction replaced Nathaniel's irritability. "Put him in the barn. We'll be there directly. Tell Mr. Dobbs I said to shuck that bastard down and string him up."

"The dogs must've worked," Griffin speculated as Thomas closed the door.

Nathaniel nodded at the observation, his expression grave. "Second time that worthless nigger's run. See to it that the patrollers are given fifty dollars, Griff. Then meet me in the barn."

Emerging from the Great House a short time later, Griffin descended the broad front steps, his booted feet echoing his passage, then headed toward the two men who stood by their horses. They were part of a band of patrollers that regularly scouted the area in search of runaways. They were dedicated, but could be, on occasion, ruthless in the pursuit of their quarry. Nearby, four hounds stretched at their leashes, tails wagging and tongues lolling in the late morning sun.

"Mornin', Mr. Kynes," the tallest of the men said. He removed his broad-brimmed hat to reveal an almost bald head.

Griffin smiled affably. "Where'd you find Jonah?"

" 'Bout six miles upriver." The man squinted in the bright sun, appearing earnest as he continued. "I'm afraid the dogs tore him up a bit. Real sorry about that, Mr. Kynes. But we got to him before too much damage was done."

"Don't worry about that." Griffin waved a hand, dismissing the apology. "When Dobbs gets through with that buck, won't be much left of him anyhow. Much obliged to you both."

Reaching into his pocket, Griffin counted out the money, giving the man the customary fifty dollars, which would be split between them. Then, politely, he invited them to stay for dinner.

But the tall man declined for them both. "Still plenty of daylight left," he explained. "We're huntin' a runaway from Four Oaks. Mr. Barrows is plenty upset. He paid twelve hundred dollars for that buck not two months ago."

Griffin inclined his head at the news, reflecting gravely that, lately, hardly a week passed that he didn't receive word from one of the neighboring plantations that one or more of their slaves had tried to escape.

Small incidents perhaps, for almost every runaway was eventually captured; it was, nonetheless, disturbing because it was happening so consistently. Like most people who lived all their lives in the South and around Negroes, Griffin had the thin thread of fear that, like a taut string on a fiddle, would suddenly vibrate into life at the mere thought of a slave revolt. Running was, of course, the first step in that direction. Not that he'd ever seen a revolt. But there were always rumors; rebellion, stealing, disobedience. Isolated, to be sure, but it paid to be on one's guard.

"I'll keep an eye out," he offered at last. He watched a moment as the men mounted their horses, then he headed in the direction of the barn, his eyes surveying the land on which he had been born.

Albemarle was not the largest plantation along the Ashley River, but to Griffin Kynes, it was the most beautiful. Covering better than nine hundred acres and fronting on the river, Albemarle lay some sixteen miles from Charleston.

Griffin could not see the fields from here. They were concealed by a stand of cypress that acted as a buffer, perhaps against those who toiled so ceaselessly on the rich, dark earth. They were Hausa and Kru, Ashanti and Angolan, Dahomean and Fanti. All were referred to as blacks or darkies or niggers, though their skin ranged from ebony to gold.

And they were all slaves.

When his grandfather, then a young man of seventeen and newly arrived from England with his bride, had first built Albemarle, indigo had been the primary crop. That was replaced in 1834 by rice, with some seventy acres devoted to sugar cane, raised mostly for their own use. For some years now, the land had been producing less and less. Last year the crop hadn't even supported expenses.

That had been only the beginning of their troubles. The failure of the crop had been nothing compared to the appearance of Aleceon Edgewood in their lives.

Probably, Griffin reflected as he walked, they would never have met the man if his grandfather hadn't been in New Orleans, indulging in his one weakness: gambling. Not that Griffin blamed his grandfather. Nathaniel had few vices and a man ought to be able to have some enjoyment out of life.

When he reached the stables, Griffin paused, watching a bright-skinned young Negro as he expertly combed and brushed a gray gelding. The animal stood patiently, flanks quivering beneath the gentle, firm strokes.

"How's Thunder doing?" Griffin came closer and ran a

hand over the horse's foreleg. The thoroughbred was scheduled to race in January.

"Fine, Masta Griffin," came the prompt reply. "Swellin's jest 'bout gone. He feelin' peppy." With a soft touch, Jude ran his fingertips along a muscle of the horse's leg, injured in a jump only yesterday. For a moment, the hands of the two men came in close proximity. Jude stared, noticing that the color of his own hand was not that much different from the suntanned skin of his young master.

Glancing up at that moment, Griffin caught the intent expression and his eyes narrowed. He didn't like Jude, although he couldn't quite put his finger on the exact cause of his enmity. Probably it was the nigger's eyes, he thought to himself. They were blue. Of all the goddamned tricks of nature, the nigger's eyes were blue. Not a dark blue, either. They were vivid, like the sky on a clear October day. Jude was a quadroon, the oldest son of Minda, the cook. He was also, in Nathaniel's opinion, a showpiece. Physically, Jude, who was almost twenty years old, was a fine specimen. Griffin couldn't argue with that. He was excellent with the horses, he was respectful, obedient . . . yet Griffin sensed—something. He couldn't put a name to the nebulous feeling, but if it were up to him, he'd sell the damned buck tomorrow.

"What're you looking at?" he demanded, his brow deepening into a frown.

Guiltily, and with a small start, Jude tore his gaze away. " 'Pologizes to you, masta, suh," he said hastily. "Jest noticin' you got a nasty cut on yore thumb."

Griffin blinked, staring down at his hand which he had accidentally cut with a hunting knife the week before. "Yes . . . well, it's almost healed." He straightened, gave the horse a pat on its rump, and without further words to Jude, turned and strode away.

Leaving the stables, Griffin walked passed the carriage house and the smokehouse, approaching the barn, the front part of which was devoted to any chastisement that might be earned by the slaves of Albemarle.

Entering the dim interior, Griffin saw the overseer, Carlie Dobbs, standing beside his grandfather. The thin, wiry man, who was in his early forties, was discussing the punishment to be meted out to the runaway slave, who, having already been stripped, now stood with head bowed and hands shackled, nervously awaiting whatever his masters decided should be his fate. A deep gash on his arm, running from his shoulder to his elbow, was bleeding profusely. Several less severe puncture wounds dotted his muscular body. The dogs, having caught his scent at dawn, had tracked him down with relentless determination. When they finally caught sight of him, they had attacked. Jonah knew perfectly well that if the patrollers hadn't shown up when they did, the dogs would have torn him to shreds.

"Griffin!" Nathaniel called out when he saw the young man. "We've been waitin' for you. Carlie here thinks that seventy-five lashes and a branding would cure this nigger of runnin'. I'm thinkin' that'll ruin him."

"Probably," Griffin agreed, coming closer. "But what's the difference? You're not thinking of keeping him, are you?"

The Negro turned in the direction of his young master, his black face gray with fear. His skin was the color of coal. The dark eyes, set deeply beneath a wide forehead, were filled with an apprehension that bordered on terror.

"Please, Masta Griffin, suh. Doan let 'em be seventy-five," he moaned. "Doan run agin me. Learnt my lesson, suh. Learnt it good."

"Shut your black mouth, Jonah," Dobbs growled, frowning at the slave's impertinence. "No one heah's askin' for your say-so." He glared a moment longer, then turned to a massive Negro who was standing nearby, and whose ebony skin gleamed in the light of the brazier he was tending. He was a giant of a man, standing a full six-feet, nine-inches. "Joe!" Dobbs gave a curt motion with his hand. "String this heah nigger up. Mebbe he'll stop his yappin' and let us get on with it."

The overseer watched only a moment as Joe, who was the blacksmith for Albemarle, secured the end of a long rope to the shackles that bound Jonah's wrists, then flung it up over a beam. He pulled on it until Jonah's arms were raised up over his head, then pulled again, until only the slave's toes were in contact with the wooden floor.

"Griff's right, suh," Dobbs said to Nathaniel after a moment. "Won't do no good to keep this one. Spend more time watchin' him than he's worth." With his thumb, he rubbed the bridge of his hawklike nose as he waited for his employer's response.

"Who said anything about keepin' him?" Nathaniel waved an impatient hand. "But he won't fetch a damn cent if he's crippled, you know that."

A slight moan escaped Jonah's full lips, but no one turned in his direction. He hung there, feeling the strain in his arms and back, but knew from experience that the discomfort was nothing compared to what lay ahead of him. The last time he had run, he had been given fifty lashes. It had almost killed him. Seventy-five, he figured, would.

"Won't cripple him," Dobbs argued earnestly with a sharp shake of his head. "Lay him up some. But it'll be months before you get a coffle together. He'll be healed by then." He viewed Jonah's muscular back, already badly scarred. " 'Course, you can always shunt him off on the next trader passin' by," he mused, pursing his thin lips. "He ain't good for nothin' but the cane fields anyway. No sense in even sendin' him to auction."

Nathaniel considered that, then looked toward his grandson. "What do you think, Griff?"

Griffin Kynes shrugged his broad shoulders. "Can't see killing him," he stated after a moment. "Give him fifty. After the branding, rub him down good with capsicum; it'll make him heal faster. Carlie's right about one thing," he turned to face Nathaniel. "Don't bother sending him in the coffle. Next trader comes along can have him at a good price. I don't like having runaways around," he went on firmly. "They're a bad influence."

Nathaniel nodded, pleased with the astuteness of the decision. "All right, let's get on with it. Don't have all day."

Dobbs turned to Joe and jerked his head in the direction of Jonah. "Get to it," he ordered briskly. "And make sure they're well laid on, heah?"

"Yassuh," replied Joe, inclining his great head, his expression placid in the face of his distasteful chore.

With practiced ease and little apparent effort, the huge Negro applied the first of the fifty lashes against the back of the runaway slave. The long rawhide whip sliced through air, then flesh, with a stinging, resonant sound.

12

At each delivered stroke, Dobbs counted, his voice a monotone that effectively conveyed boredom. Griffin and Nathaniel watched with impassive eyes as the slave screamed, helpless beneath the relentless bite of the lash.

In fact, none of the three white men present displayed, nor felt, compassion at the sight, and would have been greatly surprised if anyone did. Neither Griffin nor his grandfather enjoyed the process of disciplining their slaves; it was simply a necessity, a job that had to be accomplished. Most of the time, it was Carlie Dobbs who wielded the whip. Today was, however, an exception. It was rare for a slave at Albemarle to receive an excess of ten lashes. More than that was considered serious, and Nathaniel and Griffin always made it a point to be present on those occasions.

At last it was over. Joe released the rope and Jonah crumpled to the ground. There was little of his black skin left on his back; it was now a mass of torn and bleeding wounds.

Turning the iron in the brazier, Joe looked at Carlie Dobbs, who nodded. Moving Jonah's head to an angle that suited him, Joe quickly applied the hot iron to the slave's forehead. There was a sharp hissing sound, followed by the sickly-sweet smell of burned flesh. Jonah screamed once, hoarsely, and was still.

"Rub him down with capscium," Dobbs instructed the huge Negro. "Don't want him to bleed to death."

Picking up a rag, Joe dipped it in the pail that contained a solution of salt, water, and red pepper, then applied it liberally to Jonah's back.

"How much do you think we can get for him?" Nathaniel asked as he and Griffin walked back into the yard.

"Not much," Griffin replied, feeling the November sun warm on his back. "Be lucky if we get five hundred for him, marked the way he is."

A dark-skinned girl of about eighteen approached them hesitantly, tears streaming down her satiny cheeks. She was small boned, with an erect carriage that produced a high bosom above well rounded hips.

"Please, Masta Nathaniel, kin I take Jonah to his cabin now?" Her dark eyes viewed the old man, pleading.

Nathaniel shook his head. "Have to lock him up, Zoe," he replied, sounding regretful. "This is the second time your brother's run. . . ."

"But—"

"Go along, Zoe!" Griffin interjected sharply, annoyed by the girl's persistence.

She stood there a moment longer. Then, shoulders slumping beneath her cotton dress, which was the only garment she wore, Zoe walked away, her bare feet kicking up little mounds of ecru dust.

"That wench is too sassy for her own good," Griffin complained, watching the receding figure. "I can't understand why you won't sell her."

"She's a pretty little gal," Nathaniel replied, sounding unconcerned. "I'm hopin' that Jude boy can get her knocked up. She's real black and if she can drop a sucker with her color and Jude's blue eyes, we'll have ourselves a real fancy piece."

Morosely, Griffin reflected that the last thing Albemarle needed was another nigger with blue eyes, but he said nothing, knowing his grandfather's penchant for breeding what he considered "good stock."

They began to walk in the direction of the Great House.

14

Suddenly Nathaniel halted, putting a hand on Griffin's arm. Then he pointed at the carriage coming up the drive. It was a chaise, driven with the top down and hauled by a pair of matched bays. A Negro, dressed only slightly less grand than his master, guided the animals with a quick and sure touch, containing their spiritedness without benefit of whip or harsh words.

Neither Griffin nor Nathaniel gave the Negro driver, whose name was Ben, a second glance. Their attention was riveted on the man who was seated in the chaise and whose bearing suggested that his outing was no more pressing than a Sunday drive.

"It's Aleceon." Nathaniel frowned. "And from the looks of it, it appears like he's plannin' to stay awhile." The frown fell into a scowl at the sight of the baggage strapped to the back of the vehicle. He turned toward Griffin, noting the slightly flushed cheeks that indicated inner anger. "There's still time to change your mind," he began, but the young man shook his head.

"No," Griffin responded firmly. "I'm not turning my home over to that scoundrel." He made a face of disgust. "Wonder what's wrong with her?" he mused in a low voice, keeping his eyes on the approaching carriage.

"Who?"

"His daughter. Must be something wrong with her if he has to twist a man's arm to marry her."

Slowly, Nathaniel shook his head. "Don't know," he conceded. "Never saw her." Privately, he suspected that Griffin's assessment was probably true. A woman who was almost twenty years of age and still unmarried must have a face that would turn a man to stone. Still, once they were married, Griffin didn't have to bother with her much. He

15

had Serena, the high yellow gal that had been his bed wench for over a year now. That one would make any man forget an ugly wife.

The chaise halted before them. Alighting, Aleceon Edgewood stood there a moment regarding Nathaniel and Griffin without speaking, then nodded briefly. He wasn't as tall as Griffin, lacking a good four inches to reach that young man's height, but he was so thin that he gave the appearance of being taller than he actually was. Like the rest of his body, his face was long and angular, with an aquiline nose above a narrow mouth. His dark blond hair was thick, straight, and always neatly combed. His was a fastidious nature, and this was reflected in his clothes and bearing. Aleceon never appeared disheveled, or even rumpled, and there was that about him that could be termed an air of elegance. Even those who disliked him—and they were legion—had to admit that it was so.

Today, as always, Aleceon was dressed in a fashionable manner, his bottle-green frock coat and trousers custom made, his silk vest hand embroidered, his walking stick with its mother-of-pearl handle held at a jaunty angle.

Greeting his visitor in a barely civilized manner, Nathaniel led the way across the sun-dappled front yard into the house, heading for the study. He instructed the hovering Thomas to bring them a full decanter of bourbon. From the nature of their business, he reflected sourly, they'd all need more than one drink.

With a certain degree of familiarity, Aleceon settled himself on the sofa, accepted the proferred glass from Nathaniel, then viewed Griffin's dark and flushed face. "I take it your grandfather has informed you of my proposal?" he remarked.

"A grand name for what you've suggested," Griffin snapped quickly. "Why didn't you just take Albemarle for yourself? Why indulge in all this trickery?" His hands itched with the urge to strike the other man. Fearful of losing control, Griffin plunged them deeply into his pockets.

Calmly, Aleceon sipped at his drink, his manner languid and unhurried. But his blue eyes were alert and piercing as he viewed Griffin in silence for a long moment, apparently giving careful consideration to the question. A gambler for most of his forty-one years, Aleceon had learned the virtue of weighing his words carefully before he spoke.

"Under different circumstances, I might have done just that," he allowed at last, shifting himself into a more comfortable position. He glanced toward Nathaniel, who had seated himself behind his desk, but the older man refused to look at him.

"However," Aleceon continued, again viewing Griffin, who had remained standing, "the truth of the matter is that I know nothing about running a plantation, much less one of this size. Nor am I particularly interested in learning," he added, finishing his drink.

"Doesn't it bother you that what you are doing is . . ." Griffin raised a hand, searching for the right word, "dishonorable? Or is that expression meaningless to you?" His eyes were fierce and bright with anger.

The statement seemed to amuse Aleceon. Getting up, he casually poured himself another drink. "To a certain extent," he answered quietly, "you are right in your assumption. Honor is a useless impediment, fit only for fools."

Watching as Aleceon once again seated himself, Griffin noted scornfully, "You could not hope to understand."

Resting an elbow on the arm of the sofa, Aleceon twirled the glass in his hands, viewing it thoughtfully. It was clear to him that the young man had a mind of his own, was not in any sense a puppet of his grandfather. Whether he would, or would not, go along with this would be his own decision. Aleceon leaned back against the cushions, pleased with his assumption. He'd been a gambler all his life. This time he was playing for higher stakes than anyone knew. This time it had been Fate who had dealt the cards; a nonwinning hand.

There was a brief silence, then Aleceon said to Griffin, "When you marry my daughter, all outstanding notes will be destroyed. Albemarle will be free and clear. Thereafter, twenty percent of your annual profit will be paid to me."

"All that could be accomplished without a marriage," Griffin noted with a pronounced touch of sarcasm.

Aleceon's nod was slow. He appeared unperturbed by the young man's attitude. "Perhaps," he allowed. "But Morgana can no longer stay in school. And I've no intention of becoming tied down. She's already passed the age when she should be married. Besides . . ." he issued the cold smile that so grated on Griffin's nerves, "as your father-in-law, I'm certain that I will be welcome to make Albermarle my home. I know I don't have to tell you how attached I've become to it."

Griffin's jaw worked visibly and he turned away for a moment. There seemed to be no end to the man's audacity.

Behind his desk, Nathaniel rubbed his face with a gnarled hand, but remained silent, knowing that the decision was Griffin's alone to make.

"And what does your daughter have to say about all this?" Griffin demanded tersely, turning toward Aleceon again. His hands, back in his pockets, tightened into fists. He could feel his pulse accelerate in answer to his mounting anger.

"Morgana?" Aleceon gave a short laugh. "She doesn't even know about our ... arrangement," he replied. "I thought it better if she were to believe that you were smitten at first sight."

Griffin made a face at that. He gave momentary thought to demanding, at the very least, a physical description of the mysterious Morgana Edgewood. But then he discarded the notion. What the hell did he care what she looked like? It would do him no good if she was beautiful and stupid; nor, conversely, if she was ugly and intelligent. Neither of the choices appealed to him. Certainly she wouldn't be beautiful *and* intelligent. That would be too much to hope for. Besides, no man pawned off a daughter like that!

"What if your daughter refuses?" Griffin finally asked.

Aleceon calmly studied a well manicured nail for a moment before remarking, "If you play your part well, Griffin, I'm sure she won't. Let's hope that that situation will not arise," he observed ominously, raising his eyes slightly to meet Griffin's hot stare.

"And if I refuse this ridiculous scheme?" Griffin no longer made the effort to conceal his open distaste. Aleceon was on his fourth bourbon and seemed to swallow the stuff as if it were water. He should be drunk, but he wasn't. His grandfather had told him that one of the reasons Aleceon was so successful as a gambler was his ability to remain placid and inscrutable. Griffin was beginning to realize how accurately Nathaniel had judged the man.

Aleceon gestured with a hand that sported an ornate gold ring set with two perfectly matched emeralds. He always wore the ring. He had long discovered that it was a distraction at the card table, giving him a fraction of an advantage, allowing him to observe expressions and nervous habits while his opponent's eyes more often than not strayed to the glittering gems instead of his own face. Nathaniel Kynes had been one of those who had let his attention wander at a crucial time.

It interested Aleceon now that not once since they had begun their conversation had Griffin's eye been caught by the ring. Again, he was pleased.

"If you refuse," Aleceon replied softly, "then Albermarle will be mine—to do with as I see fit." His gaze was level and without humor. "I've already sent for my daughter," he went on. "I expect her to arrive in Charleston by the end of the week."

The cold smile returned to Aleceon's thin lips. The thought often occurred to Griffin that the man would appear only half dressed without it. It seldom, if ever, held any humor; rather, it was condescending and mocking, an attitude that was reinforced by those eyes that were the color of blue smoke.

"I think it might be a good idea if you went to fetch her, Griffin," Aleceon continued quietly, taking the other man's silence for agreement. Then he stood up and put his empty glass on a nearby table. "The long drive back will enable you both to get to know each other. I feel certain that a man of your sophistication will have little trouble in charming an innocent, impressionable young lady."

Aleceon paused, but neither Griffin nor his grandfather made any comment. He waited a moment longer, then, his bearing nonchalant, he left the study, appearing unconcerned or even aware of the hostility his words had generated.

With his departure, Nathaniel and Griffin exchanged looks—the old man's saddened, the young man's rigid with a cold, implacable anger.

Griffin turned away, feeling the determination harden within him. He had plans, plans for himself, for his sister, for Albemarle, which he intended to restore to its former position as one of the most successful plantations in the area.

As for his sister, Cammy must be given the opportunity of making a good marriage. Once she made her debut in January, he intended to persuade her to look upon Clinton Barrows with favor. The eldest son of Farley Barrows, Clinton stood to inherit Four Oaks one day. The two plantations, side by side, united by marriage, sharing resources, was a vision that was very tempting to Griffin.

First, however, Albemarle's debts must be cleared. And right now, there appeared only one way to do that.

Into the silence, Nathaniel at last expulsed a deep breath. "It's no good, Griff," he murmured, shaking his head. "I can't let you do this. . . ."

The young man came closer to the desk, mouth set tight. "You said it before, Grandfather," he pointed out as he poured himself a drink. He lifted the glass to his lips and downed the contents in a long swallow before continuing. "We'll lose Albemarle if I don't." He put the glass beside the decanter. Then, with a last, grim look at his grandfather, Griffin left the study.

* * *

Later that evening, although it was not yet nine o'clock, Aleceon retired to his room on the second floor. It was a back bedroom and, as such, did not have access to the piazza, which only the front bedrooms opened onto. But Aleceon liked it because it had windows on two walls. It was therefore bright, and, when nature offered it, had a cross breeze as well. The room was large and square, the four-poster roomy and soft with its down mattress. He wasn't overly fond of the wallpaper, which depicted overblown roses of a dark maroon color that he found depressing. But aside from that flaw, the wardrobe and dresser, as well as the several tables and chairs, were serviceable. And that was all Aleceon wanted or required.

Aleceon had stayed many times at Albemarle over the past two years, and was by now quite familiar with the routine. Because the hands began work in the fields at first light, everyone was awake and functioning at that time, with the result that, soon after darkness fell, the household quieted down for the night.

Closing the door to his room, Aleceon stood there a moment, mouth tight, a hand over his abdomen.

Then, quickly, he withdrew a small bottle from his pocket. Uncapping it, he swallowed the clear liquid. In only moments the laudanum eased the pain in his stomach. It had been growing worse in these past months—it would kill him before too many more passed, that much he knew. Six months to a year, the doctors had told him. That had been four months ago.

His suggestion that Griffin meet Morgana in Charleston had not been a whim. It was based upon the simple fact that he didn't think he had the strength to make the trip there and back, and he wanted to horde what little was left in an effort to see his daughter safely married. Once the notes on Albemarle were destroyed, the plantation should prosper, as it had done in years past. Her life, he reasoned, would be a comfortable one.

He had given Morgana little during her lifetime. Now, with death threatening his own mortality, Aleceon had tried to make arrangements for her security. And the only real security for a woman was, of course, marriage. Griffin Kynes had been far from a casual choice. Aleceon had considered and rejected a score of other young men over the past four months. They had been too old, too young, too poor, too unattractive.

And Aleceon Edgewood had too few months to live to let nature take its course.

Nor did he give any thought to the ensuing relationship between Morgana and Griffin Kynes. It would work out. Morgana was, after all, her father's daughter. Aleceon almost smiled, but then scowled at the slave who came toward him.

"Get away from me, you black viper," he growled. "Is there no place a man can have a measure of privacy?"

"Yassuh, masta, suh," the Negro replied as he calmly prepared to remove Aleceon's boots. Ben was part Ashanti, his ancestors having come from that western part of Africa known as the Gold Coast, where, it was said, there was a heavy infusion of Arab blood in the people of his tribe. While his skin was a dark and rich reddish-brown, his nose was straight and narrow, his lips well formed and only slightly full, his cheekbones set high in his angular face. His black hair, however, was kinky and lay close to his skull. He topped Aleceon's height by five inches and out-weighed him by almost sixty pounds.

Ben had been with Aleceon for over five years and, by now, knew his master as well as anyone. It wasn't so much what Aleceon said, as how he said it, that prompted Ben's responses. Aleceon grumbled and complained constantly, but in a perverse sort of way seemed genuinely fond of his slave.

Ben recognized that, and offered his master a devotion that no other white man had ever received from him. No one else knew about the sickness that daily consumed a part of Aleceon. But Ben knew. The thought at once saddened and terrified him. Even though Aleceon had already informed him that, when the time came, he would be given to Morgana, Ben knew of the coming marriage plans, and he was very well aware that it wouldn't be Morgana, but Griffin Kynes to whom he would belong.

That thought produced nightmares. At least once a year, a coffle of slaves trudged from Albemarle to Charleston, or even up to Savannah, to be sold. Who was to say that he might not be one of them?

"You feelin' bettah, suh?" Ben ventured in his soft voice as he now helped Aleceon to undress.

"Soon I will be," Aleceon murmured, grimacing. The pain was growing stronger day by day, he realized. It took all his energy and willpower to hide it from others. Only with Ben did he relax and give in to it.

"I gits you moah medicine?" Ben offered, taking a step toward the dresser.

Aleceon took a deep breath. The pain was receding to the familiar dull ache which had been his constant companion for the past two weeks. "No," he said tiredly. "I'll sleep now." As he moved toward the bed, Ben leaped forward to turn down the covers.

After his master had settled himself with a deep sigh, Ben sat on his pallet on the floor, his dark eyes never leaving the motionless, thin form. He knew that, within an hour, or two at the outside, Aleceon would need more of the clear, harmless looking liquid that allowed him to function. Occasionally, almost as a mother would do while watching over a sick child, Ben would doze, sitting up, his back against the wall. But at the slightest movement or sound, Ben would be awake, alert to the needs of the man who was not only his master, but who had once saved his life.

Chapter
2

Edith Appleby sat in her office at the Brookshire Academy for Young Women, reading the letter on her desk for the third time since she had received it that morning. It had actually arrived the day before, but yesterday, Monday, she had left her office early, retiring to her private rooms on the second floor to nurse a headache.

In her fifties, the headmistress still bore traces of the patrician handsomeness that nature had bestowed upon her at an early age, giving her a sharp-featured and sometimes forbidding demeanor. Beneath the dark blue dress made of fine lawn, her plump body was tightly corseted. Her hair, although gray, was thick and wavy, drawn back from her small ears into a sweeping pompadour. Hazel eyes, behind steel-rimmed spectacles, had the capacity to warm or chill an observer as the mood struck her.

Turning slightly, she glanced out the window. The day

was clear and cold and bright, a respite from two straight days of snow the previous week which had been followed by several more days of sub-zero temperatures and oyster-gray skies that had blanketed upper New York state with a relentless gloom.

Unlike many schools of the day that catered to females, Brookshire was academically oriented. The faculty of twenty-three—all women—were carefully screened by Edith Appleby, who demanded excellence, expertise, and a sincere desire to impart knowledge.

Not all of the young ladies had a thirst for knowledge and more than a few—parents included—thought of Brookshire more in terms of a finishing school, a label Edith Appleby considered ridiculous and demeaning.

Putting her elbows on the desk, she sighed deeply, pressing her fingertips to her temples, massaging the aching throb that was a residue of her recent migraine.

How, she wondered, was she going to tell Morgana?

Unaccountably, she recalled last Christmas Eve, when she and Morgana had sipped eggnog and eaten little almond cakes to celebrate the holidays. They had talked long and seriously, mostly of Morgana's future here at Brookshire. Unlike the rest of the seventy-four girls who comprised the student population, Morgana Edgewood always spent the holidays at school.

Ruefully, and a bit annoyed with herself, Miss Appleby realized that, somewhere along the line, Morgana had become the daughter she never had, and never would have.

Miss Appleby was not married. She had never met a man she could love enough to give up her own independence. Her father had been wealthy, arthritic, and confined to a wheelchair for the seven years that preceded his death. Her mother had died when Edith was only fourteen. From then, until her father's death some ten years later, Edith Appleby had devoted herself to his care and comfort. When he died, he left everything to his only daughter and, thirty years ago, in the spring of 1822, Edith Appleby had founded Brookshire.

In all those years she had never let herself become attached to any of her students, knowing that each in their own turn would, sooner or later, leave her.

With Morgana Edgewood, however, she had broken that rule. Now she would have to pay for that lapse into sentimentality.

Again her eyes drifted to the innocent-appearing piece of paper. It was dated the 16th of November 1852, some four weeks ago, and was from Aleceon Edgewood, Morgana's father.

Just the thought of that man caused a frown, deepening the already existing creases in her forehead. There had been rumors when he had first brought his daughter here; rumors that his wife, who had died when Morgana was born, had been of a character that was less than admirable, a woman of the streets, it was whispered.

As for Mr. Edgewood himself, it was said that gambling was one of his more respectable occupations.

Since Brookshire was highly selective and, it could be said, one of the most exclusive schools in New York, Edith Appleby quite naturally had had reservations about admitting Morgana Edgewood.

However, it had subsequently come to light that the then thirteen-year-old girl was the niece of Sarah Edgewood Enright, who practically owned the town of Taunset and the mill that bore her name. Of course, Taunset was in

Massachusetts and Brookshire was in New York, but even that distance was not so great that Edith Appleby didn't know about the Enrights. Few families were on a par with that most socially acceptable clan.

She had, therefore, with only few misgivings, accepted the girl's application.

Nor had she done the wrong thing, Miss Appleby now thought. Morgana had proved to be not only intelligent and capable, but a definite credit to the school. She was intelligent, well behaved, and conducted herself with a gracefulness that was at once both appealing and charming. She was a bit strong willed at times, but Miss Appleby, having a touch of that trait herself, saw nothing wrong with that endowment.

In fact, so impressed was Edith Appleby with this particular student, that she had—until today—entertained hopes that Morgana would join their teaching staff. It was something the girl herself had requested.

And now . . . Now this.

Laying aside the unwanted message, Edith Appleby at last sent for Morgana Edgewood.

Morgana had already finished her breakfast when she was called to Miss Appleby's office. Having been there many times, the summons didn't even move her to curiosity. It wasn't unusual for the headmistress to request her assistance in grading papers or filing or any other of several chores.

There was, in fact, nothing unusual about this morning. It was like every other weekday morning of the past six years. The bell had rung at six-thirty, announcing the start of another day. She, together with more than seventy other girls ranging in age from thirteen to nineteen, had risen, washed, brushed her teeth, dressed, and had come down to the dining room to eat breakfast. Even that had been the same, oatmeal, orange juice, hot tea laced with rich cream.

Nothing marked today as any different from its predecessors. Nor did Morgana Edgewood desire any change. (Her life contented her, her future was planned.)

When she entered the office, Morgana saw the headmistress standing by the window. The woman did not immediately turn toward her, although Morgana was certain that her presence had been noted.

Patiently, she waited. Buttery yellow sunlight crept in past the plum colored draperies, warming wood, giving a sheen to the leather upholstery and creating sharp points of light across the dark walnut desk. It was all so very familiar to her; she had even helped in the selection of the material for the draperies.

Miss Appleby turned then, regarding Morgana with a somewhat enigmatic expression, seeing a tall, slim girl with eyes so blue they could easily be termed her most arresting feature. She was dressed conservatively, without adornment, in a gray woolen dress with a white collar and cuffs. Her shining blond hair was worn severely, pulled back from her heart-shaped face and knotted in a bun at the nape of her neck.

"Be seated, Morgana," Miss Appleby murmured, still standing by the window.

Puzzled by the intent look and grave tone of voice, Morgana sat down on the straight-backed chair before the desk. She tucked her feet primly beneath her and folded her hands gracefully in her lap as she had been taught to do.

31

At last Miss Appleby walked to her desk and sat down. Taking off her steel-rimmed spectacles, she placed them carefully before her.

"Morgana," she said quietly, taking a deep breath. "I have received word from your father ..." She paused, seeing the startled look on the face of the young woman. And why shouldn't she be surprised? the headmistress thought with no little bitterness. Aleceon Edgewood had placed his daughter in this school when she had been all of thirteen years old. That had been more than six years ago. And not once in all that time had he visited or even written her. The bank drafts arrived promptly each month in payment of tuition. Twice a year, additional money arrived for clothing and other necessities. Aside from that, there had been no correspondence at all, not even on the girl's birthdays.

"Is he well?" Morgana asked, thinking of nothing else to say in the face of this unusual occurrence.

Edith Appleby wet her narrow lips. "I assume he is," she answered slowly, toying with a cameo brooch on the collar of her dress. "Quite frankly, he didn't say."

A first nudge of uneasiness coursed through Morgana, caused more by Miss Appleby's attitude than her words. She had seldom seen the woman so disturbed. Could it be, she wondered, that her father had failed to send the money for her tuition? If so, it would be the first time. But the one thing she remembered most about her father was his distressing affinity for losing vast sums at the card table. Still, she thought to herself, keeping a wary eye on Miss Appleby, she could work here if need be. She could tutor. She would even work in the kitchen if she had to. Certainly the headmistress would allow her to do that. She had only six months to go before she would become a fully accredited teacher.

Clasping her hands before her, Miss Appleby's mouth set into firmness before she again spoke. "Your father wants you to return home," she murmured, not looking at Morgana. "Right away. He has made all the arrangements for your trip to," she picked up the letter again, "to Charleston, South Carolina."

Too stunned to speak, Morgana only stared at her. A forewarning chill crept up her spine, leaving tension in its wake. She sat quietly, not moving, trying to absorb the words she had just heard.

Miss Appleby sighed deeply as she stood up. "You'll have to leave today." Although her voice remained soft, she was genuinely irritated by this sudden turn of events. She knew how much Morgana wanted to stay on, to become a teacher. And the loss would be felt by the school, too. Good teachers were difficult to find, and Morgana had the instinct as well as the intellect.

Leave? Morgana was thinking, trying desperately to channel her whirling thoughts. Her father wanted her to come home—but *this* was her home. She had never even been to Charleston. She had been born in New York and had spent what seemed to her most of her life right here at Brookshire.

Morgana's eyes strayed to the diamond-paned window. Outside, the sun glistened on the Hudson River, less than a mile away. The school was situated on the west bank of the mighty waterway, just outside of Albany. Here and there, nestled in blue shadows, were stubborn patches of snow left over from last week's storm which the winter sun's weak rays had been unable to conquer. Her gaze shifted to the big oak tree, one of many on the well tended grounds. Its branches were bare now, but how many times during the past six years had she sat beneath its leafy boughs, to read, to study, to simply daydream. . . .

"Morgana!" Miss Appleby spoke sharply, alarmed by the pallor she was seeing. "Are you all right?"

Morgana shook off her reverie. "Yes, ma'am," she managed. She straightened in the chair and made a conscious effort to relax tautly held muscles. "You said I had to leave today." She looked up at the woman before her, the woman who was more familiar to her than any member of her own family had ever been. "It's just so . . . sudden." The words emerged choked and seemed to catch in her throat.

Looking a trifle embarrassed, Edith Appleby averted her face. "I know," she whispered. "The letter took several weeks to get here. In fact, it arrived yesterday—but . . . I wasn't here when it came. I read it only an hour ago . . ." Her voice trailed off and was replaced with another sigh.

"Does he say why he wants me to . . . leave here?" Morgana couldn't bring herself to say go home. Those words had no meaning for her.

"No, he made no mention of his reasons." Getting up, Miss Appleby walked to the other side of the desk and stood before Morgana. "Do you want to read it?" she asked, offering the letter.

Morgana shook her head. She didn't even want to touch it. What good would reading it do? she thought unhappily, clasping her hands tightly in her lap. It wouldn't alter the facts, wouldn't allow her to stay.

Standing there, the older woman picked up her glasses from the desk and put them on. "You had better pack," she murmured quietly. "A carriage is coming for you in about an hour. You'll be leaving on the next boat. I'm sorry, dear," she added earnestly, sensing the girl's distress. Coming closer, she bent forward, putting an arm about Morgana in a comforting way. "I know how much it meant to you to stay on here, to become a teacher. But apparently your father has other plans for you."

"I don't want to go to Charleston," Morgana protested, unable to stem the biting edge of resentment that crept into her voice. Why, she wondered angrily, hadn't her father continued to stay out of her life! She had gotten along very well without him all these years and was certain she would continue to do so.

The words produced a frown. Miss Appleby straightened, her expression stern. "You cannot disobey your father, Morgana," she admonished firmly. Visions of her personal selfless devotion to her own father flashed through her mind. The idea of familial disobedience was quite alien to her. "If you were legally of age," she went on, adopting a softer tone, "perhaps you could make your own decision. But since you are not, the subject doesn't bear further discussion."

Morgana made no comment, but her mouth was set obdurately, effectively conveying her disagreement. She knew that, with only a slight encouragement from the headmistress, she would do just that—disobey her father.

Edith Appleby's hand reached out, hovering in the air an instant as if it were going to rest on Morgana's shoulder. Then it moved in a helpless gesture. She bit her lower lip, letting her hand fall to her side. "I do admit, though, that it distresses me that you will be living in the South. A land of barbarians," she murmured, more to herself than to Morgana. Then she brightened and, for the first time, smiled. "But you'll see your father again. I'm sure you're looking forward to that, after all this time." She nodded encouragingly as Morgana stood up.

Morgana managed an appropriate phrase as she left the office, somewhat uncertain of the veracity of Miss Appleby's last statement. It had been so long, she couldn't quite remember what her father looked like; and even if she had, certainly he wouldn't look the same. Doubtless, she thought ruefully, *he* wouldn't even recognize *her*.

Slowly, as if she did not want to reach her destination, she walked back to her room. It accommodated four girls, but was spacious enough so as not to be cramped. The beds, two on either side of the room, were narrow but comfortable. Between each bed was a table with a flowered porcelain basin and ewer. The large window, framed with a starched white curtain, overlooked the rear gardens which now, in December, appeared lifeless, the oaks and elms long since having shed their vibrant coverings.

For six years this room had been home to Morgana Edgewood. She felt safe here. Her younger years had been spent moving from place to place as whim overtook her father. There was little warning when these changes occurred, only a brief order to pack. Then they would be gone.

Morgana's eyes swept over the empty room. The others had already gone to class. Desultorily, Morgana wondered what they thought of her absence. Fortunate in her good health, Morgana had never once missed a class in six years. She fought down her resentment, having long ago reached the conclusion that certain things in life were unlikely to change and, therefore, had to be accepted.

She sat down on the edge of her bed, absently running the palm of her hand across the uneven surface of the chenille spread. She stared at the changing pattern of sunlight and shadow that rippled across the polished wood floor. Then her brow furrowed in concentration as she tried to remember her father.

She had an image of a man who was tall and thin, who wore his clothes with an unusual degree of sophistication. His thinness was not so much inherent as it was due to a bout of consumption in his early years. He had never worked a day in his life.

In her very young years, Morgana had had no idea what her father did. This was not unusual, perhaps. Not all young children knew with a certainty what their fathers did for a living. Fathers went out to work and they came home.

The difference, in Morgana's case, was that her father went out to work mostly at night—sometimes all night—while Morgana remained in the care of the current housekeeper. They came and went, nameless women with long-forgotten faces who, sometimes after only a few weeks, left in a huff, presumably having discovered that Aleceon Edgewood was not, as he claimed, in the world of finance.

Gradually, as she grew older, Morgana became aware that most of her father's time was spent gambling. There were times when he won handsomely. However, everything he made soon found its way back to the card table, leaving them, at times, in dire straits.

While her father was on his way to a life he coveted, Morgana occupied her time as best she could. She read voraciously, a lot more than any child her age could be expected to do. She also embroidered. It gave her a sense of accomplishment, although most of the things she turned out wound up in her dresser drawer or were lost in moving from place to place.

It was during one of the impoverished times that her cousin, Caroline, had so unexpectedly appeared on their doorstep. That had been when they were living in Boston. Caroline, who was the only daughter of Aleceon's sister, Sarah, had wanted to rid herself of an unwanted child. Morgana's father had made all the arrangements, "assisting" his niece in her hour of need. Then he had tried to blackmail her. When Caroline's mother, Sarah Enright, had learned of all this, she had been justifiably furious with her brother. Both Morgana and her father had been ousted from Somerset Hall, the mansion in which the Enrights lived, and to which Morgana and her father had returned some months after Caroline's visit.

Morgana remembered all of that, but of course had never told anyone about it. Certainly not Miss Appleby, who, she was certain, would have been shocked by it all.

For the short time she had known her Aunt Sarah, Morgana had become very fond of that gracious lady. She thought her aunt returned her feelings; however, she was never entirely certain of that. Once, during these past six years, Morgana had almost written to Sarah Enright. In the end, however, she had torn up the letter. Her aunt had sent them both away; Morgana could only assume that she, like her father, was unwelcome in her aunt's house.

Now, this man . . . this stranger, really . . . wanted her back in his life. And what kind of a life? she wondered with growing apprehension.

Repressing her unease in a determined manner, Morgana got up and crossed the room. Opening the door of her wardrobe, she rummaged through its dim interior. Finally, way in the back, she located her portmanteau. She observed it critically; it wasn't in the best of shape.

Briskly then, without letting her mind dwell upon the coming days, Morgana packed her few belongings.

A short while later, a knock at the door made her turn and she saw Miss Appleby standing on the threshold, a heavy woolen shawl draped about her plump shoulders.

"The carriage is here, Morgana. Are you ready?"

Not trusting herself to speak, Morgana only nodded. Picking up her wool-lined pelisse, she shrugged her arms into it, then buttoned it with hands that were surprisingly steady.

As they walked from the room, Morgana resisted the urge for a backward glance at the haven she was leaving. There was not even time to say a few final words to her friends. And perhaps that was just as well, she reflected glumly. Good-byes were so . . . final. Even now, on her way to God knew what, there was in her mind the small flare of hope that perhaps she would be able to return. The holidays would soon be upon them. Everyone would be going home. This time, for the first time since she had come here, so would she. Maybe, like the others, she too could return.

They didn't speak as they headed downstairs. Morgana was grateful that the headmistress walked with her to the front driveway. It seemed to postpone, if only for a few moments, her departure into the unknown.

But at last they reached the waiting carriage. Morgana viewed it forlornly.

"Your father will meet you at the Charleston pier," Miss Appleby was saying brusquely, handing Morgana the letter. "I'm certain he will know what time the boat docks."

She hesitated, then put her arms about the young woman, giving her an affectionate hug. "Please write and let us know how you are."

"I will," Morgana promised, close to tears.

"And take care of yourself," Edith Appleby whispered, her eyes misting. "We will miss you."

The driver had hoisted her bag inside the vehicle and now assisted Morgana in entering.

As it moved away, Morgana waved a gloved hand. Turning, she looked out the rear window until long after the plump form of Edith Appleby had disappeared from view.

Finally, she faced forward, her expression resolute. She glanced only once at the envelope in her hand. Then, without reading it, placed it in her reticule.

Morgana had never wasted time wishing for what might have been, an attitude she considered both unrewarding and unproductive. To a certain point, she was fatalisitic, but that peak was reached only after she considered her options and alternatives.

Right now, it appeared that she had no other alternative than to obey her father's injunction. Her plans for her own future would simply have to be shelved for a year or two, she decided. But it would not be forever, she told herself. When she reached twenty-one, she would be her own mistress.

Settling back then, Morgana let her calm gaze drift over the softly rolling hills, determined that this interruption in her life would be of short duration.

Chapter
3

Standing on the deck of the steamboat, its side paddles chugging slowly through the clear blue water, Morgana Edgewood viewed the Charleston Harbor with little interest.

About her, the air was warm and humid, but not unpleasantly so due to a persistent breeze that alleviated both conditions. When she had left New York, it had been cold enough to feel the bite in the frequently gusty winds of December.

Here, it seemed almost like spring. Even flowers were in bloom, creating splashes of color among the pastel shades of the houses. In the distance, she could see sunshine warming slate and tiled roofs, tipping greenery and creating an occasional glitter of light upon a window pane.

The boat neared the shore, angling effortlessly alongside the jutting wooden pier. Seagulls swooped and squawked, flashes of white against blue sky and water as they brazenly approached the many fishing boats that dotted the bay.

Leaning forward on the railing, Morgana scanned the dock for any sign of her father. He was nowhere in sight.

Some twenty minutes later she stood uncertainly, portmanteau by her side, amidst boxes and crates, coils of rope, and milling people, all of whom seemed to have a purpose, a destination in mind.

With a deep sigh of annoyance she loosened the brown woolen shawl draped about her shoulders. The temperature was in the mid-seventies and her heavy clothing clung to her in a most uncomfortable manner. She peered about for any source of shade where she could get out from beneath the blazing sun. But there was only the ticket office and it appeared crowded.

Her annoyance sharpened. There was still no sign of her father. Briefly, she glanced at the small enameled watch pinned to her bodice. It was four-twenty in the afternoon. The boat had been on time; obviously her father wasn't.

"Miss Edgewood?"

The voice startled her. Turning, Morgana regarded the young man who was striding in her direction. "Yes. . . ."

Well, Griffin thought to himself, she's not ugly anyway. He'd had no trouble identifying her. She was the only unaccompanied woman on the pier. His eyes lingered on the heart-shaped face. Her skin was fair and as smooth as cream. She had a small but well defined mouth that, right now, was set primly. Her eyes were very blue, very direct, and were fringed with thick, silky lashes.

He frowned slightly at the sight of her blond hair which she wore pulled back into a severe, most unflattering bun at the nape of her neck. The golden mass was almost hidden beneath a straw bonnet the likes of which he hadn't seen in years. Nor was he impressed by the simple brown muslin dress she was wearing; even though half concealed by her woolen shawl, he could see that it, too, was hopelessly outdated. She was tall, standing a good five-feet, seven-inches—another minus to Griffin's way of thinking. He preferred small, petite women.

When she spoke, her voice was husky, low, not at all like the breathless, somewhat musical voices of the young women he knew.

"Yes?" she said again, a bit impatiently now. She couldn't imagine why the young man was staring at her as if he were taking inventory.

He inclined his head. "My name is Griffin Kynes. Your father couldn't be here to meet you. I've come in his stead."

"Is he ill?" she asked quickly. She looked up at him with some concern.

"No more than usual," he replied, offering no further explanation, not mentioning that Aleceon had long since drunk himself into a stupor.

Bending over, Griffin picked up the shabby portmanteau, then put his hand on her elbow, intending to propel her forward. To his acute surprise, she didn't move. Beneath the slight pressure of his hand, he could feel a rigorous resistance.

Griffin faltered, more than a bit flustered, and just stood there, feeling foolish.

"I don't even know you, sir." She frowned at him, her small mouth returning to primness as she drew away from his touch.

"I just told you who I am!" he responded sharply in a voice thick with exasperation. God, the woman was standing there as if he were about to assault her. She stood very still, eyes viewing him intensely, appearing to be judging his worth. From her expression, Griffin assumed that he didn't measure up too well.

The look, so direct and challenging, unnerved him. "How would I know your name and time of arrival if your father hadn't sent me?" he demanded, mentally cursing Aleceon Edgewood and his strange daughter—whom he was expected to marry!

"My father led me to believe that he would meet me," she insisted, holding her ground. "I have his letter . . ." She began to fumble within her reticule.

Griffin removed his hat and ran an agitated hand through his dark hair. He had wasted the whole blasted day in this foolishness. The drive into the city was three hours coming and three hours going.

He watched her a moment longer, making no effort to repress his irritation. "I don't give a damn about your letter," he exclaimed at last. Ignoring her zealous and indignant protests, Griffin again grasped her arm, this time with greater firmness.

About them, Negroes had ceased their work, travelers had paused in their tracks, and all were staring at the two young people, some with broad grins on their faces.

Griffin could feel his face redden and he clenched his teeth. His eyes fixed straight ahead as he almost dragged Morgana to the waiting carriage.

"Will you be still!" he hissed. "You're making a scene." He threw the portmanteau on the seat. With no warning, he put his hands around her waist, lifted her off her feet and deposited her, none too gently, next to it. Then he got in, seating himself opposite from her.

Her back stiff and straight as she sat down in the vehicle, Morgana glared at him, her eyes shimmering with the iridescence of sapphires. "I am unaccustomed to having strange men approach me," she retorted in clipped tones, quite affronted by his boorish behavior.

He cast a black look in her direction. "I can understand that," he muttered sarcastically, happy to see the flush that crept up her slim neck and stained her cheeks. Turning, he motioned briefly to Jude, who was seated on the driver's bench.

They fell into a strained silence as the carriage moved forward.

Surreptitiously, Morgana moved her head slightly, studying Griffin Kynes. He was, she observed, dressed somewhat informally, unaware that the white shirt, tan breeches and soft leather boots was the apparel he wore most days while on the plantation. He was tall, probably just over six feet. Although he was wearing a wide-brimmed hat, she could see that his hair was black and wavy, his sideburns cropped short. His jaw was square and clean shaven beneath dark eyes that were brooding, intelligent, speculative.

He was a most handsome man—and probably knew it, she decided, feeling an irritation she was hard pressed to explain.

"You indicated that my father was not feeling well," she prompted after a while. She tried not to frown. Something in his attitude set her teeth on edge.

Griffin regarded her coolly a moment before answering. "I did?" He seemed surprised. "There's nothing wrong with your father," he replied brusquely, turning away. "In fact, I suspect he has the heart of an ox," he added in a murmured, disinterested voice. With his thumb he pushed the hat further back on his head and settled himself more comfortably.

Somewhat put off by this callous disregard for her feelings, Morgana's mouth tightened again. She'd always heard that Southerners were supposed to be polite and hospitable. If Griffin Kynes was any indication, she thought ruefully, all the stories were false.

For a time, she studied the passing scenery. The dirt road they were traveling ambled alongside the Ashley River and was lined with live oaks and cypress trees, from which moss hung like tattered gray wisps of lace.

As they passed plantation after plantation, Morgana was struck by the run-down condition of most of the houses. Even the larger ones appeared to be in a state of some disrepair, needing at the very least a new coat of paint. In the fields, she could see the bent backs of the Negroes as they labored beneath the late afternoon sun. Quickly, she averted her eyes and moved restlessly. Like most Northerners, Morgana found the very idea of slavery reprehensible.

It appeared from her father's letter, which she had at last read on the boat, that her final destination was a place called Albemarle. Morgana wondered whether it would be like the houses she could see from the road. She wondered, too, whether it was tended by slaves. It wasn't a very comforting thought.

"I suppose you were unhappy to leave school on such short notice?"

Griffin's voice claimed her attention. Pensively, Morgana regarded him for a moment, feeling a fresh surprise at his obviously unfriendly manner. Although he had addressed her, he wasn't looking at her. His attention seemed focused on the passing landscape. She wondered whether he would even bother to repeat the question if she made no answer.

"I was," she replied at last. She couldn't quite repress her bitter tone, but if he took note of it, he made no comment. "I really don't understand why my father sent for me," she added. She stared at him, hoping for some enlightenment. Who was Griffin Kynes? she wondered. And what was his relationship to her father? Although, she reflected in her usual, practical manner, the fact that she didn't know any of her father's acquaintances was only to be expected under the circumstances.

Griffin observed her with his first show of interest. He hadn't quite believed that she didn't know of her father's plans, but he realized now that she really was unaware of the reason for her being here.

"How long has it been since you've seen Aleceon?" he asked her, feeling some curiosity.

"I've not seen my father since 1846 when he enrolled me in Brookshire."

He raised a brow at that. "Six years?" he murmured, taken aback.

She nodded curtly. "Six years." She gave him a fleeting glance that was glacial in its warning to bestow no pity upon her.

Pity was the last thing on Griffin's mind. He was simply surprised, for a sense of family was deep within him. He couldn't imagine not seeing Nathaniel or Cammy—much less a child of his own—for that length of time. Settling back, Griffin fell silent again, appearing lost in his own thoughts.

Morgana hesitated, then decided not to pursue the matter further. Instead she inquired, "How much farther do we have to go?"

"A distance," he replied, without turning his eyes in her direction. "But we should reach Albemarle by dark."

Another silence descended. Weary from four days of travel, Morgana began to doze.

At last she became aware that the carriage had left the road and was now proceeding up a long driveway, lined on both sides by massive oaks, the uppermost branches of which entwined, producing a shaded, living arch.

As they neared, Morgana's eyes widened as she took in the sight of the magnificent structure that sat in a clearing, aloofly unaware of the encroaching swamp and wood that surrounded it. Three stories high, it was ringed by a verandah on the lower floor and piazzas on the two upper levels. Tall white columns rose majestically from the ground to the second story. The whole building was suffused with lilac in the gathering twilight.

The carriage halted and Griffin got out, extending a hand in her direction. "Come along," he said peremptorily, leading her up the wide front steps.

The door opened before they reached it. A tall Negro, somewhat on in years but bearing himself with a quiet dignity, smiled at them as they entered the large and spacious foyer.

Glancing up, Morgana noted with some surprise that the ceiling extended all the way to the second floor. From it were suspended two immense crystal chandeliers that splayed prismed candlelight on the parquet flooring. Several hall tables were positioned evenly on either side of the foyer, and all bore live poinsettia plants, the vivid red of the lush leaves displaying splashes of color so vibrant it seemed to glow.

"Will you be wantin' supper, masta, suh?" Thomas was inquiring pleasantly, addressing his question to Griffin, but viewing Morgana with open curiosity.

"The others have eaten?"

"Yassuh."

"Very well, we'll eat now. Put Miss Edgewood's baggage in her room." His eyes returned to Morgana. "Both my grandfather and my sister have apparently retired. I hope you don't mind if we dine alone." He said the words as if it really didn't matter to him whether she minded or not. Turning, he began to walk away.

Irked by his blatant arrogance, Morgana clasped her hands loosely at her waist and raised her chin defiantly. Surely, she thought, this man didn't expect her to follow him every time he issued a command!

"I would like to see my father first," she stated calmly, not moving from where she stood.

Halting, Griffin turned and gave her a brief glance that held more than a little exasperation. He had assumed, from the way Aleceon had spoken, that his daughter was unsophisticated, innocent, perhaps just a trifle gauche. What he found was a young woman who handled herself with a cool assurance, was candid and straightforward to an almost embarrassing degree. She seemed incapable of dissimulating, even for the sake of propriety. His mouth twitched with annoyance at his discovery. He was not especially thrilled at the prospect of being saddled with a wife who displayed such unfeminine traits.

They stared at each other for a moment longer. Griffin was the first to look away.

"Thomas," he said to the Negro, "see if Master Edgewood is awake. We'll be in the dining room." He began to walk away again, not looking back at Morgana.

With little recourse, Morgana removed her shawl and bonnet and placed them carefully on a nearby table. Then she followed Griffin across the spacious hall into a large and airy dining room.

On the south wall, she saw that French doors led out onto the verandah. The west wall was almost entirely taken up by two wide and tall windows framed by dark red velvet draperies. The high backed chairs, table, and sideboard were all made of dark, richly carved teakwood.

The only light came from two brass candelabrums that rested on the long table, which was now in the process of being covered with more food than two people could possibly eat.

As Morgana sat down in a chair held by a young Negro who could be no more than ten years old, she realized that she was very hungry. She hadn't eaten since noon, and that had been no more than a small bowl of stew so highly seasoned as to be virtually impalatable.

But as famished as she was, Morgana took the time to note the snowy white and finely embroidered linen cloth, the gleaming silver, the delicate crystal and the gold-bordered china that graced the table. She had only once before in her entire life seen such opulence, and that had been in her aunt's house at Somerset Hall.

They had no sooner settled themselves than Thomas appeared.

"Masta Edgewood is asleep, suh," he offered in his quiet

voice, his body bending forward in just the suggestion of a bow. "Shall he be wakened?"

"Oh, no," Morgana replied before Griffin could speak. "Please don't disturb him. I'll see him in the morning." Although she refrained from showing it, she was now truly annoyed with her father. He had known she was arriving today. Even if he couldn't have made it into Charleston, the least he could have done was stay awake and greet her when she had gotten here.

As they began to eat, Griffin allowed himself a small sigh, suspecting that his grandfather had purposefully absented himself, and probably had instructed Cammy to stay in her room as well. Doubtless the old man reasoned that Griffin could use the time alone with his bride-to-be.

Good Lord, Griffin thought to himself, pushing the food around his plate with his fork. How did he ever get himself involved in all this? He wasn't even sure he liked this woman. She certainly didn't know how to talk to a man, to make him feel at ease. All of the young women he knew had been carefully prepared in the social graces of conversation and flirting; they could compliment a man with a sidelong glance or a graceful flutter of their fan.

But this one ... There was a sense of independence about her that he found disconcerting.

Griffin shook his head, his lean, angular face beset with conflicting emotions. He was sorely tempted to rush upstairs and throttle Aleceon Edgewood, to evict both him and his daughter from Albemarle. Unobtrusively, he darted a black scowl at the young woman seated beside him, but her attention was elsewhere and she didn't notice.

And, viewing her almost perfect profile, Griffin made up his mind.

He *didn't* like her.

The thought so depressed him that suddenly his whole future loomed, empty and bleak. Lifting some of the food to his mouth, Griffin tasted antagonism, clenching his teeth while it settled in his stomach like an alien intruder bent on disturbing him. He wiped his mouth with his napkin and barely repressed a groan of despair.

The silence lengthened.

For a time, Morgana was unsettled by the constant presence of servants. She was unused to being waited upon in what she considered an excessive manner. The boy who had held her chair, and whose name, she learned, was Suky, was now standing behind it, waving a palmetto fan over her. Since the weather was not especially warm now that the sun had set, she reasoned that his purpose was more to keep the flies away than to offer a cooling breeze. A young, light-skinned man, about twenty, hovered constantly at her side, offering bowls and platters at intervals, refilling her cup with coffee as soon as she took a sip. His counterpart was doing the same for Griffin. Both young men were wearing black jackets with matching trousers and white gloves that could be termed no less than immaculate. At intervals, one or the other of them would disappear into the kitchen, which seemed to be just off the dining room, only to appear moments later with still more food.

There was chicken, fried, crispy, tempting; there was a huge platter of shrimp, tiny and succulent and pink; and there were mounds and mounds of rice—Morgana was to learn that it was served with every meal, including breakfast. In addition, there was red gravy, okra, corn, and sweet potatoes. Biscuits with the steam still rising from fluffy centers together with butter and jam were placed at arm's length, but Morgana never had to reach for them. They were personally offered to her by the attentive servant, who somehow seemed to know whenever she was about to make a move. And finally, there was coffee served with a cream so rich and thick it floated on the surface of the steaming concoction.

To Morgana, it all seemed a terrible waste.

Seeing her expression and apparently guessing at her thoughts, Griffin spoke.

"The leftovers go to the house servants," he told her, his tone short. "I assure you, the food will not be wasted."

She bent her head, staring at her plate, embarrassed that he had caught her disapproval. Quickly, she changed the subject. "You don't speak like a Southerner, Mr. Kynes," she observed in her low, well modulated voice. More than one of her classmates at Brookshire had been from the South. All had spoken with a soft, lilting accent that was barely noticeable in his voice.

"I'd prefer that you call me Griffin," he stated, leaning back in his chair as the plates were cleared away. "Adam, bring me a glass of Madeira," he said to one of the servants, then regarded Morgana questioningly, but she shook her head.

"I was born here in this very house," he went on in answer to her observation. "My grandfather came to the Carolinas from England. When I was seven, he hired a tutor for me. When I was fourteen, I was sent back to England, to Oxford, to complete my education."

Morgana raised a brow. "Isn't that unusual?"

"Not at all," he replied, sipping his wine. "There are no adequate schools in the Carolinas." He made a vague gesture. "And even if there were, I suspect that my grand-father would still have sent me back there. Being an Englishman, he regards all schools as inferior to Oxford."

"Your father . . ." Morgana began tentatively.

"My father died fifteen years ago, of smallpox. My mother died some years before that, giving birth to my sister."

"I'm sorry," Morgana whispered.

He regarded her for a moment, then asked, "And what of Brookshire—you did say that was the name of the Academy you attended?"

She nodded. "I consider it a fine school."

"A sort of finishing school?" he suggested with a faint smile.

Morgana heard the slight edge of condescension in his voice as he made that assumption, and couldn't help but smile at the thought of Miss Appleby's reaction to that statement. Few things had infuriated the headmistress more than having her academy classed in such a manner.

"I hardly think it could be termed that," she murmured at last, thinking of all the hours she had spent with her head bent over a book on history or geography, not to mention mathematics and classical literature.

A dark brow arched skeptically. "You were not taught how to dance or play the piano?"

She kept the smile in check, allowing her blue eyes to widen with assumed innocence. "Oh, yes. Yes, as a matter of fact, I was. I can also embroider beautifully."

He looked a bit smug, apparently satisfied that he'd been right in his assumption.

Morgana's eyes were lighted with mischievous amuse-ment as she sipped at her coffee. Looking up just then, she saw a woman standing in the doorway that led to the kitchen, her brown face wreathed in smiles.

"Wantin' to know if ever'thin' be all right, masta, suh." Although she addressed her question to Griffin, her dark eyes were upon Morgana.

Glancing at the woman, Griffin couldn't contain a rueful smile, knowing full well that the cook was merely satisfying her own curiosity. The whole household, of course, knew why Morgana was here.

"As usual, everything was very good," Griffin replied solemnly, nodding his head. He turned toward Morgana. "This is Minda," he explained. "She not only does the cooking, she runs the whole household. She's a bit of a Tartar, I'm afraid." He grinned affectionately at the Negress. "But we all put up with it because, frankly, she's the best cook in these parts."

The compliment produced such a delighted chortle that Morgana had to smile at the boisterous sound. Minda, she saw, was positively statuesque, lacking only about an inch to reach a full six feet. She was a handsome, robust looking woman, big boned, but not fat, and appeared to be about thirty-five years old. Above a red calico dress with a white fichu at the neck, her woolly hair was cropped so short that it gave the appearance of a tight black cap about her well-shaped skull.

Behind Morgana, Suky was grinning impishly at his mother, trying to suppress his ready laughter, which had a tendency to erupt at the most awkward times. Minda caught the look and scowled at her youngest son, effectively silencing any giggle that might emerge.

"Dat boy o' mine actin' uppity, suh?" Minda asked

Griffin. She had only recently installed Suky as a houseboy.

"He's doing just fine," Griffin assured her.

"He bettah . . ." Minda threw the boy an ominous look. "Paddle him so's he cain't set down fer a week iffen he doan mind his manners." She again regarded Morgana, now smiling broadly, showing a full set of white and perfect teeth.

"I can't remember when I've had such an enjoyable meal," Morgana said sincerely.

The woman looked long and hard at Morgana. Then, issuing another sound of glee, she turned and left the dining room.

In some perplexity, Morgana glanced at Griffin, who seemed to have noticed nothing unusual. He was placidly staring into space. Perhaps, she thought, it was not unusual for the cook to enter the dining room to view guests.

The room was quiet again. Griffin sipped his wine. Morgana toyed with her spoon.

After some minutes passed, she asked, "What connection does my father have with Albemarle?" The short and bitter laugh that greeted her question generated startled confusion on her part. Griffin Kynes, she decided, was the strangest man she had ever met.

"I suppose you might say that he owns twenty percent of it," Griffin observed acidly. He finished his wine, then got to his feet. "I know that you must be tired. I'll have Thomas show you to your room. Tomorrow, when you are rested, I'll take you on a tour of Albemarle."

She nodded slowly, but was still confused. None of her

questions thus far had been answered satisfactorily. It was most annoying.

Getting up, she followed the Negro—whom she assumed was a sort of butler—up the wide, curving staircase and along the landing. Finally he paused, opening a door with a smile and a bow of his graying head.

Entering, Morgana viewed her accommodations with a pleased eye.

It was, actually, two rooms. There was a bedroom of a goodly size, the wooden floor of which was highly veneered and partly covered with a braided rug, and which contained a four-poster, a wardrobe, a dressing table, and a japanned chiffonier. The ceilings were high, fully eighteen feet, she guessed. Separated by an archway was a sitting room, furnished with a wicker chair, a divan, and a writing table. This smaller room led out onto the piazza.

In some surprise, Morgana saw that her portmanteau had already been unpacked, the clothes hung in the wardrobe, her few personal possessions laid out atop the dresser.

A young woman came forward, smiling expectantly. Her skin, although dark, was not black; it was a warm brown with a slightly reddish tint to it. She appeared to be about eighteen years old.

"I'se Bella, miss," she announced, nodding her head and nervously fingering the white apron she wore over her black cotton dress.

Morgana blinked. "I . . . don't really need a maid," she protested with a small laugh of embarrassment.

The young woman put a hand to her mouth and giggled. "Ain' no maid, miss," she replied, shaking her head. "I'se yore wench. Masta Griffin give me to you."

Morgana's eyes darkened with a sudden surge of anger.

57

How dare that man assume she would accept a slave, she thought indignantly.

"Well," she retorted tartly, "you can return to *Master* Griffin and tell him that I'm quite capable of caring for myself."

The girl's nervousness increased and she took a step back. "Cain't go, miss," she whispered, almost in tears. "Masta Griffin whip me fer shoah iffen he thinks I doan take care of you prop'ly."

The girl looked so dismayed and upset that Morgana could only stand there in ashamed contrition. "I'm sorry," she murmured, quickly deciding to contain anymore impulsive comments. "I . . . of course you may stay." Morgana fought a feeling of helplessness. Oh, that man! she thought, clenching her small hands into fists. Never in her life had she met someone who annoyed her as much as did Griffin Kynes.

Appearing visibly relieved by the decision, Bella began to bustle happily about the room, turning down the bed and laying out Morgana's nightclothes with exaggerated care.

Shaking her head with resigned acceptance, Morgana walked out onto the piazza. Leaning on the iron railing, she surveyed her surroundings in mounting appreciation.

The moon had already risen, hanging in a purple sky that was lavishly decorated with brilliant stars. The moss looked silvery. Just below her room, a huge magnolia tree shone milky white.

Only a few days ago, Morgana thought to herself as she looked about, she had been in New York, feeling the biting threat of winter; now she was here, in a sort of fairyland, a place touched by the warmth of spring despite the contradiction of the calendar.

And *why* was she here? Why hadn't her father met her? Why had he sent a stranger to fetch her?

Questions bumped and jogged in her mind—and all had no answer.

Oddly, Morgana was aware of a slight stirring of homesickness. But for what? she asked herself dourly. Brookshire was a school, not a home. Miss Appleby was a headmistress, not the surrogate mother Morgana had occasionally thought her to be.

She sighed, taking a deep breath of the sweet-scented night. Griffin had made mention of a sister, she recalled. Perhaps, with another woman around, she wouldn't feel so lonely.

Then Morgana remembered Griffin's offer to show her around Albemarle tomorrow and she wondered if he felt some obligation toward her to make her feel welcome.

That thought she dismissed as soon as it came to her. Whatever else Griffin Kynes felt, it certainly wasn't the need to make her feel welcome. She couldn't remember the last time she had met such a cold, unfeeling person. He was quite insufferable, really.

And how had it come about, she further speculated, that her father owned twenty percent of Albemarle? From what Griffin had told her, he had been born here. Had Griffin or his grandfather sold a part of their plantation to her father? If so, for what possible reason?

Finally, feeling the night air cool on her arms, Morgana turned and went back inside to the bedroom, somewhat daunted by the futility of her thoughts. Everything would just have to wait until morning. There was nothing she could do tonight, she decided. She suddenly felt very tired and wanted only to sleep.

The young Negro girl came toward her. Reaching out, she calmly began to undo the buttons on Morgana's dress.

Startled, Morgana quickly raised a hand. "What are you doing?" She took a step away, holding her bodice together with both hands.

Bella was confounded by the reaction, surprise and confusion playing across her dark face. For the moment she couldn't even think of a reply.

"Helps you undress?" she said at last, the tentative response sounding more like a question than an answer.

"I do not need anyone to help me undress," Morgana declared emphatically. As if to prove her statement, she walked determinedly toward the four-poster and began to remove her outer clothes. Down to her shift at last, she paused a moment, waiting for Bella to leave the room. When the girl showed no signs of doing so, Morgana uttered a brief sigh of resignation. Doffing the rest of her attire, she quickly put on her nightdress.

When she was at last settled in bed, Bella extinguished the lamps.

With another, deeper sigh, Morgana snuggled down in the softness and fell asleep almost immediately.

Chapter
4

The following morning, Morgana opened her eyes, feeling well rested, but with a sense of it being very early. She stretched, luxuriating in the softness for a moment, then awareness came to her, making her conscious of the unfamiliar surroundings.

Outside in the rosy tinted dawn, dogs were barking, the high spirited sound being punctuated by roosters, who were not to be outdone in the greeting of a new and bright day.

Somewhere a bell was being rung with tedious monotony, and Morgana knew that this was what had awakened her.

Bella, too, got up. In some surprise, Morgana saw that the dark-skinned girl had spent the night on a pallet at the foot of her bed.

"Gits you warm water, miss," the girl announced. She

bobbed her head and quickly left the room as if to forestall any protest.

She was back in a few minutes, lugging a pail of warm water which she poured into a porcelain basin. With almost methodical precision, she laid soap and towels within easy reach, then crossed the room to the wardrobe. Opening the panelled door, Bella viewed the collection of plain dresses for a long moment, almost shaking her head in despair. In her considered opinion, not one of the garments was suitable for a lady to wear. Hesitating, she threw Morgana a questioning look.

Having gotten out of bed, Morgana was now washing herself, quite unaware that the black girl was waiting for instructions.

"What you wants to wear dis mornin', miss?" Bella finally ventured into the silence.

Pausing, Morgana regarded her, frowning slightly, hoping she wouldn't have to go through the same ritual as last night. She sighed with resignation. "The dark blue muslin will be fine, thank you," she murmured.

Bella removed the chosen dress from the wardrobe and contemplated it doubtfully. It didn't look so fine to her. Aside from the somewhat common material from which it was made, it didn't have so much as a bow or a piece of lace to relieve the plainness. Miss Cammy, she thought, would have long since discarded a dress like this one—if she had even thought to buy it in the first place.

A while later, having washed and dressed, Morgana sat at the lovely rosewood dressing table, twisting her shining blond hair into its customary knot. At the sound of a knock on the door, she looked up.

"Come in," she called out, turning.

The door opened. Tentatively, Morgana smiled at the sight of the beautiful young girl who entered. Her hair was black and very fine. Dark brown eyes fringed with black lashes were set in an exquisitely proportioned face. She was dressed in what looked, to Morgana, like a ballgown, with yards and yards of silk and lace surrounding a crinolined skirt.

"Good morning," the girl said, dimpling. "I'm Camellia Kynes—Cammy. You must be Aleceon's daughter."

Morgana acknowledged that as the girl came further into the room. She sat down on the edge of the bed, her dark eyes bright with curiosity.

Her grandfather had, only last night, told Cammy of their financial difficulties—a thing she hadn't known about until now. His reference to mortgages held little meaning for her; she had only the vaguest notion as to what that entailed. But her grandfather had been most emphatic as to her silence on this whole matter. Apparently, Griffin planned to marry this young woman, thereby solving all their problems. That was enough to gain Cammy's acceptance.

Cammy had this while been watching Morgana as she put the finishing touches to her hairdo. "Why are you doing that?" she asked at last, tilting her small head.

Turning slightly in the chair, Morgana regarded her in surprise. "Doing what?"

"Your hair," Cammy responded with a small gesture. "Bella is very good at it."

"Why, I've always done it myself." Morgana's face reflected amusement. She began to wonder if women in this part of the country did anything at all for themselves.

Cammy looked a bit surprised at that, but decided not to

pursue the matter. "Will you be staying with us?" she asked.

Morgana nodded. "I guess I will be. Is that all right?"

"Oh, yes," the girl responded with unfeigned enthusiasm. "Sometimes I get bored when we're here. Nobody talks about anything but rice and darkies. When we're in the town house, things are much more interesting."

"I presume that would be in Charleston?" Morgana speculated.

"Yes. We'll all be going there next week," the girl added. Her voice a trifle breathless with her enthusiasm over the coming event, Cammy then proceeded to tell Morgana of her coming debut at Saint Cecelia's in January.

"Perhaps I'll be staying here," Morgana noted doubtfully when she was through.

"Oh, no. No one stays at the plantation during the holidays. Or the summer months, either—it's the fever, you know."

Morgana didn't know. The imagined vision produced a trace of bewilderment. "You mean everyone goes—even the slaves?"

That produced a delighted laugh from the seventeen-year-old girl. "My goodness, no. Only the house servants come with us."

"But don't they catch the fever if they stay here during the summer?"

Cammy shook her head, her glossy black curls swinging freely with the motion. "Swamp fever doesn't affect them," she explained. "For some reason, they never get it. Of course, Mr. Dobbs, our overseer, remains here. The people can't be left unsupervised. They do nothing unless they're told to."

"What about Mr. Dobbs's health?" Morgana picked up her enameled watch from the dresser and pinned it on her bodice.

Cammy shrugged delicately, as if the thought held little interest. "He's careful, I suppose. He doesn't go outside at night." She gave Morgana a charming smile, then went on to ask, "Have you had your breakfast yet?"

"No," Morgana admitted. "Actually, I had hoped to see my father first. Do you know if he is awake?"

Cammy turned to the hovering Bella and waved a hand. "Go and see . . ." She regarded Morgana again, with a suddenly critical eye, noting that the young woman wore neither hoop nor stay beneath her plain blue muslin dress. "Is that what they wear in the North?"

It was said in such a guileless manner that Morgana issued a small laugh, unable to take offense. "Yes. Although I daresay it's a bit outdated," she added with a sigh.

Cammy pursed her rosy lips. "Well, we'll have to get to work then. You'll not be able to wear anything like that when we get to Charleston."

"Why ever not?" Morgana asked in some surprise. She looked down at her dress, which she considered quite serviceable.

"Oh, it won't do. It won't do at all." Cammy was most emphatic. Standing up, she twirled about, her hooped skirt billowing about her in a most appealing way. "Have you ever worn hoops?" she asked, standing quietly again. When Morgana shook her head, Cammy gave a small sigh. "Well then, we'll have to have a few lessons, I suppose."

"To wear a dress?" Morgana laughed delightedly at the

ridiculous notion, both captivated and amused by the young girl.

"Oh, yes," Cammy responded seriously. "If you're not careful . . . well, you'll see. My wench, Meg, is very good with a needle. We can alter some of my dresses for you until you get your own." Privately, Cammy was thinking that something would have to be done with Morgana's hair as well as her clothes, but she decided to say nothing about that right now, fearing her remarks might seem rude.

Before Morgana could reply, Bella returned with the information that Aleceon was awake and waiting to see his daughter.

Promising Cammy that they would finish their discussion at another time, Morgana hurried from her room. Following Bella's directions, she knocked on her father's door a short time later.

Entering the room, which she noted was similar to her own except that it faced the rear of the house, she saw him standing by the window. He was dressed in dove gray trousers and a white shirt, over which he wore a black silk vest. A matching cravat was tied neatly around the collar, but he was jacketless.

"Father . . ." Morgana greeted Aleceon quietly, trying to mask her shock at the sight of him.

With her first look at the man she hadn't seen in six years, remembrance flooded Morgana's mind. But how, she wondered uneasily, was it possible for a man to have aged so much in such a relatively short time? He was so thin, she doubted he weighed much more than she did. His face was drawn, almost haggard, the lines on his forehead and around his nose and mouth deeply etched. His color, too, appeared unhealthy.

Aleceon saw the look she tried so hard to conceal and met it with a wry smile. He'd had an especially bad day yesterday; even the laudanum hadn't helped. It had taken almost a full bottle of brandy to dull the pain and provide the blessed oblivion that offered a few hours respite. Most days he felt reasonably well. Only twice before during his illness had he experienced such a day, but he knew with a terrible certainty that those times would appear more and more in the weeks to come.

"I've had a bout with the fever," he offered by way of explanation. "It's a hazard in this part of the country."

Still uneasy, Morgana gave a small nod. She made no move toward him and stood there, feeling a trifle awkward. Her father was far from a demonstrative person and she knew perfectly well that he would neither kiss nor hug her in greeting. And she knew too that if she made the effort he would merely move away from her.

Aleceon studied her for a long moment, noting with a bit of surprise that she was no longer a child, that she had grown into a lovely young woman. She'd been thirteen when he'd last seen her; somehow, that last image had always remained with him.

"You're looking well," he said quietly, still regarding her.

Morgana found that she really couldn't say the same thing about him. "Are you certain that you are not ill?" she persisted, her brow furrowing in concern. She took a step closer to him.

"I'm not ill," he contradicted irritably in a tone she suddenly remembered so well.

Flustered, she looked about, her eyes resting on the Negro who stood discreetly by the door. He was dark-skinned, with gentle brooding eyes that, right now, were fixed, not on her, but on her father.

Seeing the direction of her glance, Aleceon commented, "His name is Ben. He belongs to me. We've been together for a long time."

She paled and her eyes widened expressively. "You mean you own a slave?" she exclaimed, incredulous.

Glancing toward Ben, Aleceon raised a quizzical brow. "Are you unhappy?" The thought seemed to hold some amusement for him.

The Negro's mouth stretched into a wide grin. "Not since I bin wit you, suh."

Morgana noticed that the smile didn't reach the dark velvety eyes which looked inexplicably saddened. Yet she sensed the man was telling the truth. The realization, however, provided only a small comfort. Somehow she had never envisioned her father as owning slaves, even though she knew he had lived in the South for the past six years.

Turning, Aleceon saw her shocked expression and pursed his lips. "My dear, you're no longer in the North," he pointed out dryly. "Please, for both our sakes, don't bring your abolitionist notions with you down here. I've seen men tarred and feathered for making remarks against the South's peculiar institution."

Morgana bit her lower lip. How was she going to be able to live in this strange place? she wondered. She longed for the comfort of her studies, the sameness of Brookshire, and again vowed that her absence would be only temporary.

"How is old stoneface?" her father asked then. At her blank look, he enlarged, "Miss Appleby."

Morgana appeared surprised, then her fair skin flushed

with annoyance. "She's one of the kindest people I know," she protested, upset with her father's disparaging remark.

"If you think that, then I'm glad I took you out of there," he commented with a short laugh. "The woman's a gargoyle. . . ."

Morgana's color deepened with outrage. "I will not have you speak of her that way. If it hadn't been for her, I can't imagine how I would have gotten through those first years." Her tone became accusatory. "You never came to see me, or wrote. . . ."

She fell silent at the sight of his suddenly closed look. She hadn't seen her father in six years, she reminded herself sternly. Now was not the time to argue.

"I was busy," he offered bluntly. "As for Miss Appleby's kindness, I assure you, my dear, the woman was well paid for her efforts." He gave her a sharp look. "Your tuition was higher than anyone else's. Did you know that?" he demanded. "Your precious Miss Appleby at first refused to take you; didn't think you were good enough."

At her look of dismay, his expression softened. "Well, it was a long time ago. The woman has served her purpose. But that is all behind you now."

Morgana viewed her father with a level look. "Why have you sent for me?" She sat down on a nearby chair, arranging the folds of her skirt without taking her eyes from his.

Mock surprise drifted across his face. "Don't you think it was about time?" he retorted with a rare display of humor. "Surely you didn't expect to spend the rest of your life in that school."

She lowered her head slightly. "It was so sudden, I thought there might be a reason . . ." Her expression grew intent and she inhaled deeply. "Why didn't you meet me yesterday?"

Walking toward the pier mirror, Aleceon adjusted his cravat more to his liking before commenting, "The drive into Charleston is long and tiring, as you've probably discovered for yourself. And, as I have already told you, I'm recovering from a bout of the fever. It tends to sap a man's strength for months on end."

"I'm sorry," she murmured quietly. "I hadn't realized. . . ."

"Never mind, it's of no matter," he dismissed her apology. Turning, he viewed her in silence a moment. Then, in a deceptively casual voice, he asked, "How do you like Albemarle?"

Her brow furrowed. "I haven't seen much of it yet," she replied. "Mr. Kynes—Griffin—has promised to take me on a tour of it today." She paused a moment, then went on to ask, "Are we to live here?"

He nodded briefly, shrugging his arms into the jacket held by Ben.

"But why?" She made a gesture as she got to her feet. "Who are these people? Why are we living in their house?"

"You're certainly full of questions, aren't you?" He passed a hand under his chin thoughtfully. "Nathaniel Kynes and I are . . . old friends," he explained carefully. "I've lived here, on and off, for the past two years."

"Griffin said you owned twenty percent of this . . . plantation."

He nodded again, buttoning his jacket. "I own the mortgage." He smiled at her surprise. "You are, in fact, a wealthy young woman, Morgana." Extending his hand, he took her arm, leading her toward the door. "Let's get some breakfast. There's no need for you to know the details. Down here, it's considered bad form for a young woman to interest herself in financial matters. Southern belles are far too delicate to be concerned with such things."

"I'm not a Southern belle," Morgana murmured in some annoyance, but her father seemed not to hear her words.

As they entered the dining room a few minutes later, Morgana saw that Griffin and Cammy were already at the table. The girl flashed a bright smile, but Griffin merely offered a brief nod.

The older man seated to Griffin's right she presumed to be their grandfather. He immediately got to his feet. Coming forward, he bowed slightly. Taking her hand, he raised it to his lips while Morgana just stood there in startled surprise.

The man studied her for an uncomfortably long moment, a scrutiny Morgana was at a loss to explain since it seemed more intense than the moment warranted. Then he smiled broadly.

"I'm Nathaniel Kynes," he said. "It's a pleasure to have such a lovely young lady in my home." His head bobbed in approval, and some relief. There didn't appear to be anything wrong with her that he could see. In fact, he thought her quite lovely.

Morgana returned his smile, liking him instantly, and allowed him to lead her to a chair.

Again she marveled at the repast. There were steaming platters of scrambled eggs, fried ham, oysters, and those delectable looking hot biscuits. Dainty bowls of preserves, honey, and butter rested beside grits and red gravy, which

Morgana had never before eaten, and which her father urged her to try.

"I hope your trip was a pleasant one," Nathaniel said to her as they began to eat. "It's been some years since I've been in the North," he went on conversationally, not waiting for her answer. "Too much hustle and bustle." He looked toward his grandson, who had resumed eating. "Griffin, it might be a good idea for you to show Miss Morgana about the grounds today."

Griffin nodded, a bit curtly, Morgana thought. "I plan to," he replied brusquely, then regarded Morgana with cool eyes. "Can you ride a horse?"

"No, I'm afraid not," Morgana responded with a small laugh.

"Oh, it isn't difficult at all," Cammy put in. "Let her ride Lady, Griffin," she suggested, turning briefly toward her brother. "She's very gentle, you'll have no problem," she added to an apprehensive Morgana. "I'll lend you one of my riding habits until we can have one made for you."

Tentatively, Morgana nodded, not at all certain she wanted to ride a horse. As far as she was concerned, horses were for hauling carriages and ploughs.

Later that morning, however, having donned the borrowed outfit, Morgana sat sidesaddle, holding on to the pommel for dear life, only half listening to Griffin as he gave her a few brief instructions.

"No need for you to be concerned," he assured her. He mounted his own horse with practiced ease. "Lady is so old she won't go faster than a walk no matter how you prod her on."

Morgana was viewing him with some doubt. She had the disturbing sense of being high off the ground and suffered a moment's vertigo which, thankfully, quickly passed. However, she refused to release her hold on the pommel.

Amusement flickered across Griffin's face as he watched her. She was sitting straight backed and stiffly, as though perched on something precariously fragile.

"Relax," he advised, gripping the reins of his own horse. "You just might enjoy it."

And, much to her surprise, she did. After the first frightening moments when the horse began to move, Morgana's taut muscles began to ease. After another ten minutes passed, she actually began to observe her surroundings.

The game, she noted, was extensive. Mostly small animals and a profusion of birds that was quite awesome. They swooped and wheeled, chattering noisily, creating a panorama of color that was exceeded only by the exotic array of flowers.

After they had ridden about half a mile, Griffin reined in his horse, then pointed ahead. "These are the rice fields. Each field is some fifteen acres in size and divided by those embankments."

She studied the neat, muddy patchwork. "Why are they separated like that?"

"So that one field can be flooded independently of those around it," he replied. "Unlike cotton or sugar, rice takes a great deal of water."

She regarded the scene for many moments, watching as women raked piles of rubble together, then proceeded to burn it.

Seeing her absorbed attention, Griffin went on to explain, "They're destroying what's left of the last crop, as well as any weeds or refuse that might have accumulated.

When they're through, the area will be clean and ready to receive the new seed. Come along." He nudged his horse forward.

She followed—or rather, Lady did—as he led the way through the field to another, some distance away. Here, men were ploughing, creating neat furrows that dissected the land with almost geometric precision.

"Do they work at this all day long?" Morgana was beginning to feel the heat of the sun on her back and wondered what is was like in the summer.

Griffin glanced at her. "All day," he affirmed. "Work begins at sunrise."

"When do they eat?"

"Breakfast is brought to them about eight o'clock, the midday meal about noon. Usually, they finish about four in the afternoon. After that, the remainder of the day can be spent in tending to their own patches."

"They have their own land?" Morgana asked. She viewed him in some surprise.

"Sort of," he smiled. "The land, of course, belongs to my grandfather. But we usually assign a quarter-acre to each worker to farm as his own. The produce can be kept for their own use or sold. How well they do depends, of course, on how quickly they complete their task."

"Task?"

Griffin steadied his spirited horse before he replied. "Every hand has a certain amount of work to accomplish in the course of the day. When he's finished, his day is over." He peered about, then pointed. "Look there—see those hands digging ditches?" At her nod, he continued. "They're assigned six hundred feet a day. It's a fair system," he insisted, seeing her dubious expression. "Darkies are lazy; some more than others. If we were to allow a gang to work at their own pace, some would work hard and others would laze away the day, not pulling their own weight. In this way, each one does the same amount of work in his own good time."

They continued to tour the plantation for another hour, Griffin explaining any question she might have, then they began to head back toward the Great House.

"I take it you have reservations about slavery," Griffin commented at one point. He angled his horse closer and now rode at her side.

She detected the coolness in his voice but, nevertheless, she answered truthfully. "I cannot see why you must own them," she murmured. "Wouldn't it be just as easy to hire them, to pay them a wage?"

He seemed to seriously consider that. Actually, Griffin was unaccountably filled with a sense of discomfort, of being on the defensive—and before a woman! He was torn between grim amusement and wariness. The cool assurance she displayed nudged a grudging respect from him. He knew very well that she had been impressed by Albemarle the day before. But she had entered as if she belonged, as if she were used to the scope. There was nothing in her attitude to indicate that she might be out of her element. She had lived six years in a school. No matter how exclusive, he reasoned, it was still a school. Yet she conducted herself with a comportment that struck him as—regal.

Ignoring her comment, Griffin asked, "How much do you think it costs to feed and clothe our people for one year?"

The question took her by surprise. "I . . . have no idea," she confessed, turning to look at him.

"Better than twenty-five dollars a year—for one," Griffin held up a finger. "When our people numbered three hundred, as they did two years back, that came to seventy-five hundred dollars a year to feed and clothe our . . . slaves. On their own, only a fraction of them would work," he went on, "or make anywhere near enough to be able to feed themselves. A good portion of them would probably starve if left to their own devices."

Morgana could think of no immediate answer to that and, for a time, rode in silence.

At last they reached the main compound. "And what is that?" she asked, pointing to the barn. She was sitting on the horse comfortably now, thoroughly enjoying herself.

For the first time Griffin looked uneasy and, for a moment, Morgana thought he wasn't going to reply.

"It's just . . . a barn." He averted his face and offered no further explanation.

Since he had been so accommodating and outgoing with his answers and explanations up to this point, Morgana was slightly baffled by his attitude. However, she was in much too good spirits to dwell upon it, and by the time they reached the Great House, she had quite forgotten the incident.

Again, in the light of day, Morgana admired the large and imposing structure, noticing that the kitchen, despite her first impression of the night before, was actually a separate wing, connected to the main house by a trellised portico.

Griffin dismounted, handing the reins to the waiting

Jude. Then he came toward Morgana to assist her off the horse.

Bending forward, she felt his hands encircle her slim waist. With little effort, he lifted her down.

For a timeless moment, his strong hands remained where they were as he looked down at her with an expression she was hard put to define. His dark eyes seemed to bore right through her. A tingling expectancy came over her, a feeling Morgana had never before experienced. She stood very still, allowing the pleasant sensation to wash over her.

The moment lengthened as they continued to stare at each other. Jude had led the horses in the direction of the stables, but Morgana didn't notice their departure. She was aware of nothing but those dark eyes and couldn't seem to look away from them.

At the jarring noise of a bell, they both turned toward the house to see Minda on the kitchen porch, vigorously pulling on the rope, producing the sound that summoned the family to the midday meal.

After dinner, Cammy insisted that Morgana practice wearing hoops. Amused, Morgana agreed to humor the girl. Nathaniel and Griffin had gone into the fields and her father announced that he was taking his afternoon nap.

Later, standing in her camisole and drawers, viewing what was, to her, a bewildering array of paraphernalia, Morgana was astonished.

Laid out on the bed were stays, hoops, ruffled and beribboned pantaloons, shirtwaists, petticoats . . . Surely, she thought in growing amazement, she wasn't expected to wear all that!

They were in Cammy's bedroom, which was directly

across the hall from her own. While the bedroom and sitting room was an exact duplicate of her own insofar as size was concerned, Cammy's room was done entirely in blue and yellow, even to the braided rug which was woven in those two colors. Bella and Meg, a sweet-faced Kru, assisted Morgana as she donned the waiting clothing while Griffin's sister looked on in satisfaction.

When she was at last dressed and tried to move about, Morgana quickly learned what Cammy meant. The hooped skirt, swinging from side to side, almost unbalanced her. And when she sat down, she blushed to think what would have happened if her skirt had risen up to her chin while she had been in public.

Cammy, Bella, and Meg dissolved into helpless laughter as they watched Morgana.

"Jest what you gals up to?"

Minda, hands on her broad hips, her wide feet encased in slippers, glared at them all from the doorway. "Kin heah y'all downstairs," she complained irascibly. "Sounds lak de chicken house when a new rooster comes to call."

"Oh, stop fussing, Minda," Cammy gasped between gales of laughter.

"You gals oughta be actin' lak ladies," Minda insisted, frowning, but her dark eyes glinted with affectionate humor as she took in the scene.

"You must see this," Cammy insisted. Taking a few running steps forward, she grasped the black woman's hand.

"Cain't stop fer foolishness," Minda grumbled. Nevertheless, she allowed herself to be drawn into the room.

"Piffle! It's hours until supper," Cammy pointed out. She kissed the woman's cheek, then turned to Morgana, her eyes shining mischievously. "Show her . . ." She fell into laughter again, joined by Bella and Meg.

Good-naturedly, Morgana again rose, walked unsteadily, and sat herself down with a plop that once again sent the skirt up under her chin.

"Lawd," Minda exclaimed with a great guffaw, clapping her hands. "Ain' dat be a sight fer de gen'mens to see. . . ."

Still chuckling, Minda left the room, shaking her head from side to side. With her departure, the girls again howled in merriment.

"You musn't mind Minda," Cammy said when she caught her breath. "She was my dah and thinks she owns me. I absolutely adore her, but she's always fussing and grumbling like an old bear."

Morgana regarded her curiously, wondering what a "dah" was, but before she could ask, Cammy was off again, walking about the room, her instructions and helpful hints coming fast and furious as she urged Morgana to practice.

"You must take small steps, like this . . ." Cammy minced about in what seemed an exaggerated manner. "And for heaven's sake, don't turn too fast." She twirled gracefully, looking, to Morgana, like a delicate porcelain figure atop a music box. "Slowly . . . slowly. The hoops, you see, have a tendency to sway from side to side; you musn't prod them to and fro . . ."

Obediently, Morgana followed instructions.

It was a gay and spirited afternoon, the four young women, two white and two black, time and again breaking into helpless laughter, clutching at each other for support.

Wiping the tears from her eyes, Morgana reflected happily that the stories and angry rhetoric she had heard were not at all true. From what she had seen so far, slavery was not the terrible thing the abolitionists would have everyone believe. True, the people worked, but mostly at their own pace; they were well fed, clothed, cared for, and, to her untutored eye, quite content with their lot in life.

Supper that evening was animated. The poinsettias Minda had instructed the houseboys to use as decorations added a festive touch to the meal.

The table was replete with baked ham and roast turkey with oyster stuffing, candied yams, sweet potato pie, corn, and peas. For dessert they had pecan pie, rich with rum and molasses.

Even Griffin was in a jovial mood, teasing his sister and lending an attentive ear whenever Morgana spoke, although his gaze was decidedly cool whenever it rested upon Aleceon.

Aleceon pretended not to notice, keeping his voice neutral and his face bland. He could afford to be generous. Nevertheless, he moved and spoke cautiously, well aware that Griffin's hot temper could explode with little warning, thereby ruining all their plans.

Later that night, after supper, Morgana could hear the music and singing wafting up from the slave quarters as the people indulged in their customary Saturday night partying. Not all planters allowed this, she was informed by Cammy, but most in these parts did, feeling it a good outlet after a week's labor in the fields.

And the next day, Sunday, only reinforced Morgana's newfound convictions. There was, of course, no work on this day. The people visited and gossiped, fished in the river, paid calls to friends on neighboring plantations, or simply sat in the sun, dozing.

The next week passed quickly. On Christmas day, when Morgana looked out from her piazza that morning, she was surprised to see all the slaves gathered in the front yard. The women were obviously wearing their best clothes, sporting snowy white fichus and brightly colored bandannas. Everyone seemed to be in high spirits, and there was much laughter and joking.

Later that morning, Morgana, with the rest of the household, sat on the verandah while Griffin personally distributed gifts; bolts of vivid cloth to the women, a keg of corn liquor to the men, candy and cookies for the children.

Then he, too, joined the rest of the family on the verandah while Dobbs, with the assistance of Thomas, distributed molasses, flour, and clothing to each family.

Afterward there was singing and dancing as fiddlers and banjo players produced a lively music that set Morgana's foot to tapping.

That evening, after a truly sumptuous meal prepared by Minda, they all went into the front parlor to exchange gifts. Morgana was embarrassed at not having anything to give, but Griffin gallantly assured her that her presence was gift enough for them all.

Cammy was in an especially gay mood, and when she opened her gift from her brother, jumped up to kiss him.

"Oh, Griffin," she cried out in delight. "You remembered."

He gave her an affectionate hug and watched as she held up the exquisite gold lavaliere. "I'm glad you like it, darling," he said, helping her to fasten the chain about her neck.

There was, Morgana saw, watching them, a great similarity between Griffin and his sister; same dark wavy hair, same dark expressive eyes, although Cammy's sparkled with an ebullience that seemed a part of her.

"How does it look?" Cammy asked, turning to face them all.

Everyone agreed that it looked lovely, and again Cammy threw her arms about Griffin. "You are the best brother in the whole world," she exclaimed enthusiastically.

Laughing, Griffin agreed with her. "You little imp." He tweaked her nose. "How could I have forgotten when you made certain you reminded me of it at least once a week since you saw it in the window of Kingsleys?"

She grinned, her eyes reflecting a saucy gleam, and Morgana could sense the deep feeling between Griffin and his lovely young sister.

Finally, over eggnog and rich, dark fruitcake, they all sat quietly, listening to the voices of the Negroes as they sang Christmas carols.

It was, Morgana was to think afterward, the very best Christmas day of her life.

Chapter
5

Late the following morning, they all set out for the town house in Charleston where they were to stay for the remainder of the holiday season, which, Morgana was informed, extended through the whole month of January.

Aleceon had, at the last moment, decided to stay at Albemarle. Morgana had tried to talk him into coming with them, but he had declined, claiming he needed the time to recover fully from his bout of the "fever."

Morgana couldn't argue with the fact that her father looked as though he needed a long rest, but she was uncomfortable with the thought that he would be alone with only Ben in attendance.

"Then I will stay here with you," she had told him, upset with his decision. In spite of herself, she found that she was looking forward to the trip.

For some reason, that made him angry. "Morgana, I do

not wish for you to stay," he told her firmly. "Ben is perfectly capable of seeing to my needs. And Nathaniel has given orders for a wench named Zoe to cook in Minda's absence. Believe me," he patted her hand in a reassuring manner. "A few weeks rest and I shall be as good as new."

Finally, with some reluctance, Morgana had acceded to his wishes.

Just before she left, Aleceon pressed a bank draft into her hand with instructions to use it to buy herself a new wardrobe, and at last they were on their way.

Morgana, Griffin, Nathaniel, and Cammy rode in the carriage which was driven by Jude, now resplendent in green livery. Following in the buckboard were most of the house servants, including Minda and Thomas.

The town house was located on Church, a narrow street one block east of Meeting Street. The sidewalk was made of smooth granite block from which a path of pale pink brick led to a walled garden enclosing several magnolia trees so old and so tall they reached to the second floor of the house. Along one wall were dozens of camellias, in full bloom, the flowers appearing almost too perfect against the dark leaves of the bushes.

The house itself was a lovely structure, three stories high and made of baked brick with the inevitable piazzas ringing each floor. All the panelling, including the carved mantels, were made of local cypress. The bedrooms, sitting rooms, parlors, and even the dining room were on the second and third floors, the first level being the servants' quarters and kitchen.

Morgana was absolutely delighted by it all. Having

arrived late in the day, Minda hastily prepared a light supper for them all, after which they retired.

At seven the following morning, Morgana awoke to the sound of iron wheels on the granite block of the sidewalk below. Getting up, she crossed the carpeted floor to the window and smiled at the sight of the old vendor pushing his cart, his voice a singsong announcement of the fresh shrimp he had to offer.

Bella had laid out a dress for her to wear—one of Cammy's that Meg had altered. It had a frothy white skirt made of twilled cotton with a wide blue silk sash that encircled the waist. Morgana allowed Bella to help her, for dressing was no longer the simple task she had performed all her life.

That afternoon Griffin took Morgana on a drive through Charleston and now, unlike her arrival the week before, she found herself enchanted with the beautiful city.

A peninsula, Charleston was snuggled between the Ashley and Cooper rivers, the nature of its harbor assuring it as an important place of commerce.

The first thing Morgana noticed as they drove along was that the houses were all set at a peculiar angle, with the side of the house facing the street.

They were, Griffin explained to her, situated in such manner so as to catch the breeze from the sea. Everywhere, decorative and intricately carved wrought iron railings and fences caught and held Morgana's eye. She'd never seen the likes of them before.

As they drove down the broad and cobbled thoroughfare known as Meeting Street, she marveled at the pastel colors of the houses, the steep tiled roofs with their quaint chimneys, and the pathways of exquisite pale pink brick that wended from the street through narrow walks and alleys, terminating in secluded courts and gardens that were breathtaking amidst an array of flowers and trees. She had already discovered that what appeared to be the front door of a house actually led to a covered walkway, which, in turn, took one to the real front entrance.

They drove by White Point Gardens, which Griffin promised to show her at a later date. Finally, stopping the carriage, he took her for a walk along the raised promenade that ambled along the harbor.

The day was clear and sunny and mild. Morgana felt more alive than at any other time in her life.

Looking back on the city, she could see the delicate spire atop of Saint Michael's Church. From this angle, she could see only one of its four clock faces, but could easily hear the sound of the bells pronouncing the passing of each quarter-hour.

"It's truly magnificent," she breathed at last, drinking in the sight. "I had no idea...."

Griffin gazed down at her. He had discarded his usual apparel and was attired in a fawn colored frock coat and matching trousers. A flowered waistcoat over a white ruffled shirt gave an urbane quality to his appearance.

"You're not sorry you came?" he teased.

She flushed, grateful for the cooling breeze upon her face. "No. I'm so very glad ..." She was aware that her heartbeat quickened beneath his look and was a bit surprised by her own reaction. Morgana was forced to acknowledge to herself that she was finding Griffin Kynes more and more attractive with each passing day she spent in his company. His cold indifference, so noticeable on that first day they met, seemed to have dissipated. "It's all so very lovely," she whispered.

A small smile caught and held the corners of his mouth, softening the angular planes of his face. "It's the only setting in which you belong," he murmured.

And he meant it. Dressed now in more fashionable clothes, her hair curled into soft ringlets, Griffin saw that she had a quiet beauty, quite breathtaking in its own way. She was smiling at him, and he couldn't help but stare at the transformation wrought by the ordinary expression. She had beautiful teeth, strong and white and even, and the most adorable dimple on the side of her mouth. Bemused, he noticed that it was only on the right side.

With his remark, Morgana had darted a small glance at him to see if he was serious. Was it possible, she wondered, to learn to care for a man in so short a time? She had no way of knowing, no basis for comparison.

Morgana continued to regard Griffin, who was still smiling at her. He was so very handsome, she thought, studying his rough-hewn features. He emanated virility and strength with each movement he made.

She did care, Morgana suddenly realized. The thought made her a trifle uneasy. Surely a man like this would never look twice at her, she reasoned.

"I'd like to thank you for being so kind and for showing me your splendid city," she said after awhile, when they had resumed walking.

"Oh, there's much more to Charleston than what you've just seen," he responded with a small laugh that, nevertheless, had a ring of pride in it. Just ahead of them, he noticed a group of young boys skimming stones into the water, their boisterous actions accompanied by shouts of hilarity. Griffin placed his hand on Morgana's elbow, steering her to the other side of the promenade. When they were safely past the boys, he released her. "Next month will be especially busy," he went on, glancing down at her as they strolled along. "Have you ever been to the races?"

She shook her head, not wanting to tell him that she'd been nowhere at all. She was acutely aware of his brief touch. Her arm still tingled with the contact.

"I think you'll enjoy that," he mused. "We have a horse entered. My grandfather has high hopes of winning. And, of course, Saint Cecelia's will be having its annual ball. Cammy is to be presented, as you probably already know."

"Yes," Morgana murmured, liking the sound of his voice. "She's been talking about little else. It all sounds very exciting."

"It is," he agreed. "And when we return in the summer, things will be just as exciting. There will be outdoor musicals at Orange Gardens, plays at the Dock Street Theater, concerts, parties, teas. . . ."

She laughed at his enthusiasm, tilting her head to look up at him. "How do you find the time for it all?"

"Oh, we manage." He thought her laughter was like a golden waterfall. The sound of it pleased him. "Whatever else my fair city offers, I assure you, boredom is not among the choices."

And Griffin was right. The next six weeks were a whirlwind in Morgana's mind.

Accompanied by Cammy, with Bella and Meg in attendance, Morgana shopped in all the quaint stores on King Street, spending several afternoons on the pleasurable pastime. She had never seen so many splendid dresses and accessories. With Cammy's help, she selected an entire new wardrobe, but hardly made a dent in the money her father had given her for the purpose.

The dress Morgana decided upon for the Saint Cecelia's ball was an off-the-shoulder creation made of pale blue satin. A full ten yards of material were needed for just the skirt. Cammy, of course, was restricted to white, and chose a brocade material that was to be sewn with tiny seed pearls about the neckline. Both of them would wear the traditional long gloves that rose above the elbow.

The night of the ball was to linger forever in Morgana's memory. Six hundred people attended the fashionable event. The Society had its own orchestra, the finest musicians available both locally and in Europe.

When they arrived, the orchestra had already begun to play a waltz and the music filtered down to the gallery, which was on the first floor.

Cammy led Morgana to the ladies' cloak room where they shed their outer wraps and viewed themselves in the looking glass for a final critical inspection before going upstairs to the ballroom.

When they returned to the gallery, Nathaniel brought their dance cards to them and, following Cammy's lead, Morgana looped it over her wrist. Then, curious, she read it. Except for Nathaniel and Griffin, it was filled with names she didn't even know. Griffin's name appeared only three times, for the third, ninth, and sixteenth dances.

Peering over her shoulder, Cammy giggled, then pointed to number sixteen. "It's the special dance," she whispered confidingly. In a graceful movement she raised her lace fan to shield her lips. "Reserved for wives and . . . sweethearts."

Morgana blushed furiously and made a valiant attempt

to regain her composure as they entered the ballroom. At the sight that greeted her eye, she caught her breath in delight. The huge room was a marvel. There were countless white and scented candles in the chandeliers and wall sconces. White fluted columns shone almost gold in the reflected, flickering light. Large pots of camellias had been placed around the raised platform where the musicians sat. The flowers were, of course, in full bloom. The whole room was infused with their sweet fragrance. On either side of the platform were long tables draped in white satin and holding silver bowls that were filled with sparkling punch and fresh orange slices. And there were endless platters of canapes and hors d'oeuvres.

The ambience was truly glittering. Ladies moved lissomely, gowned in their best finery and most treasured gems. The gentlemen, attired in their black dress suits, all managed to look tall and elegant, even if they were not.

With the others, Morgana watched as Nathaniel led Cammy in the Grand March, his pride visible for all to see.

Morgana found herself waiting for the third dance with an eagerness she couldn't deny. When it finally arrived, the orchestra chose to play "The Blue Danube," and as Morgana stepped into Griffin's arms for the beautiful waltz, she knew it wasn't the dance she had been waiting for, but the opportunity to be held within the embrace of those strong arms.

Effortlessly, he guided her about the large dance floor, twirling and gliding in perfect movements to the three-quarter time.

Griffin was a marvelous dancer, and Morgana felt as though she were floating. She felt almost giddy beneath his warm smile of approval as he discovered that she, too, was an accomplished dancer.

They hardly spoke, but never took their eyes from one another. The rest of the assemblage seemed to drift into the background and Morgana was left with the impression that there was no else in the room except Griffin and herself. She wished with all her heart that the dance would never end, but, of course, it did. Griffin then led her to one of the long tables. While they both sipped from glasses of champagne handed to them by one of the attentive black waiters, he smiled down at her.

"I've never danced with a partner as graceful as you are," he murmured. His dark eyes flashed with sincere admiration.

"Nor I," she responded, conscious that her ears were tingling from the flush of delight that coursed through her at his compliment.

They were still smiling at each other when Nathaniel's voice intruded.

"Come now, Griffin," the old man admonished, clapping his grandson on the shoulder. "I'll not allow you to monopolize the time of the most beautiful woman in the room." He directed a surprisingly youthful grin at Morgana. "Age has its prerogatives, my dear." He gave a courtly bow and held out his arm. "I believe that I'm the fortunate recipient of this next dance."

Laughing, flushed with happiness, Morgana put down her glass of champagne and allowed Nathaniel to lead her out onto the dance floor. While Nathaniel was not as accomplished a dancer as Griffin, he was enthusiastic to a degree that left her breathless.

The evening seemed to race by, and Morgana was astonished when the sixteenth dance arrived. Again she gave herself up to the delicious sensation aroused by Griffin's arms around her.

"Is it true," she asked him at one point, "that the sixteenth dance is a . . . special one?"

He glanced down at her for a long moment, then tightened the pressure of his hand upon hers. "Yes, it's true."

He said no more, but Morgana felt as though she finished the dance on a cloud.

During the days that followed, Griffin remained attentive. Though the only time he touched her was when they danced, his eyes sought hers more and more. Morgana was thrilled and excited by the message they seemed to hold.

So enthralled was Morgana with Griffin that she was only slightly aware that Cammy's ebullience seemed to fade in those next days, a situation Morgana was at a loss to explain. The young girl seemed most popular. The day after her debut saw the town house literally filled with flowers from admirers, most of which came from a pleasant faced young man named Clinton Barrows, who, Morgana distinctly remembered, had been penned on Cammy's card for the sixteenth dance. He arrived nearly every day, bouquet in one hand, calling card in the other. But Cammy remained distant and, at times, almost angry with the constant attention.

No doubt, Morgana reflected to herself as they at last made their way back to Albemarle, Cammy most likely had her bonnet set for the one young blade who had not shown an interest in her.

But Cammy's problem—if indeed she had one—went completely unnoticed by Morgana, for on the day after their return to the plantation, an event took place that forever changed her life.

It was early afternoon. Griffin insisted that she ride with him so that he could show her the canefields, which lay a distance away.

The planting of the sugar cane was in full progress. The roots—or ratoons as they were called—were being laid end to end in long narrow furrows cut into the dark earth.

"By July," Griffin explained to her, "the cane will be better than five feet high. It requires little care from that point until the grinding season. That should be in October. During that time, everyone works an eighteen-hour day."

"Is it so difficult to harvest?" Morgana asked. She viewed the scene with interest.

"It isn't the harvesting, but the grinding that requires constant attention," he replied, then pointed to a wooden building a short distance away. "That's the sugarhouse. When the cane is ground, the resulting juice is put into large black iron sugar kettles. It boils continually, night and day, until it granulates."

Morgana returned her gaze to the workers. "There are quite a few children in the fields," she noted. Her brow deepened into a frown of disapproval. She recalled that in the rice fields, too, there had been children among the workers.

Griffin hesitated a moment, then murmured, "I understand that the mills and factories of the North employ very young children. . . ."

Morgana's expression tightened. "I've heard that argument before, Griffin," she pointed out, fixing him with a level look.

Morgana's voice held that hint of challenge and Griffin

almost smiled. He was becoming used to it. As he looked at her it occurred to him that, when she was around, his eyes kept straying to her face. She had a proud bearing and a stubborn set to her chin. He didn't know why, but she was beginning to fascinate him. Time and again she caught him off guard, but for some reason he was beginning to find it stimulating.

"It's not all that difficult to argue with the truth," he noted, still staring at her. Was his mind playing tricks on him? he wondered. His attention had, in a sense, been forced to focus upon this young woman. Was that the reason he found her stunningly attractive? But no, he had to admit to himself. Dammit, she *was* attractive, unlike anyone he'd ever known.

"I don't see how you can compare one with the other," Morgana protested.

Griffin's response was offered in a mild voice. "Just how young are they when they are allowed to go to work in the factories?"

Her glance was a trifle annoyed. "As young as five," she admitted tersely, "but—"

"And how many hours a day do they work?" he interrupted quietly, watching her closely.

She raised her chin. "I . . . would guess the normal factory hours."

"That would be twelve to fourteen hours a day?" At her curt nod, Griffin smiled in satisfaction. "No child younger than twelve works here—at anything. And when they are sent into the fields, their task consumes only three to four hours, depending on how fast they work."

She floundered and his smile broadened. "Don't waste your sympathy on the little black rascals," Griffin said, laughing now. Gripping the reins, he moved his horse forward. "They're just quarter-hands. Their task is only twenty-five percent of what a prime hand is assigned."

As they left the fields, Griffin set a leisurely pace, angling down toward the Ashley, keeping the horses at a walk. It was a beautiful, nearly perfect day. A warm sun blazed down from a cerulean sky, unimpeded by clouds. The trees seemed greener, the moss more delicate, the very shadows appeared to have been painted with warm umber.

The river moved serenely, the tide just at the turning point when the water would flow back to the sea. Sunlight ribboned the surface, glinting and shifting, throwing darts of gold about.

A covey of birds took wing, disturbed by their approach, then soared and dipped in noisy confusion until again settling down some distance away.

At last Griffin halted and helped her from her horse. Morgana gave the animal an affectionate pat on her silky nose. She was becoming most fond of Lady.

This part of the river cut inland, creating a small sandy cove, completely surrounded by moss-laden cypress.

"It's like a little island," she exclaimed delightedly, looking about her.

"This is where I went swimming when I was a child," Griffin informed her. "And still do, on occasion. My dah used to bring me here when the weather was warm enough."

She looked up at him, recognizing the word she had heard Cammy use once before. "Dah?"

He pursed his lips. "I suppose you might say nursemaid, or nanny," he mused. "But they are, in fact, more than that. A second mother, perhaps." Griffin tethered both horses to a branch of a tree.

"And Minda is, or was, Cammy's dah?" Morgana inquired. He nodded and she went on to ask, "Was she yours as well?"

"No." He came back to her side. "My dah was a woman named Coralee. She was Thomas's wife." His voice grew low. "She died while I was in England."

She heard the sadness in his voice, and noted quietly, "You must have loved her a great deal."

He nodded again. "She was a fine woman." He raised both brows in an appealing expression that made Morgana's heart lurch. "And she never thought twice about paddling me when I needed it."

She grinned at him. "I suspect you must have needed it about once a day."

"Too close to the truth," he admitted carefully, then joined her delighted laughter.

They were standing close. As Griffin looked down at her, his laughter faded and his dark eyes grew serious.

"I'm so glad you came to us," he murmured, noticing how delicately her features were molded, sculpted into clean lines from cheek to chin. There was little, if any, soft and rounded prettiness to her face—a prettiness he suddenly considered mundane.

She was viewing him with an expression as serious as his own. "I am, too," she whispered.

He put his hand on her cheek, then, bending forward, kissed her, moving his tongue between her soft lips. His hand slipped downward and cupped her firm breast.

Morgana's arms went around his neck and she pressed closer to him, wishing the moment would never end. As he drew her down upon the soft sand, she went willingly, clinging to him.

Moving his mouth to her throat, Griffin could feel her pulse quicken. Slowly, he began to undo the lace ribbon at the top of her bodice. She murmured a small sound of uncertainty. Griffin paused for just a moment, then placed his lips back on hers, his hands now unfastening buttons.

Morgana felt her bodice being loosened. Although she made a token effort toward resistance, she knew, in advance, that it was futile. The feel of his lips on her ear was arousing a sensual quickening deep inside her. It had a mesmerizing effect on her.

His mouth now moved along her white neck to the soft hollow between her bared breasts. Against his lips he could feel the rapid beating of her heart and he felt his own body throb with an answering desire.

With unhurried movements, Griffin undressed her, stopping now and again when he sensed a resistance on her part, at those times kissing her long and deeply. His hands caressed her with feathery movements that made her tremble beneath his touch.

When she was at last unclothed, he removed his own garments and lay down at her side.

Although she had never in her life seen a man naked, Morgana found, much to her surprise, that she was without embarrassment. Instead, her eyes were delighted by the play of muscle, lean flanks, soft black body hair. He was so perfectly formed that he appeared to her a work of art, a living sculpture created by a master.

Griffin's hands were exploring every contour of her body; a satiny smooth shoulder, the clean line of her collarbone, a sweetly rounded arm.

"You're so very beautiful," he murmured, letting his eyes travel the perfection of her form. His hands were now upon her back, patiently massaging tightly held muscles that gradually relaxed beneath his practiced touch. His fingertips then traced the gentle curve of her spine, dropping to the small of her back and finding the delicious swell of her buttocks. All the while, he was kissing her face and nibbling on her sensitive ear until her whole body quivered and she could only gasp between her quickening breaths.

His hands moved to the warmth between her thighs, again hesitating, not wishing to hurry or frighten her, for he didn't need to be told that no man had ever before touched her. His fingertips found her most secret place and she moaned, gripping him tighter in an almost reflexive movement.

Gently, Griffin pushed her backward and covered her body with his own.

Entering her warmth, he met resistance, and for a moment lay still, giving her time to overcome her fear while his hands and lips continued to caress her.

When he sensed she was ready, he gave a strong thrust and broke the barrier of her womanhood. Her sharp gasp of pain was followed by a wave of pleasure that caused her to shudder with its intensity. Griffin moved slowly, controlling himself until he was certain that her level of desire matched his own.

Morgana clung to his rocking body, urging him to continue until at last her body shook with an ecstacy that tore the breath from her throat.

Afterward, he stayed within her, holding her close to him, murmuring her name, his lips on her ear, his warm breath continuing the waves of golden joy that spread throughout her.

Morgana felt the lassitude of contentment course through her, leaving a pleasant languor in its wake. She felt she could remain in Griffin's embrace forever. She was fascinated by the dark curls on his chest and kept running her fingers through the softness, delighting in the feel of it against her breast.

"I love you, Griffin," she heard herself declare fervently, mildly surprised by her own forwardness. But she had spoken the truth, she realized, gazing up at his now very dear face. She loved this man and had no intention of denying the wondrous feeling, whatever the consequence. Griffin had made her feel beautiful, desirable; it was a heady wine that she knew she must taste again and again.

Once more he kissed her, this time gently, with a lingering tenderness. For a long time they lay there, holding each other, touching, kissing, until the fires of passion blossomed anew. This time Morgana experienced only joy, and her responses were as ardent and heated as his own.

At last Griffin raised himself up on an elbow and looked down at her. With slow movements, he caressed the smoothness of her cheek, letting his fingers move down her throat to the curve of her rounded breast, still dampened with the heat of desire.

"Marry me, Morgana," he whispered, searching her face for the answer he hoped would be there.

Morgana's answer was immediate. She neither thought of, nor regretted releasing her hold on the dream of becoming a teacher. That life was now in the past. Her future was all that mattered. Her arms went around his neck.

"Oh, yes," she breathed, viewing him with love-filled eyes.

"Right away," he insisted. He drew her closer to him, burying his lips in her fragrant hair. "I couldn't bear to have you around and not make love to you each day."

"I'll marry you whenever you say, Griffin," she replied quietly. "Today, if you want . . ." The thought of being with Griffin each day caused her to again shudder in joy and she tightened her grip, letting her hands play across the muscles of his back.

That evening, just before supper when they were all gathered in the front parlor, Griffin made the announcement that he and Morgana were to be married.

Aleceon seemed greatly pleased. Morgana was relieved—if somewhat surprised—by her father's attitude. For some reason she had thought he might object; not because Griffin wasn't suitable, but because of the suddenness of it all. She had, after all, known Griffin Kynes for only two months.

Instead, Aleceon was in a rare, jocular mood, joining Nathaniel as they both congratulated the couple several times in succession.

Finally, Aleceon raised his glass of wine for a toast. "Many, many years of life and happiness to you both," he pronounced. Gazing at his daughter's happy and flushed face, Aleceon felt a momentary twinge of conscience, regretting his underhanded machinations in bringing about this union. He wondered if perhaps it would have worked out without his interference.

But no, he decided, placing the glass on a table. It was too risky to leave something so important in the hands of fate. No one knew better than he how fickle luck could be.

Still and all, he was greatly relieved that it hadn't been necessary to order Morgana to take this step.

Comforted by his assumptions, Aleceon then gallantly offered his arm to his daughter as they all made their way into the dining room.

Seating himself at the table, Griffin's eyes glinted dangerously, although his expression remained amiable enough. He felt he could almost see the wheels spinning in Aleceon's mind, could almost sense the other man's greed and satisfaction. He had never in his life hated anyone as much as he hated Aleceon Edgewood at this moment.

So strong was his feeling of antipathy that Griffin turned a cool eye in Morgana's direction, and for a fleeting moment imagined he saw the image of Aleceon superimposed upon her smiling face.

Chapter
6

The wedding of Griffin Kynes and Morgana Edgewood took place at Albemarle a week later. The minister, a portly, dour man named Henry Olive, had been summoned from Charleston to officiate.

Farley Barrows, his wife Amelia, and their three sons came from Four Oaks to attend the ceremony, but were the only outsiders in attendance.

Morgana immediately liked Farley, a bluff and hearty man in his late sixties. He had a ready smile and a charming, if somewhat garrulous way about him. Amelia, five years younger than her husband, was a thin, nervous woman who managed to frown even when she was smiling. Their eldest son, Clinton, was a gangling young man who once again showered attention upon Cammy, and looked crestfallen at her lack of response to his overtures.

During the preceding week, both Bella and Meg had

labored long hours, transforming a bolt of ivory satin into a wedding gown. Acting on Morgana's preferences, they carefully copied the gown from a picture in Godey's Lady's Book. It was long-sleeved, the cuffs coming to a sharp point on the back of the hand. Beneath a boat neckline the bodice also came to a point, hugging the waist neatly before flaring into deep folds that reached the ankle in the front and flowed into a three-foot train in the back. The headdress was really a coronet of pearls from which a delicate white lace veil fell back and across the shoulders.

Minda, too, had made her contribution, toiling in the kitchen from first light, producing a three-tiered wedding cake which she herself carried with much pride into the dining room.

All through supper that evening, Morgana's eyes went from Griffin to her gold wedding ring, seeing how it caught and reflected the candlelight when she moved her hand. It was a lovely ring. The band itself was of yellow gold. The center was fashioned into a rose blossom made of white gold and sported two tiny diamond dewdrops. The ring had belonged to Anne Kynes and was given by Nathaniel to Griffin. Morgana had at first—somewhat halfheartedly—protested that it should really be given to Cammy. But Griffin had assured her that Cammy was in possession of their mother's jewelry, which included the wedding ring that had belonged to her.

That night, in her own room, Bella having helped her to undress, Morgana lay in the large four-poster, excited anticipation coloring her cheeks with a pink glow. She had never in her life been as happy as she was at this moment. Nathaniel had promised to refurbish Griffin's room from top to bottom as a wedding present for them both. Until it was completed, they would stay here, in her room.

At last the door opened. Griffin, with a curt nod at Bella who quickly exited, looked at Morgana and his expression softened at the sight of her. In the light from the single burning lamp on the bedside table, she appeared very young. Her blond hair, unbound, tumbled about her shoulders and had the sheen of silk.

Coming forward, he sat on the edge of the bed. "Shall I extinguish the lamp?" he asked. Reaching out, he touched the softness of her hair, rubbing the strands with his fingertips.

Morgana nodded, gazing at him with adoration.

He held her gaze a moment longer, then turned down the lamp until the yellow glow faded and was gone.

In the dimness she was aware that he was undressing. Only moments later he was beside her. His hands were gentle yet insistent as he undid the buttons of her nightgown. Morgana made no resistance as he lifted it up over her head and flung it aside.

Pale silvery moonlight illuminated their bodies as Griffin bent forward, placing his lips upon hers. For many moments he kissed her, his hand caressing the smoothness of her breast, slipping to her waist and then to her inner thigh.

Now, as before, he raised her desire to a fever pitch until at last, with a small cry, Morgana's arms entwined about him as she pulled him closer to her. Her hands strayed about his body, delighting in the feel of him. She felt no shyness, no reservation as she eagerly grasped the most private part of him, guiding him into her willing warmth, once again losing herself in the exquisite sensation of being one with the man she loved.

Afterward, Morgana nuzzled against him, resting her head on his broad chest. Only moments later, her deep and even breathing bespoke sleep.

Griffin, however, lay there, hands clasped behind his head, staring up into the darkness, trying to fathom his feelings. From the time he had been fifteen and had taken his first wench, right here at Albemarle, he'd made love to many women. Most were black and didn't really count. But more than a few of them were white, for Griffin, when he chose to be, could be very persuasive.

But with Morgana it had been different. Why? he wondered. She hadn't been the first virgin he had bedded. The others had been, for the most part, unsatisfying. He preferred a woman with experience, not someone he had to coddle along. Yet both times with this woman he had reached a degree of satisfaction he'd thought impossible.

Why? he wondered again, puzzled with his own reaction. Did he love her? If so, when had it happened?

And he shouldn't love her. Her father was responsible for all their ills. . . .

The drifting, ethereal moonlight that crept in through the window found his expression set into almost angry lines. Aleceon had gotten his way—now he'd better pay off, Griffin thought to himself.

One other person lay awake far into the night.

Getting up from the corn husk mattress she shared with Jude, Zoe glanced down at him, assuring herself that he was fast asleep.

Silently, she let herself out of the cabin, then went

around to the rear. It took only a moment to locate the heavy-handled hoe she had hidden in the tall grass earlier in the day.

Tonight was, she thought, perfect. Everyone had stayed up later than usual because of the wedding and so should sleep soundly. Masta Nathaniel had graciously given them all extra rations of corn liquor to celebrate the happy event. Prudently, Zoe had touched none of it.

Gripping the hoe tightly, Zoe walked as quietly as she was able, her bare feet gliding noiselessly over the dirt road. She made her way slowly, hesitating now and then, casting a wary eye in all directions, until at last she arrived at Jonah's cabin. It had been eight weeks since her brother had been so severely beaten. He was now almost fully recovered.

Zoe knew that he would soon be sold, and not through any auction where he just might have a chance, but to a slave trader. Masta Nathaniel had made that perfectly clear. She was well aware that those rednecks bought only what nobody else wanted. Their coffles almost invariably wound up in the canefields of Mississippi or Louisiana. For Jonah, as well as for any other slave who might meet that fate, there was nothing to look forward to except death under those circumstances.

Although she was frightened, Zoe knew that she was Jonah's only hope. He would be awake and ready because, today, when she had brought his food to him, she had whispered that tonight she would come to him. She could tell him no more. As always, Carlie Dobbs hovered nearby, waiting to lock the door again after she left.

At last she stood before the small log cabin, regarding the iron padlock on the door. Studying it, she frowned.

There was no way of breaking it, she knew. But there was a chance that she could break the surrounding wood into which it was nailed.

Placing the sharp tip of the hoe between the lock and the wood, Zoe tried to pry it apart. At first, nothing happened, so she exerted more pressure. Twice the hoe slipped, and as metal grated on metal she paused, holding her breath. Somewhere a dog barked in the distance, but otherwise all was still.

Again, Zoe stuck the hoe behind the piece of metal from which the padlock was suspended, grunting softly as she strained, pushing against the wooden handle as hard as she was able. She felt it give slightly and renewed her effort. Finally, she heard the sound of wood splintering, and at last the contrivance loosened. With a bit more prying and pulling, the lock fell away.

She pushed the door inward and whispered her brother's name. Then she felt his arms go around her, hugging her tightly.

"Zoe, gal," Jonah murmured in a low voice. "Ain' nobody smart as you." He peered outside, then turned to her again. "Dis time, ain' nobody catchin' me. . . ."

She grabbed at his arm, feeling the rough cotton of his sleeve beneath her palm. "You stay offen de road," she urged strongly, frightened for his welfare. "Pat'rollers be goin' up an' down lak always. Iffen dey catches you agin. . . ." She gave a soft sob.

"Kills 'em first," he vowed fiercely, keeping his voice soft.

"An' listen fer de dogs," she pressed, tightening her grip on his arm.

"Doan worry none 'bout me," he muttered quickly,

brushing aside her concern with a wave of his hand. "Gonna walk in de water much as I kin. Dogs cain't track in de river." In the dimness, his eyes glittered with determination. "Bin hearin' 'bout de underground peoples who he'ps us'ns. Gonna find 'em iffen I kin."

Jonah glanced into the yard, assuring himself that no one was around. He hesitated a moment, wanting to take his sister with him, but knowing she would only delay his passage.

He put his hands on her shoulders. "Won't ferget you, Zoe," he promised. Bending forward, Jonah gave her a quick kiss. Cautiously, he stepped outside, almost immediately becoming as one with the black night.

Zoe watched him only a moment. Then, as quietly as she came, she made her way back to her own cabin.

The next morning, although Morgana awakened early, Griffin was already gone from her bed.

Dressing quickly, she hurried downstairs, hoping that he was still at breakfast. Excitement coursed through her each time she thought of her husband and she knew of a certainty that she would feel this way for the rest of her life. The thought birthed a smile of pure joy.

At the foot of the stairs, Morgana paused, hearing voices coming from the study, one of which she recognized as Griffin's. His voice contained an enormous amount of anger. She moved closer, the smile fading from her lips. The door was opened and she could hear the words very clearly.

"It is done!" Griffin was saying in a harsh voice she'd never heard him use. "The marriage has been effected and consummated. Just as planned. I've held up my side of the bargain, Aleceon. And I fully expect you to hold up yours. Every note, every debt against Albemarle is to be destroyed."

Standing in the hall, Morgana could feel the blood leave her face. Swaying slightly, she gripped the balustrade with hands that felt suddenly icy. She didn't comprehend it all at once, although something deep inside her realized the awfulness of what she had just heard. The words floated for a time inside her head: *the marriage has been effected and consummated. Just as planned. . . .* They hung there as if awaiting her awareness, as though her own body was making a valiant attempt to protect her mind.

Her father's answering response was a mere murmur, or perhaps, over the drumming in her ears, Morgana just couldn't hear it.

"Damn you!" Griffin shouted now. His fist came down on the top of the desk with resounding force. "Your word is not good enough. I want to see it done. Now!"

A moment later, both men, followed by Nathaniel, emerged from the study. At the sight of her, they all fell silent. Morgana looked only at Griffin. Seeing her, he halted abruptly. His face was a curious mixture of surprise and dismay, overlaid with a faint residue of anger. He blinked, drawing his breath sharply, and extended a hand in her direction.

But before anyone could speak, Morgana spun around and raced back upstairs to her room. Closing the door, she bolted it from the inside. Trembling, she rested her cheek against the carved surface. It felt cool on her hot skin.

A few moments later, when she heard the knock followed by Griffin's soft entreaty, Morgana put her hands over her ears to block out the sound. The pain she felt was so acute it struck at her very soul, threatening to destroy her.

Bella stood close by, watching her, her dark eyes solemn, silently commiserating with Morgana. At the sight of her stricken mistress, she put a hand to her lips, issuing a soft moan.

When Morgana began to sob, Bella stepped forward, putting her arms around her. "Doan you cry, Miz Morgana," she pleaded, close to tears herself. "Breaks dis gal's heart to see you takin' on so. . . ."

Raising her head, Morgana regarded the black girl's saddened face. "Did you know?" she whispered brokenly.

Slowly, Bella nodded, looking more unhappy than ever. "Ever'body know dat Masta Griffin gonna marry up wit you. Doan know why, 'ceptin' your daddy say it got to be dat way."

Upon hearing that, Morgana's tears ceased. The cold feeling returned. She moved away from the comforting arms and walked out onto the piazza. It seemed to her that her heart had suddenly turned to stone.

Looking down, she saw Griffin mount his horse, then ride off in the direction of the fields.

So much for love, she thought grimly, at that moment hating the man who was now her husband. For the first and only time in her life, she had fallen in love with a man only to see her dreams crushed beneath the harsh light of reality. Griffin had married her to save his precious Albemarle. He had lied to her, used her in the most contemptible way a man could use a woman.

Incongruously, there flashed before her mind's eye the picture of herself and Griffin on the warm sand, sheltered by the cypress and moss. She could feel her face flush, remembering her warm responses to his ardent caresses.

She had professed her love so eagerly. And now, thinking with a clear rage, Morgana realized that Griffin had never done so. Oh, his words had been sweet enough, but they had been empty.

"I love you . . ." She said the words aloud, testing them, for they were still new to her. But they were as ashes upon her tongue and she gritted her teeth.

How could she have been such a fool? she thought, feeling the anger rise and spread throughout her. She refused to excuse herself on the basis of not having had any experience with men. Time and again over the past several years she had listened to her friends, sympathizing with their heartbroken accounts of a love that had turned sour, of a man who had vowed loyalty only to betray that vow.

Probably, she reflected, Griffin now thought her devastated, broken by the revelation, for there was no doubt in her mind that he knew how much she loved him.

No! she corrected herself with sternness. Once, she had loved him; yesterday—a lifetime ago.

But she would survive. Absently, she twisted the wedding ring on her hand. Looking down at it, Morgana was of a mind to tear it from her finger and fling it across the room. Instead, she clasped her hands tightly, feeling the edge of the metal cut into her flesh. She was filled with the sense of having been manipulated, and she was furious.

Two could play at that game, she decided, staring at Griffin's receding figure with eyes that resembled mountain snow in the twilight. Then she smiled coldly, and only those who knew Aleceon Edgewood well would have noticed the eerie resemblance of that expression upon the face of his daughter.

As for her father . . . Morgana's eyes narrowed. He had obviously played a part in all this. Yet, for what possible reason?

That, at least, could be explained.

Turning abruptly, Morgana left her room. Moments later, she knocked on the door to her father's room. There was a brief pause before it was opened by Ben.

Entering, she saw her father seated at the writing table. Although she was certain that he knew she was there, he didn't turn, just continued with whatever he was writing. He had removed his jacket, but still wore his vest over a white ruffled shirt.

Morgana's gaze drifted to the fireplace, noting the smoldering ashes that were all that was left of recently burning papers. The sight of it caused the pulse at the base of her throat to throb with quickening emotion.

"Why?" she asked without preamble, her eyes returning to her father.

Looking up then, Aleceon raised a brow, the corners of his mouth tightening with what she took to be annoyance.

"Why!" she demanded when he made no immediate response.

"You are being childish, Morgana," Aleceon said with slow deliberation. He indicated for her to take a seat. With exaggerated care, he folded the paper on which he had been writing and laid it aside before again speaking. "I thought your years at Brookshire would have at least taught you how to behave in a ladylike manner," he commented.

Her eyes flashed as she seated herself on the chair before

the writing table. "We are talking about deception, Father, not ladylike manners." She viewed him stonily, her back rigid. "You are obviously the instigator in this little farce. I'd like to know why."

"You are nineteen, almost twenty years of age," he noted quietly, ignoring her agitated state. "I thought it was about time you were married."

"I find it difficult to believe that you had my welfare in mind," she shot back with heavy sarcasm. "For six years you didn't even know whether I was alive or not, and I doubt you cared. Now, suddenly, you make plans for the rest of my life without bothering to consult me." She leaned forward, intent and angry. "Did it ever occur to you that I might have had plans of my own?"

Her blue eyes were gleaming with a formidable anger, for the moment unsettling Aleceon, who suddenly recognized in his daughter a strength of will that far exceeded his own. The idea, however, did not distress him; rather, he was grateful for its existence.

"Did it!" she demanded again, feeling a hot impatience with his digression.

"Please, my dear," Aleceon murmured then, appearing pained. He passed a hand across his forehead. "Don't raise your voice." He sighed. "I can understand that you've suffered a bit of a blow to your vanity, had your feathers ruffled, so to speak—"

"Dammit! I will not be spoken to as if I were a child. Not even by you!"

Aleceon blinked, quite astonished at the outburst. Then he adopted a placating tone. "You're right, of course. I confess that I sometimes forget that you are now a woman."

She was not mollified. "I will not be put off," she said through clenched teeth. She strove to keep her temper in check. "Why was it a condition that Griffin Kynes marry me before you returned his notes of indebtedness?"

Aleceon took a deep breath and a look passed between him and Ben that, in her agitated state, Morgana didn't notice.

For just a moment, Aleceon wavered, tempted to tell her the truth. The moment passed. He didn't want her pity, didn't want anyone's pity. Dying, he suddenly realized, was a very personal thing, a very private experience. Aleceon felt he could accomplish it with more dignity if no one knew about it until the very end.

How unfortunate, though, that she had discovered Griffin's part in all this, he thought, dismayed that his carefully laid plans had gone awry. Yet she was married. And, unless he missed his guess, loved her husband. Further, unless he misinterpreted the look in Griffin's eyes, that man was not without feeling for Morgana.

Time, then. Aleceon didn't have it, but the two young people had many years of that precious commodity.

Morgana was still glaring at him and Aleceon made his decision.

"Very well," he said at last, getting to his feet. "You were put in school six years ago because . . . well, because you were troublesome. I'm sure you'll agree that a man cannot go about his business saddled with a child. Doubtless you can understand that, at least," he stated, running a hand through his dark blond hair. "And what was I to do now?" he demanded. "Certainly you couldn't have stayed in that school much longer. You must have damned near been the oldest one there."

"I was," she agreed curtly. Her attitude plainly indicated that he should continue. One part of Morgana felt restless, tingling with the desire to move, to smash, to scream her fury to the skies. But she forced herself to remain still, ignoring the self-indulgent inclination, which she knew would serve no useful purpose.

"Well, then," Aleceon went on, wetting his lips. "Was I to bring you home and have you underfoot again? Simply put, I arranged what I considered a more than suitable union for you. Griffin Kynes is an attractive man," he argued. "You must admit that."

"He is." The comment was expressed coldly.

"And he is, or will be one day, rich," he added, appearing to wait for her approval. When she made no response, he continued, a thin, shimmering strand of sarcasm threading his words. "And it certainly appeared to me, from your enthusiastic response to his proposal, that you loved the man."

"What do you know of love?" she challenged quickly. "I doubt you have ever loved anything or anyone in your entire life!"

He refused to be goaded. "We are not discussing my emotions, Morgana," he pointed out in a lazy voice.

Morgana stared at her father. Her feeling of betrayal was strong, hurtful. She had always overlooked her father's single-minded, self-centered absorption with his own well-being. She had found excuses for his strangeness, his aloofness, and accepted him as he was. But this—this was too much to accept, too much to forgive.

"And," Aleceon mused, almost as an afterthought, "I must admit to wanting Albemarle." His fingertip traced an indefinable pattern on the writing table as he seemed to collect his thoughts. "I can't run it, but I want to live here. The life of a gentleman planter appeals to me."

"So you used me as a pawn." Morgana's tone was bitter. She shifted her weight in the chair and made a conscious effort to relax her tautly held muscles. All the truths she had known about her father and had never wanted to admit to herself now rushed forward, crowding her mind with contempt. To Aleceon Edgewood, nothing was sacred—not even his own daughter; least of all his daughter.

Aleceon was now moving about the room in a disquieted manner, casting an occasional glance at her rigid demeanor. "You are a little fool!" The words erupted in a curious sound of exasperation that was at odds with his almost pleading look. He paused before her, hands in his pockets, expression now stern. "Can't you see what I've done for you? Instead of complaining, get down on your knees and count your blessings."

Morgana got to her feet, her eyes steady and unforgiving. "I have," she replied tersely. "They add up to . . . nothing."

With that, she turned and left the room without looking at him again, closing the door firmly behind her.

For long moments after she had gone, Aleceon just stood there, his face expressionless. Yet his eyes revealed a pain that had nothing to do with his condition.

"Why didn't you tell missy de truf?" Ben ventured after awhile. He had listened to the conversation between father and daughter with mounting dismay.

Turning, Aleceon glared at his slave. "And what is the truth, you black viper?" he demanded in a tight voice.

Ben hesitated, then whispered, "Dat you dyin' an' wants to make missy's life safe. . . ."

Ignoring that, Aleceon walked toward the table. Picking up the decanter, he poured himself a stiff brandy.

"Kin do dat fer you, suh." Ben came quickly forward.

"It isn't necessary for you to jump every time I make a move!" Aleceon declared irritably, motioning him away. "I'm not one of those Southern fops who can't even pour himself a drink."

Ben halted and sighed deeply. "Knows you ain'," he agreed quietly. He watched his master for a moment, then took a breath of determination. "But you should have tol' her," he insisted.

"No!" Aleceon's smoky blue eyes were fierce. "And don't you, either. Besides," he added with a flash of insight, "it's not my intentions that she's concerned with; it's Griffin's. And my reasons will not alter his. There is nothing I can say that will make her see the obvious. She will not believe that her husband loves her. And," he mused quietly, giving it thought, "perhaps Griffin himself is unaware of it." He fell silent a moment, then fixed the Negro with a hard look. "You are to say nothing of this. If you so much as say a word, I'll string you up by your heels. Understand?"

Resigned, Ben raised his hands. "My lips sealed with wax, suh. You knows dat."

Aleceon grunted as he returned to the window, then gave a deep, drawn out sigh. "I've never loved a woman," he mused idly. "Never found one that rated a second look."

"Have to be a special lady fer you to notice her, suh," Ben agreed sagely with a nod of his woolly head.

Aleceon seemed not to have heard him. He stood there quietly, almost motionless. "I married her mother because I needed her," he went on in a barely audible voice. "Kitty was a good girl. She was a whore, you know." Lifting the glass to his lips, he drank his brandy.

Ben nodded cautiously, a bit surprised at the revelation, but knowing that Aleceon was, in a sense, talking to himself.

"She was only sixteen," Aleceon went on. "But she was street wise. She died when Morgana was born."

"Must've bin a fine lady," Ben murmured in the face of that somewhat disjointed disclosure. "Miz Morgana shoah is."

Aleceon turned to view Ben. "She is, isn't she?" he demanded, as if he had just discovered that fact. When Ben fervently agreed, he turned away again to contemplate the scenery outside. "Still, I didn't love Kitty. Never found a woman I could love," he said again, with another deep sigh. "But Morgana . . . I loved her from the time she was a little girl. Always wanted the best for her. But . . ." he trailed off and morosely regarded his empty glass. He held it out and Ben moved quickly to refill it.

"Morgana was a strange little thing," Aleceon went on after taking a swallow of the fiery liquid. "Quiet, you know. Not going on at the mouth like most women. That's the thing I can't stand about them. Always preaching. Like to drive a man crazy with their sermonizing. My sister was like that. A real pain in the ass."

Ben made no comment to that. He avoided even agreeing with an uncomplimentary comment about white women.

Aleceon fell silent then, sinking into one of his frequent

dark moods of melancholy with which, by now, Ben was thoroughly familiar.

Anxiously, Ben kept an eye on the thin, gaunt back of the man who, inexplicably, had saved his life five years before. For as long as he lived, the memory would remain with him, as would his devotion for this man.

Ben had been born on a cotton plantation in Mississippi, some thirty-seven years ago. His master, a thoroughly frightening individual by the name of Warren Fiske, had beaten Ben's mother to death for malingering. Ben had been only seven at the time. At nineteen, he had married a wench named Tildy. The marriage, however, lasted less than a year. Tildy had been taken to auction and sold.

When Ben reached thirty years of age, Fiske had sold him to a passing slave trader, along with several other Negroes he considered past their prime. Eventually, Ben had wound up on a nameless plantation some ten miles out of New Orleans, where the only crop raised was sugar cane.

Toiling in the cotton fields, he soon learned, was child's play compared to the canefields, where a slave's life expectancy could be numbered in a mere five years. The work was unrelenting, from dawn to dusk, and sickness was not an excuse for absenteeism. The drivers were a surly lot, always in poor temper, always ready with the whip.

For Ben, and for the rest of the field hands, exhaustion was a constant companion, not only because of the long hours but because their diet was sadly deficient in protein. Meat was a luxury granted once a year on Christmas day, in spite of the law requiring that it be served once a week. The fact that it was a sugar plantation notwithstanding, blackstrap was doled out only every four months, the quantity so slight as to insure its disappearance after only one week. Vegetables were plentiful enough in the summer and spring, but their availability declined during fall and winter. The staples were grits and pone, enough to ward off hunger, but not enough to sustain a man for labor in the fields for eighteen hours a day. During grinding season they even worked on Sundays. Six hours was all the rest time allowed.

Ben knew, after only two years during which his health declined rapidly, that he would die if he didn't get away.

And so, for the first time in his life, he had run.

The patrollers caught him only three days later. His new master, one Samuel Carver, decided to make an example out of Ben. After giving his recalcitrant slave one hundred lashes, Carver had given orders for Ben to be staked out on a clearing in front of Slave Row as a reminder to the rest of his people of what would happen if they ever decided to run.

And there, tied down and waiting to die beneath the relentless Louisiana sun, left without food or water, was where Aleceon had found him.

Aleceon had been on his way to New Orleans and had stopped at Carver's for the night. There being no inns or any other type of public houses in the vicinity, it was customary for travelers to seek lodgings at any plantation they came across.

Thus it was that Aleceon Edgewood came to Carver's at the most crucial time in Ben's life.

Ben had been staked out for one whole day and night when he opened his eyes that morning to see the thin, aristocratic form of Aleceon Edgewood, who was viewing him somberly and listening to Carver's explanation of why his slave was being punished in such manner.

"He looks half dead now," Aleceon commented when Carver was through.

"Will be, before another day or two goes by," Carver announced in satisfaction, hooking his thumbs in his belt. He was a big and gruff-voiced man who prided himself on being able to turn out more hogsheads of sugar per acre than any of his neighbors. He went to great lengths to keep that dubious record intact.

Aleceon turned his smoky blue eyes upon his host. "How much do you want for him?" he asked casually, leaning on his walking stick.

Carver viewed him in open surprise. "He ain't for sale," he protested in his gravel-toned voice. "Gonna make an example out of this heah bastid."

"I'd say you've already done that," Aleceon murmured dryly with a brief glance at Ben's wracked body. "I'll give you three hundred dollars for him."

Pausing, Carver scratched his head. "Why in hell you wanta buy a worthless nigger like this one? He's a runner. 'Sides, like you said, he's half dead."

Aleceon shrugged and moved his ringed hand in a vague gesture. "I need a body servant," he explained. "And right now I can't afford a prime one."

Carver guffawed and hitched up his breeches. "This one ain't been trained to do nothing but work in the fields," he pointed out in a somewhat condescending voice, recognizing his visitor as a novice. "Why, he ain't even been housebroken. Wouldn't know the first thing about being a body servant." He rested a hand on Aleceon's shoulder.

"Look heah, I've got some fine young bucks. Be glad to have you inspect them, if you want."

Aleceon shook his head firmly. "No. I want this one. And I'll give you three hundred dollars for him."

Ben had listened to the conversation in growing amazement, with the wild hope that Carver would agree. He wasn't exactly certain what a body servant was, but he knew it would be a damn sight better than dying.

The bickering continued for several more minutes. Eventually, unable to resist the tempting offer of hard cash for a half dead slave, Carver had agreed.

After being untied, Ben was then carried to his cabin, being too weak to walk. One of the wenches washed and dressed the wounds on his back. After being fed and drinking his fill of water, Ben began to think that he just might live, after all.

Later that day, Aleceon came to his cabin.

Ben had made the effort to get up off his pallet, but Aleceon motioned for him to remain where he was.

"How are you feeling?" Aleceon asked, looking down at him.

"Fine, suh," Ben replied, not quite truthfully. He was awed by this man who dressed in clothes the likes of which he had never before seen, and who spoke with a curious accent that made Ben, at times, uncertain of his meaning. "Wantin' to thank you, masta, suh, fer buyin' dis no good nigger. . . ."

"You were all I could afford," Aleceon said softly with a half smile hovering about his thin lips. Then he grew serious. "Do you think you'll be able to travel in a week's time?"

"Yassuh," Ben replied swiftly, raising himself up on an

elbow to indicate his willingness. "Goes wit you now, iffen you want."

Aleceon smiled again at the obvious enthusiasm. "No. I'm not taking any chances with my three hundred dollar investment. I've left instructions that you are to be well fed and well cared for until I come back for you next week." He turned to go. Then, glancing back, he added sternly, "And, you black viper, you'd best serve me well."

Aleceon had returned, just as he'd promised, the following week. With him, he brought a mule for Ben to ride. Then the two of them had returned to New Orleans and Ben had begun to live a life he never knew existed.

Aleceon outfitted his new body servant in clothes of a quality only slightly less grand than his own. For the first time in his life Ben wore shoes—something that took a bit of getting used to. When money was won, Ben shared in the profits, for Aleceon was generous when he was lucky. When funds were in short supply, they both made do as best they could.

If it was possible for a slave to grow to idolize his master, Ben learned to do so over the next five years, to such an extent that he would have gladly given his own life to save that of the man who had rescued him from the pain and drudgery of the canefields.

Still watching the wasted form of Aleceon as he stared moodily out of the window, Ben sighed deeply, thinking of all this. The man who had saved his life was dying and Ben was helpless in the face of it.

Downstairs, at that very moment, Carlie Dobbs was pacing the verandah, glancing from time to time at Griffin, who was seated in a wicker chair.

"Goddamn that black bastid," Dobbs raged angrily, waving his arms in acute agitation. "This time I'll beat his ass till it falls off his worthless hide!"

To that, Griffin said a fervent amen. The overseer had just told him of Jonah's latest escape. After hastily writing a pass for Joe, Griffin had sent the huge Negro into Charleston to put a notice in the newspapers.

"Niggers are gettin' out of hand," Carlie muttered, still agitated. "Yestiddy, I heard Four Oaks lost another one. Disappeared overnight. Last week, Farraday had two of 'em take off into the swamp. The goddamn Underground Railroad is makin' a mess of trouble."

For a moment, Griffin made no response, having been only half listening to the overseer's rantings. Once again, as had happened all day long, his thoughts had returned to what had happened between him and Morgana that morning. He couldn't seem to get his mind off of it. Certainly he had never intended for her to find out, to be hurt. She wouldn't talk to him, had locked herself in her room all day. But she would have to come out sooner or later, he reasoned, determined to make the effort to at least try and explain the situation to her.

Aware that Dobbs had fallen silent and was regarding him curiously, Griffin brought himself back to the moment at hand. "The Underground's the least of our problems." Leaning forward in his chair, he took the glass of whiskey from the tray offered by Thomas. "There's two of those damn Yankee Abolitionists preaching in Charleston. I hear they're drawing bigger crowds each day."

"I heard 'em," Carlie said, then spat over the railing. "Spewin' their filthy venom to anyone who'll listen. We ought to tar and feather the bastids, like they did with those in Natchez." He regarded Griffin earnestly. "Run 'em right out of town on a rail, like they did. It stirs up the niggers when they heah that kind of stuff. Gets 'em riled, and to thinkin' they're as good as anybody else. Christ, Griff, can you imagine what would happen if they were freed? Randy bucks runnin' loose, rapin' and killin'? We ought to put those preaching Abolitionists in a roomful of niggers and lock the door," he pronounced with a sharp nod of his head. "They'd change their tune in a hurry."

Griffin finished his drink. "That'll never happen, Carlie," he said calmly. "Them being free, I mean. The South would never stand for it."

Carlie paused to finish his own drink, then picked up his hat which was balanced precariously on the railing. "I hope you're right, Griff," he said quietly. " 'Cause if you ain't, we're all in a passel of trouble."

Supper was over before Griffin had a chance to approach Morgana. She had spoken to no one during the meal, not even Cammy, and when she was through, she had immediately gotten up and left the room.

Quickly, Griffin went after her, seeing her about to ascend the stairs.

"Morgana, wait. You're acting foolish." He grabbed her arm, effectively halting her progress. "Look, I know how it sounded . . . I know what you think, but—"

"Do you?" The mocking words glittered icily. His attitude of patient condescension only infuriated her further. To her, he didn't look at all contrite or even sorry for what he had done. She glanced down at the hand of her arm, then up at him.

His jaw worked visibly as he withdrew his hand. He tried again. "It's not the way it seems at all."

"You didn't marry me to free Albemarle from debt?" Her voice was soft and deadly as she regarded his handsome face with exaggerated interest.

Griffin ran a hand through his hair. "Yes, but—"

"It isn't necessary to explain further, Griffin," she interrupted in the same tone of voice. "I'm not interested in your reasons or excuses!"

She spun around and grasped her skirt with both hands. Hoisting it an inch or two, she ran up the stairs without a backward glance, not wanting to give him the satisfaction of seeing her eyes bright with tears.

It took all her willpower to prevent herself from turning, from throwing herself into his arms.

Reaching her room, she entered, locked the door, and flung herself onto the bed. Burying her head in the pillow, she wept, allowing herself the tears she vowed he would never see.

Chapter
7

The next morning, after carefully avoiding Griffin at breakfast, Morgana wandered about the house in an aimless fashion, too restless to sit still. After a few tentative, sympathetic overtures, Cammy had otherwise occupied herself, sensing Morgana's need to work out her problems alone.

Toward the rear of the downstairs hallway, Morgana came across closed doors which she had not before noticed.

Hesitating only a moment, she opened them, blinking in surprise at the sight of the lovely drawing room with its molded panelling and cream colored walls. On the far side, pocket doors connected this room with the front parlor. These, too, were closed.

Entering, she saw that the furniture was of a delicate construction with fluted back- and armrests, all richly upholstered in a pale rose damask that was repeated in the draperies that covered rose-point lace curtains.

As lovely as it was, the room had about it an air of being unused. Everything was situated too perfectly. The lace doilies on the head- and armrests of the chairs and settee were not even a fraction of an inch off center. A crystal vase on top of a small table with drop leaves was positioned dead center, and empty of flowers. A candle stand sported a brass candelabra, its white candles never having been lit. In a corner, between two bow windows, was a baby grand piano with a fringed shawl draped over the top of it. Italian marble graced the fireplace, over which hung a portrait of a lovely young woman gowned in an elaborately ruffled yellow silk dress. She was holding a bouquet of white star jessamine in her arms.

Moving closer, Morgana stared, struck by the beautiful face that gazed serenely down, a slight, almost secret smile about the lips.

"Her name was Anne. . . ."

Startled, Morgana spun around to see Nathaniel. She hadn't heard him enter the room. He, too, was looking at the portrait.

"That was Griffin's grandmother," Nathaniel said softly.

"She . . . she was very beautiful."

He nodded solemnly at the observation, eyes still on the portrait.

Morgana felt suddenly uncomfortable. "I hope it's all right that I came in here. . . ."

"Oh, yes," Nathaniel quickly assured her. "This is your home now. The only reason this room has been closed off is because . . . well, since Anne died, we don't do much entertaining here at Albemarle. There have been times in years past when the house was filled with laughter and music. But with just me and Griff, and Cammy still a child . . ." He sighed.

"Anne was your wife," Morgana noted, still feeling as if she had intruded. The room was like a shrine.

"Yes." His eyes again returned to the portrait. "You would have liked her, I think. She was a bit straightforward; that sometimes bothered people. But she was honest in a way few people seem to achieve."

"I'm sure I would have liked her," Morgana whispered, not knowing what else to say. She clasped her hands together, wanting to leave, wanting to be alone with her thoughts, but she couldn't find it within herself to simply turn and leave the room. She sensed that Nathaniel had something to say to her, but she was uncertain as to whether or not she wanted to hear it.

Nathaniel walked over to the piano, rubbing his fingers across the polished surface. "This was hers. She used to play every day. The music is still there, in the bench, just as she left it." He looked at Morgana with grave eyes. "Do you play?"

"Yes. A bit," Morgana replied, still feeling uncomfortable. "I was taught at school."

He nodded again. "Then feel free to use it anytime you want. It . . . would be nice to have music in the house again."

A small silence descended. Nathaniel looked suddenly embarrassed. He turned away, staring out of the window. His hands moved restlessly, as if he didn't quite know what to do with them.

"You mustn't think harshly of Griffin," he murmured after a moment, not looking at her.

Morgana's mouth compressed. "I . . . don't think of him at all," she replied tartly. And that was a lie, she told herself. She couldn't seem to stop thinking about him.

Nathaniel turned then, his face reflecting the sort of tired sadness that only a person of his years could express. "You shouldn't blame Griffin," he entreated. His voice fell to an anguished whisper. "If anyone's to blame, it's me. Griffin did what he had to do. . . ."

Morgana raised her chin. Her eyes flashed as anger returned in full force. "He knew he was going to marry me even before I came here. Didn't he?"

Nathaniel's sigh was long and deep. "Yes," he admitted quietly. "But I think, after he met you, he wanted to."

She gave a short laugh at that. "Please, Nathaniel. I would appreciate it if you didn't play me for more of a fool than I have already been."

Unhappily, he looked down at the floor, then at her. "Is that what you think?"

"Oh, I don't know what to think," she cried out. She put a palm to her cheek. It felt warm and flushed. But then, at the sight of his stricken face, she relented. "I'm sorry. I should never have spoken like that to you."

"You and Griffin are married now," Nathaniel reminded her. "For better or worse."

She made a bitter sound which he chose to ignore.

"What you do now will set the pattern of your marriage for the rest of your life," he went on in an earnest manner. He came closer and raised a hand as if to place it on her shoulder, but then apparently thought better of it and allowed it to fall to his side. "Morgana, it would be best for all concerned if you would forget what happened, if you would put it from your mind."

"Forget?" She was astonished by his words. "Forget that my husband married me only because he had to?" She could feel the hot tears scald her eyes. Rather than display them, Morgana ran from the room.

When they sat down to eat that evening, Morgana refused to meet Griffin's eye. The conversation at the supper table was strained and awkward, with only Cammy and Nathaniel making an attempt to fill the increasing silence with bright, meaningless chatter. Aleceon had prudently absented himself, taking his meal in his room.

Morgana tried to keep a cool composure, unwilling to let them see how betrayed she felt. By "them" she meant Griffin and her father. Somehow she couldn't find it in her heart to censure either Cammy or Nathaniel, though most certainly they both had known what was going on. Cammy, she felt certain, had not really been a part of it; most likely she only found out after the arrangements had been made. Nathaniel, on the other hand, had certainly had an active hand in the plot. Still, Morgana couldn't fault him, for he had looked so unhappy, so genuinely contrite this morning, she almost felt sorry for him.

That left Griffin and her father. And even Aleceon, as angry and as exasperated as she was with him, Morgana couldn't hold entirely to blame. She had always known how he was, how he acted first in his own interests.

But Griffin . . . The end result was that all the pain she felt was caused solely by him.

That night, when Griffin knocked on her bedroom door, his voice a soft entreaty, Morgana refused to allow Bella to open it. She sat alone in the darkness with only her thoughts for company. A yawning sense of futility loomed before her as she thought of the days, the months, the years that lay ahead of her, living a life that was not of her making, living with a man she loved, but knowing she could never permit herself to give in to the feeling.

For the next three nights Morgana heard, and did not respond to, the soft knock on her door.

On the fourth night there was silence.

Morgana knew that she was alienating herself from her husband and father, to whom she barely spoke. But she was helpless in her anger and hurt to do otherwise.

Gradually, over the next two weeks, an uneasy truce was reached during the day and a certain semblance of normalcy returned to Albemarle.

Coming out of her room one morning, Morgana paused as Griffin's door suddenly opened and a young girl dressed in a plain white cotton shift that fell to her ankles emerged. Her skin was the color of honey. The girl halted abruptly at the sight of Morgana, her eyes wide, much as a startled doe when danger threatens. Even in her rising anger, Morgana had to admit that the girl was one of the most beautiful creatures she had ever laid eyes upon.

Their gazes locked for a moment, then the girl's slid away. She began to move quietly down the hall, her head lowered.

Stepping back into her room, Morgana viewed Bella with eyes like blue stone. She described the girl, then asked, "Who is she?"

Bella stared at the braided carpet on the floor as if she would find the answer there, and again, sharply, Morgana repeated the question.

"Dat's Serena, missus," came the whispered reply.

"Serena?"

"Yassum." Bella was still studying the carpet with an engrossed look.

Morgana's delicate nostrils flared. "And who is Serena?" she inquired in measured tones. She stared at the black girl, but Bella refused to meet her eye.

"Jest a wench, missus. . . ."

"I've not seen her before . . ." Morgana raised a questioning brow and her eyes seemed to turn a darker shade of blue.

Bella shrugged with increasing uneasiness. "Serena works in de kitchen. Sometimes," she qualified.

"How long has she been here?" Morgana's outer calm concealed the raging turbulence within her.

"Masta Griffin done bought her las' year, when he went to Savannah."

"He purchased a girl like that for a kitchen wench?" Morgana's tone conveyed utter disbelief. "Then what was she doing coming out of his room at this time of the morning?"

Bella bit her full lip in thought. "Doan know, missus," she decided at last with a guileless look that did nothing to deceive her mistress.

"She's Master Griffin's wench, isn't she!" Morgana demanded, taking a step closer.

Again Bella's eyes sought the carpet. "S'pose so," she admitted with another shrug. Then, glancing at Morgana's darkening countenance, hastened to add, "Doan mean nothin' though. All de gen'mens has dey wenches." She regarded Morgana earnestly.

Although she had no reason to doubt Bella, Morgana

135

was genuinely outraged. She had never heard of such a thing. Her mouth tightened. All "gen'mens" might do it, she thought, furious, but she'd be damned if she'd have such goings-on in her own home!

Turning swiftly, Morgana left the room. Walking across the carpeted hall with a determined step, she opened Griffin's door without knocking.

He was lying on the rumpled bed, only a sheet covering him from the waist down. At her abrupt entrance, he raised a brow, but made no other move.

"I will not have it!" Morgana blurted out, trying to control the urge to strike that handsome face.

A lazy smile greeted that. "Somehow, I was hoping to hear softer words from your lips than that." He threw back the sheet and she could see that he was naked. Annoyed, she felt her face flush. He patted the rumpled bed. "Come here," he said softly. "We'll talk about whatever is bothering your Northern sensibilities."

Morgana glared at him, feeling the heat on her face, but her eyes remained steady. "That . . . girl. I saw her when she came out of your room."

The black brows rose higher. "What girl?" he asked innocently.

"Damn you, Griffin!" she said through clenched teeth. "I'm in no mood for your foolishness."

He watched her for a moment, then, getting up, he crossed the room and stood before her. With some effort, Morgana kept her gaze at eye level. It seemed to amuse him, and again he smiled.

"The situation can be easily remedied," he remarked softly, the infuriating grin still in place. Reaching out, he gently traced her jaw with a fingertip. "If you will allow me back into your bed, it won't be necessary to bring anyone to mine."

Her cheeks turned scarlet, but she was uncertain as to whether it was embarrassment or rage that was coursing through her. The light touch on her face sent a flame throughout her whole body.

He took another step toward her and Morgana stiffened. "Don't come any closer," she warned, acutely irritated by the wavering tone of her voice.

Once more, amusement slanted from his dark eyes as he looked down at her, hands on his lean hips. "There's a rosy glow to your cheeks that's very becoming," he noted with a wicked glint in his eye, appearing to enjoy her discomfort. "Am I the cause, or have you been dipping your fingertips into the paint pot?"

She was infuriated. The glow deepened, heightening the blue of her eyes. "Don't change the subject!" she snapped. "I don't care what your . . . traditions are," she cried out, trying to calm her racing pulse. He was so close she could feel the heat from his body. It burned through her and her anger rose to new heights. She was furious with herself as well as with him, and she began to tremble. "I cannot believe that decent men live this way. I will not have it!" she said again, eyes blazing at him.

This time, he grinned broadly. "I never said I was decent," he protested mildly. "In fact, there are those who say I'm a regular scoundrel."

Before she could move, he grabbed her, holding her tightly against him. Even through her clothing, she could feel the hardness of him and she fought vainly against the weakness that came over her. She was certain that if he released her she would collapse because her legs seemed unable to support her weight.

He continued to stare down at her, his eyes mocking her.

With a gasping cry, Morgana tore herself from his embrace and rushed from the room. Her eyes stung with tears of impotent rage and she blinked them away quickly.

Outside, she breathed deeply, waiting for her heart to cease its pounding.

Did she still love that man after all that had happened? she wondered. She was deeply annoyed with herself and with her uncontrollable reactions to his nearness.

Yes. The thought gnawed at her, but she refused to give in to it. She had, once before, innocently offered her love and devotion. She would not make that foolish mistake again, she vowed fervently.

At last she calmed a bit. With a nervous glance back at the house, she began to walk in the direction of the group of cabins known as Slave Row. She had little purpose in mind, she just didn't want to face Griffin over the breakfast table, didn't want to see his hateful, mocking face, didn't want those taunting eyes upon her.

Approaching the slave quarters, she paused a moment, enjoying the sight of a group of black children playing in the dirt road. Their laughter was shrill and enthusiastic as they cavorted about. They were very young—toddlers really—and naked as the day they had been born.

At the sight of her, they all fell silent, eyes round. Not wishing to disrupt their game, Morgana flashed a smile of encouragement at them, then hurried on.

The cabins were small, she noticed, only one room, and made of logs. A somewhat larger cabin, consisting of two rooms, she found out later, belonged to Minda.

But the largest structure of them all was a combination hospital and nursery, and was presided over by an ancient Negress called Auntie Flora.

Despite her height, which could have been no more than five feet, and her age, which had to be in the upward reaches of seventy, Auntie Flora was an imposing sight. She stood with a proud stance, her dark eyes more direct and level than any slave Morgana had so far seen. There was an immense dignity about the woman, and if she was in any way intimidated by her status, it wasn't apparent.

The only occupant as Morgana entered was a young woman with skin the color of light chocolate. The room was sparsely furnished, containing only a table, a chair, and several husk mattresses which were positioned on the floor. There was only one small window, but the walls were whitewashed, giving one the appearance of a certain degree of airiness.

Auntie Flora nodded calmly at Morgana. She didn't appear surprised by the unexpected visit. "Dis heah's Tansy, missus," she explained, motioning toward the woman on the husk mattress. "She done had herse'f a baby gal, jest las' night."

"And where is the baby?" Morgana asked, looking about the otherwise empty room.

"Doan keep suckahs heah, missus. Dey's kept in de nurs'ry." She pointed to a closed door.

Morgana was surprised at that. "But why? Why aren't the babies with their mothers? Who feeds them?"

"Got wet nurses fer de chillens. Takes good care of 'em, we do. Doan you worry yore pretty se'f 'bout dat." She folded her fleshless arms across an almost flat bosom.

Sensing evasion, Morgana frowned. "Why aren't the

babies kept with their mother?" she asked again in a low voice.

There was no way for Auntie Flora to refuse to answer, although Morgana was, as yet, unaware of that simple fact; but the old woman's lined face looked saddened as she replied.

"Some o' de wenches," she explained carefully, "gits it in dey haids dat dere suckahs bettah off daid den slaves. An' so . . . dey kills de poor babies. Not ever'one feels lak dat," she added hastily in the face of Morgana's horrified expression. "On'y some do. But . . ." she shrugged her bony shoulders, "best fer baby an' de momma, dey be sep'rated fer awhile. Den, after de suckah a few weeks old an' de momma gits to know 'em, cain't kill 'em no more."

For a moment, Morgana was silent, feeling a sudden, overwhelming sense of depression. Then she regarded the young woman on the mattress. "Would you kill your baby?" she asked quietly.

The dark eyes brimmed with tears. "No, missus. Wouldn't do sech a thing. . . ."

Morgana smiled, then viewed Auntie Flora again. "Bring this woman's child to her." At the sight of the doubtful expression that crossed the black face, she added softly, "Please, do as I say."

Reluctantly, Auntie Flora nodded. Morgana turned away. Getting down on her knees, she put her hand on the young woman's forehead. Feeling the cool skin, she inclined her head in satisfaction.

"Has a doctor seen her?" she asked, looking over her shoulder at the old woman.

Raising both hands, Auntie Flora chortled, delighted with what she thought was a deliberate effort toward a joke. "Lawd, missus," she exclaimed. "Ain' no doctor 'round heah. 'Cept, o' cose, fer Dr. Foxworth. But he be de white folkses doctor. Doan treat us niggers."

Morgana's brow creased in consternation. "Then who took care of this woman when she was having her baby?"

Auntie Flora's black eyes grew round. "Why, dis heah ole nigger woman do it. Yassum," she nodded her head in a vigorous manner at Morgana's surprised look. "Dese wenches doan need no coddlin' when dey's givin' birf. Havin' babies easy fer 'em."

"But what if there are complications?" Morgana said quickly, upset with what she was hearing. "What if the baby is in a wrong position?"

Auntie Flora grinned broadly, displaying an almost toothless smile as she held up her gnarled hands for Morgana to see. "Kin turn 'em 'round," she stated, appearing unconcerned. "Done it lots o' times."

Morgana could only regard the old woman in amazed wonder. "And what if anyone is sick?" she ventured, half prepared for the answer.

"Treats 'em, I do," Auntie Flora offered with a shake of her gray and woolly head.

"Where did you learn to do all this?" asked an astonished Morgana.

The old woman cackled again. "Learnt in Africa. I'se an African nigger, you know, missus." She said that with a certain pride.

Morgana got to her feet, her expression reflecting confusion. "An African . . ." she made a vague gesture. "I thought you all were African."

"Lawd, missus, dat ain' so," Auntie Flora disclaimed, again exposing her gums in a grin. "Most o' dese niggers

141

borned right heah, in dis country. Doan know no more 'bout Africa den a sparrow do. *I'se* an African." She pointed a black finger at her sagging breast, again displaying pride.

"And you learned how to care for sick people there?"

"Yassum. Nacherly, has to make do wit de herbs an' barks we got heah. Works fine. Most de times," she added fatalistically, then walked slowly toward the other room.

Morgana waited until Tansy's baby was brought to her. She gave a nod of satisfaction as the young woman eagerly reached for her child. Then, smiling to herself, she left the "hospital" and the wonder called Auntie Flora.

The children were still playing in the road, having been joined by a large yellow dog. At the sight of Morgana, the animal came closer, tail wagging, ears flattened as he panted a welcome.

She paused long enough to rumple the soft fur before continuing on her way.

As she walked up the narrow street that separated the rows of cabins, Morgana saw Carlie Dobbs roughly hauling a Negro into the barn. Curious, she headed in their direction.

She heard the sound of the whip before she got there, and broke into a run.

Entering the barn a few moments later, she gasped at the sight of Dobbs ruthlessly lashing the man whose hands were tied around a wooden pillar.

Appalled, she shouted, "Stop it! Stop it!" She ran forward, "What are you doing to him? You'll kill him. . . ."

Dobbs halted, arm in midair, staring at her with open surprise. "You shouldn't be heah, Miz Morgana," he protested. "This ain't no place for a white lady. Please go back into the house."

"I want you to untie that man—immediately!" she insisted, her face reddening with indignant anger.

Striving to hide his exasperation, Dobbs muttered, "No need to concern yourself with this sort of thing."

"Untie him!"

"Can't do that," Dobbs protested, shaking his head from side to side. The overseer had recovered from his surprise at seeing her and was now regarding her with a sullen expression, only barely checking the annoyance from showing on his face. He didn't like Morgana; didn't like Northerners period. He especially disliked Northern women. They seemed to approach the question of slavery with an evangelistic ferver that raised his hackles.

She was still staring at him, angry and flushed, and Dobbs took a deep breath. "Look, I caught him stealing some tools so he could sell 'em to buy whiskey," he tried to explain. "That's an offense that calls for ten lashes. Now please, get out of here and let me get on with it."

Dobbs again raised his arm and the Negro cringed, turning his face away. Morgana quickly stepped forward, grabbing the overseer's shirt with such determination that the pocket tore beneath her grasp.

"Stop it, I say . . ." Her voice rose to a shout as she began to struggle with the man, trying to pull the whip from his hand.

"What the hell's going on here?"

Morgana turned to see Griffin and Nathaniel standing in the doorway. Both men looked angry.

"Griffin!" Morgana came toward him. "Mr. Dobbs was viciously beating this man," she exclaimed in an excited voice, pointing toward the bound Negro. "You must do something!"

Griffin looked at Dobbs, who, in an almost weary tone, explained the situation.

When the overseer was through, Griffin gave a curt nod. "Get on with it," he ordered.

Morgana's eyes widened. "Aren't you even going to question this man?" she demanded, again pointing to the slave. "Perhaps he has an explanation."

"I'm not interested in his explanations," Griffin pronounced tersely. "If Carlie says he's guilty, then he is!"

As Morgana again began to protest, Griffin took hold of her arm in a rough gesture and almost dragged her outside into the yard.

"You are, without a doubt, the most aggravating woman I've ever known," he growled. His mouth set into a grim line. "I don't want you to interfere with Dobbs again!" he ordered sternly.

In a sudden motion, she wrenched her hand away from him, her eyes blazing. "You're despicable," she shouted at him. Then she winced as she heard the whip striking flesh and the loud wail that accompanied it. "How can you do such a thing?" she demanded, close to tears.

"We do what needs to be done," he stated coldly, unmoved. "And I will thank you not to make a nuisance of yourself."

Furious, Morgana raised her hand, intending to strike him, but he easily caught her arm, holding it in a painful grip as he turned to Nathaniel.

"Take her into the house," he said to his grandfather. "And try to persuade her to stay out from underfoot." He released Morgana, who was sputtering in rage, then strode away without looking back.

Tentatively, in an almost apologetic way, Nathaniel touched Morgana's arm. "Come along, girl. Let's go into the house now," he entreated.

She resisted a moment, then, with a deep, audible sigh, followed the old man. She was still trembling with the force of her anger and outrage.

Inside the house, Nathaniel led her into his study and closed the door. Shaking his head, he remarked, "Lots you don't understand, Morgana. Sit down," he motioned. "Sit down and stop prancin' about like a restless filly."

"Now," he went on after she had reluctantly seated herself. "You got to understand how it is, and why folks hereabouts tend to keep a tight rein on their people." He sat down in a nearby chair.

"I think what I saw was a bit more than that," she began indignantly.

Nathaniel ignored her observation. Leaning back in his chair, he squinted, looking up toward the ceiling as if it would be there where he'd find the threads of his remembrance.

"It was in the summer of '22, I recall," he began slowly. "I was a young man in my thirties then. Alicia, well, she wasn't but eighteen at the time. And my wife, Anne—she was alive then, too."

He paused, a wistful smile hovering about his lips while Morgana fidgeted impatiently. She wondered if that poor man in the barn had been seriously injured and mentally cursed Carlie Dobbs for his savage brutality.

But Nathaniel wasn't to be hurried. "We were all in Charleston for the summer—fever, you know," he waited for her nod, then continued. "There was this nigger by the name of Denmark Vesey. He was a free man, or so he claimed. Well, this Vesey got it into his kinky head to lead the slaves in a revolt. Must've been planning it for months," he mused, rubbing his chin.

Morgana took a breath and shifted herself to a more comfortable position. "I hardly think that man outside was planning a revolt," she noted caustically.

"Their stealing and sabotaging are a form of it," he objected mildly, refusing to be goaded.

She looked at him in surprise. "Sabotage?"

"Oh, yes. They break tools, hide things. Left alone, they'd damage the crop if they could. They're just like children, you know."

"Since when would you treat a child like that!" she exclaimed sharply, pointing toward the window in the general direction of the barn.

"You're missing the point . . ." He fell silent a moment, trying to repress his exasperation.

"Have you?" she demanded. She leaned forward in the chair, eyes bright.

Nathaniel drew his brows together. "Have I what?"

"Ever done that to a child? Have you ever tied up a child and beat him?"

"Of course not!" Nathaniel seemed genuinely shocked by her words. He waited a moment and when she didn't speak, continued with his story. "Anyway, this Vesey managed to get close to a thousand blacks involved—from Charleston and the plantations along the Ashley and Cooper rivers. They planned to burn down Charleston, then kill as many white people as they were able to."

In spite of herself, Morgana found she was regarding him intently. "What happened?"

"Well, seems like George Farraday's cook got wind of it—he owns a plantation along the Cooper—and she told George about it only days before it was to happen."

Morgana leaned back in the chair again. "So they never actually attacked Charleston?" she observed.

"Oh, they tried, all right. Critters were armed with pikes and knives, probably made over the previous months by the blacksmiths. But by the time they got ready—the militia was ready, too. Only caught about thirty-five of them, though," he related, sounding regretful. "The rest skedaddled on home."

"And I suppose they were all killed?" Morgana noted with a sigh. "The ones that got caught, I mean."

"You bet they were," Nathaniel affirmed with a short and harsh laugh. "Hanged the lot of them. But how many of us would they have slaughtered if they hadn't been stopped?" he demanded, fixing her with a hard look.

"Well, I agree that that sort of situation could be truly frightening. Still, it was a black who saved you, wasn't it?" she pointed out logically.

"That time," he agreed with a curt nod of his head. "But the folks in Virginia weren't so lucky some years later. Ever hear of Nat Turner?"

Morgana admitted that she had not.

"No black called an alarm that time. Him and about seventy other niggers went on a bloody rampage in the summer of '31. Traveled from plantation to plantation, killin' and lootin' as they went. Before they were stopped, the bastards murdered better than fifty people. Children,

147

too—little babies. And I won't offend you by tellin' you what they did to the women before they killed them."

Nathaniel's face was grim now, uncompromising, and he noted Morgana's paleness with satisfaction.

"So, you see, girl, we can't give no quarter. Where the slaves are concerned, we've got to keep the upper hand. And it's why we put up with the patrollers," he added as an afterthought. "There's those as calls them white trash. And I'm not one to argue the point. Fact of the matter is, most of them are. But we need them. And I'm not one to chide a man on how he makes his living. Listen," he leaned forward, his eyes imploring her understanding. "Neither me nor Griff likes it when we got to discipline our people. Some do, you know." He wagged a finger for emphasis. "Ashamed to admit that, but it's so."

Morgana fell silent. She had learned things today—and not all of them were pleasant. Slavery was not a benevolent institution, despite her first impressions. It had a dark and evil side that loomed larger and larger with each new experience she encountered.

As she looked out of the window at the peaceful scene beyond, it struck her that there were six white people here at Albemarle—and more than a hundred and fifty blacks. If the slaves here ever decided to revolt . . . She gave a shudder at just the thought.

That night at the supper table, the conversation was, once again, strained. Griffin made no effort at all to ease the situation, but more than once Morgana was aware of those taunting eyes, which she refused to meet.

As soon as she was able, she left the table and went

outside. The sun was low, the western sky streaked with brilliant apricot slashes.

Griffin had watched her leave. As soon as she did, he wiped his mouth with his napkin and got up. It was time he had it out with her, he thought to himself. This foolishness had gone on long enough.

With determined steps he left the house, seeing Morgana a distance away, walking in the direction of the river.

She turned just then, the waning sun setting her hair ablaze with golden light, washing the flawless skin with a rosy color. She looked so beautiful that Griffin paused in his tracks. Staring, he caught his breath at the sight of her. How was it, he thought to himself, amazed, that he could have been so blind at the beginning?

His mouth felt dry and he swallowed. He wanted to approach her, to take her in his arms, to ravish her, consume her . . . but his limbs wouldn't respond. He felt suddenly clumsy, awkward, like a schoolboy.

The realization prompted a dark surge of anger.

Who was this woman to so provoke him? his mind demanded. Who was this damn Yankee female, with her airs and principles . . . She was his wife, by God. His wife! And as such, he was entitled to his rights, and his privileges.

He strode in her direction, full of purpose, his jaw set with new determination.

Having noted his approach, Morgana faced him, eyes cool as a sea breeze, her body relaxed, demeanor calm.

Griffin paused before her, looking down at her face as if he had never before seen it. Then he grabbed her shoulders none too gently and pulled her toward him. His mouth sought hers, forcing her soft lips to part. His tongue tasted the sweetness of her mouth and he could feel himself becoming aroused almost beyond control.

For a moment, Morgana remained passive within his embrace. Then she began to struggle, placing her small hands against his chest, trying to push him from her.

He tore his mouth away, breathing heavily. "Goddamn you," he muttered. "You're my wife. You belong to me!"

Delicate nostrils flared and whitened, and blue eyes flashed a storm warning. "I belong to no one," she spat, twisting away from him. It was a determined move, leaving no room for argument or entreaty and, sensing that, Griffin's hands fell to his side. "I'm not one of your nigger wenches," she said. The words were low and contemptuous. "You can command Serena," she declared, her eyes still blazing. "But you can't command me." She took a step back from him, hands clenched at her sides.

Griffin's face bore an expression of uncertainty that, for the moment, intrigued her. Then she turned away, unwilling to allow herself to show any interest.

"Morgana," he pleaded, as she began to walk away.

Pausing, she turned, regarding him in wintry silence before she spoke. "You got what you wanted, Griffin," she said quietly. "Albemarle is yours. But I'm not, and never will be."

Griffin heard the coldness in her voice, saw the scorn in her eyes, and in a quick motion, he turned away. He was a proud man; proud of who he was, how he lived, and, yes, proud of his Southland. He wouldn't beg for his wife's favors, or acquiesce to her foolish outbursts. He would, he decided as he walked back to the house, be accepted on his own terms or not at all.

Morgana remained where she was for a few minutes longer, then she made her way slowly back to the house.

On the way to her room, Cammy beckoned to her. After a brief hesitation, Morgana went to her.

"Come in," Cammy insisted, grasping her hand. She drew Morgana toward the bed and sat on it, pulling her down beside her. "I heard about what happened today. . . ."

For the moment, Morgana just stared at her. So many things had happened, she was uncertain which one Cammy was referring to.

"It doesn't happen often," Cammy went on, her expression entreating Morgana's understanding. "That business with Ramus . . . He's the slave you saw being punished," she went on to explain, confronted by Morgana's questioning look. "It's just that, well . . . sometimes the people get out of hand—" She broke off at Morgana's deep sigh.

"Your grandfather explained that to me," Morgana murmured wearily.

Cammy continued to regard her, then suddenly flung her arms about Morgana, hugging her. "Oh, I do want you to be happy here," she cried. "Things will work out with Griffin, too. I know it!" She said the words as though willing it to happen.

Morgana just smiled sadly and patted the slim arm, thinking of nothing to say.

"Oh, Morgana," Cammy exclaimed, close to tears. "Please give us a chance. I know it's all strange to you . . . and that business with the mortgage," she sighed, not noticing the bitterness return to Morgana's face. "I don't really understand it all," she mused, now plucking absently at the covers with her fingers. "But I do know one thing," she again viewed Morgana, this time intently. "My brother didn't marry you because he had to."

"Oh, Cammy," Morgana protested tiredly, shaking her head at the girl's so obvious attempt to smooth things over.

Cammy gripped her hand tightly, leaning forward. "I know my brother, Morgana. I know him well. The expression on his face in those days just before you were married . . ." She shook her head once, emphatically. "I've not seen that look before. . . ."

Morgana tilted her head, the sad smile returning. She was grateful—and even a bit amused—at Cammy's attempt to make her feel better. But it was useless. Words wouldn't change what had happened, wouldn't heal her bruised heart.

Griffin's sister was regarding her with such a pleading look that Morgana kissed the petal soft cheek before she got to her feet. "Thank you, Cammy," she said softly.

"Would you like to stay with me tonight?" the girl offered quickly. "Perhaps you shouldn't be alone so much. . . ."

Gently, Morgana shook her head. "I really am tired." She headed for the door. "Good night, dear."

Lying on her bed a while later, unable to sleep, Morgana could hear the sound of someone singing. The voice, rich and mellifluous, was coming from the slave quarters. It was a sad song, almost a lament, and it suited her present state of mind perfectly.

When she thought of the events of the day, Morgana realized that the anger had left her, or perhaps she was simply too weary to give credence to it. In its place was a profound sadness, a sadness for what might have been, for what almost had been hers.

She put a fingertip to her lips. Only a short time ago, Griffin's mouth had been upon those very lips. He would never know how close she had come to yielding. Agitated, she sat up in bed, motioning for Bella to remain where she was. The dark-skinned girl had immediately risen when she heard Morgana stir.

Perhaps she *was* being foolish, Morgana thought. Getting up, she walked back and forth across her room, knowing that, only a few steps away, Griffin was lying in his bed. She could go to him, lie beside him, let him quell the terrible heat he had aroused within her and which she was unable to quench. Only he could do that.

With a soft sob, Morgana headed for the door, her body trembling with its need.

Opening the door quietly, she froze. She was just in time to see Serena enter Griffin's room.

The anger returned, stronger. The cold and deadly feeling effectively doused her passion, and she clenched the knob of the door so tightly the metal bruised her palm.

Closing the door, she leaned her back against it. Her eyes narrowed with her fury, part of which was directed at herself. Once again she had almost played the fool.

"But damn you, Griffin Kynes," she whispered fiercely into the dimness, "I shall not make that mistake again."

Chapter
8

The following morning, Griffin and Nathaniel decided to ride to the neighboring plantation of Four Oaks, not only to visit Farley Barrows, who was an old friend, but to learn whether the planter had recovered his runaway slave.

From her piazza, which faced directly over the front yard, Cammy watched as her brother and grandfather rode away.

There was a subdued excitement about her as she stood there, dressed in the morning gown of blue sprigged muslin that she had worn at breakfast. Her eyes were shining and her lips were parted slightly to accommodate the quickening breaths she took.

Catching Meg's curious glance at her, Cammy brought herself under control, striving for a casualness she didn't feel.

"Get my riding clothes," she ordered preemptorily.

Turning, she went back into her bedroom. "Stop dawdling!" she exclaimed, irritated with the slave's hesitancy.

With Meg's assistance, Cammy hurriedly donned the light gray habit which was trimmed with a dark blue velvet collar and velvet-covered buttons. Disdaining the matching hat, she picked up a book from her writing table, then almost ran downstairs and out into the sunwashed day. Slowing her steps to reflect a more sedate pace, she secreted the book inside her jacket.

Arriving at the stables a few minutes later, Cammy's dark eyes swept over Jude as he groomed a horse, noting the play of muscles beneath his cotton shirt as his arms moved about. It should have been a familiar sight to her because she had seen him every single day for her whole life. But the sight of Jude was anything but ordinary to her of late.

Seeing her, Jude now straightened, his manner unexpectedly cautious.

"You be wantin' to ride today, Miss Cammy?" he asked her, laying the brush on a small wooden stool. The horse turned its head, nudging Jude's arm in a silent plea for a continuation of his attention. Absently, he moved his hand to the animal's nose, rubbing the softness, never taking his eyes from Cammy.

She frowned at his words, but nodded, following him as he walked inside to one of the stalls, adjusting her eyes to the cool dimness. There were twelve stalls, six on either side of the wooden structure which had a dirt floor. Bales of hay were stacked at the rear, and harnesses, saddles and trappings were hung on the walls and from the beamed ceiling.

Jude led a sleek, reddish-brown mare forward, then

hoisted a heavy saddle over the shiny back as if it were weightless. After he secured the straps, he cupped his hands for his young mistress.

Coming toward him, Cammy raised a small booted foot. Then, faking a stumble, she leaned her young body up against his.

Jude stood very still. Her hips pressed against him sent a flood of heat through his loins. Her white arms went about his neck and she gazed up at him, a smile curving her soft lips.

"You ought'n be doin' dat, Miss Cammy," he said in a strangled voice, keeping his hands at his sides.

"I hate it when you talk like that," she said in a low voice, but moved away from him.

"You knows I cain't talk no other way," he protested mildly.

"Stop it, I say!" She took a step back, hands on her rounded hips, her small breasts thrust forward.

He made no comment, only shook his head once, lowering his eyes. He knew that Cammy objected to his manner of speech, but knew also that to speak otherwise was to invite dire repercussions.

Jude had been born on Albemarle. His mother, Minda, was the cook. The only thing he knew about his father was the fact that he was white. When Nathaniel Kynes had first purchased Minda, she had been barely sixteen years old. She had been raped by a man who had been no more than a casual visitor at Albemarle. The result of that night had been Jude; and since Minda was a mulatto, and his father a white man, Jude was a quadroon, a high yellow. He also, thanks to Cammy, spoke better than most white people did, an accomplishment he took great care in concealing.

Watching him, Cammy bit her lip. "Come with me to the grove," she whispered.

Looking up, his blue eyes widened. "Cain't," he exclaimed, upset with her sudden brazenness. Cammy was usually very discreet about their meetings. "Not today. Got me too much to do around heah."

Glancing about to make certain that no one was within earshot, Cammy reached inside the jacket of her riding habit and drew forth the book.

"See here," she said to Jude, her tone now eager. "It's the new one by Mr. Dickens. Adam brought it back with yesterday's post. We'll read it together, just like we did with the others."

Fear momentarily paralyzed Jude, but he couldn't disguise the hunger in his eyes as he looked at the book.

Cammy returned the volume to its hiding place, then mounted her horse without assistance. She looked down at him. "Wait about five minutes, then follow me. I'll be waiting for you." She let her eyes travel insolently from his face to the bulge in his breeches, grinning impudently. Then, grasping the reins, she nudged the horse forward.

Jude managed a nod, swallowing through a throat that felt numb. He went outside, standing there for a long moment, watching until she was out of sight.

He didn't need to be told that following his young mistress was an offense that could lead to his death. Yet it was a threat that he'd been living with for years, ever since they had been children.

Only now, since last week, the danger had become

acute. He didn't quite know how it had happened, but they had made love.

Peering about him and seeing that no one was in the immediate vicinity, Jude at last walked away from the stables.

When he arrived at the cypress grove some ten minutes later, Cammy was seated on the soft grass by the river, the book in her lap.

Her face lit up when she saw him. "Come, sit beside me." She waited until he settled himself, than handed him the book. "Read it aloud," she said to him as he opened it.

For a time, Jude read, Cammy correcting him when he mispronounced a word. These occasions were few, however, for she had begun his lessons some five years before, when she was twelve and he was fourteen.

Listening to him, Cammy recalled that first day they had come here. They had slipped past Minda and run to the grove like two wild and uninhibited young animals.

Jude had gone to the river's edge. With a string and a pin, and using a small rock as an anchor, he began to fish.

Cammy kicked off her shoes, sat down, and dunked her feet in the water, wriggling her toes in the delicious feel of it.

"Gonna scare de fish," Jude had complained, giving her an irritated glance. "Ain' gonna catch nothin' iffen you keeps doin' dat."

She had looked at him, for the first time conscious of his speech. "Why do you talk like that?" she had asked him, genuinely curious with all the newly awakened awareness of her twelve years. Until that very moment she had honestly given it no thought. The sound of Jude's voice— as well as the other Negroes that surrounded her all her life—was like the sound of birds: accepted, never questioned.

Turning, he had stared at her, surprised. "Talks lak ever'body else," he had defended himself.

She thought about it, then shook her head. "No. No, you don't. You talk like a darkie."

He gave a short laugh. "What you think dis heah boy is?" Having felt a tug at the end of the string, Jude was momentarily diverted.

Not so Cammy, in whose mind sprouted the beginnings of an idea.

"If you could read, then you would know how to say the words correctly," she told him.

The notion did not immediately appeal to Jude. "Doan want to read," he stated firmly, still concentrating on the movement of the string in the water.

"Why not?" she persisted, pouting at his lack of enthusiasm.

Another of those glances came her way. " 'Cause, what good it gonna do me? Got no books anyways. 'Sides," he added in a practical vein, "gits whipped iffen masta catches me wit a book."

"Grandfather would never whip you." Cammy dismissed the very thought of such a happening.

But even at twelve she knew the rules. She knew it was against the law for a slave to read, but she didn't know why. All of a sudden it seemed like a stupid law, not worth thinking about.

Her tutor still came twice a week to give her lessons, as he had been doing for the past three years and would continue to do for the next two. Nathaniel was of the opinion that women need learn only reading, writing, penmanship, and be given a basic instruction in ciphering; perhaps a bit of music if they were so inclined. Cammy wasn't.

"I know how to read," she informed him in a tone that suggested she was imparting a secret.

"So what," he shot back, unimpressed.

"I could teach you. . . ."

"Cain't do no learnin'."

"Why not!" She became irked, then adopted an impervious manner. "Tomorrow, when we come here, I'll bring a book. . . ."

The fish Jude had been struggling with finally broke loose. Completely exasperated, he dropped the string with a muttered imprecation. Then, looking at her, he got a wicked gleam in his blue eyes. Reaching out, he grabbed her ankle with one hand, her arm with the other, and dumped her into the water, laughing at her spurious squeal of fright. Cammy could swim as well as he could.

But the very next day, despite his misgivings, Jude was introduced to the mystery of letters, letters that formed words, words that formed stories, stories that led him to places he had never even dreamed about.

After that, whenever they could avoid Minda's watchful eye, they had escaped to the grove, spending hour after hour with their heads bent over the marvelous volumes.

Jude was mesmerized, entranced. Nor had his excitement diminished even to this day.

Now, having finished the first chapter of *David Copperfield*, Jude closed the book.

The young girl, having been utterly captivated by the sound of his rich, golden voice, smiled at him. "You don't need any more lessons," she observed quietly.

"I know," he murmured, rubbing his thumb along the leather binding. "Wish I could finish the story."

"You can," she said quickly. "Take the book with you. Read it at night, in your cabin. . . ."

Slowly, he shook his head. "It's too dangerous. Not only for me, but for you as well. You know how Zoe is. That wench of mine can't keep her mouth shut about anything."

At the mention of Zoe, Cammy's eyes darkened. She hated the thought of that wench being in Jude's cabin even though she knew that Jude had no say in the matter. She was about to urge Jude to take the book anyway, but then sighed deeply, for she knew that Jude was right. She had broken a very serious law when she had taught him to read and write. But she had loved him since they were children. And so strong was her feeling that she saw nothing wrong with it, although she knew very well what would happen if her brother or her grandfather ever discovered their relationship. But that, Cammy vowed, would never happen. Not until it was too late for them to do anything about it. Griffin, she knew, had a crazy notion that she would consent to marry Clinton Barrows. But that would never come about. She had room in her heart for only one man, and that man was Jude.

Jude had started to get to his feet. Quickly, she put a hand on his arm.

"You don't have to leave yet," she protested, eyes pleading with him. "Griffin and grandfather have gone to Four Oaks. They won't be back until suppertime."

Glancing up, Jude noted the changing position of the late morning sun. There would be questions asked if his task for the day remained uncompleted. Despite her plea, he again made the attempt to get to his feet.

"Stay, Jude," she urged. "We must talk. . . ."

Sinking down again, he allowed himself a small sigh. "There's nothing for us to talk about, Cammy," he murmured. "We've been through all this before. . . ."

She leaned forward, placing her hands along each side of his face. "You know how much I love you," she said in a quiet and serious voice. "Someday, I'll find a way out for us. I promise." She moved further into his embrace, her arms tightening about him.

He was a bit saddened by her naivete. She had been saying a variation of those words for years now. But there was no way out. For him, perhaps, if he could escape to the North, but for "them," no. Even most of the Northern states had laws against miscegenation. He was light-skinned, but not enough to pass for white. No one would ever believe he was other than what he was. Sometimes, when he was dressed in livery, walking or riding through Charleston, Jude would look at the young white men about him and wonder what it was like to grow to manhood in freedom. Did they know what they had, those men on the threshold of life? Doubtless they did not, for the simple reason that they took their freedom for granted.

And, thinking of those young and white and privileged young men, Jude hated—and envied—every one of them.

"Jude," Cammy whispered, aware of his drifting attention. Her lips brushed his cheek. "What are you thinking about?"

His arm went around her, his hand caressing the small of her back. "Us," he answered. knowing that that was the answer she expected.

She murmured in contentment as he drew her closer to him, but Jude's thoughts were still turned inward. For years now, he knew that Cammy had entertained the thought that, one day, they could leave here and live happily ever after. Jude knew that was no more than a fantasy. And yet . . . if he were ever to get away, he knew it could be only with her help. Cammy was foolish and naive, but he needed her.

Nor could he delay much longer, Jude thought, only half responding as Cammy nuzzled his neck. So far, he'd been able to keep Zoe from discovering his secret, but he shuddered to think what might happen if she ever found out. Zoe loved him, although he had no feelings for her. She was no more than a convenience as far as he was concerned. But she was jealous and spiteful and he didn't even want to guess as to what her reaction would be if she found out what was going on.

His mother knew that he and Cammy occasionally met. They'd been doing it for years. Minda disapproved violently, of course, but she, like the few others who knew, thought that Cammy was only teaching him to read and write.

And, until about two weeks ago, that's just what was happening. Now, though, their relationship had moved to a different plane. A much more dangerous one.

Cammy's lips were very close to his. Moving his head forward slightly, Jude kissed her.

With a small moan, her arms tightened about him. She clung to him fiercely as the tip of his tongue sent darts of fire through her young body.

With hands that were clumsy in their haste, Cammy undid her bodice. Drawing his head to her breast, she gasped as his mouth encircled her nipple. She lay there for awhile, too weak to even move. Her breath came in whimpers as she clutched at his muscular shoulders, trying to bring him even closer to her.

She could stand it no longer. Reaching down, Cammy hoisted her skirt and shimmied out of her pantalettes, begrudging the time it took for Jude to shuck his breeches. His breath was now as quick as her own.

In a simultaneous movement they came together. Jude closed his eyes as he thrust into the willing and eager young flesh beneath his own.

About them, the droning insects and chattering birds were the only witnesses to the frenzied coupling of the two young lovers and Cammy's cry of pleasure caused only a brief cessation of nature's song before it again continued with its serenade.

When Jude returned to the stables sometime later he saw, in dismay, that his mother was heading in his direction. He barely stifled a groan, hoping he wasn't in for another lecture.

"Where you bin at?" she demanded, sounding angry. It had been Meg who had alerted her to the fact that Miss Cammy had left the house with a book tucked into her riding habit.

"Wasn't nowhere," he mumbled, not looking at her, taking care to slip back into the accepted pattern of speech.

Minda raised her hand and Jude ducked the blow aimed at his head. Over the years he had become most proficient at doing that; Minda's hand was as quick as her tongue.

"What I tell you 'bout stayin' away from Miss Cammy?"

"Wasn't nowhere near her," he protested. Despite the lie, he met her eyes squarely.

Minda's angry expression held a moment longer, then crumbled into sharp anxiety. She knew he was lying.

"Jude," she pleaded, resisting the urge to clasp the young man to her breast. "You courtin' the devil, actin' lak you do. Ain' gonna make you happy, readin' dem books . . ." She folded her hands in an almost prayerful manner. "Please, Jude. Listen to yore Momma. Knows what's best fer you, I do. An' tellin' you, you got a powerful lot o' trouble waitin' fer you. . . ."

In an attitude of disgust, Jude reached for a rag hanging on a nail just inside the door. From a shelf above it, he grasped a bottle filled with oil, then poured some of it onto the rag.

"Someday, we be free," he muttered fiercely, applying the rag to a leather harness. "Den we gots to know how to do all de things de white folks do."

Minda looked saddened at his words and her eyes brimmed with unshed tears. "Ain' never gonna be free, son," she murmured in a grieving tone. "You jest foolin' yorese'f, thinkin' lak dat. White mens bin talkin' 'bout freein' us'ns fer a long time." She shook her head solemnly. "Ain' gonna happen. Dey jest talkin', dat's all. Bin hearin' 'bout it since I wuz a li'l chile."

"Cain't believe dat!" Jude exclaimed quickly, sharply. His brow knitted into a scowl. "Iffen I do, ain' no reason to live no more."

"Jude. . . ."

"Means it, Momma!"

Minda took a deep breath. "Mebbe you right, son," she said placatingly, not for one minute believing her own words. "Dey free us'ns one day. But, till de Lawd Jesus see fit to give us'ns dat great day of jubilation, you gots to watch yore step and doan cause no trouble."

Dourly, Jude reflected to himself that the Lord Jesus had little, if anything, to do with their freedom. But he kept such thoughts to himself, knowing his mother's deeply held religious convictions. Besides, his mother was the only person in the world for whom he had feelings that could be said to approximate love. There were times, though, when he viewed her with something akin to resentment. Had she been lighter in color, had she possessed features that were not so obviously Negroid, then he might have been able to pass for white. It would have made things so much simpler, for Jude, at nineteen, had no intention of remaining a slave for the rest of his life. He had nothing but contempt for those, like Joe, who accepted their lot in life with a placid stoicism that angered and baffled him.

Standing there, Minda watched for a moment in silence as Jude worked the oil into the leather until it was smooth and pliable in his hands.

"Anyways," she stated quietly, "it doan be readin' what's on my mind. An' knows it, you do. Wuz diff'rent when you wuz both chillens. Ain't fittin' now dat Miss Cammy be a young lady. . . ."

Jude paused, glaring at her. "What you wantin' me to do?" he snapped. "When Miss Cammy tells me sumpin, gots to do what she says." There was no immediate response and he added, "Ain' it so?"

Slowly, she nodded, wishing with all her heart that Miss Cammy would find herself a nice young gentleman and get married. Only then would her Jude be safe.

Minda's sadness increased and the sorrow pressed down

upon her until she thought she could no longer bear its weight. She recognized her son's discontent. Hadn't she seen it in the eyes of the other men? Not all, to be sure. Not all men who were born slaves had the stamina or the will to fight their circumstances, even if only in their mind.

"Mebbe iffen you spend moah time wit Zoe," Minda suggested at last, "you gits dis foolishness out'n yore haid."

Jude threw the rag to the ground in a vicious motion. "Doan want dat black wench nowhere near me," he declared strongly. "She smell worse den de horses do."

Minda gave a great sigh, not for the first time wishing that her son had been born black. Then her mouth set determinedly and she again viewed Jude with sternness, hands on her hips. "Next time missy axin you to go wit her, you say no. Heah? Even if you gots to sass, you say no!" She bent her head forward, staring intently, her mouth tight.

Jude was about to retort sharply, but a look at his mother's severe countenance quickly changed his mind. He turned away from Minda's piercing eyes—those ebony pools of awareness. At times he had the feeling that his mother's eyes could peer into his soul. He shook off the disturbing feeling. His mother knew what he wanted her to know, he reminded himself sternly. She knew nothing of his plans, his capabilities. She knew only that he could read and write his name. Certainly she didn't know that he could speak as well as any white man—and better than some.

Minda was still glaring, waiting for a response.

"Awright, awright," he mumbled ungraciously. Bending over, he picked up a pail. "Gots to feed de horses," he announced. With a long stride, he walked into the stables without looking back at her.

Minda continued to stand there for many minutes, wondering if she had accomplished anything at all. Then, shaking her head in despair, she headed slowly back toward her kitchen.

Chapter
9

In April the pace of activity at Albemarle quickened. Vegetable crops were planted, fields were drained and ploughed, and in the Great House, under Minda's stern eye, spring cleaning was undertaken with a vengeance.

And, after three mornings of recurring nausea, Morgana's suspicions were confirmed: she was to have a child.

On this afternoon, she sat on the verandah in a rocking chair, a forgotten piece of embroidery in her lap. The weather was gray and dismal, holding the threat of rain and cooling the air. No breeze stirred the delicate moss as it hung motionless from the trees.

Griffin and Nathaniel had gone into the fields, and only moments ago Cammy had gone off, riding her horse as she did almost every day at this time.

Most of the hands went about their daily task. The afternoon was peaceful and quiet.

Morgana rocked slowly, her mind on the life that was, at this very minute, growing inside her. After an initial stab of dismay, she found herself more and more thrilled at the prospect of becoming a mother.

She would have to tell them soon, she thought, although the crinolined skirts were a marvelous concealment. She suspected that a woman could practically go her full term without her condition becoming noticeable.

For some reason she wanted to tell her father first, but Aleceon hadn't left his room in the past three days. A bad cold, Ben had solemnly reported to anyone who might be interested, and, except for Morgana, no one seemed to be.

She wasn't entirely certain in her own mind as to why she should even bother to tell her father anything at all. Their relationship was still strained. Oddly, she saw very little of him, even though they were both living in the same house. Aleceon spent most of his days in his room, appearing only for meals, and sometimes not even then. Although heaven only knew what he occupied his time with, she thought, sighing.

She wondered what Griffin would think when she told him about the baby, unaware that once Bella knew, the whole household became aware of the impending event.

Morgana was so wrapped up in her approaching motherhood that she never noticed Nathaniel's solicitation or Griffin's anxious glances in her direction.

Rocking to and fro, soothed by the monotonous motion, Morgana had closed her eyes and was, therefore, startled when she heard Ben's voice.

" 'Pologizes fer disturbin' you, Miz Morgana," he said to her, his stance awkward as he bowed slightly. "But axin' you to please come to yore daddy's room. He be wantin' to talk wit you."

She felt a prick of annoyance. "Why can't he come down here?" she countered with a suggestion of petulance, not wishing to move from her comfortable spot.

"Cain't, missus," Ben murmured. Sniffing, he wiped his nose with the back of his hand.

Looking at him more closely, Morgana became alarmed at the sight of his stricken face. He appeared about to cry. She ceased rocking and sat straighter. "What's wrong, Ben? Is my father feeling worse?"

"Yore daddy bin sick fer a long time, Miz Morgana," he explained in a voice that was low and grieving. "Doctor be tellin' him months ago he doan be havin' much time left. Wouldn't let me tell nobody. An' dese last three days he bin in sech mis'ry, couldn't git hisself up. An' now . . . well, he callin' fer you."

Morgana was left astonished and trembling at the report. Her father, dying? The thought was too awesome, too frightening to comprehend all at once.

Somewhat shakily, she got to her feet, heedless of the embroidery that fell from her lap. She stared at Ben for a long moment, then turned and headed for the stairs, almost running up the steps, with Ben behind her.

Outside Aleceon's door, she paused a moment, trying to catch her breath and allow her heart to return to its normal beat.

Then, without knocking, she entered her father's room.

He was in bed. Now that she could see his arms bared, his thin frame appeared shockingly wasted.

Feeling a trembling unease, she walked toward the bed, sitting on the chair that was already placed there and from which Ben had moved only rarely in the past three days, ever since Aleceon had begun to spit up blood.

"Father . . ." Morgana was appalled at the sight of him. He looked positively cadaverous, his face waxy, except for his lips, which were a ghastly white.

At the sound of her soft voice, Aleceon opened his eyes, attempted to smile, and gave it up.

"Don't feel sorry for me, Morgana," he murmured in a halting voice that was, nevertheless, a command. "I've lived my life in my own way, and I'd just as soon die without any fuss . . ." He waved a hand with a trace of his usual impatience as she started to speak and she bit her lip. "There's not much time, so you must listen to me . . . ."

"Oh, Father," Morgana cried out, unable to keep quiet any longer. "Why didn't you tell me? We can take you to New York, to Boston . . . They have the best doctors . . ." She fell silent as he raised a hand.

"I've been to the doctors, several of them," he protested weakly. "I've known for months now that there was nothing they could do."

"But there must be something!" she insisted, trying to stem her frightened tears. She had never really been close to her father, but now, suddenly, she was feeling a wrenching loss for what might have been.

"Nothing to be done . . ." An uncharacteristic sadness came upon him as he looked at the only human being he had ever loved. "I'm sorry—for all those years we were separated," he whispered. "I thought the school would be good for you. . . ."

"It was," she said quickly. She clasped her hands tightly in her lap. "I was happy there. You must believe that."

A wry ghost of a smile played at the corners of his

mouth. "I'm glad you were not unhappy there. I suspect life with me would have provided you with an education you'd be better off without . . ." He broke off, coughing, his frail chest heaving with the exertion.

Immediately, Ben stepped forward with a glass of clear liquid. Placing one massive arm about the wracked body of his master, he held him as one would a child. Then, when Aleceon calmed a bit, Ben brought the glass to the white lips.

"Drinks yore medicine, suh," he coaxed, nodding in satisfaction as Aleceon did so.

"Black viper thinks I'm his baby," Aleceon grumbled as he sank back on the pillows, but Morgana could sense the very real affection between the two men, as well as their dependence upon each other.

Then Aleceon turned to his daughter once more, his smoky blue eyes luminous with fever in his ashen face. "When I brought you here . . ." he sighed, and the sound tore at her heart, " . . . I thought I was finally doing the right thing for you." His look was pleading. "I never meant for you to find out. . . ."

"Please . . ." Morgana reached out a hand, grasping the hot, dry flesh, and was struck by the fact that it had been years since she had touched her father. She couldn't even remember him ever kissing her, or hugging her. The urge came upon her, strong, and bending over, she placed her lips upon his cheek. "Don't talk of this anymore," she begged.

"There will never be another time," he noted simply. How really fine she was, he thought to himself, carefully keeping his face bland. If he had nothing else in his life to be proud of, he could feel pride in Morgana.

Then, with more urgency, he continued. "Do you remember when we left Somerset Hall?" At her tearful nod, he went on. "Sarah wanted you to stay. I . . . wouldn't allow it." He gave a sound of disgust that was obviously directed at himself. "I would rather have seen my daughter grow up with strangers than with those who loved her," he added with deep bitterness. He closed his eyes and turned his head on the pillow, averting his face. "When you were a very young girl, you used to ask me about your mother. . . ."

She smiled, a slight, sad expression. "But you never wanted to talk about her," she noted softly.

He was silent for a long moment. Turning toward her, he seemed to search her face for something that would have meaning only to him. "You were, I thought, too young to understand," he said finally.

Her face clouded. She compressed her lips and viewed her folded hands in her lap. "Then, it's true?" she whispered. When there was no response, she looked at him, her eyes just as searching as his. "There were rumors . . ." She appeared embarrassed. "I . . . heard things. . . ."

"You always were too intelligent and too perceptive for your own good," he observed wryly, and sighed. "Your mother was a good woman," he said at last. "Whatever else she was—and circumstances forced her into a life she would not have otherwise chosen—she was a decent and caring person. I . . ." he hesitated, "I wasn't good enough for her. She deserved better. She was so young . . ." His voice trailed off. "So very young. Only seventeen when she had you. In those months before you were born, she was so excited, so looking forward to having a child. . . ."

"Did you love her?" Morgana asked from curiosity. She couldn't really imagine her father loving anyone.

In that, she was almost right. But, looking at his daughter, Aleceon found himself compelled to give only one answer. "Yes," he replied. "I loved your mother very much."

The words seemed to comfort Morgana and he was content. She would never know the feeling of pride, of overwhelming love he had experienced when first he looked upon his newborn daughter. Kitty was already dead by then. Aleceon had given her no further thought. He had married her on the spur of the moment, out of necessity. He had been, at most, fond of Kitty. She was a pretty thing, with auburn hair and a pleasing body that had accommodated many men. Over the years, Aleceon had often wondered how the two of them had produced a child like Morgana. Nature must have been very selective, he thought to himself. He had never expressed his feeling of love and pride to his daughter, for those words did not come easy to him; indeed, he rarely gave it conscious thought. It was just a feeling, lying deep within him. And even now, he couldn't find the words with which to tell her.

"It seems we are ruled by the past," he murmured, sounding dreadfully weak to Morgana. She leaned forward to catch his words. "No matter how we try to ignore it, it's always there, waiting."

His breathing sounded labored, and Morgana felt a terrifying need to do something, anything. But she just sat there, knowing in her heart that there was nothing she could do, knowing that there was nothing anyone could do now.

After awhile, Aleceon looked at her again. "If you ever need a place to go—go to your aunt. . . ."

"I will, Father. Please, don't worry about me." She gave a shaky laugh. "I'm a married woman now. And," she added, a bit shyly, "I'm not entirely certain and I've not told anyone yet, but I think I'm to have a child. . . ."

A slow, wistful smile drifted across his face. "That makes me very happy," he whispered. "I hope it eases things between you and Griffin. He's not a bad sort . . . It's just that he's a proud man, and sometimes . . . well, sometimes that gets in the way of a man's judgment." He took a deep and rasping breath. Then pain made itself felt. It was fierce, gnawing at his insides, drawing his life's breath from his body, leaving behind what felt like a pile of burning embers in his stomach. He grimaced at the now familiar intrusion, waiting until the spasm passed before he again spoke.

"Ben . . ." He motioned to the Negro and the man came immediately forward. "Show my daughter," he paused, groaning. "Show her where it is. . . ."

The black man got down on his hands and knees. Reaching under the bed, he drew forth a metal box. He placed it at Morgana's feet.

"What is it?" Morgana viewed the receptacle with curious eyes.

"Money. Gold. Keep it with you in case you ever need it."

She stared at him in some perplexity for a moment.

"Don't let Griffin know you have it," Aleceon urged, bending forward slightly. He rested a hand on her arm. "Don't let anyone know. Someday, if you should ever need it, then use it. There is more than five thousand dollars in there . . ." He fell silent at the sound of her gasp, then smiled wryly. "I'll not tell you how I came upon it. It's best that you not know." He sank back again, incredibly weary from the effort of speaking at length.

"I'll do as you say, Father," Morgana tried to comfort him. She still couldn't believe that this was happening.

After several moments passed, Aleceon found the strength to continue. "Keep it in a safe place. Here . . ." Reaching up, he removed a thin gold chain from about his neck, from which was suspended a small key. He handed it to her. "This, too, should be kept in a safe place, It's the key that will unlock the box. One more thing . . ." Aleceon glanced at the hovering Negro. Ben's dark eyes had not once moved from Aleceon's face. "This black viper is more trouble than he's worth," he said, his voice sounding raspy and dry. "But I give him to you. Over there," he pointed to the desk with a trembling finger. "You'll find his papers in the top drawer. I've already made them out in your name." He fixed Ben with a stern look. "Promise me that you will serve your mistress well and guard her life with your own."

Ben sank to his knees, tears streaming down his black cheeks. "Serves her lak I serves you, suh," he whispered in a choked voice.

Extending a hand, Aleceon patted the woolly head. "I ask for no more than that, my friend," he murmured.

Morgana frowned, not wishing to deny her father anything in his hour of extremity, but she couldn't keep silent. "I cannot own a slave," she said quietly.

Regarding her solemn, fine-featured face, Aleceon gave a short laugh at her words. "Through your marriage, you own close to two hundred of them," he reminded her. "However, if you feel that strongly, then free him. But," he admonished, raising a hand, "if you free him, make certain that he is cared for. Don't let your high ideals be responsible for further injury. Once free, how will he live? Who will provide for him?"

Confusion sank upon Morgana, who had never before thought of that. She regarded Ben thoughtfully for a long moment. "Do you want your freedom?" she asked him, leaning forward.

Ben hesitated. "Would rather be yore slave, missus. But," he added, almost as an afterthought, "doan want to be sold to nobody else."

"I would never do that," Morgana promised quickly. The thought, however, still troubled her. Then her face brightened. "I'll file the papers for your manumission," she told him. "Then, you'll be free to stay or go, whenever you decide. . . ."

She glanced at Aleceon for his approval, and the smile froze upon her face. Without even touching him, she knew, knew that the appearance of sleep was a deception, a false comfort.

For a long moment she held her breath, staring, waiting for her father to speak, to move, to smile, but, of course, he did nothing.

She shivered, feeling suddenly alone, although it was ironic that after all these years such a sensation would fall upon her. Had there ever been a time when she hadn't been alone?

A small drop of blood glimmered like a malevolent ruby at the corner of Aleceon's mouth. Removing her handkerchief from her sleeve, Morgana wiped it away, her hand as steady and as gentle as if it were living flesh she touched.

As she heard the sound of a heartbreaking sob, her hand

automatically reached out to Ben, resting on his broad shoulder. The Negro was still kneeling, his cheeks glistening wetly as he released his sorrow.

How strange, Morgana thought, aware of her own dry eyes, how strange that she was doing the comforting instead of receiving it.

Sitting there, Morgana searched her mind for memories of closeness to her father, memories to hang onto, memories to take out and savor in the years to come.

But no such time existed. Her father had never raised a hand to her in either anger or love.

Glancing out of the window, she was surprised to see the fine misty rain that had finally broken through the clouds and now fell gently and silently upon the land.

Had she ever loved her father? she wondered dully, again viewing the motionless form on the bed. It was a question she honestly couldn't answer.

Aleceon was buried the following day in the small cemetery at Albemarle. It was a pleasant spot about a half mile from the Great House, set in a clearing that was neatly enclosed by a decorative, wrought iron fence. There were only three headstones, all crafted from white marble: one for Roger Kynes, Griffin's father; one for Alicia Saunders Kynes, Griffin's mother; and one for Anne Mary Kynes, Nathaniel's wife.

It was Nathaniel who, with the aid of his worn family Bible, conducted the simple ceremony. Both he and Griffin were dressed in black frock coats over black trousers.

The air was fresh, the sun warm and bright as it sparkled on rain-washed trees and bushes. The pleasantness of the spring day irked Morgana. Everything was alive and growing, almost mocking the solemn occasion. It was, she thought, a day of death, not a day to be even thinking of such things as life and growth.

Morgana, dressed in the plain brown dress in which she had first arrived at Albemarle, remained placid through the short service, a feeling of unreality crowding in upon her. She couldn't quite accept the fact that her father was dead, that he lay in the hastily constructed wooden box that was almost completely concealed by a profusion of spring flowers.

To the side, standing in respectful silence, heads lowered, were the two slaves who had dug the grave and who now waited to fill it with earth once again. Morgana glanced briefly at Ben, hearing his quiet sobs. Beside him stood a man who was very black and whom Morgana didn't immediately recognize. He was burly and muscular with a somewhat sullen expression that dissolved into a meaningless smile as he noticed Morgana's eyes upon him.

Atlas, she thought absently, that was the slave's name. Then she returned her attention to Nathaniel's resonant voice as he continued with the simple service.

When it was over, Cammy moved closer. She had, for once, forsaken her hoops and stays and was clad in a dark blue cotton dress with a broad white collar. A bit timidly, she touched Morgana's arm.

"I'm sorry about your father," she said quietly. "It must have been an awful shock for you. I . . ." she faltered, feeling helpless. "That is to say, none of us realized how ill he was. He never said anything. . . ."

Morgana patted the slim arm. "I know," she replied simply. "He never said anything to me, either."

They began to walk back to the house, Nathaniel and

Griffin following a short distance behind. Ben and Atlas remained at the small cemetery to shovel the dirt back into the open grave.

"Were you close to your father?" Cammy asked as they made their way along the narrow path. She was well aware of the recent estrangement, but was curious as to their previous relationship.

Morgana hesitated a long moment, thinking on it. "No," she said at last. "Not really." Turning her head, she regarded Cammy, who sighed.

"I don't remember my father at all," the girl said as they walked slowly. "He died when I was two. I guess . . ." she made a gesture. "I guess both Griffin and I tend to think of grandfather in that way." She inclined her head, glancing at Morgana. "Your mother?"

Morgana shook her head. "Like yours, my mother died when I was born."

Cammy hooked an arm through hers in a silent gesture of companionship. "But you have a family now," she murmured with a shy smile. "You are the sister I never had."

When she went upstairs that night after supper, Morgana found that Ben had moved her father's trunk and the metal box into her room.

The box she shoved under her bed. The trunk she just left in a corner, not having the heart to go through his things just yet.

Another, smaller box lay upon her bed and, curious, Morgana opened it. A pair of dueling pistols rested on the blue velvet that lined the case. She stared a moment, then, not knowing what else to do with it, put it away in a dresser drawer. She wasn't afraid of guns. Long ago, her father had shown her how to load and fire a pistol. It was part of the strange education she had received while living with a man of Aleceon's character.

"Miz Morgana?"

Bella's soft voice reached her, and Morgana turned.

"Dat Ben sayin' he wants to talk wit you." She made an exasperated face. "Tol' him he got no business botherin' you at dis time, but——"

"It's all right, Bella," Morgana interrupted softly. "Tell him to come in."

Muttering to herself, Bella did as she was instructed. Ben was waiting in the hall, and when he entered stood just inside the doorway, looking awkward and out of place. He kept his head lowered, staring at the floor until Morgana spoke to him.

"Thank you for bringing my father's belongings in here." She regarded him questioningly, wondering what it was he wanted.

"Got to tell you sumpin, Miz Morgana." Ben spoke in a voice that was no more than a whisper. "Masta Aleceon tol' me never to tell you, but——" His voice broke and he wiped his nose with the back of his hand.

"Tell me what, Ben?" she prompted, taking a step closer to him.

It took a moment for the Negro to gain control of himself and Morgana could see how deeply affected he was by her father's death.

He swallowed, shifting his weight from foot to foot. "Yore daddy not tellin' you de truf when he say why he brung you heah. . . ."

She inclined her head, surprised by his words. "And

what is the truth?" she asked quietly, watching him closely.

He hesitated only a moment, then raised his head to look at her with saddened eyes. "He be knowin' fer months dat he wuz gonna die. Wantin' to see you safe before dat happen." He shook his head sorrowfully. "Wasn't true what he said 'bout you bein' underfoot. Before we come heah, yore daddy wuz visitin' lots of Great Houses, lookin' fer de right husband fer you to marry up wit. Wasn't tryin' to do you no harm, Miz Morgana," he said earnestly. "Wuz on'y tryin' to do good fer you."

At the recital, Morgana sighed and averted her face. "Why couldn't he have told me that?" she murmured. Although, she was thinking, it would have hardly made any difference insofar as Griffin was concerned.

" 'Cause den he would have to tell you he wuz dyin', an' he didn't want you to know dat. Wuz a proud man, yore daddy." Ben's dark eyes brimmed with tears. "An' he be tellin' me dat he loved you more den anybody in de world. Thinkin' on'y of you when he done what he did. . . ."

Morgana bit her lip, feeling her own eyes smart, and for a time was silent. Though she had no reason to doubt Ben, she couldn't quite believe that her father really loved her. Yet he would have no other reason for doing what he did, she realized.

"Thank you, Ben," she whispered at last. Then, in a brisker voice, asked, "Where are you staying?"

"Masta Nathaniel give me a cabin. Sayin' I kin help Joe in de smithy."

She frowned slightly. "Do you want to work there?"

Ben shrugged. "Doan mind," he answered blithely. "Laks it fine, I do," he decided after a moment.

"Very well. But I meant what I said," she told him. "As soon as I can, I will file your papers. And Ben," she added as he turned to go. "If you have any problems with Mr. Dobbs, I want you to come and tell me immediately. Do you understand?"

"Yassum."

After Ben left, Morgana walked out onto the piazza. The sun had set, but it was not yet dark. It was calm and still. The very air seemed painted in hues of lilac and gold. Morgana leaned on the railing, feeling very tired and dispirited. Restlessness coursed through her. She knew that if she lay down on her bed, she would be unable to sleep.

Perhaps a walk, she thought. Heading back inside, she reached in her wardrobe for a light shawl. Leaving her room, she went downstairs and out into the evening.

She walked along the driveway down to the carriage gate, even in her melancholy state admiring the brilliant panorama of color that streaked the western sky. Foliage and moss were outlined in black in the deepening twilight, hanging limp and still, as if at rest. Only a few yards away the river hummed softly on its journey to the sea. An early evening mist hovered over the water, thick and with a pearly translucency along the banks.

Morgana realized that, sometime during these past months, she had grown to love this land, this countryside that was so vastly different from any she had ever known in her lifetime.

The thought saddened her. She was uncertain as to what her future would be once her child was born.

Could she stay here? Could she stay with a man who didn't want or love her? There was no doubt in her mind that Griffin would honor the contract of marriage. But that was the crux of the problem: it was just a contract. Morgana was uncertain that she could live her life on those terms.

Tightening her shawl, she began to walk slowly back to the house. Ahead, she saw Griffin emerge from the stables. She called to him, waiting until he turned, a surprised look upon his face. Immediately, he headed toward her.

"What are you doing out at this time of night?" he asked, surprise turning to concern.

She shrugged, not answering that. Instead, she said, "I would like to thank you and your grandfather for allowing my father to stay here ... and for the ceremony...."

"It isn't necessary," he said quickly. "Your father was ... a fine man." The words stuck in his throat. But then, suddenly, he realized that Aleceon must have known he was dying, must have known that he would never live to see a profit from Albemarle.

Morgana's expression closed somewhat as she sensed his insincerity. Whatever else Aleceon Edgewood was, he had been her father; whatever he had done—and if his convoluted manner of thinking had produced her present dilemma—she couldn't deny that his last acts and thoughts had been for her benefit.

"I'm perfectly aware that my father made it a condition that you marry me ..." Morgana had mixed feelings about Ben's disclosures. The fact that she now understood her father's motives for bringing her here did not alter the fact that Griffin had acted with a somewhat less altruistic reason in mind. While she could class her father's deceit as benevolent, she found she could not excuse Griffin on that or any other basis.

187

"Morgana . . ." Griffin took a step closer, then halted as she raised her hand.

"Please don't," she said wearily. She took a deep breath. "If it were possible, I would leave now and release you from . . . all of it." He began to speak, but she wouldn't allow him to do so. She was in no mood for any spurious explanation he might feel it necessary to utter. "However, I am unable to leave at this time. You see," she faltered, moistening her lips, "I am to have a child."

He smiled, not wanting to tell her that he already knew. "That's wonderful," he exclaimed, taking another step forward. Her expression again halted him. Her blue eyes were viewing him with cool speculation.

"I thought you would be pleased," she murmured dryly. "I can imagine how much it means for you to have an heir . . . for Albemarle." She knew her words were sarcastic, but she couldn't help herself. No matter how her mind revolved about all that had happened, what she was left with, finally, was a feeling of betrayal. Her emotions felt like a pile of smoldering ashes waiting to spark into life at the least provocation.

Griffin fell silent a moment, his eyes searching her face. "You once said you loved me," he whispered tentatively. He longed to reach for her, but he knew if he did that she would turn him away. His pride couldn't stand that rebuff yet one more time. He knew, too, that if he told her that he loved her, she would smile that small cold smile that reminded him so much of Aleceon and would disbelieve his words.

Her brows arched. "Love is only an illusion," noted the Morgana who had lived, survived and adjusted for her whole life, mostly on her own.

A deep sigh greeted that. "We didn't know each other long enough for it to become a reality," Griffin pointed out mildly.

Morgana allowed the silence to lengthen before she again spoke. "Nor will we," she retorted coldly. Her eyes were level and unforgiving.

Then, for a moment too fast for her to see, there appeared on his face an expression of anguish that darkened his eyes and tightened his jaw. But before it was fully formed, it was gone, buried beneath a coldness that matched her own. Even though it was there, Griffin fought back his desire for this woman, this woman who had come into his life unbidden and who now had such a hold on him that he couldn't explain it even to himself.

Morgana watched him turn and walk away. Her expression retained its rigid scorn until he was almost out of sight. Then she bit her lip hard, trying to stem the rush of loneliness that engulfed her. Tears sprang to her eyes, but only the moon looked down at her bitter sadness and only the night creatures heard her sob of longing and despair.

She could not deny that Griffin had her love, although Morgana conceded that with some reluctance. She would have torn it from her heart had she been able. But her trust . . . that was not beyond her. It had once been given willingly. It would now have to be earned many times over.

Although she was certain that she would find no rest this night, Morgana walked slowly back to the house, trying vainly to free her mind of any thought of Griffin, struggling within herself to keep fresh anguish from returning. She felt emotionally battered and yearned only for the blissful oblivion of sleep.

* * *

Late the following morning, a man rode up the driveway, his horse at a walk. Behind him in a forlorn procession were six Negroes, all male, their wrists spanceled and their ankles bearing leg irons with just enough chain between each foot to allow them to take a small step.

Hearing the dogs bark, Morgana walked out onto the piazza. Looking down, she viewed the scene below with curious eyes. Motioning to Bella, she asked, "Who is that man?"

The dark-skinned girl gave only a cursory glance into the yard. "Dat's Masta Will Parkins, missus. He be a slave trader." She folded her arms beneath her breast, her expression contemptuous. "He be stoppin' by 'bout once each year. Buys on'y no-good niggers what nobody else wants."

In the yard, Nathaniel and Griffin were approaching the slave trader. As Morgana watched, she saw her husband shake his head in denial.

Then, calling to Joe, who was working at his anvil, his black skin glistening with the sweat of his labor, Griffin apparently gave instructions for the small coffle of slaves to be put in the barn, for they all now trailed along after the huge Negro.

There was more discussion, and laughter from Nathaniel as he summoned Jude, who had been waiting nearby in anticipation of caring for the trader's horse. Having dismounted, the man was peering intently at Jude, all the while talking earnestly to Nathaniel, who shook his head in an emphatic way.

At the sight, Bella issued a short laugh. "He do dat ever' time he come heah," she explained to Morgana. "Always wantin' to buy dat Jude. Sayin' he kin git a fancy price fer dat buck."

Regarding the chained and silent Negroes who were now filing into the barn, Morgana frowned. "Well, I certainly hope he won't sell Jude to that man," she mused. The sight of the chained Negroes shuffling along, heads lowered, was not a pleasant one to see. Her frown deepened.

"Oh, naw, Miz Morgana," Bella replied. She waved a hand, dismissing even the thought. "Masta Nathaniel right proud of Jude. Shows him off ever' chance he gits."

The two women watched for a while longer, then the men headed for the verandah and were lost from view.

That evening when she came downstairs, Morgana was a bit surprised to find Will Parkins at the supper table. He wasn't a tall man, standing no more than five-feet, six-inches, but he was so massive in the chest and arms that he gave the appearance of being much bigger than he was. His features were rough and coarse, his speech and manners not much better.

At first happy to see a new face at the table, Morgana found herself disliking the man before she had even finished her soup.

By the time the first course was cleared away, Parkins had sunk in her esteem to a position just below that of Carlie Dobbs. At least, she thought in growing annoyance, Dobbs didn't eat with them. He ate in his own cabin.

So far, Parkins had entertained them with tales of lynchings, public floggings, and several mutilations he considered particularly interesting.

Morgana's appetite was fast leaving her. However, as she looked about the table, she noticed that Griffin and

Nathaniel were both regarding the man with a certain degree of interest; Cammy merely looked bored, as if she'd heard it all before. As for the houseboys, they moved about quietly, faces devoid of any expression whatsoever.

"Good meal, suh," Parkins said at last. He patted his stomach and nodded in Nathaniel's direction.

"Pleasure to have you share it with us, Mr. Parkins," Nathaniel responded hospitably. "Feel free to stay with us as long as you like."

Morgana winced at that, but relaxed when she heard Parkins decline.

"Have to be movin' on," he advised. "But it grieves me that you don't have any of your stock for sale. From what I saw this afternoon, you've got quite a few prime hands. And as for that buck with the blue eyes . . ." He shook his head. "Could offer a good price, if you'll reconsider . . ." He regarded Griffin expectantly.

Seated beside Parkins, Cammy stiffened noticeably, clasping her hands tightly in her lap.

"We're not selling now," Griffin advised the man firmly, unaware of his sister's reaction. "In fact, we're getting ready to buy a few."

"That so?" Parkins fumbled about in his shirt pocket for a moment. "You might be interested in this, then." Leaning forward across the table, he handed Griffin the piece of paper which was an advertised notice of a slave auction to be held in Savannah. "Heard they got some prime ones sent down from Virginia."

Griffin read a minute, than looked up. "Thank you, Mr. Parkins. I'll look into it." He handed the piece of paper to Nathaniel and then leaned back in his chair, regarding the trader. "Too bad you didn't stop by a few weeks back. We had a buck that was a runner. Would have gladly sold him to you for a good price."

"Where is he now?" Parkins asked with a show of interest. He finished the last of his coffee with an audible smacking of his lips.

Slowly, Griffin shook his head. "Can't say. He managed to escape again."

Putting down his cup, Parkins looked surprised at that. "Didn't you hide him?"

"Gave him fifty good ones," Nathaniel put in. "We had him locked up in his cabin, but he managed to get out anyway."

"Sounds like a bad sort," Parkins contemplated, sucking at his teeth. "Best to keep runners spanceled," he advised sagely.

Nathaniel nodded ruefully. "The truth, suh. The truth."

"Although, personally, I prefer to hamstring 'em," the trader mused thoughtfully after a moment. "Cuts down on their value, but they can still work in the fields."

Unable to contain herself, Morgana eyed the man angrily, her face flushing. "Are you discussing men or animals?" she demanded, fixing him with an icy stare.

Parkins viewed her, then blinked in surprise. 'We're discussin' niggers, ma'am," he murmured, disconcerted by her tone.

"You must excuse my wife," Griffin interrupted smoothly. He cast a warning look in Morgana's direction. "She's a Northerner and doesn't quite understand the intricacies of our peculiar institution."

In an angry gesture, Morgana threw her napkin on her plate. She was furious with Griffin's patronizing tone.

Parkins raised a hand in a conciliatory manner. "No

offense taken, suh," he said hastily. "Shouldn't be discussin' these things in front of the ladies anyhow." He pushed his chair back and got up, avoiding Morgana's eye. "If y'all will excuse me, I'll check on my stock and then retire. . . ."

Nathaniel stood up. If he was disturbed by Morgana's outburst he gave no visible indication as he addressed the trader. "I'll have Thomas show you to your room when you're ready."

The two men walked toward the front hall. With an almost apologetic glance at Morgana, Cammy followed.

"I will thank you to show a bit more courtesy to our guest," Griffin said stiffly when they were alone.

Defiantly, Morgana glared at him as she got to her feet. "As you have pointed out, Griffin, I am not a Southerner. I feel no obligation to extend courtesy in the face of rude or offensive behavior."

"I saw no sign of either," Griffin shot back quickly, his brow furrowing. Standing up, he regarded her with a sternness that increased Morgana's anger. "I can appreciate your sensitivity at this time," he remarked with a brief glance at her stomach. "And I will agree that Parkins is a crude sort. But whatever else he is, he *is* a guest in my home. As such, he will be made to feel welcome. And he shall be treated with courtesy for the length of time he remains here!"

Griffin's voice had risen, and Morgana's outrage grew in direct proportion to his tone.

"In view of the fact that I feel myself unable to obey your command . . . Master Griffin," she said tartly, "I shall remain in my room until that man leaves."

Her skirts swirling from her indignation, Morgana

walked from the room, head high, leaving Griffin to stand there alone, a scowl upon his face.

Chapter 10

By the 10th of May they all returned to Charleston, with the exception of Griffin, who went to Savannah to attend the auction that had advertised the sale of prime slaves.

This time, though, Morgana's social activities were severely curtailed due to her condition. There was one thing, however, that she did do. With Nathaniel's assistance—and a few expressed misgivings on his part which she refused to heed—she filed the papers that would manumit Ben.

And Nathaniel, bearing in mind that her child was due in October, insisted that they return in September so that his first grandchild would be born at Albemarle. By then, Griffin had joined them in Charleston, and together they all returned to the plantation.

A week after the family had returned from Charleston,

Zoe was standing in the open doorway of her cabin, watching for Jude.

Directly across the dirt road known as Slave Row was the cabin shared by Joe, his wife Pearl, and the couple's three children, all of whom were too young yet to work in the fields. The three children, two girls and a boy, were a distance away at the far end of the road, playing with their friends.

The September day was uncomfortably warm, the air damp and heavy, the breeze so slight that it didn't even disturb the flies and mosquitoes; they droned incessantly, an irritating, never ending nuisance to those who had to live within their proximity.

Usually this late in the day, the breeze would quicken, providing some relief as it swept across the river, at times bringing the salty tang of the sea with it, depending on the tide. When it flowed inward it brought with it the salt water from the Atlantic. When it flowed outward, the water turned fresh. It was only at these times that the fields would be flooded with the life giving substance.

The tide had just turned and most of the hands were still in the fields. The yard was quiet and empty of inhabitants save for the children and dogs, and they, too, seemed disinclined to cavort in the heavy atmosphere.

Standing there, Zoe wiped her damp brow with her hand as she waited.

As soon as she saw Jude emerge from the carriage house, she took the food out of the bucket, spooning it onto a tin plate which she placed on the solitary wooden table. Aside from two chairs and a small, three-legged stool, the only other furnishing in the small cabin was a corn husk mattress positioned in a corner of the single room. There were no windows, but there was a small hearth for cooking and, on those occasions when it was required, for heat.

Most slaves did their own cooking in the evening, usually pone or grits, possibly pork or fish, and whatever vegetables were available in garden patches, but Zoe was able to bring theirs from the kitchen. Sometimes, when Jude went fishing—and caught some— they'd eat that, but mostly it was what Minda saved for them from the day before. Today it was cold beef, red gravy and biscuits left over from yesterday's meal at the Great House.

Zoe had been with Jude for almost a year now. They weren't married and wouldn't be until there was a child. It had been Nathaniel who had installed Zoe in Jude's cabin, a situation that had made her deliriously happy—at first. However, it soon became painfully apparent that Jude didn't want her at all. She could leave and return to her own cabin, previously shared with her brother Jonah, anytime she wanted to. The trouble was, she loved Jude too much to even consider taking that step.

But if Jude didn't love her, he seemed not to love anyone else, either. He was a loner, something rare among her people. The only one he seemed to bother with was Miss Cammy. But of course he couldn't possibly be in love with her, Zoe reflected dourly. Still, they met occasionally. Everyone seemed to know about it except for Masta Nathaniel and Masta Griffin—and certainly no black was going to tell them.

Jude thought that she didn't know, but Zoe heard things: Minda whispering worriedly to Thomas, one day; a few of the house servants discussing it, another day. They all fell silent when she approached, but Zoe had heard enough to piece some of it together.

She was consumed by curiosity over the nature of these meetings. It didn't happen often, but today it had happened again, for the first time since he had returned from Charleston a week ago. Not being a house servant, Zoe was never included in these trips.

And today, Zoe was bound and determined to find out what was going on.

Jude entered, his handsome face set in a scowl. He was wearing his usual attire of a linsey-woolsey shirt and breeches that were string tied at the waist. Like Zoe and everyone else save the house servants, he wore no undergarments. In town, of course, he wore his livery. But as soon as he returned to the plantation, he gave that splendid outfit to Minda, who personally washed and ironed it, then put it away for the next time.

Zoe watched Jude as he now sat down. He viewed his meal, but made no move toward it. His silence wasn't all that unusual; he spoke to her only when he had to.

"Jude, man," she said at last in a low, cajoling voice. "Eat yore supper. You bin frettin' fer days now, ever since you come home." Her dark face turned anxious as she wondered if perhaps he was ill. Usually his appetite was good and he ate whatever she put in front of him. But lately he seemed too preoccupied to even eat his food.

"Jude. . . ."

With a grunt of annoyance and a quick irritated glance at her, Jude began to eat.

For a while, she stared at him. Lawd, but he was a powerful handsome buck, she thought, her own expression wavering between anger and dismay. If only he would let her, she would love him with everything she had to give to that emotion. As it was, it was bottled up inside her with no means of escape, and, like a festering wound, was causing her more and more distress.

"Gits you grits wit sweet'nin', iffen you wants," Zoe offered after a bit. She took a step toward the table.

He didn't bother to look up. "Doan want none."

With a sigh, Zoe moved back to the doorway. She leaned on the frame in a careless attitude. "Looked fer you dis mornin'," she murmured, absently viewing her bare feet. "Noticin' you wuz gone off somewheres. . . ."

Jude tensed, but kept on eating. "Ain' no business of yourn what I do," he muttered. He wished she wouldn't talk so much. He would rather be alone with his own thoughts. How was a man to think with a prattling woman around him all the time? He hunched over the tin plate, shoveling food into his mouth without really tasting it.

"Thinkin' mebbe it is my business," she contradicted. She stared outside at a lone chicken scratching in a tuft of grass. "Seen Miss Cammy when she go off, ridin' her horse." She turned slightly and gave him a sidelong glance. "An' seen you goin' in de same direction on'y a few minutes after dat. . . ."

Startled, Jude looked up at her, glaring. "You ever say a word 'bout dat, I'll shet yore black mouf forever."

She was a bit disconcerted by his fiercely angry look, and a bit surprised by the force of it. But she was also determined. After a moment she worked up enough courage to ask, "What you doin' when you meets Missy?"

"None of yore goddamn business," he snapped, returning his attention to his plate. He picked up a biscuit, rolled it around in the red gravy, and ate it in two bites.

Zoe's broad nostrils flared indignantly at his tone.

"Wants to know," she insisted. She folded her arms across her high bosom and viewed him with level eyes.

In a violent motion, Jude threw the wooden spoon on the table where it landed with a clatter. Then, getting up, he began to pace the small cabin, casting angry looks in her direction.

"What you thinks we doin', heh?" he jibed. "What you thinks?" His chin jutted out and his breath came heavy, expanding his broad chest until it strained against cotton.

Her gaze slipped away. "Doan know," she mumbled. "But wants you to tell me."

"Well, wants to know, do you?" he muttered savagely. His blue eyes glinted like an approaching storm. He knew Zoe well enough to know that, like a dog with a bone, she wouldn't cease her questioning until he answered her. She would hound him for days, even weeks, until she got what she wanted. And under no circumstances must she learn the truth, at least that part of it that was so dangerous to him.

"Awright," he said at last in a tone that suggested compliance. He took a deep breath. "Tells you. Missy teachin' me to read." He nodded at her suitably shocked expression.

A fearful look came into Zoe's dark eyes. "You crazy?" she hissed. "Wants to git yorese'f kilt? You gots to stop it now! Doan learn no more. . . ."

His laughter was harsh as he viewed her stricken face. "I already know how to read and write," he informed her softly, dropping the idiom that had become so hateful to him.

She stared blankly at the sound of his voice, unable to believe her ears. Even the timbre of it had changed. Had she closed her eyes she would have thought that it was a white man talking.

"Did you hear me, Zoe?" he asked in the same soft tone. He brought his face close to hers, enjoying her unsettled state. "You wanted to know what we were doing; now, I think you know."

"Sweet Baby Jesus," Zoe gasped as fear knotted in her throat. "You stop talkin' lak dat! Stop it dis minute, 'fore someone heahs you . . ." She stood there, breathing deeply, peering about the small cabin as if it were suddenly peopled by unseen demons. A slave could be sold, shipped to the canefields, if it was even suspected that he could read, much less write. A slave who could write could easily pen himself a pass. She'd heard stories of slaves who had had their hands chopped off for possessing such a skill.

At last she regarded Jude, her own fury mounting. What he was doing could get them all in serious trouble. White men were not selective when their anger was aroused.

"An' what you think you gonna do wit dat learnin'?" she demanded, her brow furrowing in consternation. Her breath came so fast that her words were rushed. "Cain't use it nohow. Masta thinks you bein' uppity, he take de skin offen yore back."

Raising his chin, Jude's blue eyes narrowed. He knew he shouldn't tell her anymore, but the temptation was irresistible.

"With Miss Cammy's help, I'm going North," he stated at last, his voice barely a whisper. He glanced through the open doorway to assure himself that no one was around. Then he viewed Zoe again. "It won't be long before all slaves are freed. When that time comes," he pointed a thumb at his chest, "I'll be ready."

"Freed?" She gave a short, bitter laugh, expressing heavy skepticism. Jude moved to the other side of the table. Zoe walked away from the doorway, coming closer to him. One corner of her mouth curled downward as she looked at him. "You daft in de haid, honey man. Ain' no white folks gonna free us'ns. Think dey's gonna do de plantin' and de ploughin' all by deyselves?" She put her hands on her hips and viewed him with open scorn.

He grimaced at her ignorance. "They'll pay us to work, you little fool," he growled. "But I don't aim to work in any field. . . ."

He appeared so confident, Zoe faltered, feeling uncertain. "You really thinks it gonna happen? Thinks we gonna be free?" The thought scared her a bit, for Zoe, at eighteen, had known no other life than the one she lived at Albemarle. She had never even been to Charleston. Her mother, Linny, had been pregnant with Zoe when Masta Nathaniel had bought her. Linny had died when Zoe was thirteen years old. Jonah had been two years older than that. Since then, Zoe had been doing just what she did now: the washing and ironing for the people who lived in the Great House and helping Minda in the kitchen in the afternoons. The work she wouldn't miss at all. But where would she go if freedom actually came? Who would supply her food, her clothes? She didn't even have a husband. . . .

"It will happen," Jude was affirming strongly, inclining his head in a solemn manner. "It's not only books I read, I read the newspapers, too." He couldn't prevent the pride that crept into his voice with the statement.

Zoe considered that for a long moment, the possibility at

204

last beginning to excite her. Her mind ran wild with the possibilities. She could go anywhere, do anything she pleased. There would be no one to stop her, to give her orders, to threaten her with a beating if she refused.

Eager now, Zoe reached out and clutched at Jude's sleeve. "Den, takes me wit you," she begged, her eyes imploring. "When you goes, takes me wit you. . . ."

Impatiently, he brushed aside her hand. "You?" The word was threaded with a shimmering strand of mockery that caused Zoe's lip to tremble. He laughed at the thought, shaking his head from side to side.

Zoe clasped her hands tightly, her dark eyes never leaving him. "Won't be no trouble." Her voice wavered with anticipation. "Promises you. Do ever'thin' you tells me . . ." She broke off when the laughter continued. The sound of it struck at her heart like a heavy fist.

"Don't plan on spending the rest of my life with the likes of you," Jude pronounced firmly when he had his amusement under control. "Besides," he added, turning away from her, "you'd only get in my way. I'm not going to saddle myself with an ignorant black wench like you." He didn't dare tell her that Cammy was planning to run with him. As her coachman, no one would question him when they rode away from here.

Zoe fell silent, more hurt and bitter than at any other time in her life. She watched with quiet resentment as Jude shucked his shirt and breeches and lay down on the husk mattress.

She should be there, at his side, but knew it would be futile. The heat would spring up, flooding her belly with desire. But Jude, as she knew from experience, would probably turn away, muttering disdainfully. He did that more often than not.

Having completely forgotten Zoe, Jude lay, hands behind his head, staring up at the ceiling, impatient for his plans to become a reality. He could, of course, write his own pass anytime he wanted to, had even practiced forging Master Griffin's bold scrawl, always being careful to burn the papers afterward. But, having given it great and deep thought, Jude was also too smart to try it. He knew very well that he would have only one chance at freedom, only one; therefore, his escape would have to be foolproof.

If he did forge a pass, it would get him as far as Charleston. Then what? Having been born and raised on Albemarle, Jude had never been further than Charleston. He did know the quickest means of travel North was by boat. Only a fool like Jonah would attempt it overland. Jude had no doubt that sooner or later Jonah would be caught again, despite the fact that he had remained at large for almost seven months now. Probably the fool was hiding in the swamp, he thought contemptuously.

However, to get on a boat, Jude reflected, still staring up at the ceiling, one needed money as well as a pass. He had saved some, but he didn't want to spend it until he had to.

No, the only foolproof way was with Cammy. Once North, he would of course have to send her back home. He wouldn't put it past Griffin to come after his sister with murder in his heart. Jude would never feel safe if he had to continually look over his shoulder, waiting for Cammy's brother to suddenly appear. On his own, he could mix and blend in with the free colored community until such time as freedom became a fact.

But Cammy wouldn't suffer too long, he reasoned. It

was to be expected that her brother and grandfather would raise holy hell for a while. Then they'd marry her off to some respectable white man and the matter would be ended.

And so Jude daydreamed, his thoughts turned inward, seeing with his mind's eye the stories he had read, the pictures he had seen. Oh, it would be a good life, he thought in satisfaction, a broad lazy smile finding its way to his full lips. And, best of all, he would be free.

The next morning, Zoe emerged from the washhouse, lugging a basketful of freshly washed laundry, muttering to herself as she went to hang it up.

All day long, it seemed to her, she washed and ironed, then had to help Minda in the kitchen.

"An' you would think," she said out loud, though there was no one around to hear, "dat after you wuz done, Zoe gal, you could at least count on yore man to pleasure wit you. But naw, dat buck got his mind someplace else . . . an' ever'body knowin' jest where."

She dropped the basket on the ground. Straightening, she stood with her hands on her rounded hips, a sour look on her black face.

"An' jest what he doin' when he follows missy to de grove?" She gave a sharp, unpleasant laugh. "Readin', he sez," she continued with her solitary monologue. "So when he gits Nawth, he kin be somebody . . ." She gave a snort of disgust.

Picking up a ruffled white shirt that belonged to Nathaniel, she shook it out, snapping it, then secured it to the wash line with wooden clothespins.

For a time she continued with her task, her mind filled

with thoughts of Jude and how she could persuade him to take her along when he made his escape.

Even thinking on it, Zoe doubted that she could change his mind. But that wouldn't prevent her from trying, she decided firmly. Whatever peril was involved, she would willingly share it with him.

Perhaps, she thought, pinning a petticoat to the line, she could threaten Jude into changing his mind. Tell him that she would reveal all she knew about his plans unless he took her along with him.

The basket was now empty. Peering in the direction of the stables, Zoe's black eyes narrowed. Jude was nowhere about. Most days at this time she could see him grooming horses, repairing straps and harnesses or otherwise making himself useful.

But today he was nowhere around.

Glancing about in the late morning quiet, Zoe moved furtively in the direction of the wooded area that surrounded the main compound. Last night, Jude had told her that he was getting ready to run. Did he already do it? she wondered. Or was he with Miss Cammy again?

She would, Zoe suddenly decided, see for herself just what kind of lessons missy was giving her Jude.

Sometime later, Zoe stood, concealed by moss and the heavy, drooping branches of a great gnarled cypress. And what she saw filled her with an anger so great, she could hardly contain herself.

They were naked, the rich golden color of her man's skin in sharp contrast with the white and flawless skin of her young mistress.

The look on the face of Jude as he found a sudden release from his passion was one that Zoe had never seen.

On those rare occasions when Jude condescended to couple with her, it was a quick and brutal thing he did, as if he couldn't wait to get it over and done.

No wonder she hadn't conceived in all these months, Zoe thought, enraged. That Jude was dumping his seed before he ever got to her.

Cammy still had her white arms about Jude, kissing him, teasing him, her laughter trilling through the grove like that of a contented bird. Jude laughed, too, as she tickled him and playfully bit on his ear. Grabbing her, Jude held her tight against him, murmuring words Zoe couldn't hear. And then there was silence as the lovers kissed, deeply and passionately.

Zoe compressed her lips tightly, afraid that the angry thoughts in her mind would come rushing out through her mouth. With effort, she swallowed, then turned away, unwilling to witness the couple's heated embraces. As quietly as she had come, Zoe now made her way back to the yard.

Unaware of anything amiss, Cammy finally sat up, smoothing her hair with her hands. She stared down at Jude, stretched out languorously on the blanket. With her finger, she traced the muscles on his shoulder, trailing down the smooth, golden skin to his flat abdomen. The feel of his bare flesh caused her to shudder in delight.

"Cammy . . ." he murmured warningly, not opening his eyes.

She gave a soft laugh, then lay down beside him, putting her head on his warm chest.

After a bit, she glanced up at his still closed eyes. "Jude . . ." she whispered, then bit her lip. "There's something I've got to tell you. . . ."

He grunted but made no move. He was half asleep.

"I'm going to have a baby. . . ."

Beneath her body, Cammy felt him go rigid. In a slow movement, he opened his eyes, then raised himself up on an elbow, almost tumbling her off of him.

She was frightened at the look of him, never having seen such a truculent expression upon his face. "It will be all right," she tried to assure him. "We'll just have to leave sooner than we planned, that's all."

His blue eyes stared steadily, almost hatefully, into her own. His hands balled into fists. For a long moment, fear and anger battled within him. Fear proved stronger. He turned from her. Drawing up his knees, he folded his arms across them and put his head down in an attitude of utter dejection.

Cammy placed a small hand on his arm. "Listen to me, Jude," she entreated earnestly. "I know exactly what we're going to do. I'm going to tell Morgana."

He raised his head, staring at her in dumb astonishment. "You can't tell nobody!" he protested hoarsely. "You want to see me get killed? Oh, Jesus," he muttered, turning away again. The fear spread throughout him, leaving him breathless with the force of it.

"Will you please listen?" she begged. "Morgana will help us. I know she will. And besides, she comes from the North. She can tell us the best place to go. . . ."

Jude listened dully to her plans, too overwhelmed to do anything else. For having been taught to read, he could be sold. For this . . . When they were through with him, death would be a welcome blessing. His mind presented increasingly grotesque possibilities to him. His body actually cringed at the thought of the indignities that would be visited upon it. How many strokes of the lash did it take to kill a man? he wondered, growing more frantic. He shuddered, feeling icy cold beneath the warm sun.

Finally he turned, aware that Cammy was shaking his arm.

"Are you listening to me?" At his brief nod, she said, "And once we get there, we can be married..." She paused at the look he gave her and her lips trembled. "Don't you want to marry me?"

He gave an impatient gesture, summoning his remaining strength to bring himself under control. "Yes, of course," he lied. "But how do you plan to keep the baby a secret until we leave?"

She looked down at her almost flat stomach. "Nothing shows," she observed. "We have at least a month to plan—"

"A month!" He couldn't wait that long, he thought distractedly. He was filled with the urge to run, right now!

She nodded, eager again. "Morgana won't be able to come with us until she has her own baby. You and I can't possibly go into Charleston alone," she explained patiently, although she knew he was perfectly aware of that simple fact. "But Morgana and I can go on the pretext of doing some shopping. You will, of course, drive us."

He gave her a doubtful look, the fear still crouched in his belly, waiting to spring up in his throat. "What makes you think she'll do all this?"

"I know she will," Cammy insisted firmly. "You don't know her like I do."

"Have you talked to her yet?" he asked skeptically, relaxing only slightly.

"Not yet," she admitted. "But I will, today," she added

211

quickly, seeing his expression close again. She put her arms around him. "Please trust me, Jude," she whispered, her mouth against his neck.

Jude's only answer was another deep sigh. He had, he reflected dispiritedly, no other choice.

Back in her cabin, Zoe's anger spewed forth and boiled over like a pot of unwatched milk. She prowled the small cabin like a caged cat seeking escape. Occasionally, she paused by the open door, peering across the yard to the stables. Jude had still not returned.

Within her frail body, hate took shape and grew, spreading throughout her like water poured on sand.

"Goin' Nawth, is he?" She clenched her teeth as she stared outside into the sun-dappled yard.

She knew now why Jude had been so confident. Probably, she thought in rising agitation, even if Jude was caught trying to run, Miss Cammy would see to it that the whip wouldn't scar that handsome body.

Not like her brother, Jonah. Poor Jonah was too ignorant, too dumb to get away. He had run twice and been caught both times; though, this time, luck seemed to be with him. But he didn't have a white lady to help him. Miss Cammy wouldn't look twice at a buck like Jonah. Her brother didn't have blue eyes and his skin was black as night. Jonah was a nigger, but Jude. . . .

Well, goddamn them all, Zoe thought in the heat of her rage. Jude was just as much a nigger as Jonah. Maybe it was time for honey man to learn that. . . .

Chapter 11

It was hot. The late September air was heavy and humid and uncomfortable, as it had been all week long since their return. In the distance thunder rumbled against a sullen sky. Creatures in the woods and swamps paused a moment, hearing in the ominous sound a prelude to the approaching storm.

After the cooling breeze that had been present in Charleston, Morgana found Albemarle stifling. Both Griffin and Nathaniel had urged her to stay indoors, at least until the danger of fever had passed. But as she sat in her room, fanning herself in an effort to find some relief from the heat, Morgana couldn't resist going out onto the piazza, having instructed Bella to move the divan out there.

Supper was over, and here in the privacy of her own room, Morgana had discarded hoops and stays, wearing no more than a cotton nightgown over which she wore a thin wrap of the same material.

Sitting herself down, Morgana viewed the darkening sky, studying the silvery mist that crept up from the river, hovering almost caressingly about the trunks of the cypress and oaks. She fervently wished for October, and her baby, to arrive.

Feeling disgruntled, Morgana sighed deeply. Lately, *waiting* seemed to fill her life.

Bella brought her lemonade, offering yet another admonishment against sitting in the night air. Garbed in her usual black dress and white apron, Bella wore a red bandana about her head, tied in such an intricate manner that it suggested a fashionable turban.

"Shouldn't be heah, Miz Morgana," she grumbled. "Best you go inside." Putting the glass down on a small table, she stood with hands on her hips, viewing her mistress as though she were a naughty child.

"It's so very warm," Morgana protested tiredly, waving a hand. "At least there's a bit of a breeze out here."

Bella clucked her disapproval. "It's de breeze what comes from de river dat brings de fever," she advised solemnly, nodding her turbaned head for emphasis. "An' when de fever gits a'holt of you, doan let go. Keeps comin' back. Makes a body right sickly, it do."

With a certain wariness, Bella turned and eyed the bronzed sky with a flicker of apprehension. She always breathed a sigh of relief when September, and the chance of hurricanes, passed. The first year she had come to the Carolinas, September had birthed just such a fearsome spectacle and she hoped to never again see the likes of it.

Watching her, Morgana smiled with true affection.

Bella was, she thought, a godsend. The girl constantly hovered, alert to Morgana's needs, whether it was a cool drink of water or a change of perspiration-dampened clothing. Morgana had long since put herself in Bella's capable hands, and had actually grown very fond of her.

"I promise I'll go inside in just a few minutes," she said at last in an effort to placate her.

"Iffen you doan, Masta Griffin paddles me fer shoah," Bella murmured darkly with an audible sigh.

Morgana regarded the black girl with a suddenly intent look. "Have you ever been . . . paddled?" She felt angry at just the thought.

"Not since I come heah," Bella replied offhandedly. She went inside, emerging a moment later with a palmetto fan in her hand.

Morgana was looking at her in surprise. "I thought you were born here. . . ."

"Oh, no, missus. I wuz borned in Virginny." She made a vague gesture with the fan. "Doan rightly know where dat is, but it's a long ways from heah. Took days an' days fer us'ns to walk to New Orleans. Dat's where de auction wuz," she elaborated.

"How long ago was that?"

Bella screwed up her face in thought, mentally counting the plantings, then, finally, held up three fingers. "Dat long ago."

"You were about fifteen when you were sold?" Morgana speculated.

" 'Spects so," Bella agreed blithely. She laid the fan on the table within Morgana's reach.

"Is that where my husband bought you?'

Straightening, Bella shook her head. "Wasn't Masta

Griffin. Was Masta Dabney Pritchard what bought me."
At Morgana's look of confusion, she went on to explain,
"Masta Dabney lost dis gal while he wuz playin' cards.
An' it wuz Masta Nathaniel who won me."

Leaning back, Morgana gave a sigh, but made no comment. She wondered how long it was going to take for her
to get used to this sort of thing.

At the sound of a knock on the door, Bella went inside
again. Morgana sipped a bit of the tangy lemonade, then
looked up to see Cammy.

"I . . . just wanted to talk to you," she said, sounding a
bit breathless.

"Of course," Morgana responded quickly. She patted
the divan. "Come, sit beside me. I'm grateful for your
company." She noticed that Cammy was still wearing the
gown she had worn at the supper table, a ruffled and
beribboned pale blue merino creation over a wide, crinolined skirt. Just the sight of it made Morgana feel warm.
Reaching out, she picked up the palmetto fan from the
table beside her.

Cammy hesitated a moment, then turned to Bella.
"Leave us alone." She waited until the slave left, then sat
herself down. She was silent for a time, twisting her
handkerchief with nervous movements.

At last Cammy turned toward Morgana. "How are you
feeling?" she asked. She was perched on the edge of the
divan as if she were about to take flight.

"Except for being a bit uncomfortable with the heat, I'm
fine." Morgana gave a rueful smile. "I certainly hope that
you're not going to tell me to go back into that hot room,"
she murmured, fanning herself. "Bella's been hounding me
since I came out here."

Cammy smiled at her, a stiff parody of that expression, too bright, too affected to be meaningful. "You like Bella?" she asked.

A bit surprised by the question, Morgana laughed. "Of course I do. At first I was unsettled by having someone around me all the time," she admitted. "But now I confess that I'd be lost without her."

Turning away, Cammy was quiet for a long moment and when she did speak, Morgana was again, jolted by surprise.

"Do you think that slavery will ever be abolished?" the girl asked in a deceptively casual voice.

"Why, I don't know," Morgana answered slowly, considering it. "I certainly hope it will be, one day." She took another sip of the lemonade.

"You don't regard the darkies as inferior?"

"Certainly not," Morgana stated, turning to look at her. "They are uneducated, but that's hardly their fault, is it? There is a big difference between being ignorant and being uninformed."

"It's against the law to teach Negroes to read or write," the girl mused. She regarded Morgana with some curiosity. "Do you believe that, if they were educated— informed—they would be just like we are?"

Morgana shrugged. She put the fan back on the table, feeling too weary to even use it. "I don't see why not." She gave a short laugh. "Of course, I wouldn't want to argue the point with your grandfather," she murmured wryly, inclining her head. "He seems to feel they are like children."

Cammy looked down at her lap and managed to keep her voice steady. "I used to think that way, too," she whispered. "Does everyone in the North feel as you do?" she asked after a bit, not looking at Morgana.

"I can't speak for everyone," Morgana responded quietly, wondering at the seriousness of the girl's tone. She had the oddest sensation that Cammy was talking about one subject and thinking of another. The feeling was disconcerting, but transitory. The heat was stifling even her reactions. "But, yes. I think that most Northerners agree that slavery is a terrible thing. Some, in fact, are quite outspoken in their beliefs."

"Then, if a Negro were to live there, no one would bother him, is that right?"

Morgana frowned in perplexity. "Cammy, what are you getting at?"

The girl wet her lips, hesitated, then mopped her face with the crumpled handkerchief. "I need your help," she murmured, turning her dark eyes on Morgana. "You're the only one . . ." Her mouth set into a tense line. This morning, when she had thought it all out, it had seemed so simple. Now, faced with the moment of truth, Cammy found herself searching for the right words.

Studying her young sister-in-law, Morgana felt a prodding of unease. The girl was pale and her eyes seemed darker and larger than usual. Her face was grave, troubled, displaying none of the usual mischievous energy that Morgana was used to seeing. The handkerchief in her hands had been reduced to an undefinable wad. "I'll do whatever I can," she said quickly, alarmed. "But first you'd better tell me what this is all about."

"I . . . I'm in love with someone, and . . ." Cammy bit her lower lip, shifting her position restlessly on the divan.

The smile returned to Morgana's lips and she relaxed

once more. So that's what all this was about, she thought in relief. "That's wonderful," she began, then her brow creased in thought. Since no young man had called here at Albemarle, obviously Cammy's young man was in Charleston, or perhaps at a neighboring plantation. "Is it Mr. Barrows?" she prompted, thinking of the young man who had called most often while they were in the town house.

Cammy stared blankly a moment, then shook her head. "No. No, it isn't Clinton. . . ."

"Someone that your grandfather doesn't approve of?" Morgana probed tentatively when the girl showed no sign of continuing.

Cammy swallowed. "It's . . . Jude." Her voice was so low, her words were barely audible.

It was Morgana's turn to stare blankly. "Jude?" For the moment she didn't even recognize the name, trying as she was to place it with one of the fresh young faces she had seen in Charleston.

"Jude." Cammy was staring in a determined manner.

Morgana blinked. "I don't—" she began, then fell silent. Her blue eyes suddenly widened with comprehension. "You mean . . . *our* Jude?" At Cammy's brief nod, Morgana felt a rush of dismay so strong that it produced a feeling of nausea in her throat. She took a deep breath in order to fight down the unpleasant sensation, then closed her eyes in an effort to assimilate her thoughts. For the immediate present she was too stunned to speak.

Cammy continued to watch her closely, almost holding her breath in anticipation of Morgana's reaction.

"But you can't marry him," Morgana breathed at last. She gripped Cammy's small hand. "Neither your grandfather nor Griffin would ever allow it." Whatever could the girl be thinking of? she wondered distractedly.

"I know," Cammy quickly agreed with a brief nod of her head. She appeared almost relieved now that the first hurdle had been accomplished. "That's why we must leave here."

"Where could you possibly go?" Morgana was astounded by the girl's calm statement.

"North. I've never been there. Neither, of course, has Jude, so you must tell us where to go. But first, we must return to Charleston. I can't go by myself, with only Jude driving. Grandfather would never allow it. But if you came with us. . . ."

Bewilderment settled upon Morgana as she tried to follow the rush of words. She tried to make sense out of what she was hearing, but her mind couldn't absorb it all. Cammy seemed to have entirely forgotten that she was unable to travel.

"We'll have to wait until after your baby is born," Cammy said quickly, sensing her thoughts. "We had planned to wait until next year, but—"

"You cannot run away with Jude," Morgana interrupted firmly. She straightened. "You mustn't even think of such a thing! Your grandfather . . ." She made a gesture, feeling helpless in the face of just the thought of Nathaniel's reaction to this situation. Cammy herself had noted that her grandfather would not allow her to drive into the city with only Jude in attendance. Whatever possessed the girl to think that Nathaniel would accept this!

"But I love him," Cammy cried out. At the sight of Morgana's freshly stricken face, the girl exclaimed, "You don't understand. Jude and I—we grew up together. I've known him all my life. He's the kindest, most gentle person in the whole world."

"I'm trying to understand," Morgana offered patiently. She took another deep breath. "But—"

"Oh," Cammy made a sharp, disparaging gesture with her hand, "how could you understand? You're a Northerner, a Yankee . . ." Her eyes brightened with a sudden anger and she regarded Morgana sharply. "Or is it just that when your convictions are tested, you find yourself lacking. . . ."

Stung, Morgana frowned in consternation. "That's not it at all," she protested strongly. "You're being unfair! We are not discussing abolition. Even in the North, feeling would run high against a marriage of this sort—"

"I don't care," Cammy interjected heatedly, her back rigid. "I don't care what people think."

Upset, Morgana's finger went to her lips in an effort to caution Cammy, whose voice had risen. Getting up, she went to the iron railing and peered into the yard. It was quiet, with only the usual sound of the dogs barking and an occasional laugh that wafted up from Slave Row.

It was completely dark now, the black sky unrelieved by stars, which were hidden by the clouds. The air hung still and unmoving, the slight breeze having retreated in the calm before the storm.

Satisfied that there was no one in the immediate vicinity, Morgana walked back to the divan. "You don't mean that," she objected softly as she sat down again.

Cammy's eyes were bright. "I do. I do mean it! And besides," her voice fell to a whisper, "if I stay here, Griffin will make me marry Clinton Barrows." Absently, she plucked at the tatted edging of the handkerchief, unraveling it. "At least he will try," she added grimly, her mouth tightening. "And I will not do that. I cannot abide him."

"Is that why Clinton came to call so often while we were in Charleston?"

Cammy made an exasperated face and put what was left of the handkerchief on the small table. "Exactly. They seem to think I'll change my mind eventually. I've told Griffin that I would not consider Clinton Barrows under any circumstance." She sighed. "My brother patted my hand and told me I'll see things differently in a year or so."

"He seems like a nice young man," Morgana ventured tentatively.

Cammy was silent a moment, studying the changing pattern of light on the piazza floor created by the flickering oil lamp in the bedroom and the deepening shadows outside. Then, turning her head, she regarded Morgana with a level look. "I cannot marry Clinton because..." Her resolve deserted her and she reached out to take Morgana's hand, holding it tightly. "You've seen Jude. He's not like the others. Nor," she went on, "is he ignorant, as he pretends to be. I've taught him. From the time we were children, I've taught him. He can read and write. And," she continued with a trace of bitterness, "he speaks as well as you or me. He's just afraid to, you see." She was watching Morgana closely, her lips trembling, her brimming eyes pleading for understanding.

Morgana sensed the unbridled, unspoken emotion. Cammy, she had long since learned, was never casual about anything, and if ordinary things goaded her toward excitement, what would love do?

In a quick motion, Morgana clasped the girl in her arms,

giving her a hug. "Oh, my dear Cammy. If it were up to me, you and Jude could marry this instant. Please, don't think I'm censuring you."

Cammy's expression turned eager. "Then you'll help us?"

"What can I possibly do?" Morgana responded sadly, leaning back against the soft cushions again. Her finely drawn features displayed unutterable sympathy. "Even if you ran away, you know that Griffin would follow you and bring you back here."

"He won't if we are already married."

"I doubt that even that would stop him," Morgana replied with a shake of her head. She knew perfectly well how much Griffin thought of his sister. She had, this while, been thinking of Nathaniel's reaction, but now she realized that Griffin would be just as angry, if not more, were he to learn of all this.

The girl drew away, her face hardening. "He'll have to." She got to her feet, hands clasped at her waist, and looked down at Morgana. "I'm to have Jude's baby."

A muted, rolling sound of thunder punctuated her statement. White-faced, Morgana just stared at her.

"Oh, dear God," she murmured, putting a hand to her pale cheek. She glanced at Cammy's waist, but the crinolined skirt gave her no indication. "How long. . . ."

"Not for more than four months yet. That's why it is so important that we leave as soon as possible."

"Does anyone know? Have you told Jude?"

Cammy nodded slowly. "Just this morning. No one else knows. I think I've been able to keep Meg from discovering it, but I'm not entirely certain. I have an idea she suspects.

However," she added hastily, "Meg would never tell, even if she did know."

Cammy continued to watch her, waiting for a response, but when Morgana didn't speak, a cold feeling of abandonment crept over her. She rubbed her bare arms, feeling suddenly chilled. She hadn't realized until this minute just how much she had been counting on Morgana's help.

"There must be another alternative," Morgana said after a brief pause. "To your running away, I mean."

"There is no other way," Cammy stated flatly, then sighed. "I've known for a long time that one day I would have to make this decision."

Morgana leaned forward, still unconvinced. "Is there any chance, any chance at all, that your grandfather could be persuaded to free Jude—" She broke off at Cammy's mirthless laugh. "But surely, under the circumstances, he would at least consider it. The baby might change his mind."

The girl shook her head firmly. "If he or my brother ever found out before we could get away . . ." She averted her face as if to escape the sound of her own words. "They'd kill Jude." Her voice ended on a strangled sob.

Startled, Morgana's eyes widened. However, despite the girl's conviction, she couldn't believe that that was a possiblity. They might sell Jude, she thought, and that would be bad enough, but they would never kill him. The idea was out of her realm of imagination.

"Cammy," she said after a bit, "are you sure, very sure, that this is what you want? Once you take this step, there will be no turning back."

"Morgana, I love Jude," Cammy whispered softly, almost sadly. "I know it's difficult for you to understand, but I've known him all my life. To me he isn't a slave, or black. He's just . . . Jude."

Looking away, Morgana felt despair crowd in upon her. She wished she could refute Cammy, point out the illogic of the whole situation. And, if it weren't for the coming child, she might have made the attempt in spite of Cammy's plaintive words.

"Morgana, will you help us?"

Overwhelmed by the heat and by Cammy's distressing tale, Morgana just sat there. Absently, she glanced at the sky, noting the approaching storm with distant eyes. She didn't know what to do or what to say. She had a sudden longing to rush from the room, to creep into Griffin's strong arms and rest there, sheltered. What matter if he didn't love her? she thought wildly, brushing the dampened tendrils of her hair from her forehead. She loved him—wasn't that enough?

But it *did* matter, she told herself sternly, upset with her inclination. She wasn't about to throw herself into Griffin's arms whatever the provocation. She had done that once and she had learned a bitter lesson for her rashness.

Coming forward, Cammy touched her arm, shaking her out of her reverie, demanding, with her eyes, Morgana's strength and fortitude.

The moment of weakness passed and Morgana sat up straighter as she gathered her inner resources about her, forcing herself to think clearly.

A thought began to form in her mind, and as Morgana considered it, she felt certain that it would work. Both Griffin and Nathaniel would be angry; that was only to be expected. But she sensed that Cammy was prepared to go through with her plan of running away with or without her help. On their own, she reasoned, they would probably be caught before they even left Charleston.

"I have an aunt in Massachusetts," she said at last, turning to look at Cammy again. "Perhaps you and Jude can go there. The two of you can be married and stay there until the baby comes, and until you both decide where to live, and what to do."

"Would your aunt allow us to stay?" Cammy asked excitedly, bending toward her.

Morgana pursed her lips. It was a question she could not, or course, answer with any degree of accuracy. "I'll write to her tomorrow," she decided with a firm nod of her head. "I've been meaning to do it ever since my father died. When we receive her answer, we'll know what to do." She glanced down at her swollen stomach; her child wasn't due for another three weeks. "I'm not entirely sure I'll be able to go with you. But if it's at all possible, I'll take you there myself."

The more Morgana thought about it, the more feasible it sounded. Besides, she thought, it would be good for her to get away from here for a while. Decisions would have to be made and she needed time and a haven to think clearly.

Cammy's dark eyes flared with hope. "Oh, if only it could be so . . . ." She pressed a trembling hand to her lips.

"Of course it will," Morgana tried to assure her. She sighed deeply. "I can't say I approve of what you have done . . . ." Her voice trailed off. My God, Morgana thought to herself, suddenly ashamed of her words. Who was she to talk? She had given herself to the man she loved before they were married. What right did she have to condemn anyone else?

First one, then another fat drop of rain began to pelt her

shoulders, and Morgana finally got to her feet. Cammy, she thought, had been right about one thing: Morgana felt that Cammy was the sister she never had. The thought was, in some ways, at once disturbing and demanding. Still and all, she felt a very real responsibility for this girl's welfare. Morgana knew she couldn't let Cammy down, whatever the cost to herself or her marriage. That last caused her mouth to twist in irony. What marriage? she wondered. When a man marries a woman under a threat it is no true marriage, it is a desecration of vows.

Putting an arm about Cammy, Morgana spoke briskly as they walked back into the bedroom. "Now, don't you worry. Everything will turn out all right."

Morgana felt certain of her words. But Morgana hadn't lived in the South long enough to realize just how improbable her statement was.

That night, Morgana lay on her rumpled bed, tossing and turning for more than an hour. The rain had cooled the air a bit, but had increased the humidity, adding to her discomfort.

At one point Bella got up from her pallet. Reaching for the palmetto fan, she began to wave it over Morgana. Morgana motioned the slave away.

"Just because I'm restless is no reason for you to spend a sleepless night," she protested, insisting that Bella return to her pallet.

After that, Morgana made the attempt to lie still, her thoughts on Cammy. Running away and getting married was one thing. But what, she wondered worriedly, would the two young people do afterward? Could Jude earn a living? Could he support a wife and child? Morgana took some comfort in the fact that she could give them some of the money her father had left her. But what would they do when it was gone? Perhaps by then, she thought, Nathaniel would relent and allow them to return home.

Hearing the sound of a door open and close in the hall, Morgana raised her head, listening. She figured it was well after midnight; time and more for the whole household to have settled down.

She put her head back on the pillow and compressed her lips tightly, certain that it was Griffin's door that had issued the noise. And there was only one reason for someone to be entering his room at this time of night. It must have been Serena.

Even though it was quiet now, Morgana buried her head deeper into the pillow, imagining it was possible for her to hear the sounds of lovemaking from across the hall.

Morgana's moan of despair was muffled in the downy softness. How did Griffin make love to that . . . wench? Was it an expression of love or sex? Was it a hurried act to relieve his need or did he enjoy it? Did he spend endless minutes caressing her? Morgana couldn't erase the imagined pictures from her mind no matter how she tried. Visions tormented her, goading her still further toward wakefulness; Griffin's strong muscular arms about the satiny smooth, honey colored skin; his mouth pressed upon rose-tinted lips . . . .

"Oh, God," she murmured, suppressing a sob of longing.

At the foot of the bed, Bella's head again appeared as she sat up, peering anxiously through the dimness at her mistress. She waited a full minute, but Morgana remained quiet. Presently, Bella lay down again, falling asleep almost immediately.

But Morgana lay there, wide awake, listening to the

pattering of the rain that continued almost until it was light. Not until she heard Griffin's door open and close again did she fall into a restless, troubled sleep. She dreamed of Griffin, dreamed that she continually reached for him only to have him laughingly elude her outstretched arms.

At last the morning dawned, clear and fresh and sparkling. Morgana awoke feeling as tired as if she had not slept at all.

Bella regarded her with a worried frown, noting the dark smudges of weariness beneath Morgana's eyes. "You jest stay in bed, Miz Morgana," she urged. "Brings yore breakfast up heah."

Before Morgana could protest, Bella was gone. She sank back against the pillows, and before Bella had returned, fell into a light and dreamless sleep.

She awoke some time later feeling much better and ate heartily of the bacon and eggs Bella put before her.

After having eaten and dressed, Morgana took a stroll in the direction of the stables, relieved to find Jude alone at his chores.

When he saw her, his blue eyes turned suddenly wary. Even so, Morgana had to admit, now that she studied him with care, he was a very handsome young man. He possessed features that were almost Caucasian—his lips perhaps a trifle full, his nostrils only slightly flared. His black hair, while tightly curled, wasn't kinky. If it wasn't for his coppery gold skin ... Yes, she decided in that instant, she could understand Cammy's attraction, if not her love.

"Miz Morgana," he murmured respectfully as she neared. "Kin I do sumpin fer you?"

She smiled slightly, although there was little humor in

the expression. "I was told that you could speak English as well as I can," she commented dryly.

His eyes grew round and fearful and he took a step back from her.

"I mean you no harm," she exclaimed quickly, seeing his reaction. "I . . . just wanted to be certain." She looked about to assure herself that no one was around. "Cammy told me everything last night," she said, dropping her voice to the merest whisper.

Jude studied the ground for a moment, then met her eye. "And what are you going to do?"

"Help you both, if I can," she responded quietly. Even though prepared, Morgana felt a slight shock at the difference in his voice.

With her words, Jude seemed to relax, although his attitude remained cautious.

"Do you love Cammy as much as she loves you?" Morgana asked then.

Gravely, he nodded his head. And the beginnings of new hope surged through him. Jude had no misgivings about using white people when the opportunity presented itself. "I'm so glad you understand," he murmured, striving for sincerity and hiding his jubilation. With both Cammy and Morgana helping him, freedom was assured. The thought was intoxicating.

"Do you have money?" Morgana asked him.

"Some," he admitted. "About three hundred dollars."

She raised a surprised brow.

"I don't spend my money on foolishness," he supplied quickly, sounding a bit pontifical. "Whatever I make, I save."

She nodded once, satisfied. "It will not, of course, be

enough. But I have some money of my own. I'll be glad to give it to you and Cammy."

He looked grateful. "Will we be going North?" Jude asked. At her nod of affirmation, he was sorely tempted to enlist her aid in leaving immediately. Wisely, he checked himself. "Cammy said you would know what to do," he whispered. "I thank God for your help...."

When Morgana left Jude, she was completely certain that she was doing the right thing. It was so obvious, she thought, that the two young people were in love. There was no one else who would help them, she realized. In spite of the ensuing repercussions—and Morgana did not fool herself into thinking that there would be none—she knew that she would have to be the one.

Returning to her room, Morgana sat down at her writing table and carefully penned a letter to her Aunt Sarah. Then she gave it to Adam, the slave who made the trip into Charleston twice a week to pick up mail and newspapers. She could make no further plans until she received a reply. Morgana hoped it would arrive quickly, for all their sakes.

Chapter
12

With few exceptions, notably coffee and tea, salt and flour, shrimp and beef, most of the food consumed at Albemarle was grown right on the premises. The land abounded with game, the river with fish, the soil generous with its constant supply of vegetables, rice, sweet potatoes, and sugar cane.

It was not so unusual, therefore, that the kitchen was large and well stocked. When Nathaniel had first built Albemarle, he had taken great care in the selection of a suitable site. The pantry, which was an addition to the kitchen itself, had been constructed directly over an underground spring, with the result that, even in the hottest weather, the room, having two-foot-thick walls, remained cool.

There was even a wood burning stove, but Minda preferred the brick hearth with its roomy bake oven on one side for creating most of her culinary achievements. The kitchen was her domain. Since the death of Anne Kynes, Minda had ruled supreme. She'd had a few misgivings when she first learned that Masta Griffin was planning to take a wife, but Miz Morgana, like Miss Cammy, was content to leave things under Minda's capable jurisdiction.

Mostly she worked alone, but in the late afternoon Zoe came in to help with supper. Occasionally, Serena would appear. But, Minda often thought grumpily, that yellow gal was no more than a hothouse flower. Couldn't boil water if her life depended on it. In truth, the only reason Serena even came into the kitchen was to give her the semblance of a task. The girl really had only one function to perform, and being a scullery maid wasn't it. She was here for the sole purpose of giving pleasure to her master whenever he chose to summon her to his room. He never did that directly, of course, he always left word with Thomas when he desired her company.

On this bright and sunny Saturday afternoon, Serena was nowhere in sight. Minda was happy for that state of affairs because the girl had a tendency to chatter in an endless fashion while accomplishing absolutely nothing.

Absorbed in her chore, Minda's large brown hands were kneading dough with a fierce determination. Now and then she glanced toward the young black woman seated at the well scrubbed kitchen table, peeling potatoes in a lackadaisical manner.

"Doan got all day, Zoe," Minda muttered with a show of irritation that wrinkled her normally smooth brow. "You shoah bin draggin' yore butt aroun' lately." Straightening, she wiped her hands on her apron and scowled. "You knocked up or sumpin?"

Zoe's glance at Minda was sullen. "Ain' knocked up," she mumbled, the irascible expression on her face destroying what prettiness she possessed.

"Well, you lookin' peaked enuf to be," Minda commented sarcastically as she put the dough into the pan. Walking to the open back door, she stuck her head outside. "Suky!" she called out with lusty enthusiasm. "Suky! Git yore black ass to movin'."

The young boy was supposed to be cutting and stacking firewood, but the day was too warm, so he had been merely sitting beneath a tree, dozing. At his mother's call, he reluctantly got to his feet and ambled slowly in her direction.

As he passed her, Minda's brown hand shot out and delivered a sharp slap to the kinky head of her youngest son.

"Ashes up to de ceiling an' you sittin' lak you wuz roy'lty or sumpin," she scolded the boy, who only grinned at her. With a semblance of diligence, the lad began to rake the hearth clear of ashes.

Minda watched him a moment, then moved back to the table, her slippers flapping on the wooden floor with each step she took. With a heavy sigh, she sat down, fanning herself with her apron. "Lawd, it gits hotter each year," she commented to no one in particular. Then she peered sharply at Zoe, who had ceased working altogether and was just staring out of the window. "You shoah you ain' knocked up?" she demanded, her eyes narrowing.

Her attention captured, Zoe made a face, but didn't bother to answer the question again. "Be a miracle iffen I wuz," she declared in an acid voice. "That worthless nigger son of yourn ain' good fer nothin'. Thinks he be too fine fer me."

"What you talkin' about, gal?" Minda demanded sharply, eyes flashing beneath her broad forehead. Her regal bosom heaved with indignation. She was outraged that anyone would speak disparagingly of her eldest son. "Jude's de finest buck you'll ever see. Thank de Lawd Jesus you got him. Cain't do no better."

"Dat so? Humph." Zoe's slim shoulders jerked with her agitation. "Ain' no man a'tall, dat one." She opened her mouth to say more, then thought better of it. Besides, she knew what she was going to do and Minda wasn't going to stop her. She picked up the knife again and savagely attacked the potatoes.

Minda watched her suspiciously for a moment, but, as always, the preparation of food claimed her first attention. Supper was due in just over an hour and Minda wasn't about to ruin it because this black gal was acting strangely.

Getting to her feet, she crossed the room to the oven, carefully removing a ham that was glistening with molasses and cloves. She regarded it with a critical eye for a moment, then, satisfied, put it on the table.

Zoe was crazy anyway, Minda decided as she sliced the moist pink meat. It was no wonder her Jude didn't pay her no mind. It was too bad that Masta Nathaniel had insisted that Jude take Zoe for a wench, she thought to herself. He was too good for the likes of her.

Suky had completed his simple chore and Minda now gave him a sugar cookie, prodding him out the door again with firm instructions to refill the wood bin before supper. Then, walking to the cupboard, she reached for the tin can that held the brown sugar. Strewing a generous portion of the sweet stuff into the pan drippings, she commenced to stir it vigorously with a wooden spoon.

Minda was troubled about her oldest son, but that wasn't anything new. Jude had been different from the day he had been born. She faced that fact with a certain amount of pride, but was wise enough to realize that a slave who was different could arouse more than admiration from his masters. And as fond as Masta Nathaniel was of her boy, Minda knew with a certainty that he wouldn't take kindly to what had been going on right under his nose for years now.

When Jude and Cammy had been children, Minda hadn't minded so much. It wasn't that unusual for children—black and white—to play together, especially when the family was in residence on the plantation. The fact of the matter was that there were no other children, except black, to play with, and so everyone viewed the association with a tolerant eye.

But while, from Minda's viewpoint, Miss Cammy was still little more than her baby, Jude had long since left his childhood behind. The situation was now fraught with danger—for Jude.

The only reason they had been able to get away with it for so long, Minda reflected, adding a bit of flour to the gravy, was that there had been no white mistress to take charge of Albemarle. Men had their own concerns, and the fields and crops were what occupied most of their waking hours. Minda had tried, even in the beginning, to discourage the association of Jude and Cammy. Unfortunately, trying to outwit her had become almost a game to the two children. Nor had Minda ever dared to ask Masta Nathaniel to intervene. By that time, young Masta Griffin had been packed off to England and there was, in effect, no one to gainsay the wishes of Miss Cammy.

She had tried to talk some sense into Jude, pleading with him to cease his dangerous pastime. He wouldn't listen. But then, Minda was forced to admit, he couldn't very well refuse his young mistress, either. Although what her son would do with his book learning escaped her. It was all, really, a waste of time.

As Minda moved about her kitchen, her mind on her own worrisome thoughts, Zoe surreptitiously watched the front yard, knowing full well when Griffin returned from his afternoon rounds. When she was certain that Minda was otherwise occupied, Zoe slipped outside, and by the time Griffin reached the front steps, she was waiting for him.

"Masta, suh," she said to him in her most deferential tone of voice. "Kin I talk wit you?"

Griffin looked down at the slight figure, taking a moment to place the name with the face. He registered surprise. "Zoe! What the hell are you doing here? Aren't you supposed to be in the kitchen?"

"Yassah." Zoe seemed a bit breathless, and, in point of fact, she had never before addressed her master on a personal basis. She was more than a bit frightened, but her anger at Jude had climbed to monumental proportions, making her careless of any consequences that might befall her.

Griffin displayed exasperation. He was hot and tired, and wanted a cool drink before he ate. "Dammit, gal. Speak your piece or get back into the kitchen where you belong."

Zoe swallowed nervously, shifting her weight from foot to foot. "Please, suh. Gots to talk wit you. It's 'portant dat you knows. . . ."

."Know what?" He glared, then his expression suddenly softened. "You knocked up, is that it?" His grandfather, he thought, would be pleased. It had been almost a year now. They were both beginning to think that Zoe might be barren, or that Jude had no sap in him. "You'll get a silver dollar if it's a boy," he assured her, smiling. He patted her shoulder.

Lawd Jesus, Zoe thought in growing exasperation. Why did everyone just look at her and pronounce her knocked up? "Ain' dat, suh," she said at last. Taking a deep breath, she continued in a resolute manner. "Wants to talk wit you in private . . ." She pressed her full lips together, giving the appearance of obstinacy.

The frown returned.

"It's 'bout my Jude, suh," she went on before he could protest. "He . . ." She paused and glanced about them. There was no one within earshot that she could see, but she knew very well that didn't mean a damn thing. If someone saw her talking to Masta Griffin, they'd make every effort to learn what was going on.

"What about Jude?" Griffin plucked a handkerchief from his pocket and, removing his hat, wiped the back of his neck. Damn all niggers, he was thinking. A man needed the patience of a saint when dealing with them.

"Masta, suh," Zoe entreated in a stronger voice, close to tears of frustration. "Shouldn't be talkin' 'bout it heah, in de open."

Griffin issued a long, drawn out sigh. "Christ," he muttered. "Come inside. At least I can have a drink."

Obediently, Zoe followed him, her eyes avid as she took in the spacious and opulent surroundings. It wasn't often that she got past the kitchen. Once, when there had been guests, she had made it into the dining room. But when she had clumsily spilled a tureen of soup, Minda had banished her forever from anything but the most menial of chores.

At last Griffin paused, looking into the study. Seeing that it was empty, he beckoned to her. "In here. And, by God, Zoe, it had better be important or I'll see to it personally that you can't sit down for a week."

With a deep sigh, Griffin settled wearily in a chair and flung his hat on the desk. Seeing Thomas standing in the doorway, he ordered him to fetch a bourbon and branch water.

After the door had closed, Griffin viewed Zoe again. Impatience furrowed his brow. "Now, get on with it. You've wasted enough of my time."

The girl plucked at her cotton shift with nervous fingers. "Masta Griffin, suh. Jude's got hisself a . . . another gal . . ." She faltered, biting her lip.

Muttering an oath, Griffin passed a hand across his eyes. He hated to involve himself in his people's squabbles. "Well, just what the hell do you want me to do about it?" he demanded at last. "You said it was important!" He glared at her. "Damn your black hide, you need your ass warmed by the paddle."

Zoe's large dark eyes glistened with frustrated tears. If only he'd let her tell him in her own way. She was about to speak again, but at the sound of a discreet tap on the door and Griffin's booming voice as he shouted at Thomas to enter, she fell silent.

The butler deftly removed the glass from the small silver tray he was carrying and set it in front of Griffin. It was a tribute to his many years of service that Thomas did not look in Zoe's direction. But his heart thumped painfully as he left the room, closing the door again, because he, as did just about every house servant at Albemarle, knew all about Jude and Cammy, knew that she had been teaching him to read and write. That was not a secret that could be kept. If Zoe was about to tell Masta Griffin that, then Jude was in serious danger of being sold. That, he knew, would break Minda's heart.

In the hall, Thomas hovered close enough to hear voices in the study. Taking a handkerchief from his breast pocket, he carefully began to dust an already dust free table.

Inside, Griffin took a long, appreciative sip of his drink, then regarded the black woman, indicating for her to continue.

"It's de woman, suh," Zoe said, desperate now. "She's . . . she's a white lady." Her voice fell to the merest whisper and her trembling began, increasing until her frail body began to shake as if she had the fever.

Griffin just stared at her. His face paled and flushed as his emotions rose and ebbed with the force of his outrage. For one small moment in time, he credited Zoe with lying. The thought was, however, short-lived. No matter how riled, she would never dare lie about anything like that.

His anger settled into a cold knot in the pit of his stomach. "You've just killed Jude," he noted in a quiet, flat voice. "You know that?"

"Yassuh." Zoe looked down at the floor, scuffing her bare toe in the softness of the carpet.

"You hate him that much?"

She swallowed again, visibly, wiping her mouth with the back of her hand.

"Answer me!"

"Yassuh, masta, suh."

"Then why am I to believe that you're telling me the truth?"

She looked up at him. "Doan lie, suh," she protested, shaking her head. "Saw it wit my own eyes." Her voice ended on a dry sob. "Dey wuz in de grove, de two of 'em . . ." She couldn't keep her hands still, and now clasped them behind her back. Although she knew that Griffin was staring at her, she couldn't bring herself to look at him and kept her head lowered.

Griffin's eyes had narrowed dangerously. "And what, exactly, were they doing in the grove?" His voice was deceptively soft.

"Dey wuz . . ." She looked up now, feeling helpless. He continued to stare at her, waiting for her answer. His hand, still clutching his drink, had tightened to the point where the glass was in jeopardy of being broken.

"Answer me." The voice was still soft.

"Dey wuz . . . pleasurin' wit each other. . . ."

For a moment, Griffin thought of that day when he and Morgana had first made love. Had they been spied upon, too?

"You little bitch," Griffin growled in a menacing voice. Getting to his feet, he approached her until he was standing right in front of her. Then he slapped her, hard. She flinched, reeled, but stood her ground.

"Whips me iffen you likes, suh, but it doan change de truf," she insisted stubbornly, again staring at the floor.

Griffin felt he could have killed her then. With great

effort, he stayed his hand. He turned away from the black woman, trying to collect his turbulent thoughts.

Jude hadn't left Albemarle since last May, when they had all gone to Charleston. Zoe, of course, had remained here, as she always did. That was four months ago. Obviously, Zoe wouldn't be coming to him now unless it was someone right here, in the house. And there were only two white women. Cammy, he dismissed immediately, without even giving it conscious thought. That left. . . .

"Morgana." He wasn't even aware that he had spoken the name aloud. This was her way of getting even with him, he thought, enraged. A chilling thought struck—she was pregnant. By Christ, he'd kill her.

Zoe was watching him, by now almost paralyzed with fear. Even her trembling had ceased. "Naw, suh," she managed with great effort. "Ain' Miz Morgana. Ain' yore wife. She's a fine lady, Miz Morgana is. . . ."

Griffin spun around to look at her, his face really dreadful to see. For the moment Zoe closed her eyes to blot out the sight.

Griffin grabbed her by the shoulders and shook her so violently that the breath left her lungs and she gasped.

"Do you know what it feels like to have a hundred lashes?" he demanded in a loud voice. "Do you? You little black bitch!" His voice rose to a shout. "If it wasn't my wife, then who?"

"Miss Cammy," Zoe whispered, really terrified now. Masta Griffin looked like a madman, his eyes wild and staring, his nose pinched and white. His mouth was compressed so tightly that the nerves in his jaw pounded in protest against the enforced restriction.

Griffin stopped shaking her and stared for a moment

suspended in eternity. Then his fist shot out, landing on her jaw. Zoe fell, feeling the blood filling her mouth where her teeth had loosened. In a black rage, control gone, Griffin kicked at her helpless form.

"Griffin!"

Nathaniel's voice cut through his rage and Griffin turned to stare at his grandfather.

"What the devil's going on here? Can't a man get a quiet drink before supper?" Nathaniel viewed Zoe's crumpled form and frowned. "What's that black wench doing in the house? She causin' trouble?"

The comment was so ludicrous that Griffin almost laughed aloud. He opened his mouth to speak, but could find no words to express the appalling charge made by Zoe against his sister. He just stood there, hands clenched at his sides, gripped with a feeling of mute helplessness.

"Griff, boy. You feeling sick? What's the matter with you?" Nathaniel glared at Zoe. "Get up, gal. I want to know what's going on, and I want to know it now!"

"Jus' tol' Masta Griffin de truf, suh," Zoe mumbled, getting to her feet. Her jaw was beginning to swell and she touched it tentatively, wincing as she did so.

"What's this wench talkin' about, Griff?" Nathaniel looked toward his grandson, but Griffin had sat down at the desk, his head in his hands, and he made no reply.

Nathaniel again viewed Zoe, his expression commanding an answer.

The black woman hesitated as long as she dared. Then, in a halting voice, she repeated her tale.

Nathaniel looked like he was about to be ill. "Get out," he yelled in a strangled voice when she was through. "And if you so much as breathe a word of this, I'll have your tongue cut out. Then I'll feed the rest of your black carcass to the hogs!"

Zoe stumbled from the room, not looking at either man. She wasn't sorry for what she had done. Jude deserved whatever was coming to him. In spite of Masta Griffin's words, Jude wouldn't be killed; she knew that. He was the pride and joy of Masta Nathaniel, who showed him off every chance he got. But Jude would get a whippin' the likes of which he'd never had before. And serves him right, Zoe thought in grim satisfaction. As for Miss Cammy— nothing would happen to her, Zoe reasoned. She was a white lady.

When the door closed, Nathaniel turned to view Griffin, who hadn't moved since the last time he'd looked at him. "You think that wench was tellin' the truth?" he murmured. He came closer to the desk.

Griffin's answer was a deep, despairing sigh. He had no doubt that Zoe was telling the truth. There was, in fact, no reason for Zoe to lie. If Griffin had been informed that his sister had committed murder, he could have more easily accepted that deed than the one that had taken place.

"Goddamn women," Nathaniel muttered angrily. He slapped the desk with the palm of his hand. "Black or white, they don't have the sense God gave a turnip." He walked around the desk and put a hand on Griffin's broad shoulder. "We'll have to send her away, Griff," he said quietly. "Cammy can't stay here now. If that black wench knows, then they all know." He gave a sharp sound of disgust. "Their blasted grapevine will have the news all over the state." When he received no response, Nathaniel frowned. "Griffin! Snap out of it, boy. You know as well as I this is not the first time something like this has happened.

245

The thing's over and done with. We've got to think about your sister now...."

There was a soft knock at the door and Nathaniel cast angry eyes in that direction. "What is it?" he called out irritably. His anger turned to surprise as he saw Morgana enter the room.

The "grapevine" Nathaniel had spoken about was already in action: Thomas to Minda and to Meg—who had been in the kitchen, sipping a companionable cup of coffee with the cook. Minda had collapsed, moaning in fright. Meg had raced upstairs to her mistress, who had fled to Morgana in hysterical tears.

"We're busy right now," Nathaniel began awkwardly, attempting a smile.

"I know why Zoe was here," Morgana informed him quietly, closing the door again. Her face was grave and solemn as she viewed the old man. She had already dressed for supper when Cammy had burst into her room, and was clad in a pale green silk dress over a wide crinolined skirt that almost concealed her advanced pregnancy.

"Jesus," Nathaniel muttered with her comment. He ran a trembling hand through his silver hair. "I sometimes wonder who owns who," he sighed, sinking heavily into a nearby chair. "Where the hell is my granddaughter?" He viewed Morgana, who bit her lower lip.

"She's upstairs. She's ... very upset."

"Upset!" Nathaniel was visibly incredulous. "She wrecks havoc on us all— and she's upset!" He got up again, too agitated to remain still for any length of time. "Well, she won't be much longer," he declared with firmness. "We're going to send her away. England, maybe." Pausing, he glanced at Griffin, who still appeared to be in a state of shock. He hadn't even looked up when Morgana came into the room.

"I . . . don't think that would be wise," Morgana said in the same quiet tone. Mentally, she tried to prepare herself for the furious anger she knew her words would generate. "At least, not now."

Griffin looked up then, his dark eyes hot and anguished. "Oh, she'll go," he said suddenly, harshly, before Morgana could respond. He gave his wife a hard look. "You tell that—my sister, to have her bags packed and be ready to leave in the morning." He finally stood up and his face was implacable as he continued. "And between now and then," he advised in a tight voice, "I don't want to set eyes on her!"

"Now, Griff . . ." Nathaniel began placatingly. The young man turned a fierce gaze in his direction.

"I don't want to see her!" Griffin shot back. "She has thrown away whatever future she may have had." And, he thought in silent despair, a part of his own dream as well. No white man would marry Cammy now, certainly not Clinton Barrows. The young man's father would never permit it. Clinton himself would probably balk at such a union, Griffin thought, further distressed.

Morgana was about to angrily remind him of Serena, but then thought better of it. Instead, she took a deep breath. "Cammy will be unable to travel for at least four months."

The words hung there as the two men turned to look at her. Their expressions were blank, uncomprehending at first.

"You mean . . ." Nathaniel couldn't quite speak the

words. His color had turned ashen and his lips trembled visibly.

Morgana's nod was solemn. "She is to have a child."

"Oh, my God," Nathaniel groaned, sitting down again. His shoulders slumped and he suddenly looked every one of his seventy-one years. "Hate to lose that Jude," he mumbled to no one in particular. He covered his eyes with a hand and seemed to sink further into the chair.

"That nigger won't live out the day," Griffin stated grimly. He headed for the door with long strides, brushing past Morgana as if he didn't even see her.

Morgana's eyes widened. "Wait! No . . ." But Griffin was gone and so she turned to Nathaniel. A heavy feeling of apprehension settled in the pit of her stomach and she fought off a dizzying sense of nausea. With some effort she gained control of herself once more. Going to Nathaniel's side, she knelt before him, taking his cold hand in her own warm one. "What is Griffin going to do?" she asked fearfully.

Lowering his other hand to the armrest, Nathaniel's eyes were glazed as he viewed his grandson's wife. He appeared a bit surprised that she was still there.

"Nathaniel!" Morgana squeezed his hand in an effort to gain his attention. "What is Griffin going to do?"

"Do?" the old man repeated inanely. "No buck can live after rapin' a white woman." He turned away and sighed.

In a sharp movement, Morgana shook her head. "No, no. It wasn't like that at all," she protested. She tightened her grip on his hand. "They're in love. . . ."

Nathaniel blinked, his pale skin reddening with her words. "Don't you be talkin' like that, young woman!"

"But it's true," she insisted, desperate for him to understand. "They've loved each other for years." He made no answer, so she continued. "When Cammy leaves, you must allow Jude to go with her," she urged strongly. "They can go North, or even, as you said, to England. . . ."

In a curt gesture, Nathaniel withdrew his hand and glared at her. "You think I'd give my granddaughter to a black buck?" he exclaimed, incredulous at the thought. "I'd see her dead first."

"You are a hypocrite, Nathaniel!" she shouted at him, getting to her feet. Tears of anger threatened, but Morgana kept herself under control.

Startled, he turned to look at her.

"What about Serena?" she demanded, her mouth tightening. "What about your grandson and that . . . black wench! I've never heard you speak out against that." She waited for his answer, but Nathaniel merely looked embarrassed and made no response. Softening her voice, Morgana said, "Cammy is not the first woman to have a child out of wedlock. . . ."

Nathaniel was now regarding her with pity, as though she were a child who simply did not understand. "I wish it were as simple as that," he murmured at last, looking away.

"There is nothing difficult about it," she declared firmly. "At least Cammy acted out of love."

Nathaniel moved restlessly in his chair, refusing to meet Morgana's level, accusing eyes. Then, in a quieter voice, he said, "Love has nothing to do with it, Morgana. It has to do with the children." He looked at her again. "If Serena ever has a child," he explained carefully, "it will be black—and a slave." He paused for a moment, then added,

"In the eyes of the law and society, the child my granddaughter will have—will also be black. And a slave."

Appalled, Morgana could only stare at him. "Why can't you let them go away?" she cried, desperate now. "What you are about to do will destroy Cammy. Let them alone," she begged. "Let them be married, if that's what they both want—" She broke off at his suddenly fierce look.

Nathaniel got to his feet, his face an even darker shade of red than before. At his temple, a pulse throbbed with his agitation. "No granddaughter of mine is going to go before a judge and swear she's got colored blood!" At the sight of Morgana's surprised face, he nodded curtly. "That's how it's done, girl. She'd have to claim *she's* a nigger."

Nathaniel turned then, and with slow steps left the study without a backward glance.

Chapter
13

For a long moment after Nathaniel left the study, Morgana just stood there, feeling drained. She had expected both Griffin and Nathaniel to be angry and upset with what had taken place. But she had not expected the cold fury Griffin had displayed nor the dark despair evidenced by Nathaniel.

Quickly then, heedless of her condition, Morgana ran into the hall. She glanced once at the stairs, torn between wanting to go to Cammy and wanting to try to prevent Griffin from killing Jude.

The immediacy of one was more important than the other, she decided, heading for the front door.

On the verandah, she halted abruptly, puzzled by the activity she was seeing. Only a few feet from where she was standing, Nathaniel stood quietly, his face expressionless as he viewed the preparations taking place. The sun was low now, the front yard ribboned with gold and lilac.

It seemed to Morgana that every slave on the plantation was suddenly gathered in the yard. Even the children were there, eyes wide with fear as they viewed the unusual happenings. Of Jude, though, there was no sign. Perhaps, she thought with a surge of relief, he had managed to escape.

But a glance at her husband dashed that hope. Griffin was watching everything, his demeanor, to all outward appearances, calm, if grim. He stood with his feet planted wide, holding his riding crop with both hands. He issued no instructions, yet the slaves were working in silence beneath his black scrutiny, apparently knowing what to do.

Wood and brush had been gathered and laid out in a sort of rectangle, about seven feet long and about two feet wide. It was just now being ignited. It burned smoky at first, but then, as the wood caught and held, the low blaze burned clear.

Dear God, Morgana thought, her heart beating wildly. Were they going to burn him? She put a hand to her throat at the thought. But, she tried to console herself, it wasn't a very large fire. . . .

Then, at each end of the rectangle of fire, Morgana saw a slave place a stout oaken pillar, the top of which had been carved into a U-shape.

A high thin wail broke the unnatural stillness as Minda suddenly rushed forward, skirts billowing with her haste. Her eyes were round, filled with a terror that made her motions stiff and clumsy. She ran past Griffin, who never even turned his head, and fell at Nathaniel's feet.

"Doan let him kill Jude," she cried out piteously. She

clutched at his boots with hands that were shaking. "Please, Masta Nathaniel, doan kill my boy..." Tears streamed down her black cheeks and her great bosom heaved with the force of her anguish.

Nathaniel looked down at her. For the first time since this business had started, Morgana thought she detected a look of pity on his face. But it was gone in an instant.

"Get back to the kitchen, Minda," Nathaniel said, not unkindly. Then, hands behind his back, he raised his head and stared over her, refusing her any more of his attention.

For a while, Minda didn't move. She crouched, sobbing as if her heart would break. At last, Suky approached his mother, his step hesitant, his large dark eyes looking fearfully at Nathaniel, who paid him no mind.

Grabbing Minda's sleeve, the ten-year-old boy urged her to move, terrified that whatever punishment had fallen to his brother would somehow be visited upon his mother as well.

For a time, Minda resisted, or perhaps she was just too weak in her grief to move. But at last, in a quick movement that seemed almost desperate, she clasped her young son to her breast. Getting up, she lifted the boy off his feet, holding him so tightly that his small body squirmed in discomfort.

Then, still sobbing, Minda stumbled away in the direction of the kitchen.

The group of Negroes parted now and Morgana finally saw Jude. He was held fast by two slaves on either side of him, his face fierce, eyes bright, although with anger or fear, she wasn't able to tell.

Behind the trio came Joe, who was dragging the trunk of a tree in his wake. It was freshly cut, about seven feet long, and in some confusion, Morgana watched as a few of the slaves began to douse the wood with water.

Finally, under the direction of a grim-faced Carlie Dobbs, who had brought up the strange procession, Jude was stripped of his clothing and lashed to the tree trunk, stomach down.

After the leather thongs were tightened, the huge log was then raised to the oaken pillar, each end resting snugly within the U-shaped tops.

As the full horror of what she was seeing washed over her, Morgana gave a shrill cry and started forward, only to be caught by Nathaniel, who gripped her arms with surprising strength.

"Get back into the house," he ordered in an angry voice, unaware that she had been standing there.

"You can't!" Morgana cried out. Her voice sounded thin and unrecognizable even to her own ears. "It will take hours for him to die . . ." Her breath was coming in short, rapid pants, as if she couldn't get enough air into her lungs. Her pulse throbbed and drummed in her ears and a cold dread weakened her limbs.

"He'll be roasted like the piece of worthless meat he is," Nathaniel said to her in a gruff tone. "Now, go back inside. You can't stop anything." Regarding her, his face softened a bit at the sight of her wide and horrified eyes. "Go to Cammy," he whispered, bending forward slightly.

Cammy! Oh, dear God, Morgana thought, breaking away. Her bedroom was directly over the front yard. As she raced up the stairs, Morgana reflected bitterly that that was probably the reason why Griffin had chosen the site.

Pausing before Cammy's door, Morgana took a moment

to catch her breath, both hands on her swollen stomach. She listened, but heard nothing. And so she entered.

Relief flooded over Morgana when she saw Cammy on the bed. Clad only in a camisole and pantalettes, she was lying on her back, staring up at the ceiling. Morgana had expected to find the girl in hysterics, but she appeared almost calm. Too calm, perhaps.

"Cammy," Morgana murmured softly, coming forward. She felt overwhelmed with pity.

"Do you know why they saturate the tree trunk with water?" Cammy asked tonelessly, not turning toward her.

Startled by the question, Morgana sank down on the bed. She stroked the girl's hair. "Don't think about it. Please...."

Cammy turned slightly to look at her. "It's so the wood doesn't catch fire and burn." She spoke the words as if teaching a young child a lesson.

"Oh, please, Cammy," Morgana cried out, fighting her tears. She took the girl's hand in her own. It felt like ice and she began to chafe it. "Let us get out of here," she begged, fearing the girl was in shock. "Let's go for a walk. Or we can get the carriage—I'll tell Ben to drive us into Charleston...."

But Cammy made no move. She just lay there as though she hadn't heard a word Morgana said. Her face was so pale she looked like a fragile porcelain doll.

"No," she murmured at last. "I can't leave until it's over. Jude will know that I'm here. He'll know that I'm with him to the end. Then I'll go." A note of raw bitterness crept into her voice and her small hands balled into fists. "I'll stay until my baby is born. Then I'll go and never come back. I hate them. I hate them both, Griffin and my grandfather. I hate them!"

Morgana was about to take the girl in her arms in an attempt to comfort her when the first anguished scream rent the September air. It was a horrifying sound, the long drawn-out howl of an animal in mortal distress.

Cammy froze, her slight body stiffening. She didn't even appear to be breathing. Only the pulse at her throat indicated life. Another scream followed as Jude cried out in agony.

Although Morgana tried to stop her, Cammy insisted on going out onto the piazza. The girl stumbled on legs that appeared wooden and unresponsive. Weakly, she leaned on the railing, her dark eyes riveted on the terrible scene being acted out below.

Coming to her side, Morgana looked down, unable to suppress her revulsion. Except for Jude's hysterical screams, there was a great and awful silence in the yard. Morgana saw Zoe standing to the side. Confronted with the fruits of her treachery, the woman's face was gray and tormented.

Bella and Meg were there, too, holding onto each other in their fear. Even Serena was in the crowd, her delicate hands covering her face, shielding her eyes. Morgana began to understand why all the slaves were gathered. Obviously, they had all been commanded to attend.

A movement caught her eye. Unable to believe what she was witnessing, Morgana saw two of the slaves turn the tree trunk slightly.

My God, Morgana thought in horror, catching her breath, they're roasting him like a pig! Revulsion left her, swamped in a wave of anger that grew to awesome proportions.

She glanced down at Cammy, who had sunk to the floor in a crumpled heap, her hands gripping the iron bars of the railing. Her lovely face was ghastly in its paleness. She looked so small, so vulnerable, that Morgana's heart twisted in compassion.

Enough!

The thought presented itself, and Morgana acted. She knew she couldn't prevent Jude's death—but she damn well could prevent this senseless torture, she thought, enraged.

She gave little thought to what she did next. She acted on emotion alone, and that emotion was a pure, white-hot anger.

Leaving Cammy's room, Morgana went to her own, trying without much success to shut out the piercing, blood-curdling screams that rose and ebbed with chilling repetition. Flinging open dresser drawers with a furious carelessness, Morgana located her father's dueling pistols, making certain that they were loaded.

Then she went downstairs quickly, her hand at her side, one of the guns concealed in the folds of her skirt.

As she emerged outside, no one turned to look at her. It was completely dark now, the glow of the embers lighting in a grotesque manner the horror that was Jude. Nathaniel had moved from the verandah and now stood quietly at Griffin's side. All eyes were on the writhing, groaning form of Jude as he struggled futilely against the thongs that bound him so securely in place. He had passed the point of being able to scream.

Morgana saw that the wood and brush had burned down

to glowing, red-hot coals, not as high, but hotter than actual flames. There was no hesitation in her, no questioning as to right or wrong.

Morgana came as close as she dared, close enough to feel the shimmering curtain of heat that wavered in the still air, distorting images as one peered through it. Then, raising the gun, she pointed it directly at Jude's head.

When the shot rang out, there was no immediate reaction. Eyes blinked, viewed the spreading stain of blood that flowed from Jude's forehead, then, in an almost concerted movement, turned in her direction.

But no one moved.

Morgana's hand, still holding the gun, dropped to her side. Then she released her hold, allowing it to fall to the ground. She turned her furious gaze upon her husband—and met an anger that matched her own.

Slowly, Griffin began to walk toward her, his face a rigid mask of fury, the riding crop clenched in his hand as though it were a weapon.

Morgana stood where she was, facing them all, her expression daring them, challenging them to take exception to what she had done. And, although she didn't notice it, every black face was regarding her with a gratitude that bordered upon veneration, including Zoe's. Even Nathaniel's expression had fallen into a strange look of relief. Only Dobbs and Griffin appeared angry at what had taken place.

At last Griffin stopped before her. She raised her head slightly, so as to meet his smoldering eyes with her own cool gaze.

"You—" he choked, unable to get the words past his tightened throat. Twin spots of color appeared in his cheeks, testimony of the rage he was barely able to contain.

Morgana continued to look up at her husband, one part of her mind wondering if he were going to strike her, but feeling no fear at the prospect.

For an endless moment, the silence lengthened. Griffin was still staring at her. He seemed incapable of speech.

Suddenly, Morgana's eyes widened as she felt a sharp and searing pain. Unable to help herself, she gasped with the force of it. It began in her lower back, then quickly, with a vicious stab, it worked its way forward to her abdomen. She wrapped both arms around her stomach and gasped again, bending forward until her head almost touched Griffin's chest.

In a reflex motion, his hand shot out to steady her. Morgana moaned as the pain came again, stronger, Stupidly, Griffin just stood there.

With quick steps, Nathaniel came to Griffin's side. He took one look at Morgana, then exclaimed, "It's the baby! Get her upstairs, Griff. I'll send for Doc Foxworth."

Hesitating only a moment, Griffin dropped the riding crop. Reaching for Morgana, he carried her into the house and up the stairs to her room, where he laid her carefully on the bed.

He motioned to Bella, who had followed him and now stood uncertainly in the doorway. "Do something!" he cried out anxiously, aware that his hands were shaking.

Quickly, Bella moved forward and began to undress Morgana, pausing when her mistress groaned and turned on her side.

Feeling utterly helpless, Griffin backed from the room and closed the door.

When the contraction passed, Bella removed the rest of Morgana's clothing. Then, moving efficiently, she tore a sheet in half, tying one strip on either side of the bedpost. Knotting the ends firmly, she placed one in each of Morgana's hands.

"Now, you pull on dat," she crooned, wiping Morgana's glistening brow with the tip of her apron. "Pull hard—and you jest holler all you wants. . . ."

Bella kept up the meaningless, comforting chatter, praying for the doctor to arrive soon.

But it wasn't the doctor who delivered Morgana of her daughter some four hours later—it was Auntie Flora, hurriedly summoned when it became apparent that the physician wasn't going to make it in time.

Morgana's recovery was slow. Although her labor had been brief, it had been violent, and when the doctor arrived almost an hour after the baby had been born, he found Morgana in a severely weakened condition, bleeding heavily and only half conscious.

After examining her, he packed her with linen gauze, showing Bella how to change it at intervals when it became saturated. Then he gave her a sleeping draught. For the next two days, the doctor stayed at Albemarle, until he could safely pronounce Morgana out of danger.

Tansy was summoned to the Great House to serve as a temporary wet nurse until Morgana was strong enough to take over that function for herself.

At times during those two days, Morgana thought she saw Griffin's anxious face hovering over her. But by the time she came fully to her senses, she was uncertain as to where the line between imagery and reality began and ended.

It was on the third day when Cammy came to visit her.

The girl appeared wan and drawn as she approached the bed. Clad only in a nightgown and cotton wrap, her hair was twisted into one long, thick braid. Morgana wondered if she'd had any sleep at all during the previous two nights. From the look of the dark and purple smudges beneath Cammy's eyes, she sincerely doubted it.

For a moment the two young women stared at each other. Then, with a wrenching sob, Cammy threw herself forward, embracing Morgana.

"Can you forgive me?" Morgana whispered to her sister-in-law.

Cammy raised her head and with tear-filled eyes, attempted a smile. "Forgive you?" She gripped Morgana's hand tightly. "I get down on my knees and thank you. You were the only one with courage enough to do what had to be done . . ." The sobs came again. For a time, Morgana held the girl until she calmed.

At last Cammy sat up, wiping her cheeks with the back of her hand. She gave a deep, shuddering breath.

"Cammy," Morgana said quietly. "You have your whole life ahead of you." She placed a hand on the girl's arm. "From this day forward, you must live for yourself and for your child. . . ."

Cammy gave a small, sad smile, accompanied by a slow nod. "I thank God for the baby," she said simply. "That, at least, cannot be taken from me." She held Morgana's eye a moment longer, then turned, looking toward Bella. "And where is my new niece?" she asked with an attempt at brightness.

Bella summoned Tansy from the sitting room. The girl came forward, holding the child in her arms.

Her face softening, Cammy reached for the infant. "Oh, she's so beautiful . . ." She glanced toward Morgana, who was unable to contain the smile of pride that curved her lips. "Have you decided what to name her?"

Morgana nodded. "Anne."

Cammy offered a small smile that never reached her eyes. "That will please my grandfather," she murmured. She bent her head, putting a cheek against the softness of the infant.

Watching her, Morgana was greatly relieved. Cammy would be all right, she told herself, refusing to believe otherwise. She was strong and she was young. In time, perhaps, she would forget. . . .

Later that day, Griffin entered her room. Tansy, who was breast feeding the baby, smiled up at him.

"Shoah is a fine li'l chile, Masta Griffin," she said enthusiastically as he looked down at his daughter. The baby was contentedly suckling, a tiny white hand against a full brown breast.

Tansy was quite happy with her new position, even if it was only temporary. She was eating better than she ever had. For the first time in her whole life, she was eating the same fare that was served to her masters. Of course, she had to feed Anne first, before she fed her own daughter, but so far this was not creating undue problems. At present, she was producing enough nourishment for both infants.

Griffin nodded, but didn't bother to answer her. Finally, he turned and walked slowly toward the bed, regarding Morgana as she rested against the softness of two downy pillows. Her shimmering blond hair was unbound and tumbled about her shoulders in appealing disarray. Her blue eyes were level as she looked at him.

"Are you feeling better today?" he asked in an almost formal manner.

"Yes," she replied, aware that her own response sounded just as stilted. "Although I will be glad to be up and out of this bed," she added, still watching him.

"The doctor said you must rest for at least ten days," he reminded her sternly.

She sighed, then gave a brief nod of acquiescence. "Griffin," she murmured, sitting up a bit straighter. "I know you are angry over what has happened, but—"

"This is not the time to discuss it," he said shortly, interrupting her.

"I don't see why not," she flared hotly, annoyed by his pompous attitude. "We can't ignore it . . ." She fell silent at the look of his angered eyes and compressed mouth. Then she leaned back against the pillows again, feeling exhausted by just the small effort she had expended. Perhaps he was right, she thought wearily, seeing him turn and leave the room. In any event, she didn't seem to have the strength to speak at length, much less argue at this time.

She had no intention of justifying her actions, anyway. Morgana couldn't prevent the unwanted picture of Jude's last agonizing moments that taunted her memory. She shuddered, wincing in pain as her muscles reacted against the sudden intrusion. Still, it was there; the coppery skin disfigured by horrible blisters, the black hair singed and smoldering. . . .

No! she thought with renewed determination. She had

done the right thing, the only thing under the circumstances. Griffin wouldn't hesitate to kill a horse that was suffering in pain, yet he had committed that terrible act against another human being. Even now it amazed her.

Nor did he seem to feel that he had acted wrongly. In a very odd way, that was the only thing that kept her from judging Griffin too harshly. He actually thought that he had been performing a necessary function. Going over in her mind what Nathaniel had said to her, Morgana realized that he, too, felt the same way.

Morgana shifted her weight in bed, restless, wishing that she could relax, wishing that she could sleep. She felt empty and alone. Finally, with a cry of despair that she couldn't repress, she beckoned for Tansy to bring her baby to her.

The brown-skinned woman got up, came forward, and gently placed Anne in her arms. The child was now sleeping peacefully, a small fist against her pink lips.

Comforted by the warm little body against her own, Morgana at last slept. Tansy took the baby from her then. Bella tucked the light blankets closer around Morgana.

For a moment, both black women stood there looking down at the sleeping form of their mistress. At last Bella shook her head slowly.

"Dem two peoples got deyselves a powerful anger 'tween 'em," she mused quietly. "Hopin' Miz Morgana doan git it in her haid to take her chile an' leave heah. Wouldn't want to be 'round Masta Griffin, nohow."

Tansy nodded solemnly at the observation. Like everyone else, she was still shaken by what had taken place earlier in the week. "Seems lak white folks got deyselves moah trouble what dey kin handle," she agreed, rocking

Anne in her arms. "Wonder what Masta Griffin gonna do when Miss Cammy has her baby. . . ."

Bella rolled her eyes and raised both her hands. "Lawd, doan even want to be thinkin' o' dat," she declared. "Had us enuf trouble to las' dis heah gal fer a lifetime."

The two women moved to the sitting room. Tansy placed Anne in the cradle, then sat down.

"Thinkin' Miss Cammy really wantin' to marry up wit dat boy?" Tansy asked musingly after a while.

Bella shrugged. "Doan know. She wuz learnin' Jude his letters, dat's fer shoah. Ever'body knowed dat. But it doan do him no good now."

Tansy leaned forward, lowering her voice. "Dat Meg tellin' me dat Miss Cammy real upset by all whats happened. She jest cry all de time, Meg sez. Waitin' till her chile be borned, den she goin' away."

Bella shifted in her chair, giving her friend a sharp look. "Where at she goin'?"

"Doan rightly know. Prob'ly Nawth."

Bella snorted as she leaned back again. "How dat li'l gal gonna git herse'f Nawth? Cain't git herse'f to Charleston, lessen somebody he'ps her."

Tansy made a vague gesture, not responding, and for a time the two women sat quietly.

"Seems lak it all dat Zoe's fault," Tansy muttered resentfully after some minutes went by.

"Humph. Dat gal hidin' in her cabin, she is. Doan dare go in de kitchen. Minda gonna carve her hide up, right pretty lak." It didn't strike Bella as odd that Minda blamed not her masters for the death of her son, but Zoe. "Wouldn't su'prise me none iffen dat gal gits herse'f sol'," Bella concluded with a firm and righteous nod of her head.

"An' serve's her right," Tansy declared quickly. Then her light brown face fell into a thoughtful expression. "Gots to admit, though, dat Jude boy wuz a powerful handsome buck." Catching Bella's somewhat disapproving look, she hastened to add, "Nacherly, he not as handsome as my Adam. Jest means dat he wuz a pretty boy. Mebbe kin un'erstand why Zoe done it."

Bella made a wry face and crossed her arms under her breast. "Yore Adam heahs you talkin' lak dat, gonna be de las' time you talkin' 'bout anythin'," she advised darkly.

Tansy looked sheepish, then broke into a wide grin.

Putting their hands across their faces to stifle the noise, both young women began to giggle.

Despite her early appearance, Anne was a sturdy child with rosy cheeks and a mop of fine, wispy black hair that covered her small, well shaped head.

When, after two weeks, it became apparent that Morgana wasn't producing enough milk for the child, Nathaniel hurried off to Charleston in search of a suitable wet nurse, returning a few days later with a sixteen-year-old girl named Celia, whose child had recently died. Morgana was immediately taken with the girl, who was a light-skinned Kru with a ready smile and amiable manner.

The sitting room was hastily converted into a nursery and, for a time, Bella was a bit put out by what she considered an invasion of her territory. But it soon became apparent that Celia, when she put her mind to it, could charm the birds out the trees, and it wasn't long before she and Bella were fast friends.

Another week went by before Morgana was well enough to get out of bed. Each day, Griffin visited his wife and his daughter, but Morgana had the distinct impression that he came more from a sense of duty than anything else. He seemed, to Morgana, to be a changed man. He was quiet, withdrawn, uncommunicative.

Griffin studiously avoided speaking to his sister, a situation that didn't seem to bother Cammy at all, for, as she told Morgana, she didn't have anything to say to her brother.

While Griffin refused to speak to Cammy, he was barely civil to Morgana, and not once did he refer to or even agree to discuss the incident with Jude.

Nathaniel urged patience. But Morgana was discovering that she was far from a patient woman. More than once she considered leaving Albemarle. However, her daughter and Cammy were powerful inducements for staying. In any event, the baby was too young to travel, and, of course, she couldn't possibly go without Celia, who was not, strictly speaking, her property, but belonged to Nathaniel.

As for Cammy, she would need all the help and support Morgana could give her when her time came. Nathaniel seemed to have softened in his attitude toward his granddaughter, although he showed no inclination of directly crossing Griffin, and any words of kindness or understanding came when his grandson was absent.

At the beginning of November, Cammy took to her room and refused to leave it, ignoring Morgana's pleas to get out of the house for at least an hour each day.

"You need your exercise," Morgana urged, distressed by the lethargy she was seeing. "You cannot lie about all day long like this. . . ."

But Cammy refused to listen. She seemed to have sunk

back into the depression she had experienced just after Jude's death.

One day, during the latter part of November, Meg came to Morgana's room in tears.

"Missy won't eat," Meg cried unhappily, wringing her hands as if it were somehow her fault. "Dat Minda makin' all kinds o' vittals she thinkin' will tempt Miss Cammy. But dat chile jest doan even look at it. Jest lays dere an' cries lak her heart bin broke. Den she sleeps. When she wakes, it start all over agin. . . ."

Morgana listened to the report, tight-lipped. When Meg concluded, she walked into the nursery, looking down at her daughter for a long moment. Then, lifting Anne from her cradle, Morgana went to Cammy's room, her face set with severe determination.

Cammy was in bed. Although it was past four in the afternoon, she hadn't bothered to dress and still wore her nightgown.

Morgana hesitated a moment. Then, her mouth set firmly she walked across the floor. Bending over, she deposited Anne in Cammy's arms.

Startled, the girl automatically held the infant. Anne was awake, her eyes bright and darting. She squirmed, making baby noises and, reaching out, rested a tiny hand on Cammy's chin.

Standing at the foot of the bed, Morgana viewed her sister-in-law with uncharacteristic sternness, hands on her hips, brows drawn down in open disapproval.

"This is what you carry inside of you," she said shortly. "A child. Your child. You can deprive yourself, Cammy, but can you deny your baby?" Her voice lowered a bit, became almost pleading. "I can hand Anne to Celia," she noted quietly. "But right now, your child has no one but you. . . ."

The baby continued with her gurgles of happiness, then began to kick her legs, her small feet pushing at Cammy's abdomen.

If the image of Jude's last moments had plagued Morgana, they were etched indelibly in Cammy's mind. It was permanently seared into her memory, just as if it had been branded there with a hot iron the way Dobbs marked runaways. She had only to close her eyes to see it. So strong, so intense was her remembrance of those awful minutes that even the recollection of their pleasant times together could not compensate, could not erase that horror.

For a long time Cammy looked down at the child in her arms, her expression unreadable.

Then the tears began to slip down her cheeks, silently, unstoppable, until finally Cammy gave a great sob, burying her head against the child. Frightened by the change, the baby now began to cry with lusty indignation. Quickly, Morgana motioned to Meg, instructing her to take the child back to Celia.

Sitting down on the edge of the bed, Morgana held Cammy while the girl sobbed as if her heart would break. Morgana made no attempt to calm her; she allowed the solace of weeping to run its course.

But the ploy had worked. Cammy finally roused herself. While she still stayed in her room most of the day, she not only ate, she walked about the grounds with Morgana for about an hour each morning.

At the beginning of December, Morgana finally received an answering letter from her Aunt Sarah, who apologized profusely for the delay, explaining that she had just returned from Europe. The letter was lengthy and expressed the feeling that Morgana was welcome anytime she chose to return to Somerset Hall. The invitation, Sarah was careful to explain, included anyone that Morgana might wish to bring with her. After reading it, Morgana put the letter in a drawer of her writing table and did not mention its arrival to Cammy.

It was the day before Christmas when Cammy at last went into labor.

Morgana had come to Cammy's room to fetch her for their morning walk. But Cammy, in her nightgown, was clinging to the wooden post of the bed, her face contorted with pain.

"De baby's comin'," Meg announced somewhat unnecessarily. She was rubbing Cammy's back.

Morgana moved closer and Cammy managed a smile. "It's true," she whispered. She appeared almost relieved.

"I'll send for the doctor." Morgana began to walk toward the door.

"No!" Cammy reached out a hand. "No doctor. Meg has already sent for Auntie Flora."

Morgana paused, uncertain.

"Please," Cammy pleaded. "I want Auntie Flora ... and you." Another spasm gripped her and for the moment she was unable to speak.

Morgana remained uncertain a moment longer, but then, remembering Auntie Flora's gentle touch upon her own body, nodded. And, though she hated to admit it to herself, she thought there was a chance that Griffin and Nathaniel would probably refuse to send for the doctor. They both still had the ridiculous notion of keeping this whole thing a secret.

With a brisk step, Morgana returned to Cammy's side and helped Meg get her back into bed. She didn't bother to send word to Nathaniel or Griffin, knowing that they would realize what was happening soon enough.

Nine hours later, Morgana bent over Cammy's straining body, her eyes frantic with worry. Meg was diligently sponging her mistress's sweating brow.

Turning, Morgana regarded Auntie Flora, who didn't appear the least concerned. "Is she all right?"

The ancient Negress cracked her toothless grin. "Missy havin' a baby, missus. She ain' sick."

"But she's so narrow." Morgana gave another worried glance at the girl on the bed, wondering if there was still time to send for the doctor.

Just then, Cammy gave a great shriek and Auntie Flora bent over her. "It's comin' now. Kin see its haid." Her gnarled hands reached for the emerging infant, and only moments later she held the child up for view. "It's a boy!" she pronounced triumphantly, severing the cord with a knife.

Cammy's smile was as triumphant as the old woman's tone as she reached for her son. She clasped the baby close to her breast and wept happy tears.

Cammy named the child Jamie. He had black curly hair, much like Cammy's own. And his eyes were blue. His skin was almost white, with only the barest hint of a golden hue to mark his heritage.

"A mustee," Nathaniel breathed as he viewed his grandson for the first time the next morning. Shaking his head, he left the room.

Griffin refused to look upon the child.

Chapter
14

The December night was quite cool but calm. Only the drone of insects and the flickering fireflies disturbed the quiet, somehow intensifying the silence instead of alleviating it.

At the edge of the clearing, Jonah stood quietly, his black eyes straining through the darkness as he surveyed the Great House that sat on a rise about a hundred feet away from him.

Clad in a light jacket which he had stolen, Jonah still wore the same cotton shirt and breeches that he'd had when he left Albemarle. On his feet he wore a pair of brogans. The roughly made shoes, usually worn by slaves only in the winter months, had also been stolen.

Beside him stood another runaway named Zack. A head shorter and nowhere near as muscular as Jonah, Zack had been a field hand at White Manors, the very plantation they were now viewing.

Behind them, the wooded area led into the swamp where, together with eight other runaways, they had built crude shelters for themselves amongst the cypress and gum trees.

Jonah had come across Zack while stumbling through the swamp some three days after his escape from Albemarle. Zack, who was thirty-four years old, had been at large for seven weeks, leaving the relative safety of the swamp only to steal food and, when he could manage it, tools. He had watched Jonah's progress for more than an hour before he had felt safe enough to approach, assuring himself that the newcomer was not being followed by the patrollers.

At that time Zack had no more than a lean-to, a few boards hastily lashed together to keep the rain from falling upon him while he slept. With Jonah's help, a cabin had been constructed.

Others, subsequently, had joined them.

As the days passed, hope had risen. For the most part, the patrollers avoided the swamp, fearing the quicksand that lie in wait for the unwary. Too, the place was alive with cottonmouth moccasins, coral snakes, and even alligators. Under the circumstances, the dogs were virtually useless and would themselves be placed at great risk. Only the desperate or the determined, ventured into the swamp. Jonah and his cohorts were both.

Jonah's previous inclination of finding the Underground and heading North had been temporarily put aside. At first, there had been only Zack and himself. But before too long a time had gone by, they had been joined by other runaways. Soon their number would increase until there were enough of them for a full-scale revolt.

They had weapons of a sort; knives, hoes, scythes. But they had no guns. However, Tampa, the brooding Fanti who had run from Four Oaks, assured them that he knew where Farley Barrows kept his guns. When the time came and their number assured success, that would be their first stop.

Albemarle, Jonah insisted, would be their second. Not only did he want to rescue his sister, Zoe, he had scores to settle. His scarred body was a constant reminder, lest he forget his goal.

Now Jonah took a step forward. It was after ten o'clock and the Great House was dark and silent.

"Mebbe we could git into de kitchen," he speculated, thinking of the tempting array of knives that was no doubt just lying about.

"Naw," Zack shook his head sharply. They had come here with the express purpose of raiding the toolshed and he didn't want to press their luck. "Too dangerous with jest us'ns. Masta Whitney got hisself five sons, all growed. An' dey mean bastids. Seen one of dem beat a wench till she up an' died 'cause she wouldn't come to his room lessen she wuz dragged."

"Doan call him masta," Jonah insisted, bringing his face closer to Zack. "Doan call no white man dat no moah. We our own mastas now."

Zack shrugged, but made no comment. While the thought of an insurrection gave him a great deal of satisfaction, he was unable to drum up the zeal that infected Jonah, a zeal that had made the man, in effect, their leader.

"Ain' dere no white lady?" Jonah asked him, glancing at the house again.

"Yeah. But Miz Whitney bin poorly fer years. Stays in her room most times. Doan rightly know what's goin' on."

"When we git ready, mebbe we come heah first," Jonah suggested. "Could kill 'em all iffen we wants."

Zack considered that tempting possibility for a long moment. His mental process was sluggish, but then, until recently, he hadn't had to think for himself. But he remembered all the whippings he had endured since he had arrived at White Manors as a boy of twelve, remembered all the hours, the endlessly hot and bitter hours, he had toiled in the fields. There would be great satisfaction, he thought, in seeing his white masters die. However, without guns, they wouldn't stand a chance. Zack's father had been one of those slaves who had joined the insurrection led by Denmark Vesey more than thirty years ago. And there were valuable lessons to be learned from the abortive attempt at freedom.

No, they needed guns. One pistol, one rifle was worth more than a hundred knives and hoes.

"Naw," Zack said finally. "Dat Tampa's right. Wouldn't do no good to come heah. Four Oaks is where de guns is at. Collects 'em, dey do. An' Farley Barrows got on'y three sons, one of 'em jest a baby, an' another no more den a saplin'. Naw," he repeated with a firm shake of his head. "Best we stay wit de plan."

"Doan dey got guns heah?" Jonah asked after a moment, reluctant to give up on the possibility.

Zack grunted an affirmation. "But dey ain' in one place. Each one got his own and keeps it in dey room." Seeing the hesitation on his companion's face, Zack grabbed his arm.

"Tells you, Jonah, it be too dangerous. Let's go! We git de tools, den we go back."

Jonah resisted a moment. In the velvety darkness of night his eyes seemed to glow, reflecting an inner light that was ignited by visions only he could see. And that vision was total insurrection, every plantation burned to the ground, every slave—man, woman, and child—set free.

And it was a possibility. Overall, the blacks outnumbered the whites by more than four to one. In some areas it was, of course, many times higher than that.

Jonah had no doubt that most of his people would heed the call to freedom. There would be those, he knew, who would resist out of fear or some misguided feeling of loyalty. Those would have to be killed. But it was, he thought, a small price to pay for what would eventually be accomplished.

"Come on, Jonah," Zack urged in a stronger voice, sensing the other's continued hesitation. "Doan want us'ns to git caught, do you?"

Shaken from his introspection, Jonah viewed his friend a moment, then nodded slowly. He followed the other man as they both hugged the shadows on the edge of the clearing, making their way toward the toolshed.

Jonah moved with care. He wasn't about to be caught. This time, he thought with grim fortitude, this time he would fight to the death.

And before they were through, Jonah vowed, clenching his massive fists, he would see Carlie Dobbs and Griffin Kynes in hell.

Chapter
15

It was the first week of the new year, and Morgana hoped that 1854 would be a more pleasant one than its predecessor. It had been mutually and tacitly agreed that, this year, they would all forgo the trek into Charleston. Cammy had recovered quickly from her confinement and the joy of having her son had greatly restored her spirits. She seemed, for the time being, to have achieved a certain degree of contentment. Unlike Morgana, Cammy was able to nurse her own baby and refused to allow anyone to take over that most enjoyable task.

The morning dawned clear, if a bit cool, and Morgana awoke to the sound of Anne's fretful cry. Before she could get up and don a robe, Celia had already taken the child to her breast.

Although it was still early, not yet seven-thirty, Morgana decided to get up, in view of the fact that she was now wide awake.

Bella seemed subdued and quiet as she assisted Morgana in dressing, but Morgana made no comment on the somewhat unusual state of affairs, reasoning that if Bella had a problem, she would come to her in her own good time.

Having washed and dressed, Morgana walked into the sitting room and kissed her daughter, who was now back in the cradle. Hearing the rumble and creaking of a wagon, she walked out onto the piazza. In the distance, a group of about ten slaves, all in the back of the buckboard, were being driven through the gates and along the road to Charleston. Morgana's brow wrinkled in perplexity as she watched the little scene with curious eyes.

"Dey's bein' sold," Bella murmured, coming to stand at Morgana's side as the buckboard rumbled away.

Morgana glanced at the black woman. "Why?"

"Do it ever' year," Bella responded, then cleared her throat. "Miz Morgana . . ." Agitation took hold of her and she bit her lip, which had begun to tremble.

Morgana now turned to study her more closely. "What is it, Bella? What's wrong?" she asked in consternation, noticing that the young woman seemed nervous and upset.

"Oh, Miz Morgana," Bella cried out, wringing her hands and close to tears. "Masta Griffin whips me fer shoah . . . Sez de first one who breathes a word gits skinned alive. . . ."

Morgana frowned at the recital. "Bella! What on earth are you talking about?" She put her hands on the slim shoulders. "If there is something I should know," she said quietly, "then you must tell me."

Bella regarded her mistress with wide, fearful eyes. "You won't tell Masta Griffin I tol' you?" she pleaded, sounding truly distraught.

"Of course not. Nor," Morgana added, mouth tight, "will I allow him to whip you."

The assurance was enough for Bella. Like most of the slaves at Albemarle, Bella had learned to trust Morgana. Still, her words came in spurts, between small sobs. "It's de baby, Miz Morgana. Oh, Lawd Jesus, what Miss Cammy gonna do when she finds out?" Bella put her hands to her face and wept in earnest.

"What are you talking about?" Morgana exclaimed sharply. Reaching out, she took hold of the girl's wrists, pulling them away from her black face. "Tell me! What about Jamie? Is he sick?"

"No, missus. He ain' sick." Bella glanced outside. The coffle was out of sight. "He's wit Tansy," she whispered. "Masta Griffin gonna sell 'em both. Gave Tansy Miss Cammy's baby. Gonna sell 'em as a pair . . . Sellin' Zoe, too, but Miss Cammy's baby too light to be passed off as her'n, so he give it to Tansy." Bella's voice ended on a wail.

The blood left Morgana's face. "Oh, my God . . ." She turned and hurried from the room, almost colliding with Celia in her haste.

She screamed Griffin's name as she ran down the stairs, only to be informed by Thomas that her husband had accompanied the coffle to Charleston.

Dismayed, she ran outside, skirts swirling around her ankles. There, on the verandah, she spied Nathaniel. Though it was barely eight o'clock in the morning, he was seated in the rocking chair, sipping a drink. He didn't seem surprised to see her, but he avoided her eye as she stormed in his direction.

"How could you have let this happen?" she demanded angrily, sounding breathless. She was dumbfounded that Griffin would have done this in the first place, and further shocked that Nathaniel had made no move to stop it.

Nathaniel took a long sip of his toddy before replying. It was his third and it helped blunt his thoughts. "Damned grapevine," he complained irascibly. "Can't understand how the hell they do it."

"Nathaniel!" Morgana spoke sharply, resisting the urge to shake the old man. "You must send someone after that child. I will not allow this to happen."

"Can't stop it now," Nathaniel said. Although his voice was quiet enough, his chest rose and fell more quickly than if he had in truth been calm. He downed his drink. "Thomas!" he shouted, waving his glass. "Damned buck's never around when you want him." He hunched lower in the rocker.

"Nathaniel—" Morgana broke off as Thomas brought another toddy. The Negro cast her a look full of despair as he retreated.

"Can't do nothin'," Nathaniel mumbled. Turning slightly, he gave her a brief glance. His eyes appeared sunken, shadowed with pain. "Boy's a nigger, just like the rest of them." He turned away again.

"That child's no more black than you or I," Morgana all but shouted, then fell silent as she heard the scream. It was loud, piercing, as if the person who had uttered it was in mortal anguish.

With one more glance at Nathaniel, who seemed not to

have heard the commotion, Morgana ran back into the house.

She was about to go upstairs when she saw Cammy coming down. The girl's hair was disheveled. Her cotton robe was untied, revealing the white flannel nightgown she wore underneath it. She was standing a few steps down from the landing, leaning on the banister, a crazed look upon her face. In her right hand, a pair of scissors gleamed dully. Behind her, Meg hovered anxiously, hands outstretched, but not daring to touch her mistress.

"Cammy . . ." Morgana tried to keep her voice quiet and steady. She started up the stairs. The girl looked down at her as if a stranger were approaching.

"I'll kill him!" she cried out in a low and ragged voice. "I'll kill my brother for this!" She raised the scissors in a threatening gesture.

Morgana paused. She took a deep breath, forcing herself to be calm. Her heart was beating painfully fast, causing a throbbing in her ears. Slowly, she climbed, one step at a time, never taking her eyes from Cammy's distraught face.

"We'll get him back," Morgana murmured in the same quiet tone. She extended a hand. "I promise you, we'll get your baby back. . . ."

Drawing away slightly, Cammy regarded her with bright, suspicious eyes. "He sold my baby. He took him away and sold him!" She repeated it over and over, as though she herself couldn't believe it.

Coming closer, Morgana put her arms about the slim figure, and turning her around, led her back to her bedroom. Cammy went docilely enough, but wouldn't allow Morgana to take the scissors, which she clung to in a fierce, determined manner. Her face was a curious mixture of dazed, hysterical anger.

After the door closed, Morgana sat Cammy gently down on the bed. "Listen to me," she murmured in slow, measured tones. She bent forward to better see Cammy's face. "I will bring your baby home. Cammy," she shook the girl, trying to gain her full attention. "I will bring him back to you. But to do that, I must leave you and go into Charleston." She peered closer. "Will you promise me you will do nothing foolish while I am gone?"

Cammy finally looked directly at Morgana, the words at last penetrating her fogged state of mind. "How?"

Morgana gave a small breath of relief. It was the first thing Cammy had said in a coherent manner. "You leave that to me." She cupped Cammy's chin with her hand. "Do you understand everything I've said?"

Slowly, Cammy nodded, and this time made no protest when Morgana took the scissors from her grasp and handed them to Meg.

Straightening, Morgana regarded the frightened slave. "I want you to stay with your mistress," she instructed the wide-eyed Meg. "Don't leave her for a moment. Do you hear me?"

"Yassum," Meg replied readily. She took a step closer to Cammy as if to indicate her willingness to comply. "Stay's by her side, ever' minute. Promises you."

Morgana nodded, satisfied. Then she regarded Cammy again. She was sitting on the bed, her shoulders slumped, hands loose and limp in her lap. "I'll return as soon as I'm able. Although," she stressed, "I doubt that I'll get back today."

As Morgana turned to go, Cammy's murmured voice

halted her. "He won't listen. You can talk as much as you want, but Griffin won't listen. He's going to sell my baby . . ." Her voice broke as she began to sob. Meg came closer and put her arms around her mistress, appearing as if she, too, was ready to burst into tears.

Morgana's lips curved into a humorless, cold smile. "I have no intention of trying to change Griffin's mind," she stated. She continued toward the door where she paused, looking back at Cammy. "I'll be leaving in a little while. When I return, Jamie will be with me."

As she closed the door, Morgana closed her eyes and offered a brief, fervent prayer that her words were true. Feeling an acute sense of urgency, she summoned Bella and Ben to her room.

A while later, Morgana rummaged through her father's trunk, finally locating a leather poke among the contents. Then, with Ben's assistance, she dragged the locked metal box from beneath her bed. Kneeling on the floor, she unlocked it, then began to stuff the gold into the poke.

Glancing up at Ben, she asked, "How much does it cost to buy a slave?"

"Depends, Miz Morgana," he answered, scratching his woolly head. "A prime buck kin bring eighteen hun'erd." He looked sheepish then. "Masta Aleceon bought this worthless nigger fer only three."

Morgana frowned at him. "I don't ever want to hear you say that again, Ben," she admonished sternly. "You're not worthless."

"Yassum."

"But a baby, Ben," she went on. "How much does a baby cost?"

Ben shook his head. "Dey doan sell suckahs by

deyselves, Miz Morgana," he said slowly. "Always wit a wench."

"Well, how much then?" she demanded, growing impatient.

He shrugged. "Kin go fer, mebbe eight, nine hun'erd. Depends on de wench."

Morgana chewed her lower lip in contemplation, still on her knees. "Well, there's about two thousand dollars in the poke. That ought to be enough." She got to her feet, brushing her skirt with her hands. "Ben, you go and get the carriage ready."

Bella stood by, regarding her mistress doubtfully. "You plannin' on goin' to de auction, Miz Morgana?"

"Yes," she answered shortly, giving the woman a brief nod. "And I'll outbid any man there if it takes every cent I've got," she added grimly. Going to the wardrobe, she took out a shawl.

Bella's doubt increased and her expression turned skeptical. "Never seen a white lady theah before, Miz Morgana," she mused slowly. "Thinkin' dey's holdin' sep'rate auctions fer 'em."

Morgana halted abruptly, staring at her. "You mean they don't allow women at these . . . auctions?"

"Never seen one, Miz Morgana," Bella responded. "But I on'y bin sol' once. Jest not shoah."

Morgana hadn't considered that obstacle. She stood, pensive, her mind working with its usual agility. Then her eye lit upon the open trunk and she gave a slow smile.

"Well, we won't take any chances," she murmured softly. Removing her shawl, she threw it carelessly on the bed. "Come, help me." She walked over to the trunk and began to pick up first one, then another article of clothing.

Thank God her father had been so thin and gaunt, she thought, as she began to undress.

Bella watched her actions with wide, incredulous eyes.

Morgana pulled on a pair of fawn colored trousers, at first over her pantalettes. Looking at herself in the mirror, she frowned at the bulge of material. Without hesitation, she stripped down to her skin. Again the trousers went on, this time fitting smoothly, just a bit loose in the waist, and about an inch too long.

"Hurry, Bella," she said, waving a hand. "Get your needle. Just tack the cuffs. I'll pin the waist. No one will see it beneath the jacket anyway."

She stood with as much patience as she could muster while Bella accomplished the few stitches on either side of the cuffs. Grabbing one of her petticoats, Morgana hastily tore it lengthwise, then put one of the pieces across her breasts. Turning, she said to Bella, "Tie it." She looked down. "A bit tighter."

A white ruffled shirt went on next, and completely confused by the intricacies of the cravat, Morgana submitted to the ministrations of Bella, who deftly accomplished the task. She could not, she realized, wear the boots. They were too big. Her own would have to do, but the trousers would hide the tops.

Bella helped Morgana into the frock coat that matched the trousers. It fit surprisingly well. The shoulders were a bit large, but not noticeably so.

Viewing her, Bella shook her head and pursed her full lips. "Ain' nobody gonna think yore a man wit dat hair," she noted wryly, gesturing at the golden mass.

Morgana looked into the pier mirror and gave a short

laugh. "I daresay you're right. Is there a hat in there?" she pointed to the trunk.

"Yassum," Bella replied after a brief search. "An' a walkin' stick, too."

Quickly, Morgana piled her hair atop her head, pinning it securely. Then she put on the hat. "There. Is that better?"

Carefully, Bella studied her mistress from head to toe. "You wait jest a minute, Miz Morgana," she said.

Before Morgana could protest, Bella hurried from the room, returning a short while later with a piece of coal. With light, deft strokes, she began to darken Morgana's eyebrows, thickening them slightly, then did the same with the bit of hair that was visible just in front of her ears.

Viewing herself once more, Morgana smiled delightedly. "Hand me the walking stick, Bella. I'm going to Charleston."

It was late in the day when Morgana finally reached the city, grateful that Ben knew the way to where the auction would be held. But then, why shouldn't he know? she reflected angrily. She doubted there was a slave in the South who didn't know where the auctions were held in their area.

The carriage halted on the cobbled street before what looked like a common warehouse. Morgana got out and approached the front entrance, which was securely locked. Then, in dismay, she read the posted notice on the door. The auction was not to be held until ten o'clock the following morning.

"But where are the slaves now, Ben?" she asked worriedly, looking about. There was no one around; the whole area seemed deserted.

Ben pointed to a one-story building across the street from where they were standing. Several citrus trees and a huge wisteria vine did little to conceal the structure's delapidated condition. "Dey's in de jail, Miz Morgana," he answered, turning to look at her. "Dat's where dey spen' de night. Calls it a barracoon, but it's jest a jail."

Morgana started to move across the street, then stopped in her tracks. She realized the only way to purchase a slave right out of the barracoon, without attending the auction, would be to deal directly with the owner. In this case, Griffin. That was a chance she couldn't possibly take. With a sigh, she viewed Ben, who nodded, having sensed her intentions.

"Best you waits fer de auction, Miz Morgana," he advised solemnly. "Be a crowd of peoples aroun' den. Safer dat way."

Morgana nodded, then gave him a sharp look. "Ben, you must call me Master Morgan. Please, try to remember."

"Yas, Miz—ah, Masta Morgan."

"Good. Until this is over, you call me that even when we're alone," she instructed firmly. "Understand?"

"Yassuh, Masta Morgan, suh." He grinned broadly at her nod of approval.

"Now. Where can I stay until morning?"

Ben pondered. "Dere's a place on Meetin' Street where de ladies stay, an' it's mos' respectable. Nobody bother you dere."

She made a face at the suggestion. "I can't walk into a place like that, dressed like this," she reminded him.

That produced a sheepish grin from Ben. "Yassum— Masta, suh. Gen'mens stay at de Charleston Hotel."

"All right." She began to get back into the carriage, then paused, glancing at him. "Can you stay there?"

He nodded in affirmation. "Got a place in back by de kitchen," he assured her, closing the carriage door as she settled herself.

"Fine. Then that's where we'll go."

A while later, Morgana entered the crowded lobby of the fashionable hotel, Ben following a few steps behind her. She was nervous and her eyes darted about, scanning the red velvet chairs that were positioned amongst the potted plants. What if she met Griffin? The thought caused her stomach to tighten as she approached the front desk.

"I'd like a room for the night," she said to the clerk. She tried to lower her naturally husky voice and carefully avoided eye contact.

However, the clerk, a thin, pasty-faced individual in his early thirties, gave her no more than a cursory glance. He was always busy at auction time because of the swelling numbers of out-of-town clientele that the function generated.

"Three dollars," he mumbled brusquely, pushing a key in her direction. Looking toward Ben, he added, "Your nigger stayin'?"

She nodded.

"Want him fed?"

"Of course!"

"Another six bits," he informed her, barely stifling a yawn.

She paid the money, then turned away, feeling weak. A

group of men were discussing the auction in loud and raucous tones. She walked quickly passed them to where Ben was standing by the front door. "You know where to go?" she asked him, coming closer.

He nodded. "Doan worry 'bout me, suh."

"I worry for us both," she replied with a small laugh. "Come for me in the morning, right after breakfast." She glanced at the key she held in her hand. "Number twenty-four."

"Be there . . . suh." Ben gave a slight bow.

She turned then and walked hurriedly across the carpeted lobby. She looked neither right nor left and prayed that she wouldn't come across her husband. She was hungry, but didn't dare go into the dining room. That, she thought, would be tempting fate too far.

Walking up two flights, Morgana located number twenty-four. Closing the door behind her, she leaned against it, a deep sigh following soon thereafter.

It was not a large room, but the bed appeared comfortable enough. After a moment, she took off her hat, placing it on the mahogany dresser. The jacket she put over the single chair. Then she removed her boots. She would never be able to retie the cravat, she thought tiredly, and lay down on the bed with the rest of her clothes on.

Although it was not yet dark, she felt weary, both in mind and in body. Wistfully, she thought of Griffin—not the Griffin of today, but the one she first knew and loved. Sometimes her yearning almost got the better of her; her treacherous body remembered, even if her mind sought forgetfulness.

What she was about to do would again anger him, she realized, taking a deep breath of resignation. She closed her eyes, unwilling to face that, knowing in her own heart that she was doing the right thing.

She turned over on her stomach and plumped the pillow with several vicious jabs before resting her head on its dubious softness.

Oh, Griffin, her mind silently cried out, even with all that's happened I still love you so. . . .

Morgana knew that she had given herself countless excuses for not leaving Griffin. In the beginning she told herself she could not leave because she had no money. After her father died, she told herself she could not go because of the coming child. Yet, deep inside herself, Morgana was aware of the gentle deceptions her heart offered as excuses for her staying at Albemarle.

During the week before she and Griffin had been married, Morgana had had many daydreams of what their life together would be like. They had been such pretty dreams, she thought sadly, and now they lay like broken toys, mangled in the grip of an ill-tempered child. Nothing had turned out the way she had imagined it would. Nothing.

What kind of a charade had her life become? Morgana thought miserably.

Although she was very tired, Morgana laid there for hours, her mind filled with thoughts of Griffin. It was well after midnight before she finally fell into a restless sleep.

When she awoke, bright sunlight was streaming in through the window. She sat up quickly and peered about the strange room, taking a brief moment to orient herself.

What time was it? she wondered frantically, struggling into her boots. Hastily, she donned the jacket and hat. The mirror over the dresser was cracked, but she was reassured by what she saw. She looked the same as she had yesterday.

Opening the door, she blinked as she saw Ben. He was seated on the floor. When he saw her, he smiled as he got to his feet.

"What time is it?" she asked him worriedly.

"Jest a bit after eight, suh. Plenty o' time. You eat yore breakfast . . ."

She shook her head as she closed the door. "If Griffin is there. . . ."

"Ain' dere," Ben assured her. "Seen him, I did. 'Bout thirty minutes ago. He long since gone. You eat yore breakfast," he repeated with a patient nod of his head.

"Have you eaten?" she asked as they walked down the hall.

"Yassum . . . suh. Doan you worry none 'bout Ben." He chuckled, following her down the stairs. "Got me some grits wit molasses, I did. Dat gal whats in de kitchen, she knows a fine buck when she sees one."

"All right," Morgana was unable to repress a smile. "I'll get something to eat. But I won't be long," she stressed. "Be in the carriage when I get there."

"Be there, suh," Ben promised solemnly.

In spite of Ben's assurance that Griffin was not around, Morgana entered the dining room a few minutes later with no little trepidation. She crossed the carpeted floor and found a small table in the corner. As she seated herself, she let her gaze travel the room. There were only a sprinkling of women, most of the occupants were men. Griffin wasn't among them.

A waiter appeared, a spurious smile appearing carved into his black face.

Morgana glanced briefly at the bill of fare and ordered scrambled eggs, bacon, and coffee. Then she waited, feeling a gnawing sense of impatience. She hoped fervently that she would be able to accomplish what she had set out to do. She had never in her life attended an auction—much less one where they sold people. She hadn't the faintest idea of what to expect.

When the waiter finally put the plate in front of her, Morgana bolted her food down in a most unladylike manner. As she wiped her mouth with a linen napkin, she couldn't help but wonder what Miss Appleby would think of her performance . . . Then the frivolous thought fled her mind as she rushed outside.

Ben was there, waiting. But despite her early confidence, Morgana began to tremble with what lie ahead.

Chapter
16

Unlike yesterday, the street was now filled with horses, carriages, liveried servants, well dressed—and some not so well dressed—men. The air was cool on this January morning, but the sun was warm, the breeze so slight it barely nudged the leaves.

When they arrived, Morgana sat in the carriage for a full two minutes studying the crowd.

A group of Negro drivers and servants congregated near the hitching rail, to which were tied a dozen or so horses. For them, she could see, this was not an auction, it was a social event. News was being exchanged, gossip from the Great Houses, which of their friends had been, or were to be, sold, who had been punished and why.

Listening to their muted voices and laughter, Morgana's eye finally lit upon Atlas, and she frowned. The burly Angolan had been installed as groom and stableboy in place of Jude. He was standing somewhat apart from the others, engaged in conversation with one of the liveried drivers. So far he had not noticed her arrival.

Motioning to Ben, Morgana called his attention to the slave. She didn't think he would recognize her, but he would certainly recognize Ben.

"He doan see us'ns yet," Ben noted quietly. He glanced across the cobbled street, squinting slightly in the sun. "Drives de carriage behind de jail, an' waits fer you dere," he suggested.

Taking a deep breath, Morgana nodded in agreement, trusting Ben. Then, not seeing Griffin anywhere in sight, she finally got out of the carriage and headed for the entrance. Nobody gave her a second glance.

The building in which the auction was to be held was a one-story wooden structure, some sixty by a hundred feet in size, the only notable structural achievement being the white-pillared portico in front. Inside it was furnished with true spartan frugality. Against one wall was a wooden platform about two feet high with steps on one side. Along the same wall stood the slaves that were to be sold this day.

Except for a rickety table where a clerk sat, prepared to make out the bills of sale and collect the money, the room held no other furnishings.

Most of the men were standing in small groups, conversing, laughing, gossiping. The front doors had been left open, as had the two windows on either side of the room, but already the air was dense with cigar smoke. Gauzy sunlight streamed in through one of the windows, producing slanting, wavering rays as it cut through smoke and dust.

When Morgana entered, her gaze swept the crowd in search of Griffin. He was standing with two other men, deep in conversation. Quickly, she moved to the other side of the room, putting as much distance between them as she could.

Selecting her position, Morgana stood quietly, leaning only lightly on the walking stick, trying her best to adopt the stance of some of the men she was viewing. She was nervous, but not unbearably so; rather, her attitude was one of caution. She was more concerned about the baby than she was about herself.

She wondered how Cammy was faring and prayed that the girl would do nothing rash while left alone. Although, in truth, Morgana couldn't blame Cammy. It didn't take much on her part to realize what her own reaction would be if she were in the same predicament.

The room was becoming crowded now. Morgana was certain that even if Griffin glanced in her direction he wouldn't see her. There were so many bodies between them she had to peer around heads to catch a glimpse of him.

Relaxing a bit, she studied the slaves, easily recognizing Zoe. The young woman was standing in an attitude of utter dejection, her eyes lowered. Next to her stood Tansy, who was holding Jamie in her arms. There were only seven women and they all stood together. They were obviously wearing their best clothes, black calico dresses with white fichus. All had bright red bandannas tied about their heads.

The rest of the slaves were men, about twenty-five in all. They were clad only in cotton breeches. All the men wore iron spancels on their wrists.

Morgana found the sight terribly depressing. Shifting her position a bit, she tried to avoid looking at the forlorn group of men and women who, through no more than a happenstance of nature, had to live in such a harsh environment.

The auctioneer, a short, balding man with a potbelly and quick, birdlike movements, now mounted the platform. He gave a brief announcement, informing the gathering that the sale would begin in about twenty minutes. "And if any of you gentlemen wish to examine any of the wenches in private, we've a shed just outside for your accommodation," he concluded, rubbing his hands together in an anticipatory manner.

There was a slight flurry of movement as a few of the men now stepped forward to avail themselves of this service. Zoe and one other Negress were led outside. In some relief, Morgana noted that Tansy had remained where she was standing, possibly because of the encumbrance of the baby in her arms.

"Now, that's a likely lookin' buck, wouldn't you say?"

Startled, Morgana turned to the man who had come up beside her, then quickly averted her face.

"See the one I mean?" he persisted, pointing to a tall and muscular Negro. "Ashanti, I'm thinkin' . . . Make good fighters." He turned to Morgana. "Pearson's my name, suh." He nodded his head in a friendly greeting. He was a heavyset man with a paunch that caused the buttons on his yellow silk vest to strain with each breath he took. His graying sideburns were sparse and crept down his cheek in a tentative manner, disappearing at his jawline. Age had plucked the hair from the top of his head, leaving a shiny pate that gave him the appearance of a benevolent friar.

Morgana gave him only a brief glance. "Morgan, sir," she offered at last, still not looking directly at him. "George Morgan."

He moved closer. "Do you live in Charleston, Morgan?"

"No. I'm from . . . New Orleans."

"Ah," he beamed, rocking on his heels. "Fine city. Visited there about two years ago. Had the time of my life. Not many cities to compare with that one."

Morgana wet her lips, wishing the man would go, but he showed no inclination of doing so.

"You lookin' for a buck or a wench?" he went on after a minute's silence.

"A . . . wench."

"Aha. Thought so, suh. Fine lookin' young fella like yourself." He nudged her with his elbow, jerking his head in the direction of Tansy. "Notice that little high yaller? Pretty a piece as I've ever seen. Well tittied out, too." He sighed wistfully, not noticing how the "young man" beside him blushed hotly. "Wife'd never let me bring that one home," he mused, hooking his thumbs in his vest pocket. "Here to buy a fightin' buck, myself. Wife doesn't approve of that, either," he added sourly. "But I told her a man's got to have some enjoyment out of life." He turned again to Morgana, who had managed to get herself under control. "You a married man, Morgan?"

"No."

Pearson nodded his head in an almost approving manner. Reaching into his coat pocket, he brought forth a cigar, bit off the end, and stuck it in his mouth, unlit.

"Must be plenty of fine wenches for sale in New Orleans," he speculated casually after a minute, his words coming a bit garbled as he chewed on the cigar. When there was no immediate response, he regarded Morgana questioningly.

"I suppose there are," she offered shortly. She was growing irked by his insistent prattle, but she dared not take the chance of moving away.

"Had me a quadroon once," Pearson went on, much to Morgana's annoyance. "She was sixteen. Fanciest little wench you'd ever want to see. Bought her right here, in Charleston. Gave me two bright-skinned suckers. Had to sell the lot of 'em when I got married, though. That was about seven years back." He expulsed his breath in a deep sigh. "Sure wish I had them to sell now. Price of niggers keeps going up and up. Why, today, I could've asked twice the price and got it easy."

Morgana's hand tightened on the walking stick. She had an almost uncontrollable urge to hit the pompous oaf over the head with it. Bright-skinned suckers, indeed, she thought with rising fury. The man had actually sold his own children, yet his only regret seemed to be that he could have gotten more money had he waited. It was on the tip of her tongue to ask if one of the children had been a girl. Had he sold his own daughter, sold her so that she could be purchased for the same intentions as had her mother? Morgana decided she didn't really want to know the answer.

"Excuse me, sir," she said finally, aware that her voice was tight and angry. "I think they're about to begin."

Morgana moved quickly, afraid that her temper would

get the better of her, but was cautious enough to keep an eye on Griffin's whereabouts. She moved closer to the platform so she would not have to shout when the time came to bid. Griffin, she noticed, had not moved and, fortunately, had his back to her.

Zoe and the other young black woman had been returned to the group and once again the auctioneer mounted the wooden platform.

The first slave to be sold was the huge Negro that Pearson had pointed out as a likely fighter. The man was so black his skin had little, if any, highlights; from head to toe he was unrelieved ebony. He was tall, an inch, perhaps two, over six feet and had broad, muscular shoulders. Dressed only in cotton breeches, he stood quietly, almost proudly, despite the incongruity of the iron manacles on his wrists. He displayed no fear as a few of the men crowded close while the auctioneer began to extol the prime condition of his merchandise.

Pearson was among the men. Reaching up, he motioned for the Negro to bend down and open his mouth. Poking his pudgy fingers into the dark cavity, he diligently inspected the man's teeth. Apparently satisfied, he ran his hands over the muscular body, prodding at the man's genitals, squeezing the thighs, punching at his abdomen with quick jabbing thrusts. One or two of the other men were doing the same thing as the auctioneer continued with his enthusiastic spiel.

The bidding, begun at eight hundred dollars, was intense and energetic, and ended with Pearson's bid of nineteen hundred and fifty dollars. Looking immensely pleased with himself, Pearson then stepped up to the table to claim his bill of sale.

The whole process made Morgana ill. For a moment, she turned away. It took all her control to stand quietly and watch, to avoid calling attention to herself by berating the egotistical men about her who were displaying such a careless superiority.

As unobtrusively as possible, she continued to keep an eye on Griffin. Thankfully, he wasn't milling about. He was still with the same two men she had seen him with when she had entered.

Listening to the proceedings, Morgana couldn't help but wonder what would become of the slaves that were being sold. At least one, she knew, was destined to become a fighter. But the rest—where would they end up? Would they be ill treated? She shook herself away from her wandering thoughts, forcing herself to concentrate on the moment at hand.

An hour passed. Tansy, the baby still in her arms, at last mounted the platform, her eyes cast down. Zoe had already been sold. For once, Morgana had watched the process with dispassionate eyes, uncaring of the fate in store for the young Negress.

"Look lively, gal!" The auctioneer gave Tansy a poke in the ribs with his finger. While his tone was jocular enough, his little black eyes narrowed menacingly.

Tansy straightened, a bright smile plastered upon her face. Even from where she was standing, Morgana could see the girl trembling.

The auctioneer laughed heartily, then addressed the

group in an almost conspiratorial manner, his voice at the level of a stage whisper.

"This little yaller can warm my bed anytime," he informed them all with a broad grin.

Frowning, Morgana began to understand why white women were not welcome in a gathering of this sort.

Amidst the good-natured laughter that followed the auctioneer's remark, Morgana glanced once at Griffin. However, his back was still toward her and she couldn't see his expression. He didn't appear to be laughing, although the two men he was standing with were displaying high amusement. The auctioneer continued, and Morgana returned her attention to the platform.

"Now this heah's Tansy," the man pronounced, raising his voice slightly to indicate that he was getting down to serious business. "She's unmarked and docile. Only eighteen years old, but already a fine breeding wench, as you can see." He made a brief gesture toward the child in her arms. "She'd make a fine wet nurse for any of you gentlemen as has such a need in your family. She's primarily a field hand, but young enough to be housebroken." He glanced down at his notes to refresh himself. "Tansy comes from Albemarle and is the property of Mr. Griffin Kynes, who wishes to sell her at this time." He looked out upon the crowd expectantly.

One of the men bid three hundred dollars. Morgana quickly upped it to four.

"Four-fifty," came the return bid.

Taking a deep breath, Morgana raised a hand. "Six hundred."

There was a brief pause, then, "And fifty!"

"Eight hundred," Morgana called out, still taking care to distort her voice as much as possible.

After that, there was silence.

Gazing about the smoke-filled room and seeing no other indications, the auctioneer shouted, "Sold!" Then he quickly proceeded to the next slave.

Morgana moved through the crowd, making her way to the table. She paid the money and collected a bill of sale, keeping her back always in the direction of Griffin, who, at any rate, hadn't shown undue attention to the person who had bought Tansy and her supposed child.

Beckoning the brown-skinned girl to follow her, Morgana then walked out into the bright afternoon sunshine. Crossing the street with hurried steps, she went to the rear of the jail, where Ben was waiting beside the carriage.

Morgana entered and motioned for Tansy to get in. The girl halted abruptly, recognizing both the carriage and Ben, then stared stupidly at Morgana.

"Get in!" Morgana instructed sharply, anxious to be on their way.

When Tansy finally did, the carriage moved forward at a smart pace. Tansy couldn't take her eyes off Morgana, still not recognizing her, until, at last, Morgana spoke in her normal voice.

"It's Miss Morgana, Tansy," she murmured quietly.

There was no immediate reaction. Then the girl's eyes grew round. "Lawd Jesus, missus," she breathed. "What you doin' heah, dressed lak dat?" Her eyes grew even wider as they surveyed Morgana from head to toe, unable to believe what she was seeing.

Bending forward, Morgana checked to see that the baby

was all right before she answered. Satisfied that he was sleeping peacefully, she said, "Tansy, how would you like to go North, to be free?"

Turning somber, the girl just stared at her, dark eyes turning wary. She knew perfectly well what she was supposed to say anytime anyone asked her that question. For a slave to admit to wanting freedom was to invite consequences too awful to even think about.

"Wants to be yore slave, missus," Tansy replied dutifully after a moment's consideration. She gave a short nod of her head for emphasis, then shifted the baby to a more comfortable position in her lap.

The answer confounded Morgana, who was, for the moment, at a loss for words. She heard Ben chuckle. Then the Negro glanced over his shoulder at Tansy.

"Best you speaks de truf, gal," he noted quietly. "Miz Morgana meanin' what she says."

Again the girl regarded Morgana, still uncertain, still unable to believe her mistress was serious. It wasn't that she didn't trust Miz Morgana; she did. But she knew very well that white folks were to be trusted only so far. Tansy glanced at Ben, whose attention was again centered on the road. Miz Morgana, she knew, *had* freed Ben, although, for reasons of his own, he continued to serve her.

Morgana was regarding Tansy quizzically, not understanding the hesitation. "Do you want to go North?" she repeated in a stronger voice.

The girl looked away for a moment, then back at Morgana, still a bit uncertain. "How do I git dere?" she responded at last.

Morgana patted the slim brown hand. "You just leave that to me."

"Kin I take my baby?" Tansy spoke hesitantly, not wishing to jeopardize her sudden good fortune.

Leaning back on the seat, Morgana looked dismayed at the suggestion. Good Lord, she had forgotten all about Tansy's baby. She bit her lip. Then, determined, she nodded. "Yes. Yes, we will take your baby with us."

They fell silent then. Occasionally, Morgana turned around and glanced out of the small rear window in the carriage, hoping and praying that she wouldn't see the buckboard on the road behind them. She consoled herself by reasoning that Griffin would surely stay until the end of the auction. When she had left, there were still seven slaves to be sold. Taking a deep breath, she tried to relax.

When they arrived at Albemarle some hours later, Nathaniel was standing on the verandah. Incredulous, he watched as Morgana stepped out of the carriage, followed by Tansy and the baby. Having gone into the fields shortly after he spoke to Morgana the previous morning, he hadn't even known she was gone. Cammy hadn't left her room and Nathaniel had supposed that Morgana was with her.

"What the hell," was all he could think to say as Morgana removed the hat, allowing her golden hair to tumble about her shoulders.

As she walked toward him, Morgana felt a pressing need for haste. She was, at best, an hour or two ahead of Griffin, and knew she couldn't leave until after the household settled down for the night. The next few hours would be critical.

Just then, Cammy came rushing from the house, still in

her nightgown, her wrap billowing and flapping about her slim body as she raced down the broad front steps. Laughing and crying at the same time, she reached for her son, burying her face in the child's soft and warm neck.

Morgana allowed them a brief moment, then she stepped close to Cammy. "We are leaving in a few hours," she said quietly. "Do you want to come with us?"

"Oh, yes. Yes!" Cammy cried out, still clutching her son to her breast.

Morgana placed a hand on her sister-in-law's arm. "Tansy and the baby will have to stay in Ben's cabin until we're ready to leave," she said. "You stay in your room until then. Pack only what you can put in one bag. And remember, Cammy, it will be cold where we're going."

Unable to speak, Cammy only nodded, reluctantly handing the child back to Tansy.

Morgana turned. "Ben, you put the carriage and horses in the barn. But be ready to leave when I come for you."

"Yassum," Ben nodded smartly. He climbed back up on the driver's seat and prodded the horses forward.

Then Morgana turned to Nathaniel, who stood with his mouth open, still unable to believe what he was seeing. Taking him gently by the arm, she led him inside to the parlor.

Closing the pocket doors, Morgana faced Nathaniel, almost amused by the look of dumb astonishment on his face.

Still staring at her, Nathaniel sat down heavily, as if his legs would no longer support him. "How the hell did you do that?" he asked, waving a hand in the general direction of the front yard.

Morgana couldn't repress the small smile that found its way to her lips. "I admit that I never thought I would be buying slaves," she commented dryly, with a slight shake of her head. "But it appears that I have just bought two of them."

"But ... but how?" he sputtered. He wanted to comment on her attire, but he couldn't seem to find the words, so he just stared at her.

Quickly, and in as few words as possible, Morgana told him.

"But the money," Nathaniel persisted, raising both brows. "Where did you get the money?"

That, too, she told him. When she was through, Nathaniel regarded her in silence for a long moment, then slapped his knee. "By God," he exclaimed, giving a great guffaw of a laugh. "By God!" He repeated that several times, laughing until the tears came. "You're some kind of a woman, Morgana," he said when he caught his breath. Fumbling in his pocket, he brought forth a handkerchief and wiped his eyes.

Then he quieted and grew serious. "But what're you going to do now? When Griff finds out about all this ..." He shook his head, his lined face reflecting deep concern. He knew how hotheaded his grandson could be when provoked.

"I hope he won't find out until we have already left. And that's up to you, Nathaniel," Morgana added quietly, watching him closely. At this moment the fate of them all rested with this man. Morgana prayed she had not misjudged him.

"Leave?" Nathaniel raised his head, eyes widening. "Where are you going?"

"I'm taking Cammy and the baby, as well as Tansy and Ben to my aunt in Massachusetts. They'll be safe there. But Griffin mustn't know until we're gone." She took a step closer, her voice falling to a whisper. "Please, Nathaniel, say you'll help us."

He looked at her for an agonizing moment. Then, almost sadly, he nodded.

She came to his side and kissed his weatherbeaten cheek with true affection. "Thank you," she murmured, squeezing his arm.

As she reached the door, his voice halted her. "Are you coming back, Morgana?"

She turned to look at his anxious face.

"Please come back," he entreated. "We need you."

Chapter
17

An hour later, Morgana stood on the piazza just outside her bedroom. Hidden in the shadows, she watched for Griffin's return, tightening the woolen shawl about her shoulders. The sun had set and the air had turned chilly. Although she had discarded the jacket and cravat, she had not taken the time to change the rest of her clothes and still wore the outfit she had worn to the auction.

She was a bit tense with the enforced wait, even though she knew it was necessary. She couldn't chance leaving now and meeting Griffin on the road. Her nerves were taut and she prayed that Nathaniel would keep his promise and remain silent. He had already gone to his room and she took heart from that.

Now all she had to do was hope that no one else would tell Griffin. She didn't think anyone would; still, she knew very well that she wouldn't relax entirely until they were actually on the boat and away from here.

Morgana refused to allow herself to dwell upon the future. Right now she had committed herself to getting Cammy and her baby to safety. After that, she could work on her own problems.

At Morgana's side, Bella was fearful and agitated. While she greatly admired what her mistress had done, Bella wished she could be anywhere else but here when Masta Griffin found out about all this. The fact that Masta Nathaniel seemed to have tacitly agreed with what was going on offered only small comfort. Her young master was a man with a fearful temper and it was best to stay out of his way when he was riled.

Time and again Bella's eyes anxiously sought her mistress. She was trembling and longed to sit down, but she knew that she couldn't do that unless Morgana did. So she stood, clasping and unclasping her black hands, murmuring audible prayers until, at last, with rising impatience, Morgana ordered her to be quiet.

Turning, Morgana glanced into the sitting room. Anne was in the cradle, sound asleep. Celia was standing beside it, twisting her apron with nervous hands. Occasionally she reached out to rock the cradle and peer at the sleeping child.

Morgana's heart wrenched at the thought of being separated from her daughter, even for a short period of time. But the journey would be difficult enough with two babies in tow, and she herself couldn't nurse Anne. Tansy could, but if and when Morgana returned, Tansy wouldn't be with her. She shook her head. No. Anne would have to stay. Resolutely, Morgana returned her attention to the yard, hoping that Griffin would get back soon. What, she wondered distractedly, would they do if Griffin decided to spend the night in Charleston?

Twilight had deepened into a purple haze by the time the buckboard, driven by Atlas, creaked up the driveway.

With little expression, Morgana watched as her husband got down from the bench seat and strode wearily into the house. She wondered if he had regrets about what he had done, or tried to do. Somehow, she doubted it. As with Jude, Griffin probably reasoned that he was doing the right thing for all concerned.

It seemed to her that an eternity went by before she finally heard Griffin make his way up the stairs.

Standing behind her closed door, ear pressed against the solid wood, Morgana thought he paused outside her room, but couldn't be certain. Nevertheless, her heart pounded until, finally, she heard his door close.

Glancing at Bella and Celia, she put a finger to her lips, cautioning them against making any kind of a sound. Then, carefully, she opened her own door and peered into the empty hall, listening. The whole household had settled into a hushed quiet.

She waited then, a full hour before she felt safe enough to leave. During that time she dressed herself in the brown woolen dress she had arrived in. It was the warmest she owned. Over the matching pelisse she draped a woolen shawl. Then, with a last look at her daughter—one that caused her heart to ache within her breast—Morgana left her room.

The hall was dark and silent. Not even one candle burned in the wall sconces. She stood quietly a moment, letting her eyes adjust to the dimness. Then she walked slowly, hand on the wall, until she reached Cammy's room.

A light tap on Cammy's door brought an immediate response. Without words, dressed in a wine colored pelisse and carrying a heavy cloak she had never even worn, the girl fell into step. Both of them had, earlier, had Ben pick up their baggage and take it out to the carriage.

Noiselessly, they both made their way down the stairs and out to the barn without incident, although by now there was only one person on the plantation who didn't know what was going on.

Tansy was already waiting for them, having left her cabin when she saw the light extinguished in Griffin's bedroom. Both infants were, thankfully, asleep.

From the barn to the road, Ben walked beside the horses, holding the bit of one of them in his hands, allowing the animals to move only at a very slow walk.

On the road at last, he climbed up onto the driver's seat, then prodded the horses forward at a rapid pace.

Three hours later they were back in Charleston.

By now it was after one o'clock in the morning. They all, with the exception of Tansy and the two babies, had no sleep.

Morgana directed Ben to drive to the pier. The ticket office was, of course, closed, a posted sign in the window informing them that it would reopen at six A.M.

Wearily, she suggested that they all sleep as they could in the carriage. It was pointless, she thought, to go to a hotel at this ungodly hour.

Outside it was dark, and the moon had already risen from its resting place. The whiteness was pale and thin, dusting the bay with a silvery glow that melted into blue shadows along the shoreline.

Eventually, Cammy slept. Ben, stretched out on the driver's seat, dozed intermittently.

But for Morgana sleep was a luxury she couldn't afford. She became uncomfortably aware that five people were depending upon her, at least three of them for their very lives. It was a responsibility that weighed heavily.

She wondered what Griffin would do when he found out about what she had done. With a little luck—and Nathaniel's help—there was a possibility that he could go a day, or even more, before he discovered Cammy's absence. But what about her own absence? That he would most likely discover before the day was gone.

Morgana wished that she'd had time to write to her aunt and let her know they were coming. In a way, she supposed that Sarah was expecting them, for she had written about Cammy and Jude. But Sarah didn't know when they would arrive; now there was no way for Morgana to let her know.

She sighed, watching the first faint rays of the pearly dawn lighten the sky.

Quite a few boats were anchored in the harbor, not an unusual state of affairs. Vessels from such faraway places as London, Glasgow, and the West Indies put in here to load indigo, turpentine, and tar, as well as rice, corn, and other produce.

Small fishing boats were now coming in, some of them from James Island, their catch heading for the market which opened at five-thirty in the morning.

There were at least two steamboats that she could see. Morgana said a quick prayer that at least one of them would be heading North—and that there would be space available for all of them.

As soon as the sun tipped the horizon, the activity began as Negroes set to loading and unloading the various cargoes. Seagulls spread great white wings, swooping between tall masted ships in hopes of gleaning their morning meal.

The ticket office opened, finally, at six-fifteen. Morgana was first in line. Happily, one of the steamboats was headed for New York. From there, they could transfer to a packet going to Boston.

The boat, however, was not scheduled to leave until ten o'clock.

Morgana had Ben take them all to the Charleston Hotel where they had breakfast. From the hotel, Ben drove the women and children back to the pier. He then drove to the livery stables, leaving the horses and carriage there, requesting the owner to send word to Albemarle in a day or two and have someone come and fetch the rig.

Then he walked back to the pier.

Shortly after ten o'clock, the *Delta Fox* began to move, its side paddles slicing neatly through blue water as it headed out toward the Atlantic.

Tansy, as supposed "dah" for Jamie, had been allowed to share the stateroom occupied by Cammy and Morgana. Ben, however, had had to be booked into a lower cabin, in an area set aside for Negroes.

Standing on the deck beside Morgana, Cammy viewed the receding shoreline, unable to repress a small sigh of relief. After a while, she turned to Morgana, a worried frown creasing her brow. "You didn't have time to let your aunt know we were coming, did you?"

"It will be all right," Morgana assured her with a firm

nod of her head. "I don't want you to concern yourself with that. She was most emphatic in her letter. I know we'll all be welcome at Somerset Hall." She put a hand on Cammy's arm. "Come, let's go down to our cabin and see how Tansy and the children are doing."

The cold was absolutely chilling when they arrived in Boston four days later. Prodded by a howling wind, it seemed to penetrate the heaviest clothing.

After Ben had collected their luggage, Morgana secured a hired cab and instructed the driver to take them to Taunset, seven miles distant.

Cammy was silent for most of the trip. At first, she had just been glad to leave Albemarle, to get away from her brother, to get her child to safety. But in these past few days the enormity of her predicament left her quite shaken. She had, in effect, cut herself off from her family, had no money, no means with which to support herself and Jamie. She hoped that Morgana was correct in her assumption that they would all be welcome at Somerset Hall. If so, then she and Jamie would have a safe haven— at least for the immediate future.

And Cammy refused to think beyond that.

Her aunt looked just as Morgana remembered her. Time had been very gentle with Sarah Enright. At forty-seven, her chestnut brown hair was still rich in color and texture, even if dusted with silver at her temples. Her gray eyes were still clear and brilliant—and right now wide with surprised pleasure.

"Morgana!" she exclaimed, embracing her niece. "How good it is to see you." She drew back, her dark green satin gown rustling softly with her movement. "I was sorry to hear about your father . . ." Her lovely eyes shadowed. "As you know, my brother and I were not close in these past years. But," she smiled sadly, "I confess to having loved him, despite his faults. His death came as a shock to me."

"He spoke of you . . . at the end," Morgana murmured as her aunt led them into the rear parlor. "I think he regretted many things. . . ."

Sarah patted Morgana's arm in a consoling way. "You and I will have a long talk, dear," she whispered. Then she motioned to the three people waiting in the large, well-furnished room. "Do you remember your cousin Benjamin?" Sarah looked at Morgana.

"Yes, of course I do." Morgana smiled at the man who came forward, kissing her cheek. At twenty-nine, Benjamin Enright had an appealing face and an engaging smile beneath a shock of red-gold hair. His blue eyes welcomed her, as did his quick hug of affection.

"The last time I saw you," he said, studying Morgana's face, "you were just a little waif with big and somber eyes."

Morgana laughed delightedly at the description of herself as a child. "You haven't changed much, Benjamin," she commented, viewing him.

He grinned, gesturing to the young woman standing by his side. "My wife, Hannah."

Morgana clasped the outstretched hand, smiling at the delicate, fine-boned young woman with the silver-blond hair and vivid green eyes.

"And, of course, Nicholas," Sarah interjected, nodding at her younger son. "He is now a lawyer," she added with an unabashed touch of pride.

Younger by some four years than his brother Benjamin, Nicholas Enright had dark hair and dark eyes set in a good-looking, even featured face. The brothers didn't resemble each other very much, Morgana noted. Even their taste in clothes seemed to be at odds, Nicholas tending toward a conservatism that was expressed by a dark gray frock coat and a somber black cravat. Benjamin, on the other hand, was wearing a buff colored jacket and his vest was a bright red with tiny yellow flowers embroidered on the fabric.

Despite his courteous welcome and cousinly kiss, Nicholas Enright's attention seemed to have focused upon Cammy, and he only briefly nodded at Morgana's acknowledgment.

"Come along," Sarah said, placing a hand on Morgana's shoulder. "I know you'll all want to freshen up before supper."

Morgana was led to the room she considered her own, it having been the one she had stayed in when she lived at Somerset Hall more than seven years ago.

For a time she walked about, touching the furniture, an ache growing in her throat with her memories. She remembered everything about this room. Her fingertips felt for the nick in the rosewood dresser top. It was still there. The large four-poster looked just as it had when last she slept in it, even to the brightly colored patchwork quilt that covered it.

This room had been a sanctuary to her—but it had lasted such a few short weeks before she had once again been uprooted. Now, she thought to herself, it was once again a sanctuary.

Later, having rested and changed their clothes, Morgana and Cammy met the others in the dining room. Tansy and Ben were in the large kitchen having their supper with the household staff.

As the conversation flowed smoothly, Morgana happened to glance at her cousin Nicholas. She raised her napkin to her lips in an effort to conceal her smile. The young man was gazing at Cammy with such unconcealed admiration and interest that his face positively glowed. He couldn't seem to look away and appeared oblivious to everyone else at the table.

Cammy, of course, couldn't help but notice. Her cheeks flushed prettily as she tried to ignore the intense scrutiny.

When they were settled in the parlor again, the talk turned to more serious matters.

Sarah informed her niece that, despite the threat of secession by several Southern states, it was only a matter of time before abolition became a fact.

"But surely the North cannot feel so strongly that it would actually take the chance of having the Southern states secede?" Morgana protested at one point.

Sarah, who had changed into a mauve silk gown for supper, shrugged. "Right now, the Abolitionists are in the minority," she conceded, then made a vague gesture with a ringed hand. "But there are very powerful people dedicated to the cause." She looked at Morgana. "Mr. Garrison, as you well know, is tireless in his efforts to abolish slavery."

A maid entered the parlor just then, carrying a large silver tray with a pot of coffee and a plate of butter cookies studded with nuts and raisins. With practiced ease, she placed it on the low, glass-topped table between the two settees that faced each other.

"The South will never abolish slavery," Morgana murmured with a shake of her head. Glancing at Cammy, she saw the girl's nod of agreement.

"They'll have to, if it becomes law," Hannah interjected solemnly. The young woman was standing by the fireplace and now moved toward the settee. "As for secession—I sincerely doubt that they would go that far." She began to pour the steaming coffee into the delicate porcelain cups.

"But they would!" Morgana insisted, recalling everything she had seen and heard this past year. "I've lived there, I know they would. And it wouldn't surprise me in the least if South Carolina was the first state to secede," she added grimly, reaching for the cream pitcher.

Sarah extended a hand toward her niece. "Morgana, you must not return to the South. Stay here with us," she begged.

"I can't," Morgana replied with a deep sigh. She stirred the coffee once, then rested the spoon on the saucer. "My daughter—"

"Bring her back here," Sarah interrupted, leaning forward. "Nicholas will be glad to escort you."

"I will indeed," Nicholas offered promptly, with a nod of his head. "Sooner or later, this situation will become acute. I'm certain of it." He shook his head as he picked up his cup. "And I fear the time is not all that far distant."

Cammy regarded the young man frankly, and a bit depreciatingly. "There has been talk of abolition for years," she pointed out, still viewing Nicholas, who blushed with her attention. "I've been hearing arguments on that subject since I've been a little girl."

Seated beside Hannah, Benjamin cleared his throat, his face somber. "Have either of you heard of the new party that's been organized?" Both Cammy and Morgana indicated they had not, so he continued. "A Major Alvan Bovay out in Ripon, Wisconsin has formed a new political group—they're calling themselves Republicans."

Morgana gave a mirthless laugh at the news. "There have always been new parties, Benjamin," she stated, reaching for a cookie. "The American Party has been trying to unseat the Democrats and the Whigs for years."

Benjamin nodded at the observation. "I agree, the Know-Nothings are a small threat. But, in increasing numbers, they are joining the Republicans. And now that Horace Greeley is beginning to show an interest, the movement seems to be gaining momentum. They're going to hold their first formal convention in July and plan to name candidates at that time."

Morgana frowned at the report as she wiped her hands on the provided napkin. "But why do you think the Republicans are different from any other fledgling party?" she asked her cousin.

"Because their main platform will be to abolish slavery," Benjamin replied. "In all states. I seriously doubt that they can win the next election. They're not yet that strong. But if they manage to select a man who is in any way forceful and charismatic, then I believe they have a good chance at the presidency."

"And you think that such a man would actually pass a law, abolishing slavery in the South?" Morgana asked, finding it difficult to believe.

Benjamin's nod was serious. "Yes, I do."

Morgana paled. "They'll never stand for it!"

He nodded again, slowly, his lips pursed. "I'm afraid you're right. And if there is a move toward secession, the government would have no alternative but to take up arms. Of course, if it were only South Carolina, the fighting would be brief. However, if the rest of the South joins with them . . ." He turned away, viewing the darting flames in the tiled hearth before again facing Morgana. "I don't even want to think of what might happen."

When Morgana retired later that night she felt an unease that threaded its way through her mind, stopping just short of outright fear.

She'd heard nothing of all this at Albemarle. There, day followed placid day, the river rose and ebbed with the tide, crops were planted and harvested. . . .

But no one spoke of abolition as anything other than a hypothetical occurrence—one they all agreed the North would not be so foolish as to instigate.

Fretful, she tossed and turned for some hours before she finally fell asleep. Her last thoughts were of Griffin. By now, he must know what she had done. She didn't need to guess that his reaction would be anger. She knew that. What she did wonder was if her absence mattered to him. She had thought that, once away from Albemarle—and her husband—she would be able to see things with a more circumspect eye; so far, that had not happened.

But of one thing she was certain. What she had done would not help matters in her relations with Griffin anymore than had the incident with Jude.

Chapter
18

A week after their arrival, Cammy, having borrowed a heavy, fur-lined cloak and matching muff from Hannah, took a walk around the vast grounds that comprised Somerset Hall, enjoying the sting of cold upon her cheeks.

She was fascinated by the snow, the New England countryside, and the invigorating weather. About a mile from where she was standing, the Taunton River appeared just as gray as the day itself. Somerset Hall was situated on a gently rolling hill about two miles from the milltown of Taunset, but a silvery mist precluded her from seeing anything more than vague outlines in the distance.

Light snow had been falling since early morning and the January day had a dim yet luminous look about it. Flakes were fluttering about like so many feathers, taking their time before they reached the ground.

Tansy refused to set foot outside, claiming the cold gave

her aches and pains in places she never knew she had. Cammy didn't insist upon her company, rather enjoying the quiet solitude.

For the first time in many weeks she felt safe. She grieved for Jude, but it was now a quiet sorrow, not the overwhelming despair she had experienced at the beginning. She had Jamie, who was a part of Jude. Cammy made a silent vow that her son would grow up to know his father and to cherish his memory. Just as she would.

She had gone only a short distance when the sound of boots crunching in the snow made her turn around. In some surprise, Cammy saw Nicholas Enright heading in her direction. He was wearing a greatcoat and a hat of some soft material, the bright red woolen scarf around his neck offering the only vivid slash of color in his otherwise somber attire.

Approaching, he smiled a bit hesitantly, as if fearing he might not be welcome. "Miss Kynes, may I walk along with you?" he asked.

She nodded. "Of course, Mr. Enright."

"I hope I'm not intruding . . ." He fell in step, matching her slow pace.

"On the contrary, I would be pleased for the company."

For a time they walked in silence, Nicholas occasionally looking down at her, until at last Cammy paused at the end of the driveway. She gave Nicholas a shy glance, disconcerted by the intense way he was looking at her.

"I'm sorry," he murmured, embarrassed as he caught her questioning look. "I didn't mean to stare at you. It's just that . . ." He gave a soft laugh, his warm breath hanging in the frigid air for a fleeting second. "I've never seen anyone quite as beautiful as you are."

She flushed a rosy tint and lowered her eyes. "That's very kind of you, Mr. Enright," she murmured graciously.

"Oh, I meant it," he hastened to say. Nicholas couldn't look away from her. A few of her dark and shiny curls peeped out from under her bonnet, tantalizing him with their softness. The blue cloak—which he recognized as belonging to Hannah—set off the incredible perfection of her ivory tinted skin. And her eyes . . . Nicholas was certain that he could easily get lost in their fascinating depths.

At last he cleared his throat. "Ah . . . I was wondering if you would care to attend a lyceum with me this Saturday night—if you like that sort of thing." He watched her expectantly, unaware that he was holding his breath.

Cammy grew somber, not quite meeting his eyes. She felt a sudden heaviness around her heart. The young man seemed so sweet, so innocent to her. She felt bowed down by the weight of experience. "I . . ." She bit her lip, then regarded him with level eyes. "You do . . . know about me, don't you?" she whispered. She raised a hand and brushed a few snowflakes from her cheeks, but she kept her head up to look at him.

"Yes," Nicholas replied quietly. He admitted to himself that his initial reaction had been one of shock when he first heard Cammy's story. He and his brother Benjamin had been in the room when Morgana told his mother of all that had happened. Following soon on the heels of his first shock had come a rush of pity; the girl was so young, so vulnerable, he thought. It didn't seem right that she should have suffered so much. Then pity, too, dissipated, for each time he looked at Cammy, be became more and more mesmerized.

"It doesn't matter to me," he said in a rush, when she

remained silent. "What's in the past is over and done with."

She contemplated that for a moment before observing, "There are not too many gentlemen who would feel that way."

Nicholas took a breath. "You must have . . . loved him very much." The words seemed to cause him pain. He turned away, studying the white scenery. When she didn't answer him, he turned to her again, his eyes searching her face. "If you don't want to talk about it, I understand," he said quickly.

Cammy shook her head. "No, it's all right." She met his eye. "I did," she said. "I loved him very much."

Nicholas nodded gravely at her words. "Then he must have been a fine man," he stated sincerely.

Cammy's eyes moistened and she blinked rapidly against the hot sting. "He could have been—if things were otherwise."

Nicholas seemed about to reach for her, but then thought better of it. "I think you did the right thing," he said to her in a low voice. "To bring your son here, I mean. He's a fine boy."

Her breath was a soft shudder as they turned and began to walk back to the house. On either side of the driveway, tall poplars dropped beneath their burden of snow. Cammy thought they looked like silent white sentinels.

"You like children, Mr. Enright?" Cammy asked after a while, when her emotions were again under control.

"I certainly do." He glanced down at her. "I hope that someday I will have a houseful. . . ."

His enthusiasm brought a smile to her lips. "Then I'm surprised you have not yet married."

Nicholas grew serious again. "I have not yet married for the simple reason that I've not found a woman with whom I wish to share my life. Until now," he added in a barely audible murmur. He didn't look at her as he said that. He seemed to be profoundly interested in the tips of his boots.

Wonderingly, Cammy glanced up at him, but made no comment.

Just before they reached the front steps, Nicholas paused, regarding her with dark, searching eyes. "I know it's too soon to speak of these things," he began. "I'm certain you need time to forget your loss . . . But, if you would consider it, I'd very much like to get to know you better."

Her smile was tremulous, warm. "I'd like that, too, Mr. Enright."

His grin made him appear suddenly boyish. Extending his hand, he put it on her elbow. "Let me help you, Miss Kynes. The steps can be slick. . . ."

Another week passed. One day, as soon as she opened her eyes in the morning, Morgana knew she would have to return to Albemarle.

She had been wrestling with her thoughts and options for days; remaining here, returning with Nicholas and bringing her daughter back North—or just returning and staying.

This morning, almost as if her subconscious mind had made the decision for her during sleep, Morgana awoke knowing the answer. Whatever problems existed between her and Griffin, they had Anne to consider now. Morgana hadn't wanted to admit just how much she missed her daughter, but when she looked upon Jamie her arms ached with a longing that cut right through her.

She would return—but she would not ask for Griffin's forgiveness for what she had done.

As expected, Sarah immediately tried to dissuade her. "From what you've told me about the man you married, I cannot understand your decision to return to him," she exclaimed, truly dismayed. "I thought you would be glad to get away. After all he's done, I shouldn't think you'd ever want to see him again."

"There have been times when I felt that way," Morgana admitted with a nod. "And yet," she smiled softly, "I think I knew from that very first day I saw Griffin that there would never be anyone else for me. And as for Anne . . ." Her sigh caught in her throat, ending in a sob. "Oh, I miss her so. . . ."

"Of course you do." Sarah gave Morgana a quick hug. Then she sighed with resignation. "I feel I have found you only to lose you again," she murmured softly.

Morgana gripped her aunt's hand. "You are so very dear to me," she whispered. "I can never thank you for all you've done. . . ."

Sarah bit her lip. "You will come back to visit?"

Morgana smiled through her tears. "I promise I will."

After her discussion with her aunt, Morgana sought out Ben. She found the Negro in the back yard, splitting firewood—a task he had taken upon himself for want of anything better to do.

As she approached, Ben gave a final chop, leaving the ax buried in the log. Then he straightened, smiling at her.

"I'm going back home, Ben," she said quietly.

He nodded as if he'd known that all along. Sitting down on a log, he wiped his brow on the sleeve of his jacket.

Despite the cold, the work had produced a thin film of perspiration on his black face.

She watched him a moment, then suddenly asked, "Ben, how old are you?" Sitting down beside him, she arranged her heavy woolen skirt about her ankles.

"Doan rightly know, Miz Morgana," he answered. "Thirty-seven, I reckon; mebbe thirty-eight."

"Have you ever been married?"

The question didn't seem to cause him any surprise. "Had me a wife once, but she got sold. Never seen her agin." He sighed heavily, although from his words or his recent exertion, she couldn't tell.

Morgana shifted her weight a couple of times until she felt comfortable on the hard wood. "Does that mean you're still married?" she asked him.

He shook his head. "Naw, Miz Morgana. Ain' married no more. When de preacher sayin' de words of marriage, he say, 'until death—or distance—do you part.' " He spoke the phrase slowly and clearly, as if he had memorized it.

Morgana struggled with the anger which, of late, seemed her constant companion. "You mean a marriage is dissolved whenever the husband or wife is . . . sold?"

"Yassum," Ben acknowledged with a nod of his head. " 'Spects my Tildy got herse'f another husband by now," he speculated.

"Do these . . . separations happen often?" she inquired, a bit astonished at how little she knew about how these people lived, even having been in their proximity for more than a year now.

Ben shrugged. "Iffen you got a good masta, it doan happen so much. But my ole Masta Fiske . . ." He shook his head slowly from side to side. "He be one fearful man. Kilt my momma, he did. Whipped my Tildy, sayin' she sassed him. Den he sol' her."

Morgana turned away and bit her lip, not wanting to hear anymore. For a time they sat in silence.

"What do you think of Tansy?" Morgana asked after a few minutes had gone by.

"She be a right pretty gal," he answered after a moment's thought. "She spirited."

Morgana turned to look at him. "Would you be willing to marry her?"

Ben seemed to consider that. "Marries her iffen you want me to, Miz Morgana," he said at last. "But goin' back wit you when you goes home," he added firmly.

"You mustn't do that!" Morgana exclaimed quickly. "Here, you're free. But even with your papers, once you go back there, you'll be in danger of becoming a slave again." She was astounded and dismayed that he would even consider such a thing.

"Knows dat, I do, Miz Morgana," Ben replied solemnly, inclining his head. He tightened the scarf around his neck, pulling it up to cover his ears against the cold.

"Don't you like it here?" she persisted, bending toward him.

"Lak it fine," Ben assured her. "Pretty, wit de snow an' all. An' dese people bin good to me. Yassum, laks it fine," he repeated, his full lips curving into a smile.

She sighed, feeling exasperated. "They why won't you stay here?"

Ben regarded her for a long moment, his expression turning serious. "Promised yore daddy I watch over you," he said in a low voice. "Cain't go back on my word to dat man."

Morgana smiled slightly, touched by the simple statement. "You were very fond of my father, weren't you?" she asked softly. Reaching down, she picked up a handful of snow, absently fashioning it into a round ball.

"Yassum," Ben responded with quiet conviction. "Saved my life, he did. Was wit him fer five years, an' it wuz de happies' time in my life. Traveled lots, us. An' I wuz dressed fine all de time." His dark eyes sparkled with his memories. "An' ever' time Masta Aleceon won at de cards, he give Ben some of de money to spend." He chuckled, slapping his knee. "Dem gals in New Orleans would do dey fanciest struttin' ever' time dey seen Ben comin' along."

She was silent a moment, then sighed deeply as she lobbed the snowball at a tree. It landed with a soft splat, shattering into a spray of white.

"Very well," she said at last, brushing her hands against one another. "It isn't for me to ask you to marry anyone. And since you are now a free man, I can no longer tell you what to do." She got to her feet. "If it's your decision to return with me, I won't try to change your mind."

Later that day, Cammy burst into tears when Morgana told her of her decision. But Cammy's welfare no longer troubled Morgana. She knew that Sarah would let her stay indefinitely, and it didn't take much perception on her part to see that Nicholas and Cammy were growing more and more attracted to one another with every day that passed.

"But you can't," the girl cried out, persisting even in the face of Morgana's firm decision. "Please, Morgana. Send for Anne. Stay here . . ."

"Cammy, I must go back," Morgana retaliated, not

fully explaining even to herself why she felt it necessary to return to Albemarle.

In spite of everything that had happened, Morgana knew that she loved Griffin Kynes as much today as when she had married him, more than a year ago. There was that to be said, and no more. It was not something she could change at will, however much she may have wanted to. Somehow, some way, she would have to pick up the threads of her life and begin anew.

And her life was with Griffin.

Two days later, with expressed misgivings on the part of her family and copious tears from Cammy, who clung to her, weeping, Morgana and Ben left Somerset Hall.

Chapter
19

The February evening was damp and cold. Outside, the rain fell steadily, without let up, as it had been for the past two days now.

Standing by the window in the study, hands in the pockets of his tan breeches, Griffin contemplated the silver rivulets of water that coursed down the diamond-shaped panes of glass, eventually forming small gullies that threaded through the front yard.

The rain, he thought to himself worriedly, was starting much too early. The ground was already so saturated that the new water wasn't running off easily. The fields were becoming flooded under the onslaught. If the weather didn't clear, and soon, the crop would be irreparably damaged.

"Masta, suh . . . Yore supper's ready," Thomas reminded him in his soft voice as he entered the study for the second time in the past fifteen minutes. When there was no immediate response, he added, "Masta Nathaniel already sittin' down." He waited hopefully.

Without looking at Thomas, Griffin nodded then. With one more look at the gray and wet weather, he headed for the dining room.

In the hall, Griffin paused abruptly, seeing Serena about to ascend the stairs. She was dressed in the red silk gown with its black lace overskirt that he had purchased for her on an impulse when last he had been to New Orleans. It was her one piece of finery, and she wore it every chance she got. Her long black curly hair was piled atop her small head and secured with an onyx comb, another gift he had given her.

Viewing him with her dark and beautiful eyes, the girl whispered a question. "Waits for you in yore room, suh?"

Serena's expression was a silent plea, for she was very much in love with her strong and virile master. Like everyone else on that night four weeks ago, Serena had known that Morgana was about to leave Albemarle. She had hugged the knowledge to herself in secret joy, feeling that now she would have Griffin all to herself.

From the very day he had purchased her in Savannah more than two years ago when she had been sixteen, Serena had loved Griffin Kynes. She had been a virgin then, terrified of what her fate was to be.

Fortunately—or perhaps unfortunately for her— Serena's fate had been to fall in love with her master. She had no aspirations of rising above her station. She asked for nothing other than to be his slave.

Even though Griffin, in these past weeks since his wife had left him, had, for some reason, been unable to make love to her, Serena couldn't find it in her heart to censure him. Just being allowed to lay at his side was bliss enough for her.

Now, one delicate hand on the balustrade, Serena continued to wait for his answer, her eyes bright with anticipation.

But Griffin frowned at her, an expression Serena had seen often of late. His voice emerged unintentionally gruff. "No. Go back to your cabin."

Her eyes filled with tears as she turned. Although the sight would have, at one time, caused him to relent, Griffin said no more as the girl withdrew. With slow steps, he continued on to the dining room.

As he sat down at the table a few moments later, Griffin thought to himself that he wasn't very hungry. He viewed the chicken, fried just the way he liked it, the platter of tiny shrimp, the bowls of rice, the tempting golden mound of biscuits, and, sighing, picked up his glass of Madeira.

To Griffin's right, Nathaniel sat, eating with his usual appetite.

Although it was not yet seven o'clock, the lowering and sullen weather had already brought with it the darkness of night. Both of the silver candelabrums sported lighted candles and the two brass lamps on the sideboard were turned high, casting a flickering yellow glow that prodded at shadows in the corners.

The room was quiet with just the two of them there. It seemed empty despite the presence of the four houseboys who moved about on slippered feet. One of them offered the platter of chicken to Griffin, but he shook his head, moving his hand in a curt dismissal.

"You're not eatin', boy," Nathaniel observed, wiping his

mouth with his napkin. He gestured to Adam and the light-skinned Hausa immediately spooned more rice and shrimp onto the empty plate.

"I'm not hungry," Griffin replied, sipping his wine. "Too much pie for dinner."

The old man snorted. "You didn't eat enough to fill a bird," he contradicted. He picked up his fork again and plunged it into the rice.

Griffin just shrugged and motioned for his glass to be refilled.

"Got to drain the west fields tomorrow," Nathaniel noted after a while, scraping the last of the shrimp from his plate.

"I know."

Eventually, Nathaniel put down the fork and leaned back in his chair. He viewed his grandson for a long moment with a worried eye. "You got to talk about it sometime, Griff," he murmured at last.

Griffin's eyes were steely as he darted a quick look at the older man. "Talk about what?"

Brows drawn down, Nathaniel pushed his chair back and got to his feet. "Come on, boy. I could use a brandy and so could you."

Griffin issued a deep sigh of resignation, but got up and followed his grandfather into the study.

The night was cool and a small fire had been laid in the grate. Nathaniel sat down in one of the two wing chairs before the comfortable blaze, rubbing his hands together in satisfaction while Griffin poured their drinks.

"Feels good," Nathaniel murmured in contentment. "Cold seems to reach my bones more than it used to. Think mebbe I'm gettin' old."

Griffin smiled slightly as he handed Nathaniel a glass. Then he sat down. "You're not so old."

"Almost seventy-two now; that's not young." Nathaniel took a deep sip of the brandy and felt the warmth settle in his stomach. Then he put the glass on the table beside his chair. He sat back, fixing Griffin with a level and knowing look. "Got to talk about it, Griffin," he said again, this time more firmly. "It's been weeks now and you're actin' like nothing happened. Can't keep it bottled inside you. Bad for the digestion," he pronounced sagely. "No wonder you can't eat." He leaned forward, clasping his work-worn hands between his knees. "What're you going to do about Morgana?"

Griffin's expression closed as annoyance tugged at him. He didn't even want to think about her, much less talk about her.

"What're you going to do about your wife?" Nathaniel persisted in measured tones, undeterred by his grandson's attitude.

"What the hell do you want me to do?" Griffin exploded in exasperation. He ran a hand through his dark hair. "She's gone. And good riddance," he muttered, draining his glass.

Nathaniel's mouth hardened into a thin line of censure. "You don't mean that, boy," he murmured, shaking his head in an almost sorrowful manner. "You got the look of a man who's lost something mighty precious to him. Man wants to get rid of his wife, he looks relieved when she goes; he don't look like you."

"After what she's done, I don't want her back!"

Griffin's fierce look was meant to silence Nathaniel who simply ignored it. He was determined to have his say. He was not one for interfering between man and wife, for some things are better left to the principals involved. But this situation was different than most, Nathaniel reasoned. He himself had had a hand in it, and so had a right to speak.

"What did she do?" he asked finally. At Griffin's glowering look, he repeated, "I mean it, Griff. What did she do? Think about it." He waved a hand. "Saved the life of your sister's child? Put a buck out of his misery? Hell, that woman's got more gumption than any ten put together."

Having had his say, Nathaniel rested back again and, for a time, neither of them spoke.

Outside, the rain quickened, driven by a wind that bent branches and whistled along the eaves of the house.

Nathaniel stared into space, thinking of his wife, Anne. With her at his side, he had discovered the meaning of life. She had joined him on his trip to America, sharing his determination for a new life in a new country. All that any man could desire had been in Anne. In Morgana, he recognized the same type of woman. Difficult—but impossible to live without. They made it all worthwhile, gave meaning to a man's life and accomplishments.

Nathaniel had never even considered taking another wife after Anne's death. She had been too perfect a mate to ever be replaced. She had struggled and toiled by his side when they had come to this new land. And she had died before fully reaping the rewards from both their efforts. When their son Roger had fallen ill with smallpox fifteen years ago, Anne had nursed him day and night in her own tireless and courageous way. On the very day Roger had died, Anne had come down with the dreaded disease, and before the week was gone she, too, had succumbed.

Turning his head slightly, Nathaniel viewed his brooding grandson. Griffin, from the day he had been born twenty-six years ago, had found a special place in Nathaniel's heart. Although he had never told a living soul, Nathaniel had always been somewhat disappointed in his own son. Roger had been a soft spoken man with an intellect more suited to a poet than a planter. He'd been a dreamer all his life, and the only thing of worth his son had ever accomplished—in Nathaniel's eyes—was his marriage to Alicia Saunders, a beautiful and gentle-bred Charleston girl whose family now lived on James Island. William Saunders, a retired lawyer, had been violently opposed to the marriage of his only daughter to Roger Kynes, whom he considered unworthy of the lovely and gracious Alicia. In that, Nathaniel had to admit, the old barrister had been right.

But Griffin . . . From the beginning, he had been the recipient of his grandfather's love and pride. Nor, Nathaniel reflected ruefully, had Griffin ever disappointed him. Until now.

"Reminds me of your grandmother," Nathaniel mused at last, putting his thoughts into words as if his mind had never left the subject. "Your mama, now, she was a sweet little thing." He cast a quick look at the young man, who continued to remain silent. Griffin was sunk deep in the chair, legs stretched out before him. "You remember your mama, boy?"

Griffin muttered a brief affirmation. He got up, poured himself another drink, and sat down again. He continued to stare moodily into the little blaze in the grate.

"She was a fine lady," Nathaniel continued with a slow nod. "That's what she was—a lady. But your grandmama ..." A soft smile crept across his lined face. "Ah ... She was a woman." He peered sharply at Griffin's averted face. "You know the difference, boy?" he demanded.

Griffin groaned inwardly. The old man just wasn't going to give up, he thought. But his only answer was another deep sigh.

"You got yourself a woman." Nathaniel gave a small chuckle and took another sip of his brandy. "Takes a man to handle one of them," he declared knowledgeably. He gave his grandson a sly, sidelong glance. "Want to know how she did it?" He spoke in a deceptively soft and casual voice.

Griffin at last looked directly at his grandfather. "Did what?" he asked, although he knew very well to what Nathaniel was referring. He *had* wondered how Morgana had managed to buy Tansy and the baby, then spirit them away. All Nathaniel had told him was that she bought them, then took them North. Upon hearing that, he had flown into a black rage, refusing to even speak of her again.

Nathaniel gave another chuckle, pleased with the response he had received. "You should have seen her," he murmured, his eyes lighting with remembrance. "Never seen a woman dressed like a man before ..." He rubbed his chin, unobtrusively watching the younger man.

Griffin's brow creased in perplexity. He wondered whether his grandfather had had too much brandy.

Seeing the look, Nathaniel nodded his head, his expression positively gleeful. "That's how she did it!" he exclaimed, sitting up straighter, aware that he now had Griffin's full attention. "Dressed herself in her daddy's clothes—walkin' stick and all. Then she took herself off to Charleston, went to the auction and, cool as you please, outbid every man there." He laughed in sincere delight, then finished his brandy in one long swallow.

Dumbfounded, Griffin just stared at him.

"Yessir!" Nathaniel gave a vigorous movement of his silver head. "Brought 'em all back here. They were here when you came home," he confided. "Then, after you went to bed, she had Ben drive them to Charleston where they took the next boat North."

Sitting there, Griffin tried to conjure up the sight of Morgana dressed as a man. But his imagination failed him, projecting an image so ludicrous that, in spite of himself, the corners of his mouth softened in the beginnings of a smile.

Noting that, Nathaniel's eyes gleamed in satisfaction. "Now—what're you going to do about that woman of yours?"

Griffin made no immediate answer. He was thinking about that day when Morgana shot Jude. Approaching her, he had been about to strike her with his riding crop. The defiant look in her eyes had stayed his hand, made him incapable of carrying out his intention. And, knowing her as he now did, he realized that even if he had struck her, she wouldn't have flinched; she probably would have struck back.

He felt his chest expand with unconscious pride as he thought that, even though his mouth was twisted with a grim sadness. He sighed, turning morose again.

"There's nothing I can do," he said at last.

"You love her?" Nathaniel peered intently, his dark eyes bright with speculation. He knew the answer, had for months, but he wondered if Griffin knew.

Griffin hesitated, then nodded slowly.

"Well then, seems like you oughta tell her that."

"It wouldn't do any good," Griffin replied quietly. "Besides," he averted his face, "I . . . tried to tell her once, but she wouldn't listen."

Nathaniel's sound of disgust was sharp and he shifted his weight in the chair, displaying agitation. "No woman alive who wouldn't listen to a thing like that," he muttered. Then, frowning, he jabbed a finger in Griffin's direction. "You ought to go after her, tell her. . . ."

Griffin turned to look at the old man. "Where, exactly, would I go?" he asked impatiently and just a bit sarcastically.

Nathaniel's frail shoulders slumped as he sank back in his chair. "Don't rightly remember," he admitted sadly, then thought on it for a long moment. Finally, he snapped his fingers. "Massachusetts! That's it. To an aunt in Massachusetts."

At that, Griffin gave a short, humorless laugh. "That's a pretty big place," he noted wryly, again picking up his glass.

A silence descended as the two men each fell into their own thoughts. The baby began to cry, the sound of her fretful wails carrying easily downstairs and through the open door of the study. Abruptly it ceased as, upstairs, Celia took the child to her breast. Then it was quiet again, with only the sound of the rain to punctuate the passing minutes.

"Seems to me that a woman like that wouldn't leave her baby for too long a time," Nathaniel mused at last. His gaze rested upon Griffin, who had again sunk into a dour contemplation of the darting flames. "Wouldn't surprise me a'tall," he went on quietly, "if she were to come back soon, if for no other reason than to see her baby. . . ."

Having offered that assumption, Nathaniel leaned his head back, absently contemplating the shelves that marched up the wall on either side of the tiled fireplace. They were filled with an assortment of volumes that Nathaniel had collected over the years and which he had always intended to read when he found the time. But time, for Nathaniel Kynes, always seemed to be at a premium, and so most of the books languished, unread.

But he would get to them one day, he thought, closing his eyes.

The warmth of the fire and the brandy combined to prod Nathaniel toward sleep. After only a few more minutes passed, his head began to nod until, finally, his chin came to rest on his chest and he slept.

Griffin continued to sit there, staring at nothing, his thoughts alive with Morgana.

The anger really hadn't left him, but it was becoming unfocused. Was it directed at himself? Morgana? Cammy? He wasn't sure. He wasn't sure about anything anymore. At the time he had punished Jude and sold Jamie, he had felt very strong in his convictions. The fact that Morgana had thwarted him both times provoked a righteous rage within him that continued to simmer long after the events had taken place.

But in these past two weeks, he had become aware of a new emotion, one he had never before felt: loneliness. And loneliness, Griffin reflected morosely, was not something a person got used to. Suddenly, nothing seemed very important anymore. The very house seemed to echo with emptiness. As much as possible, he had avoided thinking about Morgana. But at odd times of the day, her image would invade his mind, provoking a bleak despair that almost made him physically ill.

As for the nights . . . During the four weeks that Morgana had been gone, he had summoned Serena to his bed on more than one occasion. To his utter dismay, even her young and warm body couldn't rouse him from his lethargy.

Against his will, he found himself remembering things, how the solitary dimple in her smooth cheek deepened when she was amused, the flash of her eyes when she was angered, the rare golden laugh that haunted him with its never-to-be-forgotten sound, and the soft and white body, so pliant, so willing beneath his touch. . . .

"Oh, God," he moaned, unable to bear the memories that stalked through his mind. He had never realized it was possible to love so deeply. And the realization had, for him, come too late. At night, in the darkness of his room, even with Serena at his side, he kept hearing Morgana's voice. "I love you, Griffin," she had said. "I love you." Griffin felt the despair churn within him. Would he ever hear those words again? Ever hear them from the only person who mattered?

Leaning his head back, Griffin closed his eyes. Weariness etched his face, somehow more profound because it was of the mind, not the body.

He was more than a little drunk, and the lack of food wasn't helping matters. But then, in these past weeks, that had been the only way in which he was able to summon the comfort of sleep. And oblivion.

Just before he drifted into the void of blackness that beckoned so invitingly, Griffin wondered whether his grandfather had been right.

Perhaps Morgana would come back—if for no other reason than their daughter.

Chapter
20

This time when the boat docked at Charleston, Morgana felt as if she were coming home. The soft and gentle breeze, tangy with salt spray, kissed her cheeks in welcome. Almost avidly, her eyes took in the now familiar sight of slate and tiled roofs, the beautifully decorative ironwork, the majestic spire of Saint Michael's Church. She breathed deeply of the sweet and pungent March air that was filled with the scent of flowers and citrus.

After collecting their baggage, she sent Ben to rent a carriage. A while later, they were on the road to Albemarle. She felt deliciously giddy at the prospect of again seeing Griffin, even though her feeling was tempered with cautious restraint.

Since the boat hadn't docked until after five in the afternoon, she knew they wouldn't get to their destination until well after dark.

And what would her reception be? Morgana wondered, a bit nervously. Nathaniel would be glad to see her, she knew. But what about Griffin? Would he welcome her—or would he send her away again?

Although she was tired, Morgana couldn't relax enough to sleep. She was, therefore, wide awake about two hours later when she felt the carriage come to an abrupt halt.

"Where you goin', Nigger!"

The menacing voice boomed from the darkness, shattering the quiet evening.

Startled by the gruff and sinister voice, Morgana looked outside to see the patrollers approaching. There were more than twenty of them. Some were carrying torches, the wavering golden glare cutting sharply through the black shadows along the dirt road. All of them held guns.

"What do you want?" Morgana demanded, upset by the delay. "Who are you?"

The leader peered suspiciously, then relaxed, but only slightly. Angling his horse forward, he came closer.

"Sorry, ma'am," he apologized. He removed his broad-brimmed hat in an almost deferential manner. He was of medium height, his body thick and compact without an ounce of spare flesh upon it. A high-bridged nose dominated an otherwise unprepossessing face. "Name's Drover. Jake Drover. Excuse me, ma'am, but you shouldn't be out tonight. . . ."

"What are you talking about?" Morgana frowned at the man. She knew patrollers were necessary, but she didn't like them. They were a rough and mean sort, their numbers drawn from the so-called poor white trash. "Get those men out of the way," she ordered, waving a hand at the others. "They're blocking the road."

His expression didn't change, nor did his attitude of tense watchfulness. Although his rifle wasn't pointed at her and was being held with an outward display of casualness, Morgana noticed uneasily that it was aimed directly at Ben.

"You shouldn't be out tonight, ma'am," he repeated firmly. "There's trouble. . . ."

"Let us pass!" Morgana was growing exasperated with the man's stubbornness. "We're on our way to Albemarle."

The man cast a hard look at Ben, who was nervously trying to maintain his composure.

"You trust this heah buck?" he demanded of Morgana.

"Of course I do!" she retorted angrily. "You have no right to stop us this way. . . ."

"Didn't mean no disrespect to you ma'am," he hastened to say, but the hard expression remained. "There's a gang of niggers on the prowl, led by a renegade buck named Jonah. We caught one of the black devils about an hour ago. But the rest of 'em headed into the swamp. Killed one of my men and set fire to Barrow's house over at Four Oaks." He looked closely at Morgana, who had paled at the report. "That's only about six miles from Albemarle, ma'am," he reminded her in a quiet voice.

Sobered, Morgana nodded slowly. "Well, we can't go back," she decided. She was silent a moment, then viewed the waiting patroller. "You said they headed into the swamp?"

"Yes, ma'am. But no tellin' how long they're going to stay there. They're crazy . . . and they're likkered up, too. You better ride along with us."

"Where are you going?"

Drover pointed back in the direction from which she had

come. "One of my men lives about an hour's ride from here. We're going to get his dogs, then come back again. Can't do no tracking in the dark without the dogs."

Morgana chewed her lower lip thoughtfully. "That's almost clear back to Charleston," she pointed out. She shook her head firmly. "No, Mr. Drover. We'll continue on. Besides, we'd only hold you up."

The man saw the truth in that. He gave a slow nod and put his hat back on his head. "All right," he agreed, but with reluctance. "I'll send two of my men to ride along with you. Although," he added, "I doubt it'll be too much protection for you. When the renegades left Four Oaks, they stole some guns. They're not only crazy, they're armed."

After assigning two men as an escort, the patroller rode off into the night, the rest following closely.

Ben removed the whip from the whip socket to the side of the driver's seat and flicked it over the rump of the horses, spurring them forward, this time at a quicker pace as they hurried toward Albemarle.

There was no thought of rest now as Morgana anxiously looked out into the dark night. There wasn't even a moon to alleviate the relentless blackness. One of the patrollers had insisted that Ben extinguish the small lamps bobbing atop the carriage, and now there wasn't even that bit of light to guide them. Ben was apparently trusting to the horses' instincts to stay on the road. Morgana could only hope that his confidence was not misplaced.

The two patrollers were only a small comfort, she realized uneasily. If they were suddenly attacked by a gang of renegade slaves, the two men could easily be overcome. Then what? The stories Nathaniel had told her came rushing to her mind and she shuddered at the prospect of what might happen.

Supposing they had already attacked Albemarle? She bit her lip and moaned, thinking of her child. Babies, Nathaniel had said. They had killed helpless babies. . . .

Why did they seem to be going so slow! And why hadn't she thought to send word she was coming?

"How far away are we?" she called out to Ben, her anxiety growing.

"Jest a couple of miles, Miz Morgana," Ben answered over his shoulder, not bothering to turn around. He, too, sounded worried. "Be there soon."

But it seemed to take forever.

She smelled the smoke before she saw the flames.

Little by little, the blackness became invaded by an ominous glow. Four Oaks, Morgana thought, recalling that the patroller had told her that the house had been set ablaze.

Before they had gone another half mile, however, Morgana realized that the flames she could see shooting up into the moonless sky came, not from the neighboring plantation, but from Albemarle. . . .

Vague and frightening fancies tormented her in those harrowing minutes; Griffin slain, her child murdered.

Oh, God! She put her trembling hands to her face. Better she were to die as well, rather than live with such a horror waiting to be envisioned each day of her remaining life.

When they at last drove through the gates, Morgana could see that it was not the house, but the barn, that was on fire.

Now she could hear screams, shouts, the sound of gunfire. The terror pressed down upon her. People were running back and forth, all of them black. She wondered frantically if the slaves of Albemarle had joined the revolt. If so, they were all doomed.

The carriage was careening forward. Ben was standing up, gripping the reins in his hands, shouting for everyone to get out of the way.

A figure leaped out of the darkness and tried to jump up on the carriage seat, but a well placed shot from one of the patrollers caught the man in the chest. With a wild yell, he fell backward.

At last they reached the Great House. Before Ben could get to her, Morgana had opened the carriage door and was racing up the steps.

Griffin, Nathaniel, and Carlie Dobbs were on the verandah, rifles at ready, and were soon joined by the two patrollers.

There was no time for amenities or greetings as Morgana, followed by Ben, ran into the house and up the curved staircase.

Entering her room, Morgana gave a sob of wild relief. Both Celia and Bella were huddled in a corner, shielding the baby with their bodies, their faces terror-stricken in that moment before they recognized Morgana and Ben.

At the sight of her, they both began to wail, clutching at her as if for protection.

Quickly, Morgana tried to calm them down. She then went for the mate to the pistol she had once before used. Checking to see that it was loaded, she regarded the two cringing women.

"Lock the door when I leave," she instructed in what she hoped was a calm voice. "Let no one in until I return."

"Has to git over my daid body to git to dis heah chile," Celia cried out in a high, thin voice. She clasped Anne tightly to her breast.

Morgana attempted a smile, but managed only a weak grimace. Then she and Ben went into the hall. She waited until she heard the sound of the bolt. Nodding at Ben, they both went downstairs.

The five men were standing close to the front door, attitudes wary and cautious as they watched the rampaging Negroes. So far, they hadn't approached the house.

Catching sight of her, Griffin snapped, "Get back into the house!"

"I can help," Morgana informed him quietly, producing the gun. "I . . . know how to use it," she reminded him.

She couldn't define the look he gave her, but it was brief, then he returned his gaze to the yard.

"Some of those bastids got guns," Carlie noted grimly, peering at the renegades with narrowed eyes.

"Got 'em at Four Oaks," one of the patrollers commented. "Mister Barrows got a whole collection of 'em, but most don't work. And even if they did, wouldn't be enough ammunition, 'cept maybe for two or three of 'em."

"Is Farley all right?" Nathaniel asked quickly. He gave the man a searching glance as he inquired after his old friend.

"Don't know, suh," the man replied. "Was when we left."

"Where are the patrollers now?" Griffin asked angrily, then listened to the man's words with a disgusted expression. "They should have stayed here, dammit!"

"Thought they headed into the swamp," the patroller

tried to explain in a voice that hovered on the edge of a whine.

"Well, they're not in the swamp now," Griffin muttered through clenched teeth, gripping the rifle in his hands.

The renegades had this while been whooping and hollering in glee at the sight of the burning barn. Their laughter sounded maniacal. Finally, with a thundering retort, the structure collapsed to the ground in a shower of brilliant sparks.

Morgana moved closer to Nathaniel. "Are our people involved in this?" she asked quietly. She was amazed at her own calmness.

Nathaniel shrugged his thin shoulders. "Hard to tell, girl," he murmured. "Certainly, not all of them are. . . ."

"Why don't we bring those who aren't up here with us?" she suggested.

Turning slightly, he gave her a wry smile. "How're you gonna tell the difference?" he wanted to know. "Besides, we can't give them any guns, it's against the law." His expression softened and he touched her arm, giving it a slight squeeze.

Morgana felt the sincere welcome. Tears burned her eyes, but she couldn't give in to them. So far, Griffin had shown her no indication of his feelings about her return. He looked worried, tense, but she knew that had nothing to do with her.

"That nigger's makin' me nervous," one of the patrollers complained, looking at Ben, who was standing at Morgana's side.

"He stays here," Morgana stated firmly. She stared at the man until he turned away with a muttered oath. Griffin glanced at her again, but made no comment. His expression was inscrutable and it unnerved her. She couldn't tell what his reaction was to her return. He looked noticeably thinner to her and she felt a small stab of alarm, wondering if perhaps he had been ill.

Then Morgana heard Nathaniel draw in his breath sharply. She turned toward him.

"They're comin'," he said in a strained voice. He raised his rifle. "They've had their fun. Now they're comin' after us. . . ."

Looking into the yard, Morgana saw that he was right. They had grouped, crouching low in the waning embers of the fire. But as yet they made no move forward.

"They're waiting for the fire to die out," Griffin observed tersely. "It'll be really dark then. We'd better get into the house."

Carefully, they all backed in through the front door, Ben positioning himself in front of Morgana.

Turning, Griffin raised his rifle in a threatening gesture, aiming it at Thomas, who had suddenly appeared.

The terrified Negro quickly raised his hands. "Doan shoot, masta, suh," he cried out fearfully. "Comin' to help you. . . ."

"Get the hell out of here," Griffin ordered harshly, not lowering the rifle nor taking his eyes from the trembling man.

"Where I gonna go?" Thomas wailed, looking miserable.

"Let him alone, Griff," Nathaniel said. His brows dipped into a severe frown. "If Thomas is gonna attack, he'll have to fight me first."

A shot rang out and they all started as the ball crashed into the outside wall.

With a shriek of animal fear, Thomas bounded up the stairs, heading for the attic.

Griffin, Nathaniel, and the two patrollers aimed their rifles at the front door, which Griffin had locked. Carlie Dobbs, his attitude tense, moved a few steps forward, standing with his back against the wall.

Morgana, pistol in hand, was a bit disconcerted to find her target was the back of Ben, who was still standing in front of her.

There was a sound of a sharp retort as something slammed with great force against the front door. Again and again it sounded, and they all knew that the door would soon be broken down.

Griffin looked toward his grandfather. "The study. It has a door that locks, and a window if we need it. Let's not barricade ourselves in a room we can't get out of."

In a sudden movement, Morgana turned and began to run up the stairs.

"Where are you going?" Griffin shouted after her.

"To get Anne!"

Morgana was only halfway to the landing when the front door caved in under the constant battering onslaught.

For a timeless moment, they all froze as Jonah, the other blacks crowded close behind him, stepped into the hall.

In that instant, Morgana saw that most of the blacks were carrying knives and only three had guns: Jonah, a Negro she didn't recognize—and Atlas, the burly Angolan who had replaced Jude and who had apparently joined the renegades.

Then, everyone began to shoot at the same time.

The next agonizing moments were an incoherent jumble in Morgana's mind. Ben raced up the stairs. A shot caught him in the back just as he reached her and he fell heavily against her, knocking her down.

One of the patrollers fell, blood streaming from his forehead. The force of a ball in his chest slammed Carlie Dobbs against the wall. Only two of the renegades were cut down.

After the first volley of shots, the blacks came rushing forward with a yell, overpowering Griffin, Nathaniel, and the remaining patroller.

"Now I gonna whip his white ass to death," Jonah shouted triumphantly. He was holding Griffin in a vicelike grip.

Atlas was making his way up the stairs, crouching like an animal, a hideous grin on his black face.

For the first time, Morgana looked upon a Negro and thought him less than human. Indeed, the black face of Atlas his eyes wild and savage, thick lips drawn back in a parody of a smile, appeared more beast than man to her.

Terrified, Morgana tried to push Ben off of her, struggling with the weight of him across her lower body. She had dropped the gun when she had fallen, and now frantically groped around, not daring to take her eyes from Atlas.

At last her hand closed around metal. But before she could aim it, the Negro dived at her, knocking the pistol from her grip.

Lying almost on top of Morgana, Atlas leered down at her, bringing his black face so close she could smell his whiskey-laden breath. That, combined with his musky body scent, made her gag. She put both hands on his chest and pushed with all her strength.

Her effort produced no more than a laugh from the muscular slave. Bending down, he put his mouth on hers.

The terror rose up in her throat. Morgana could feel the steps cut into her back and lower spine as she struggled. She was aware of his hand fumbling with her skirt as he tried to push it up, but the weight of his own body was impeding his progress.

"Bring dat wench down heah!" Jonah called out. "Wants her to see what a hun'erd lashes look lak on a white back!" When Atlas gave no indication of hearing the command, Jonah raised his voice to a shout. "Goddamn you, nigger! Iffen I come up dere, gonna crack yore kinky haid open!"

Atlas turned then, casting a sullen look in Jonah's direction. Then he got up. His hand went around Morgana's wrist in a grip so tight it made her wince in pain. With a yank, he pulled her up, then began to walk downstairs. "We has our fun later," he muttered to her, dragging her along.

In the yard, there wasn't a soul about. Atlas was the only Albemarle slave who had joined the rebellion. The rest were all in their cabins, doors shut tightly. They would not join, but they would not help, either.

The smokehouse and the carriage house had been set afire and the combined blaze threw shafts of golden light about that danced crazily in the black shadows of night. The air was acrid with the smell of smoke and burning wood. In the stables, the horses were hysterical, their neighing cries shrill with terror as they smelled the smoke.

Morgana resisted the urge to look up toward her room, praying that Bella and Celia had had sense enough to get out of the bedroom. Using the back stairs, they could get out through the rear door. The renegades had not yet fired the house, but she knew they soon would.

Right now, however, they had other things on their mind.

Three of the oak trees that lined the driveway now sported a man lashed to the trunks. Griffin, Nathaniel, and the patroller had all been stripped to the waist. Each one of them was now tied to a tree.

Griffin turned slightly, trying to catch a glimpse of Morgana, his expression reflecting anguished concern for her safety. He struggled against his bonds, sweat beading his face with his effort, but was secured as strongly as was Morgana, held in the grip of Atlas.

Nathaniel was still and, as much as was possible under the circumstances, stood with dignity, his mouth grim.

The patroller, however, was cursing loudly in a furious rage, struggling against the ropes that bound him.

Grinning, his face appearing evil in the shifting firelight, Jonah stepped slowly toward him, a rawhide whip coiled in his right hand. His eyes were gleaming with triumphant satisfaction. All his plans were coming to fruition. He had tasted freedom and found it sweet. Revenge, he thought, would taste even sweeter. He still felt the rage that had flooded him when Atlas had told him that Zoe had been sold. It was yet one more score to settle.

"Thinkin' you makin' too much noise, *masta, suh,*" Jonah said to the patroller in a voice that was laced heavily with sarcasm.

The patroller's answer was a string of invectives so vitriolic and expressive that Morgana had never even heard most of the words he used.

Jonah only kept on smiling. Even after the first stroke

drew a screeching yell from the man, he kept the smile in place.

The rest of the renegades howled in delight, urging Jonah onward and begging for a chance to use the whip.

"When I gits tired, y'all kin have yore turn," Jonah assured them magnanimously. He again raised his arm.

With each blow of the whip, Morgana could feel her insides cringe, her mind imagining that it was Griffin's back receiving the punishment.

Frantically, she looked about the yard. There were over one hundred people little more than a stone's throw away—where the hell were they?

Glancing down at her, Atlas grinned, then pulled her in front of him, her back against his chest. His arms went about her waist. He was holding her so tightly against him that she could feel his arousal even through her voluminous skirt.

"Ain' nobody gonna save you, missy," he whispered, his mouth against the back of her neck. "Dese people knows enuf to stay in dere cabins. Dey come out, we kills 'em. Knows it, dey do."

Morgana bent her head in an effort to get away from his searching mouth, but he raised a sinewy arm to her throat, forcing her head back again.

"You watch," he ordered softly. "Gonna see how it is to be a slave." He nuzzled her neck. "Den I gonna teach you how it is to be a wench. Likes it, you will. Promises you."

Morgana took a deep breath, then swallowed in an effort to keep from screaming. She refused to allow herself to sink into the hysteria that was threatening to overwhelm her.

Her eyes darted about, viewing the renegades. They

362

were all, she saw, very drunk, and getting more so. Having raided Nathaniel's stock of whiskey, the Negroes were now passing the bottles around, each man drinking long and deeply before handing it to another.

Watching them, she was astounded at how she had been fooled by their attitude of subservience, of gentle good humor, of apparently genuine regard for their masters. It had all been a hoax. These were no more than savages who lay in wait for the first opportunity to torture and murder.

In the midst of these sharp and bitter conclusions, there came the thought of Ben, and Morgana felt ashamed. That man lay dead on the stairs because of her. He could have easily joined the renegades. He could have easily stayed in Massachusetts. Instead, he had chosen to give his life to save her own.

The patroller had ceased his cursing, crying out now only in agony as Jonah, appearing tireless, continued with the savage beating.

Then, over the screams of the patroller, the howling of the renegades, and the whispering, menacing voice of Atlas, Morgana heard the faint sound of yapping dogs.

She ceased her struggles and stood very still, for the moment not even breathing. The sound was coming closer. But so far, no one seemed to have noticed. She reasoned that she could hear it because she and Atlas were standing a distance away from the mob of men, who were now so drunk and noisy it would take a cannon shot to capture their attention.

But Morgana realized that, even if the majority of them hadn't yet heard, Atlas soon would. He was drunk, but not sodden. Somehow, she would have to keep him engrossed with her for a few minutes longer. If the blacks heard the oncoming patrollers, they would probably kill Griffin and Nathaniel before they ran—and probably take her with them!

She began to struggle again, this time with purpose. Each time she moved, she rubbed her buttocks up against him until Atlas was breathing so heavily only the sound of his own gasps reached his ears.

At last he spun her around to face him and Morgana allowed him to do so, all the while keeping the pretext of fighting him. She began to scream now, placing her mouth close to one of his ears, putting a hand against his head, palm over his other ear.

Atlas was now wild with desire. With clumsy hands he began to tear at her clothes.

Morgana could feel herself tiring. She knew she couldn't fight him off much longer. Her body felt like a mass of aches and bruises.

With a grunt and a sudden movement, Atlas sank to the ground, dragging her down, cursing at the impediment of her skirts.

A shot rang out, but Atlas paid no mind. Beneath her, Morgana could feel the drumming sound of horses' hooves vibrating through the ground.

She began to fight in earnest, clawing at Atlas's face, her nails leaving trails of angry red scratches in the black skin.

Men were shouting, shots were being fired, dogs were growling fiercely as their canine teeth sunk into black flesh, and still Morgana fought, her breath now coming in whimpering, gasping sobs.

Tiring of the little game, Atlas put his hands about her neck, squeezing, his eyes inflamed with lust or murder, she couldn't tell. For the moment her vision blurred. Even the hateful black face lost its outline and blended in with the shadows behind him. Her throat muscles strained, grew rigid. As if in the distance, Morgana thought she heard her name being called with a terrible urgency.

Suddenly she saw Griffin, his face rigid with fury as he came up behind Atlas. Jumping on the man's back, he put his arm about Atlas's throat, bracing his knee against the slave's spine. Increasing the pressure of his grip, Griffin forced Atlas's head backward, straining until the muscles in his temple throbbed with the effort.

Morgana had managed to squirm out from under Atlas and now sat on the ground, too weak in her relief to even get to her feet.

Griffin then placed the palm of his free hand on Atlas's forehead, pushing the Negro's head even further back. He again increased pressure until, at last, with a sickening crunch, he broke the man's neck.

Griffin held him a moment longer, then released him. Atlas's lifeless body crumpled, his head at an awkward angle.

Morgana began to sob, unaware that she was doing so. Coming toward her, Griffin picked her up in his strong arms and carried her into the house.

He walked up the stairs, stepping around Ben. Morgana continued to sob, clinging to him, her tears falling in droplets upon his bare chest. Reaching her door, Griffin kicked at it with his foot.

"Open it, dammit!" he shouted.

Recognizing his voice, Bella hastened to obey, her eyes round with fear.

Walking toward the bed, Griffin gently laid Morgana

upon its soft surface. Straightening, he glanced at Celia, who was holding the sleeping Anne. Then he addressed Bella.

"See to your mistress. Don't leave her alone." He looked down at Morgana, who had calmed somewhat and was lying there, an arm across her eyes. She appeared utterly exhausted. Then he left the room.

On the steps again, Griffin stooped down and turned Ben over so that he was face up. Bending forward, he placed his head on the black man's chest. There was a faint, thready heartbeat.

Calling for Thomas, who had finally come out of hiding, Griffin gave instructions for Ben to be carried to Auntie Flora's cabin.

"Then fetch the doctor," he added, continuing on downstairs.

The patroller in the hall was dead. So was Carlie Dobbs. Briefly, Griffin viewed the two dead Negroes. Then, with a grim expression, he headed outside. He saw Nathaniel conversing with the newly arrived patrollers and he headed in their direction.

Of the twenty renegades, eight had been killed outright, including the two in the front hall. Another four were seriously wounded. The remaining eight, including Jonah, were standing in quiet dejection, hands tied behind their backs. They were guarded by several patrollers and the dogs, who occasionally strained at their leashes in an effort to get to their quarry.

The patroller who had been beaten was now lying on the grass, being tended to by several of his friends. He was cursing once more with vivid enthusiasm.

Nathaniel, having taken the time to put his shirt on

again, turned as Griffin neared. "I've told Joe to round up some of the hands and clear away the bodies. They'll bury them in the swamp." Griffin nodded and Nathaniel went on to ask, "Is Carlie dead?"

Griffin nodded again. "And so is one of your men," he added with a look at Jake Drover.

"We'll take him with us," the man responded. "Now, where can we string up these niggers?" He motioned in the direction of the renegades. "Jonah's your buck, ain't he? Want to handle him yourself?"

"No," Griffin responded quickly, before Nathaniel could reply. Right now, he felt as if he'd had enough killing to last him a lifetime. "Get them all out of here, including Jonah. Do what you have to, but do it elsewhere."

Jake Drover shrugged, nodded, then went to join his men.

"How is Morgana?" Nathaniel asked. His lined face reflected concern as he buttoned his shirt.

"She's resting. I've already sent for the doctor."

The words were no sooner spoken than Griffin looked up to see Daniel Foxworth's buggy rumbling up the driveway.

"I was over at Four Oaks," the doctor explained as he climbed down. He was a tall man, but on the lean side, which gave him an appearance of lanky uncoordination. His black moustache was full, looking somewhat oversized for his face. "I saw the flames and figured you might need help," he went on, reaching back inside the buggy for his satchel. "Is everybody okay here?"

Griffin regarded the man in gratitude, then quickly explained the situation. "I want you to take a look at my wife first," he said as they headed for the house. "After that, there's a buck that's needing attention. I put him in Auntie Flora's cabin."

The doctor chuckled and gave a short shake of his head. "He's in good hands then," he observed blithely. "Sometimes I think that old wench of yours is a witch."

Normally, Foxworth did not treat slaves. His reasons, however, were strictly pragmatic and not from any sense of prejudice. The doctors who tended slaves—and for the most part they were a motley crew, drunk more often than not—were immediately classed as "nigger doctors." The only time a white person would submit to their ministrations was in a time of emergency.

The reverse was also true. In times of emergency it was quite acceptable for a doctor of Foxworth's standing to treat Negroes.

The doctor went upstairs and Griffin poured himself a drink while he waited in the study. Looking out of the window, he saw the patrollers ride away, the renegades in tow. Those that couldn't walk were strapped on the horses like oversized saddlebags. Griffin knew that each and every one of them would be hung.

The bodies had been removed and Nathaniel had organized a bucket brigade to douse the remaining fires. The carriage house and the smokehouse were gutted. The barn was burned to the ground.

Only now did the full import of what had taken place make itself known to Griffin. They could have all been killed. When he thought of Morgana in the grip of that black buck and what could have happened to her, his hands began to shake.

Griffin had finished his drink when the doctor came downstairs again.

"She's all right," Foxworth reported. "A few cuts and bruises, but nothing serious. I admire the way she's got herself under control," he added, rubbing the back of his neck in a gesture of weariness. "Most women would be in hysterics after what she's been through. Had to dope up Amelia Barrows. Couldn't quiet her down at all."

Griffin viewed the doctor with a serious expression. "Any casualties over at Four Oaks?"

Foxworth shrugged. "Nobody killed, if that's what you mean. Farley took the missus and his sons and got the hell out of there when he saw them coming. But the bastards did plenty of damage before they left. Well," he said, heading for the door, "I'll see to your buck now."

"He's not mine," Griffin explained as he walked with the doctor into the hall. "Used to be Morgana's, but she freed him."

Pausing, the doctor turned, staring at Griffin in some surprise. Most people in these parts refused to even consider such a step, regardless of the circumstances. Certainly no slave of Albemarle had ever been freed.

"Do the best you can for him," Griffin went on. He appeared almost embarrassed. Few were as outspoken as he when it came to manumission. "He saved my wife's life."

When the doctor left, Griffin went upstairs slowly. Outside Morgana's room, he paused a long moment before entering, motioning for Bella and Celia to leave.

Morgana wasn't in bed. She was seated on the chair by her dressing table. Dark bruises on her throat and upper arm were the only outward indication of what she'd been through. She had changed her clothes and brushed her hair. It lay soft and shining about her shoulders. Like everything else about her, Griffin thought it incredibly beautiful.

She was watching him, but she wasn't smiling as he came closer. Her expression was one of quiet contemplation.

Viewing her, Griffin felt such a rush of love for this woman, that, for the moment, he couldn't even speak. There was pride and there was strength, he could see it in her bearing and in her face. Both he recognized as a mirror image of his own pride and strength. A man needed those in a woman, he thought to himself. Needed them almost as much as gentleness and softness.

But above all, he needed love. To feel it or give it—Griffin somehow thought the former the necessity. To give love was rewarding; to feel it was to feel life itself.

For a few tense minutes, neither of them said anything. But the very air seemed charged with emotion, with the sort of tingling expectancy that one senses before a summer storm.

Although thoughts and words crowded his mind, what Griffin finally said, was, "So you came back...."

"Yes," she whispered. Her eyes were level as she continued to watch him.

He gave her a sharp look. "Was it because of Anne?" His breath seemed to still within him as he waited for her reply.

She hesitated, viewed her folded hands in her lap, then raised her face to him again. "Not entirely."

A small silence descended. Once or twice, Griffin opened his mouth to speak, then closed it again. Morgana continued to sit calmly, making no effort to break the awkward quiet.

Griffin began to move about the room, hands in his pockets. "When I discovered what you did," he said after a while, his voice barely audible, "I wanted to thrash you to within an inch of your life. . . ."

"And now?" she asked softly, tilting her head slightly.

Pausing, he turned toward her. "Oh, Morgana," he murmured with a small, sad smile. For a moment he seemed incapable of speech. Moving across the room, he sat down in a chair across from her, elbows on his knees, face in his hands. "At first, I was so angry, I couldn't even think straight. And then . . . I'm glad you got them away," he whispered, his voice muffled. "That child . . ." He looked up at her, expression anguished. "I never meant him harm. I was just so wild with the thought of Cammy. . . ."

"Your sister and her child are safe," she assured him quickly, smiling. "In fact, I believe that she and my cousin have discovered a mutual attraction for each other. I hope it works out for them. He seems genuinely fond of the baby, too."

Griffin continued to regard her for a long moment, wanting to know more about his sister's welfare. But he couldn't quite bring himself to ask. Not yet. Perhaps in time. Right now the thought of Cammy was like an open wound.

Finally, Griffin got up and came toward her. Kneeling at her feet, he took her soft hands in his own. "We got off to such a bad start . . ." His voice caught and he wet his lips. "But . . . I love you, Morgana," he whispered. "You must believe me. Whatever else I am or have done, I love you very much. . . ."

Her eyes shone with tears as she looked down at him. "That's the first time you've ever said that to me. . . ."

Reaching up, Griffin put his hands on each side of her face and looked deeply into her eyes. "Can you learn to love me again?"

Her eyes sought and found his, and it was as if they looked into each other's soul.

"I have never stopped loving you," she replied simply.

His breath seemed to catch in his throat and it was a moment before he could continue. "And can you forgive me? For everything?"

She nodded, not trusting herself to speak.

"That day when we first made love . . ." Griffin's voice was halting, as if he were searching for the words. "I want you to know that, for me, it had never been like that before. . . ."

"Oh, my darling," she murmured with a gentle laugh. "That was the easy part." She squeezed his hand. "For us, it will always be the easy part." Her smile was warm as she gazed into his eyes. "It's the loving with your heart and with yourself that takes time and understanding. . . ."

"And can we?" he asked with urgency, his dark eyes never leaving hers. "Can we learn the difficult part?"

"I think we already have, my darling," she replied softly. "I know that nothing will ever destroy the love I have for you."

His heart seemed to swell within him as he heard the words he thought he'd never hear again. They were like cool spring water to his parched and arid senses. Getting to his feet, Griffin raised her up, embracing her. "Promise me," he said huskily, holding her tightly against his bare chest. "Promise that you'll never leave me again. While you were gone, there was nothing—nothing at all. Everything became meaningless..." His voice broke. "I'd thought you'd gone forever...."

"I'll never leave you again, Griffin," she replied, feeling the joy blossom within her. She felt his love like a tangible thing, enveloping her with its warmth and security.

He hugged her tightly, feeling a contentment he had long been without.

Then, hearing his named called, Griffin went out onto the piazza, Morgana at his side. He looked down into the yard as Dr. Foxworth waved at him.

"The buck's going to be all right," the doctor shouted, a hand cupping his mouth. "Be sore for a few weeks, but he's going to make it."

Griffin nodded, smiling, and returned the wave of the departing physician.

"Thank God," Morgana murmured, her eyes glistening.

"Ben will have a home here for as long as he wants it," Griffin assured her. "In fact, I'll deed him a few acres of land to work as his own...."

She couldn't prevent the few tears that coursed down her cheeks with his words.

His brows drew together. "That's something I don't ever want to see again," he murmured, tracing the silvery rivulets on her face with his fingertips. "There'll be no more tears for you, not ever..." Gently, he prodded the corners of her soft mouth until the dimple appeared to tantalize him. Bending forward, he put his lips on the adorable indentation, and in response, Morgana smiled tremulously. "That's better," he said, still holding her close, his chin against her hair.

For a long moment they stood within each other's arms,

bodies pressed together, feeling the warmth that flowed through them with the contact.

Drawing back slightly, Griffin looked down at Morgana, searching her eyes for the answering response to his growing desire.

Without speaking, he picked her up and carried her to the bed, helping her to undress. When he had removed his own clothing, he lay down beside her and drew her into his arms. Beneath his lips, her skin felt like satin and tasted the way he imagined a rose petal would taste.

They came together naturally, without restraint, each delighting in the texture of the other, in the sensations aroused.

They made love sweetly, tenderly, and, at last, with the remembered passion each had to give to the other.

Afterward, as they lay quietly, arms entwined, Morgana looked at Griffin, wanting to tell him all she had learned, of the dark clouds brewing both in the North and South—but she knew he'd never leave his beloved Albemarle. She knew, too, as she rested her head on his chest, that whatever the future held for them, they would face it together.